WONDROUS STRANGE

WONDROUS STRANGE

The Life and Art of
GLENN GOULD

KEVIN BAZZANA

Copyright © 2003 by Kevin Bazzana

National Library of Canada Cataloguing in Publication

Bazzana, Kevin
    Wondrous strange : the life and art of Glenn Gould / Kevin Bazzana.

Includes bibliographical references and index.
ISBN 0-7710-1101-6

    1. Gould, Glenn, 1932-1982.   2. Pianists – Canada – Biography.
I. Title.

ML417.G69B365 2003   786.2'092   C2003-902969-7

We acknowledge the financial support of the Government of Canada through the Book Publishing Industry Development Program and that of the Government of Ontario through the Ontario Media Development Corporation's Ontario Book Initiative. We further acknowledge the support of the Canada Council for the Arts and the Ontario Arts Council for our publishing program.

Typeset in Janson by M&S, Toronto
Printed and bound in Canada

McClelland & Stewart Ltd.
The Canadian Publishers
481 University Avenue
Toronto, Ontario
M5G 2E9
www.mcclelland.com

1 2 3 4 5   07 06 05 04 03

Photo on endpapers: Gould trying out pianos in Columbia Records' 30th Street studio in New York, April 1957. (*Photograph by Don Hunstein. Sony Classical.*)
Photo page ii: Gould in a CBC studio, 1962. (*Photograph by Herb Nott. CBC Still Photo Collection.*)

to Sharon, Sophie,
and Blossom – my family

Merry, and tragicall? Tedious, and briefe? That is hot ice,
And wondrous strange snow. How shall we find the concord
Of this discord?

– William Shakespeare,
A Midsummer-Night's Dream

CONTENTS

Opposite: Gould's famous folding chair and his practice Steinway in the living room of his midtown Toronto apartment shortly after his death. *(Photograph by Lorne Tulk.)*

POSTLUDE

(In the Form of a Prelude)

A POSTHUMOUS LIFE

He died, it is true, on October 4, 1982, shortly after his fiftieth birthday, but few classical performers have ever remained so *alive* so long after death. On the bitterly cold afternoon of October 15, at an ecumenical memorial service in the largest church in Toronto, St. Paul's Anglican, it was already clear that affection for Glenn Gould ran deep, that his sudden, untimely death had shocked and moved many people. He once said he would like to attend his own memorial, to see who – if anyone – came. Three thousand people, it turned out, from around the world: family, friends, colleagues, government officials, fans. Gould did attend after all, and as usual got in the last word. At the end of the service, the closing Aria from his then new recording of Bach's Goldberg Variations was piped in. He was playing his own requiem.

His death stimulated new, widespread demand for his work, which coincided with the advent of commercial CDs. CBS Masterworks (which became Sony Classical in 1990) began re-releasing his recordings at once, and posthumous Grammy Awards – his first as a pianist – attested that he was "hot." In the 1990s, Sony Classical released all of his studio recordings and many of his concert, radio, television, and film performances in a massive *opera omnia* on CDs and video, and CBC Records and other labels (including pirate labels) have released many more CDs over the years. His recordings sell better today than they did when he was alive. By the time he died he had sold around one and a quarter million records, but by the end of the millennium he had sold almost *two million* copies of that new Goldberg album alone. When both of his Goldberg recordings were repackaged for the umpteenth time in 2002, as *Glenn Gould: A State of Wonder*, the compilation became one of the bestselling classical releases of the year. "Dying," a Sony Classical executive joked, "was a great career move for him."

Only after his death did many people realize how much besides performances his legacy included. The films and television programs he made to promote his ideas, and his innovative radio documentaries for the CBC, have had international exposure. A *Glenn Gould Reader* was published in 1984, and other collections of his writings – articles, scripts, letters, interviews – followed. A year before the *Reader* appeared, a volume of writings had already come out in France, and editions followed in Germany, Holland, Italy, Japan, Spain, and Sweden. His few original compositions, even little piano pieces he wrote as a teenager, have been performed around the world, recorded, and enshrined in a critical edition by the prestigious German music publisher Schott. Many composers of far greater accomplishment would kill for such attention.

Since his death, the literature on Gould has grown exponentially. Today it rivals that of classical performers as prominent as Callas and Toscanini, even of some fairly important composers. He has been the subject of a vast periodical literature and of dozens of books in many countries – those already mentioned as well as Poland, Finland, China. (His posthumous reception has itself inspired some literature.) "Canada has always been a cool climate for heroes," wrote Northrop Frye, and while Gould is a national treasure at home he really is something like a hero – a revered and studied and influential figure – outside the English-speaking world. He said in 1980 that his highest per capita record sales had long been in Japan, followed by the German-speaking lands; today he also has passionate followings in France, Italy, Scandinavia, Russia, Armenia, Israel, Australia, Brazil. It was symptomatic that a Glenn Gould Society first arose in Groningen, The Netherlands, and that the Toronto-based Friends of Glenn Gould, founded in 1995, would attract members from some forty countries.

For half a century he has been one of Canada's attractions for the rest of the world. Mikhail Baryshnikov admitted that when he defected in Toronto in 1974 he knew "precisely three things" about Canada: it had great hockey teams, it grew a lot of wheat, and it was home to Glenn Gould. In 1991, I ran into a Canadian musicologist who had just returned home from Vienna, and she showed me a photograph she had taken of one of the major Viennese music shops, which had prominent window displays on either side of its front door. This was, keep in mind, the big Mozart Year – the bi-centennial of his death – yet only one of the window displays was given over to Mozart; the other was devoted to Gould.

Outside the English-speaking world Gould is taken a little too seriously at times. The 1998 Radio-Canada documentary *Glenn Gould: Extasis* was typical of his reception in Quebec: full of talk about the soul and the absolute and the incorporeal, about emanating light and music's disappearing into its own appearance. (Typical quote: "*L'âme est emporté, jusqu'à la jouissance de Dieu.*") The French writer Michel Schneider, too, was moved to purple prose in *Glenn Gould piano solo*: "*Chez lui la musique est un autre état du silence, la lumière une leçon de ténèbres*" – and so on. I once saw a lecture in which a Parisian scholar sought to categorize and analyze Gould's flamboyant physical mannerisms at the keyboard, purportedly in order to gain insight into his performances; as a further area of research he suggested, with a straight face, a typology of Gould's eyebrow movements.

Most of the literature is less baroque. There have been three major biographies, a "biography for young people," three coffee-table books of photographs, and reminiscences by people who knew Gould. There have been broad surveys of his work as well as more focused studies, and scholarly reference books: a discography, and a catalogue of his papers, acquired by the National Library of Canada in 1983. Just about every aspect of his life, personality, work, and thought has been put under the microscope at some time, even his notorious singing at the keyboard.

His biographer Peter Ostwald, a psychiatrist, while insisting that Gould did not fit any one psychological or medical category, noted that some of his childhood and adolescent behaviour resembled Asperger's syndrome, a mild variant of autism whose symptoms include deficiency in social skills, obsessive rituals and routines, unusual sensitivity to sensory stimuli, and (sometimes) extraordinary gifts in a particular area. This subject has since been pursued by Timothy Maloney, who shared his detailed research with me; his findings have not yet been published, though the admittedly colourful notion of Gould as autistic has already been taken up, rather too eagerly, in the popular press. So far I have not been persuaded that such a diagnosis really fits the biographical facts or is necessary for making sense of Gould.

The posthumous attention has extended to public events large and small – film festivals, lectures, panel discussions, travelling exhibitions – in cities all over the world. There have been five major conferences, which have ranged widely – scholarship, testimony, ceremony, hagiography. At the CBC, Gould has been the subject of specials and portraits on radio and television as well as documentaries about his radio work, his tour of Russia, and his affinities with "things Japanese"; the small concert hall in the CBC's Broadcasting Centre, in downtown Toronto, is named Glenn Gould Studio. NPR, the BBC, NHK, and all of the major European networks have broadcast programs about Gould, and his unique style of "contrapuntal radio" has spawned some imitators. (In 1999 the American writer Edmund Morris acknowledged "contrapuntal radio" as an influence on his use of fictitious alter-egos in *Dutch*, his controversial biography of Ronald Reagan.) Gould, who tends to attract young people and technophiles, is a popular figure on the Internet, the subject of fan sites, discussion groups, databases, and much more. He has been the focus of several interactive hypermedia and CD-ROM projects, and I know of a handful of college-level courses devoted to him.

A Glenn Gould Foundation was established on the first anniversary of his death, and it awards a triennial Glenn Gould Prize in Music and Communication. (Laureates to date have been R. Murray Schafer, Yehudi Menuhin, Oscar Peterson, Toru Takemitsu, Yo-Yo Ma, and Pierre Boulez.) There is a Glenn Gould Park near his old apartment building, and Toronto has declared the house in which he grew up to be a historic site. There is a scholarship in his name at the University of Toronto, a Glenn Gould Professional School at the Royal Conservatory of Music, an annual Glenn Gould Lecture in New York. His name was attached to the International Bach Piano Competition in Toronto, in 1985, despite his disdain for all forms of competition. Canada Post issued a stamp honouring him in 1999, though he was later rejected for a spot on the new paper currency: according to government polls the public considered him too eccentric, "neurotic to the point of being damaged."

Composers have paid homage to him in music, and his name sells: Alexina Louie's *O Magnum Mysterium: In Memoriam Glenn Gould* is one of her most often performed pieces. His Goldberg recordings have inspired several transcriptions of the piece as well as original works like Christos Hatzis's *Gouldberg Variations*. He has inspired new works by painters and sculptors, including a whole exhibition, *The Idea of North*, in New York in 1987. Choreographers have made dances inspired by his image and his recordings (usually the Goldberg Variations). Poets all over the world have sung of Gould; a whole book, *Northern Music: Poems About and Inspired by Glenn Gould*, appeared in 2001. He has been featured in short stories by writers including Joy Williams, Lydia Davis, and Joyce Carol Oates, and in novels: Thomas Bernhard's *Der Untergeher* (published in English as *The Loser*), Richard Powers's *The Gold Bug Variations*, Joe Fiorito's *The Song Beneath the Ice*, Thomas Harris's *The Silence of the Lambs* (Gould was the pianist of choice for the psychopathic killer Hannibal Lector). He also inspired *The Maestro*, a novel for young people by Tim Wynne-Jones, and Anne Chislett's children's play *Not Quite the Same*. David Young's play *Glenn*, which had its premiere in Toronto in 1992 and played at the Stratford Festival in 1999, features four actors portraying different eras in Gould's life and different aspects of his psyche. François Girard's feature film *Thirty Two Short Films About Glenn Gould*, released in 1993,* includes interviews with those who knew Gould as well as dramatized vignettes. The film earned near-universal acclaim, though it is more naive than insightful, a salad of unexamined legends and clichés, and is stylistically too arty for its own good. Girard's insistence on elevating rather than humanizing his subject – "ARTIST, PHILOSOPHER, MADMAN, GENIUS," the ads proclaimed – yielded some sequences that I find embarrassing to watch.

There is some trade in Gould relics. Half a century ago he inscribed a page from the manuscript of his String Quartet to the critic Eric McLean: "Allow me to bequeath to you this particularly tattered page which comprises Bars 226–241 in the revised critical edition. I trust it will be carefully preserved with due regard for a future generation's clamor for authentic bits of Gouldiana." He was joking, but Gouldiana now sells for real money. In the United States, letters (even typed letters) have fetched prices above three thousand dollars, and an old signed photo can sell for even more; a recently discovered teenage composition was professionally valued at perhaps fifteen thousand dollars, perhaps a great deal more.

Then there is the phenomenon of "Gould tourism." Since his death an astonishing number and range of people have made the

---

* The producer, Niv Fichman, recalled that late one night around 1980 he and two friends – all young film students and rabid Gould fans – saw the pianist emerge from a Toronto hotel with a garbage bag and set off in his Lincoln Continental. The trio followed him for half an hour, until he stopped at a bus shelter, dropped his bag into a garbage can, and drove away. They could not resist retrieving the bag, which contained nothing but grapefruit peels and back issues of the *Globe and Mail*.

pilgrimage – some repeatedly – to Toronto to visit sites related to Gould. His childhood home, the schools he attended, the churches and halls in which he played, his apartment building, the hotel where he kept a studio, the diners he frequented – all have become sacred ground. Gould's is the most visited gravesite in Mount Pleasant Cemetery, in which rest many other celebrated Canadians. By some accounts it is the most visited gravesite in all of Canada. Fans have also been drawn to the "Gould country" around Lake Simcoe and along the north shore of Lake Superior, and to the National Library of Canada, often not to study Gould's papers as much as to see and touch them. Some visit the library hoping to play his piano, or sit in his famous folding chair, which now rests behind glass, the object of much veneration. (The curators have always been uneasy with the library's status as a de facto Gould museum.) In 1998, an Ottawa newspaper reported that Gould's papers – the most consulted collection in the whole library – were in danger of deteriorating from overuse; they have since been microfilmed.

Gould has inspired a cult of personality of a kind rarely seen in classical music since the days of Liszt and Paderewski, and for which figures like James Dean and Elvis Presley offer better contemporary equivalents. He had groupies, mostly women, from his early concert days. Many women wrote to him as though he were an old friend, because they heard "something" that spoke to them in his playing. Most were harmless, like the woman who wrote about her prize-winning petit point copies of his photos and album covers, though some sought meetings and even marriage, or imagined relationships with him, and grew bitter when he did not reciprocate. One rebuffed fan wrote threatening letters that he forwarded to the RCMP. Another woman, who "communicated" with his album covers, wrote to him prolifically in his last years to share the minutiae of her day-to-day life, because, she said, she had no one else to write to. Some of these women actually tracked Gould down, to his alarm, and his father recalled chasing one persistent fan from the family cottage with a hose.

I have never seen a parade of schoolchildren in Arthur Rubinstein's honour, and doubt I ever will, but I have seen one in Gould's honour, and have stopped being surprised at the forms of adulation he provokes. A piano student in England once sent me photographs of her back, on which she had tattooed the main theme from Gould's String Quartet, and I was once assured that his name can be found encrypted in the Bible Code. He has crept into the popular culture – how many other dead classical musicians have been mentioned on *The Simpsons?* When the newsmagazine *Maclean's* named its 100 Most Important Canadians in History, Gould ranked Number 1 among artists, ahead of the Group of Seven, and Number 5 overall, just behind Samuel de Champlain. A Gould recording of a prelude and fugue by Bach was one of twenty-seven samples of Earth's music on a special phonograph record affixed to the two *Voyager* spacecraft launched in 1977 – a fact of great significance for some fans, even though a Pygmy girls' song and "Johnny B. Goode" are also on that record.

In death as in life Gould broke the rules: a cottage industry is not the usual fate of a classical performer, dead or alive. (Nor was it, by his own admission, something Gould desired.) For the vast majority of performers, recordings and broadcasts and films are adjuncts to a concert career, and almost always even a major performer's reputation and record sales and presence on the music scene decline, sometimes precipitously, after he is no longer around to generate fresh publicity. But Gould gave up concert life at the age of thirty-one and spent half of his professional career disseminating new work while staying out of the public eye, maintaining his presence through a conspicuous absence. Generations of listeners knew him only through the electronic media, so there was no public Gould to disappear when he died. It is not surprising that he of all performers should maintain a high profile for years after death. Indeed, his own posthumous life is the best evidence for some of his most cherished beliefs about the validity of an artistic career pursued through the electronic media.

Gould's personality has certainly fuelled his posthumous appeal. His eccentricity made him fascinating, his isolation made him mysterious, his personal modesty made him lovable, and his apparent sexlessness paradoxically gave him sex appeal among some female (and male) fans, even as it invited speculation about his private life. (At a conference in Amsterdam, in 1988, a woman in the front row listened patiently to a sober talk about one of Gould's films and then rose to ask, "Was he gay or what?") His family and friends and colleagues, people who barely knew him, even people who have merely written about him, have been much sought out by his fans.

Of course, he was a great pianist, too, among the most naturally gifted of his day; that will always assure some kind of following. And he was a powerful communicator of deeply personal, sometimes shocking and subversive, but always compelling and entertaining interpretations, which he put across with great conviction. Performances so unique will probably always sound fresh and unconventional and retain their power to attract new audiences. The controversies that made Gould a fascinating as well as infuriating performer in his day have not abated, though he provokes less outrage than he once did. His place in the pianistic pantheon seems to solidify with time, as new generations discover his work unhampered by the critical baggage that attended him while he lived.

He has had some influence on younger generations of musicians, especially in Bach, though the very uniqueness that continues to attract new fans means that he is unlikely ever to be widely influential. Even his Bach playing is in some ways a historical artifact, an exemplar of a mid-twentieth-century high-modernist approach to music whose heyday has passed. The principles of historically informed performance are now much more influential than Gould – he is not quite so *inevitable* in Bach as he once was – though some pianists, of the order of Evgeny Kissin, are still unwilling to tackle Bach because of the standard he set.

His posthumous reputation has been enhanced by the aura of the explorer, the rebel, the outsider that surrounds him despite his mainstream success. His eccentric interpretations, his garish on-stage demeanour, his abandonment of concert life, his dropout lifestyle – all imply a stubborn resistance to authority and conventions that makes him an immensely attractive figure, even a role model, especially to young musicians engaged in their own battles with teachers and traditions and the clichés of the classical-music business. He was refreshingly irreverent in a business whose conservatism and formality and pretentiousness have always alienated many people, especially the young. Moreover, his championship of recording technology and other media made him a conspicuously *modern* artist, and his ideas are still relevant, still discussed, today. Like Marshall McLuhan, he made predictions about technology that made him seem a kook in the sixties but a visionary after his death: he foresaw implications of technology that are only now, well into the digital era, being realized in mainstream musical life. This is the more remarkable considering that his first recordings were made in monaural sound just a few years after the end of the 78-r.p.m. era and the introduction of magnetic tape and the long-playing record.

A major source of Gould's posthumous reputation, particularly among laypeople, is the perception that he was something more than a piano player. He has demonstrated, even after death, a remarkable ability to capture people's imaginations, sometimes with the force of revelation, especially people with no preconceptions about classical music. Many musically literate people, too, hear important intellectual and critical discourses in Gould's playing, and the literature includes books and articles in which his work is assessed from philosophical, ethical, theological, anthropological, political, and other broad perspectives.

Gould inspires real devotion in some people – like the Québécois woman who published a book-length love letter to him, *Glenn Gould: Mon bel et tendre amour*, filled with poems, pictures, and unclassifiable reflections. In some quarters he is received as a kind of guru or monk, a holy man, a Platonic ideal – the posthumous reception really does get this airy. I have heard him spoken of with the kind of "moral awe" that psychologists have noted in people's reactions to figures like Gandhi, whose indifference to worldly things is taken as proof of purity and nobility. In fact, when Gould was fifteen and had just given his first professional recital, his father wrote to a friend,

> My wife and I have always prayed that Glenn's music might be able to touch men's hearts in such a way that it would be a turning point in their lives. In some measure our prayers have been answered. One mother telephoned us after her nineteen year old son had heard Glenn play in October [1947]. She said that her son came home after the concert and said: "Mom, you've been telling me that there was such a thing as a hereafter and a life eternal. I never really believed it until I heard Glenn Gould play tonight. Now I know." She went on to say that the boy, who was given to swearing, hasn't been heard to swear in the days following the concert. So even instrumental music can have great power over men's lives, when it has God's blessing.

For all the uncritical idolatry in Gould's reception, those who profess to hear "something" in his playing are not crazy; often, in fact, they are hearing precisely what Gould intended to communicate. He considered his performances to be not just readings of pieces of music but documents of his world view, and he insisted that even the most seemingly mundane matters of performance practice and recording technology had larger implications, especially ethical implications. He thought that artists had a "moral mission" and that art had enormous potential for the betterment of human life; as a performer he aimed not only to play well but to do good. The unity of theory and practice does come across in his recordings – and the rest of his output – even to laypeople, and his fans include many people who take seriously the ideas they perceive embedded in his art.

Still, an urge to canonization remains among some fans, and has been abetted by gaps and misunderstandings in the biographical literature. After all, it is easier to sustain an image of Gould as an autodidact, hermit, and puritan when his biographies neglect to stress that he was fundamentally influenced by his one piano teacher, enjoyed the company of other people, and had sexual encounters. One great drawback to the posthumous cult has been a reluctance to see him in any kind of context, as though any status but heroic iconoclast did injury to his achievement. Most glaringly absent from the biographies has been Canada. Otto Friedrich, in the preface to his authorized biography, commissioned by Gould's estate, admitted that he was contractually bound "to be sensitive to, to look carefully into and to give close attention in the Biography to the impact of the country of Canada and way of life of Canada on Glenn Gould's development, life and work." Yet Canada ended up a bit player in his book: he devoted less than 10 per cent of it to the first twenty-two years of Gould's life, the years in which his personality and piano style and aesthetic ideas were formed. Like many, outside Canada anyway, he saw Gould as an unclassifiable entity who came out of nowhere in 1955, the year he first performed in New York. Only a few later writers, like the Japanese scholar Junichi Miyazawa, have properly acknowledged the importance of the theme of Gould as Canadian. It was, in fact, the starting point for my own biographical research, though my motivation was not patriotism but simply accuracy, comprehensiveness.

An old proverb bears keeping in mind when it comes to Gould: "What's Bred in the Bone Will Not Out of the Flesh." His origins had a great deal to do with who and what he was. For all his originality he was identifiably a product of the country, the province, the city, the very neighbourhood – and the times – into which he was born. Many of his admirers seem unwilling to believe that a milieu as apparently bland and provincial as middle-class Anglo-Protestant Toronto between the wars could have yielded so wondrous strange an artist unless his relationship to his upbringing was entirely one of resistance. In fact, he remained, all his life, in fundamental ways, an Old Toronto boy – he never did leave town – and his work incarnated Canada in unmistakable if sometimes unusual ways. I have begun this book at the end, so to speak, because today no one comes to Gould's work except through a haze of posthumous glorification. But to find the themes and motifs that make sense of him, the threads that bind his life and work (if not always neatly) together, we must get beyond the cult and the cottage industry. We must look back, first, to a sleepy, leafy street in Depression-era Toronto.

Opposite: The thirteen-year-old prodigy at home, at 32 Southwood Drive in Toronto, making music with his beloved dog, Nicky, and his bird, Mozart, February 20, 1946. On the music desk of the piano: Bach's partitas and *Well-Tempered Clavier*. Another photograph from the same session ran above a profile of Glenn in the next day's *Toronto Daily Star*. Of Mozart, he told the *Star* reporter, "He can't talk yet, but he knows his music." *(Photograph by Gordon W. Powley. Archives of Ontario.)*

PART ONE

BEACH BOY

The Prodigy, 1932–47

"I was born in Toronto,
and it's been home base all my life."

He grew up in a small country – physically vast, rich, imposing, but a small country nonetheless. When he was born, in 1932, Canada had barely 10 million people spread out across a land mass larger than all of Europe, and though not young it was culturally imma- ture, still beholden to the venerable empire out of which it had sprung while increasingly pressured by the newer, more powerful empire to which it was linked by an immense open border. Gould's hometown was hardly small – in 1932 the population of Toronto was a little over 630,000, with almost 200,000 more in the metropolitan area – but it was not the cosmopolitan city it is today. It was still a proudly provincial city, an enormous small town, whose cultural standards had not kept pace with its physical and economic growth. Margaret Atwood once described Toronto in the thirties and forties as "anglophone culture at its most yawn-inducing," and it was in just this milieu that Gould's personality and the foundations of his art were forged.

It was overwhelmingly British, for one thing. When Gould was born, half of Canada, three-quarters of Ontario, and more than 80 per cent of Toronto was British, and a colonial mentality prevailed:

a Torontonian could do no better than to strive to be British. The city was established by the English – as the town and fort of York and the capital of Upper Canada – in 1793, and in many respects it remained, metaphorically, an English fortress. In Gould's day it was still rife with propaganda that reinforced Canada's place within the British Empire; in school, children sang "Rule, Britannia!" and "There'll Always Be an England" and learned to draw the Union Jack. The abdication crisis and the Royal Tour were big news in the late 1930s. Sometimes, it is true, this loyalty was tinged with resentment, and throughout the early twentieth century, especially after each of the world wars, there was much talk of Canada's growing independence and national identity, yet the country did not have unilateral authority over its own Constitution until 1982, the year of Gould's death.

Now the most multicultural city in the world, Toronto in Gould's childhood was among the most homogeneous cities of its size, and loyalties – racial, religious, political, cultural – were resolutely defended. Three-quarters of the population was Protestant, including, overwhelmingly, the elites that controlled the city's politics, economy, justice system, culture, and almost everything else. Groups like the Orange Order, a militantly Protestant fraternal organization, wielded great influence (the novelist Robertson Davies called Toronto "the Rome of the Orange Order"). Anglo-Protestant values were reflected in both public and private life – in political conservatism, cultural provincialism, moral prudishness. Well into the twentieth century there were still remnants of a High Victorian genteel tradition – Italian immigrants coined the term *mangiacake* ("cake-eater") to describe the city's WASPs – and to many locals, dowdiness was a badge of moral superiority. It was a highly repressed city; behaviour was strictly regulated according to Protestant codes. The temperance movement was strong, as it was throughout Ontario, and even when cocktail lounges and jazz clubs became legal the police patrolled them with Cromwellian vigilance. Law and custom conspired to guard the peace of the Sabbath. Nothing was open on Sunday except churches, and there were still locals for whom playing outdoors or eating candy, reading a novel or taking a bath, even singing or laughing on Sunday was sacrilege. Censorship was widespread in the media, and the police were on hand wherever people congregated, enforcing moral and political standards even where they had no legal right to do so (liberty was often sacrificed to order). Davies called this "the bony, blue-fingered hand of Puritanism," and it made Toronto the subject of ridicule to world-lier visitors, including the wicked hedonists of Montreal.

All of which sounds suspiciously like every cliché of the Old Toronto of legend – Toronto the Good, Toronto the Blue, the City of Churches, the Queen City – and even seventy years ago that was not the *whole* city. There was always some ethnic mix, always a darker, bawdier town beneath the prim exterior, always some dan-gerous hypocrisy alongside the official morality – nicely exposed in some of the early novels of Morley Callaghan and by the local nov-elist Hugh Garner, who wrote in 1949 that Toronto's quiet Sundays were really a consequence of Saturday hangovers. Moreover, the empire to the south was undermining the influence of the Mother Country in many quarters, even between the wars. But it was pre-cisely the ethnic Toronto, the bawdy Toronto, the American Toronto from which Glenn Gould was (mostly) shielded as he grew up. The Toronto that he knew, that informed his personality and his art, that he himself rosily recalled in later life – "I always felt that 'Toronto the Good' was a very nice nickname" – was the puritani-cal Anglo-Protestant city whose image so many Torontonians have longed to shed. When, as he liked to do, he called himself "the Last Puritan," he was proudly and self-consciously maintaining the legacy of the city of his youth.

Until he was almost thirty, Gould lived in the Beach, a cozy, peaceful neighbourhood of leafy streets and crescents in the east end of Toronto, bordered by Lake Ontario to the south, Woodbine Park to the west, and Scarborough, the adjoining suburban municipality, to the east. Depending on which local you believe, the Beach extends as far north as Danforth Avenue or Kingston Road or only as far north as Queen Street, the neighbourhood's main commercial strip. The Gould family lived in a modest, two-storey brick house at 32 Southwood Drive, a short street that runs from Williamson Road, two blocks from the beach, north up the brow of a steep hill to Kingston Road. Originally the Beach was countryside and farmland, but from the 1870s, when steamboats and streetcars began to bring day trippers and holiday makers, it was transformed into a summer-cottage and resort area offering pleasure gardens, amusement parks, picnics, regattas, boating, summer and winter sports, music and dancing, a racetrack, and a boardwalk. By the turn of the century, now home to a growing number of permanent residents, it was considered a part of the city, and the east end's various villages were eventually annexed to Toronto, a process completed in 1909. The neighbourhood's days as Toronto's Coney Island came to an end around 1925, but it remained an attractive part of town, with parkland abundant even by the standards of a city whose streets, as the humorist Stephen Leacock wrote, "were embowered in leaves."

In the old days, Torontonians had loved the Beach for its beautiful views, its breezy summers, its woods and creeks and ravines – and its permanent residents fiercely protected its greenness. In an autobiographical essay he began in the last year of his life, Gould wrote that his "first dream-like images of childhood" were "images exclusively of trees – trees shrouded in morning mist, trees heavy with snow on a winter afternoon, trees, above all, whose branches served to filter the waning twilight of a summer evening."

In other respects – emotional, intellectual, political, cultural – the Beach was a less idyllic nurturing ground for a sensitive child with an artistic temperament. Many of Toronto's features were magnified there, beginning with its racial makeup. When Gould was born more than 90 per cent of the Beach's residents were of British heritage; his was the most British neighbourhood of the most British major city in the most British province of a former British colony. The Beach was an enclave in which Others, as residents or visitors, were not welcomed. Downtown, on the other side of the Don River – that was where the immigrants, the workers, the poor lived. Such exclusivity, of course, breeds a sense of superiority and entitlement, a narrowness of vision, and bigotry. "We were living then – I am speaking of the 1940s – in what was already a big and interesting city, but we talked among ourselves like villagers," wrote the journalist Robert Fulford, who also grew up there. "We knew no culture but our own, and not much of that. In my public school there was exactly one Jew, in my high school there was exactly one Negro (he was called 'Snowball')." Catholics were "Papists," and subject to prejudice. The neighbourhood's newspaper of choice, the conservative, influential *Evening Telegram*, fiercely defended British laws and Protestant customs against their perceived enemies – the United States, Quebec, communism, Jews.

The Beach in those days was a sleepy neighbourhood, dowdy, unfashionable, and complacent even by Toronto standards. Horses still drew bread and milk wagons, and lawn bowling counted as excitement. Fulford thought it a "constricted little world in which art, imagination and genuine politics played no part at all," and one might wonder that it would be home for more than half a lifetime to a musician renowned for radical ideas and an eccentric character. But there had been advantages to Toronto long before Peter Ustinov famously described it as "New York run by the Swiss." Condemnation of its dullness and philistinism and oppression has always been balanced by praise for its orderliness and cleanliness, its stability and security, its peacefulness and pleasantness. Fulford wrote that in his youth "Toronto was a city of silence, a private city, where all the best meals were eaten at home and no one noticed the absence of street life and public spaces." It was a culture of homebodies in which the herd instinct was suspect. Callaghan considered Toronto a good place for a writer to work, because people weren't always breathing down your neck, and the literary scholar Northrop Frye quipped that "Toronto is an excellent town to mind one's own business in."

Gould felt the same way. "Toronto is essentially a truly peaceful city," he wrote in 1978, one of those few cities that "do not impose their 'cityness' upon you." It is for this reason that Toronto, for all its provincialism, and despite a reputation for being inhospitable to artists and intellectuals, was the ideal city to nourish an artist as iconoclastic as Gould. Raised quietly as a typical middle-class Toronto WASP, he was not smothered creatively, but rather left alone to cultivate his highly individual ideas and practices, unmolested and free of oppressive traditions. He was sheltered, but *productively* sheltered – and, by choice, continued to shelter himself as an adult. For an artist of Gould's sensitive and unconventional temperament, a more vibrant and cosmopolitan culture might have bruised the creative ego, but in the comfortable insularity of Toronto he developed a self-confidence that steeled him against outside influences and allowed him to carve out his own niche.

Toronto, Gould wrote, has "always been rather like a collection of village neighbourhoods," and one reason it did not impose its "cityness" on him was that the Beach was a kind of self-contained village within the city. Gould, we might say, grew up in a small town in Toronto. Moreover, his roots on both sides of his family were in small-town Ontario, and though he was a child of the big city he was a small-town boy at heart. Both sides of his family had lived in Southern Ontario since the early nineteenth century. His paternal grandfather, Thomas George Gould, was born in Paisley, Ontario, in 1867, the year of Canada's Confederation, and his family relocated to Uxbridge when he was a teenager. Gould's father, Russell Herbert Gould, known to family and friends as Bert, was born in Uxbridge on November 22, 1901. His mother, Florence Emma Greig, was born in Mount Forest on October 31, 1891, and was always called Flora or Florrie. The Greigs relocated to Uxbridge, about sixty kilometres northeast of Toronto, around the time of the First World War, and there are still Goulds and Greigs living there. Thomas Gould's business was in Toronto, and he kept rooms in town, but his home and social life were in Uxbridge, to which he commuted by train and eventually retired in the early thirties. (He died there in 1953.)

Uxbridge was settled in the first decade of the nineteenth century, mostly by Pennsylvania-Dutch Quakers, Germans, and Scots. Leacock, who taught briefly at Uxbridge High School in 1889, described it as a small town "situated nowhere in particular on the high ground between Lake Ontario and Lake Simcoe, one of those agricultural centres that grew up around a gristmill and a saw-mill when the settlers moved in, grew to a certain extent, and then planted trees in the street to replace the shattered forests and fell asleep under the trees. . . . It had the usual equipment of taverns and churches but was a clean, bright, orderly little place, dull as ditchwater but quite unaware of the fact." It was still a small town when Gould's parents met there, and even after they married, on Florence's birthday in 1925, and moved to Toronto, they retained close ties to Uxbridge. Their two families knew each other well and shared church and social lives. Gould's parents also owned a cottage north of Toronto, to which the family retreated on weekends and in the summer. Situated on the northeast corner of Lake Simcoe, where tourism had been a mainstay, increasingly, since the dawn of the automobile era, the Gould cottage was within walking distance of the hamlet of Uptergrove, a sort of glorified intersection serviced by an all-purpose country store, though cottagers got most of their supplies about ten kilometres away, at the north end of the lake, in the town of Orillia.

In Uxbridge and Uptergrove and Orillia, Gould absorbed the same conservative Anglo-Protestant values he did at home. Angela Addison, who knew him in his student days, wrote that the people of Uptergrove "tended to be plain-spoken, hard working, abstemious, and caring," and the same was true of a town like Uxbridge, where the centre of social life was the church. Orillia's most famous resident, Stephen Leacock, a notorious "character," a hedonist at war with religion, and an unrepentant drinker in one of the driest towns in Ontario, was regarded by the locals with considerable suspicion. Frye noted that such physically and culturally isolated towns, necessarily close-knit, developed a sort of "garrison mentality" in which "moral and social values are unquestionable," though, once again, from Gould's perspective this was a milieu that, while narrow, had attendant blessings: tranquility, security, simplicity – and natural beauty. Leacock, though he satirized Orillia and its residents in *Sunshine Sketches of a Little Town*, a classic of Canadian literature first published in 1912, rhapsodized about "the smiling beauty of the waters, shores, and bays of Lake Simcoe and its sister lake, Couchiching. Here the blue of the deeper water rivals that of the Aegean; the sunlight flashes back in lighter colour from the sand bar on the shoals; the passing clouds of summer throw moving shadows as over a ripening field, and the mimic gales that play over the surface send curling caps of foam as white as ever broke under the bow of the Aegean galley." Between this vision and Toronto lay a hundred kilometres of rolling hills and dark woods and granite ridges, small lakes and wide valleys, cool air and open sky and mist, the landscape dotted with villages and farmland and evidence of the tourist trade.

This sounds like a typically Canadian pastoral myth evoking nostalgia for the peaceful, protected, leisurely life of a small-town childhood, but it was a reality of Gould's early life, and it nourished him. He loved the pleasures of the cottage – cycling, playing games, exploring the woods. "He swam like a fish," his father recalled, and he was "never happier than when on the water with his boat." Sometimes, Bert would find his son in the boat miles up the lake, alone or with his dog or a friend, "coming at full speed through a very heavy chop," soaking wet, "holding the tiller in one hand and conducting an unseen orchestra with the other, and singing at the top of his voice." (Gould fantasized about operating a fleet of water-taxis on the lake when he grew up, or living on a houseboat.) Bert could afford the luxury of heating at the cottage, and Gould loved snowy winter weekends; already as a child he felt a powerful attraction to all things northern. "Heroes and heroines of much of Canadian life take their source on these waters," the novelist Hugh Hood wrote of the lakes north of Toronto, and Gould was one of them. Close, frequent contact with the cottage country in childhood bred a lifelong love of nature. Toronto may have been "home base," but it was the countryside that really sustained him; even in the city he would take long walks along Balmy Beach and the other eastern beaches. As an adult he would make frequent trips to the cottage, and to other, more distant retreats, in order to recharge his creative batteries. As he told a journalist in 1956, "I gather my inner resources from the outdoors."

"When people ask me if I'm Jewish, I always tell them that I was Jewish during the war."

He was born, at home, on September 25, 1932, and his birth certificate gave his name as "Gold, Glenn Herbert." The family name had always been Gold, and when his grandfather, who had worked as a furrier in Toronto since 1902, established the family business in 1913, he gave it the name "Gold Standard Furs" (pun presumably intended). All of the documents through 1938 that survive among Gould's papers give his surname as "Gold," but beginning at least as early as June 1939 the family name was almost always printed "Gould" in newspapers, programs, and other sources; the last confirmed publication of "Gold" is in the program for a church supper and concert on October 27, 1940. The whole family adopted the new surname, and ancestors were retroactively rechristened.* When asked about the name change, a lifelong Uxbridge resident who had been Glenn's nanny at the cottage in the summer of 1938 while Florence recovered from an illness, answered, with perfect Upper Canadian reticence, "Well, I shouldn't really say this . . ."

Xenophobia was among the less admirable by-products of Toronto's homogeneity, and the city was notorious for anti-Semitism between the wars. Jews counted as the largest non-British population in Toronto, and Jewish immigrants were widely perceived as "foreigners" and sources of unrest. After the First World War their numbers were curbed by a new immigration policy that observed a strict racial hierarchy, a response to overt lobbying to "keep Canada British" by not "polluting" the indigenous stock. By the 1930s, Jewish immigration had slowed to a trickle. The Depression

---

* Name-change searches requested from Ontario's Office of the Registrar General revealed that Bert formally changed his name only on December 5, 1979, so that he could legally marry his second wife under the surname Gould. The searches turned up no information on Gould or his father or grandfather from the period around the start of the Second World War, suggesting that the family's change of name was informal and that Gould was still legally Glenn Herbert Gold when he died.

offered a convenient pretext for scapegoating Jews, and anti-Semitism grew alarmingly, even at the highest levels of the Canadian government (as the diaries of Prime Minister Mackenzie King reveal). Discrimination in the form of bans and quotas, either overt or tacit, was pervasive, often legal. After Hitler came to power in January 1933, a more malignant strain of *Judenhass* could be detected in Toronto in the increase in hate literature, pro-Fascist groups, and harassment of Jews. In the Beach, where, Robert Fulford recalled, a petition was taken on his street during the war to keep a Jewish family from purchasing a house, bigotry was often disguised as concern for order and propriety. Jews, it was said, had loud parties and littered and changed clothes in their cars when they picnicked at the beach. Locals recoiled at this want of Anglo-Saxon reserve, and restrictive signs – "ONLY GENTILE BUSINESS SOLICITED," or, more pointedly, "NO JEWS OR DOGS ALLOWED" – appeared on the eastern beaches. In the summer of 1933, youthful "swastika clubs" in the Beach provoked anti-Semitic incidents that culminated, the night of August 16–17, in one of Toronto's worst riots. Moreover, of the Western democracies Canada had by far the worst record for giving sanctuary to Jewish refugees from Nazi Germany. In early 1945, a senior Canadian official, asked how many Jews would be admitted after the war, notoriously replied, "None is too many."

The Canadian fur business, like the garment industry, was home to a large proportion of the Jewish labour force, nowhere more so than in Toronto, where, in 1931, 60 per cent of those employed in fur and fur-goods manufacturing were Jewish, and where dozens of businesses were owned and managed by Jews. In both the fur and garment trades, poor working conditions and anti-Semitism spawned a politicized, militant labour force disposed to socialist and Zionist causes that influenced the trade-union movement between the wars. As Jewish labour grew increasingly fractious (strikes and riots were common), and Jewish life generally became more dynamic, many fearful Torontonians came to associate all Jews

with revolutionaries and communists, and Jews were often subjected to brutal persecution by the police or to racially motivated
deportation. In 1937, the charismatic, rabble-rousing communist
leader of the militant Fur Workers Union in the United States came
up from New York to investigate the scrappy Toronto local, and
ended up inciting gang warfare among downtown fur workers that
lasted sporadically until the outbreak of war in fall 1939. His name
was Ben Gold.

In short, there were reasons why two Anglo-Protestant
Torontonians named Thomas and Russell Gold, who manufactured
and sold fur goods downtown, might have felt, on the cusp of the
Second World War, that their surname was a liability. Gould himself
once told a friend that his family considered their surname "too
Jewish," especially because they were in the fur trade. The Goulds
were not alone: many Torontonians at this time, Jews and Gentiles
alike, changed surnames that sounded "too Jewish" (Grunwald to
Greenwood, Levy to Lloyd, and so on). Student friends of Gould's
remember flashes of pique on the subject, from Thomas as well as
from Gould's parents, who were quick to correct firmly the whis-
pered assumption among some people that the family was Jewish.
Thomas, according to Bert's brother Grant, did not want to be
associated with the Jewish element in his business and was not well
disposed toward them. Obviously, the family was to some degree
caught in the prevailing anti-Semitism of interwar Toronto, or, at
least, was squeamish enough on the subject to take action. Of
course, there were Jews named Gould, too, in Toronto. But Gould
was also, in the words of the former nanny, "a good Uxbridge
name," for the town's wealthiest and most distinguished resident
had been a businessman and politician named Joseph Gould
(1808–1886). Ironically, Joseph Gould was himself born "Gold":
he changed his surname as a child, and his amused elders followed
suit. To make matters more confusing, Thomas, Glenn's grandfather, was married twice, the first time to Josephine E. Gould, a
granddaughter of Joseph Gould. She died in 1894, and in 1900

Thomas married Alma Rosina Horne (1871–1961), Bert's mother.*

The Gould literature has left open the possibility that the Golds'
ancestry *was* Jewish, and Gould (who, according to Peter Ostwald,
was not circumcised) sometimes made jokes on the subject, like the
remark quoted as a heading above. But at least as far back as the
mid-eighteenth century there were no Jews in this particular Gold
lineage, and in fact Gold was a commonplace surname among both
Gentiles and Jews in England and Ireland. Thomas's father, Isaac
Gold, was born in Maine, in the United States, in 1833, and died in
Stayner, Ontario, in 1884. According to a short handwritten biography now in the Uxbridge-Scott Township Museum and Archives,
Isaac was educated in England and "converted at the age of 23" –
converted, that is, to Methodism. He was ordained as a Methodist
minister in 1863 in Quebec, and later served in Paisley and Uxbridge,
but he had been born into the Church of England. Isaac's own father,
also named Isaac Gold (1807–1873), was born in Fordingbridge, in
the county of Southampton (today Hampshire), England, though
he, too, died in Stayner. The villages of Fordingbridge and later
Basingstoke, also in Hampshire, were home to the Gold family
throughout the eighteenth century, until the family emigrated to
the United States, presumably around the 1820s, and all of the
eighteenth-century ancestors were christened in the Church of
England. Other paternal ancestors lived elsewhere in England
(including Yorkshire), and Bert noted in an interview that there
were some United Empire Loyalists and Pennsylvania Dutch in his
background, too. His ancestors settled in various places in
Southern Ontario – Uxbridge and nearby towns like Greenbank,

---

* To make matters even *more* confusing, Gould's first name is frequently misspelled
as "Glen" in documents (including official ones) dating back to the beginning of
his life, and Gould himself used both spellings interchangeably throughout his life.
In fact, it is difficult to find a specimen of his signature in which a second *n* is clearly
discernible. To his record producer Andrew Kazdin, Gould offered a lame explanation: he had discovered early on that if he started to write the second *n* he would
be unable to stop and would end up writing three *n*'s.

Epsom, Saintfield, and Cobourg, starting in the very early nineteenth century.

"On the whole I think I was a happy child."

At the heart of the Goulds' milieu was religion – Methodism on the Gold side of the family, Presbyterianism on the Greig, both traditional middle-class faiths that (along with Congregationalism) were largely folded into the United Church of Canada, formed in 1925 just a few months before Bert and Florence were married. In both families religion was a priority, and in this respect they were hardly unusual. In Toronto it was essential to be devout, though unseemly to be *too* devout. In religion as in all things, discretion was crucial: overt displays of piety were associated with fundamentalist, "backstreet" faiths (Baptists, Jehovah's Witnesses), and considered to be in bad taste.* The Goulds and Greigs were sincerely devout. For them, the church was more than a centre of social and cultural life. Thomas Gould was a prominent and beloved figure in the Methodist and United churches, with a reputation, as one obituary put it, for "consistent Christian living." In his early days in Uxbridge he had been a Sunday-school teacher and lay preacher, and in 1908 he founded the Business Men's Bible Class there, which held weekly meetings as well as social events, including large annual banquets and rallies. For thirty-five years Thomas led the class, one of the largest such groups in Canada, and both Goulds and Greigs were involved with it. Both of Gould's parents came out of traditions that were steeped in the social gospel and that stressed personal faith and morality, respect for the authority of the Bible, community service, and the belief that God should be manifest in all aspects of life. Gould's conservatory friend Ray Dudley remembers often coming

---

* The aggressive evangelism of nineteenth-century Methodism certainly influenced Gould's grandfather (who was born in a Methodist parsonage, the son of a minister) and probably influenced Bert, too.

across Bert alone reading the Bible, and Gould himself noted, in a eulogy for his mother, that "Florence Gould was a woman of tremendous faith and, wherever she went, she strove to instill that faith in others" – including her son Glenn, whose childhood and early adolescence were bound up with church life. At his death he still had books his parents had given him, with titles like *The Wonderful Story of Jesus*, *Proverbs to Live By*, and *An Argument for Evangelism through Your Vocation*. The family was strict about the Sabbath, too: there was no fishing at the cottage on Sundays.

For Gould, who was born on a Sunday, the church was more a sanctuary than a source of religious dogma. As he wrote near the end of his life, his vivid childhood memories of churches "have to do with Sunday-evening services, with evening light filtered through stained-glass windows, and with ministers who concluded their benediction with the phrase 'Lord, give us the peace that the earth cannot give.' Monday mornings, you see, meant that one had to go back to school and encounter all sorts of terrifying situations out *there* in the city. So those moments of Sunday-evening sanctuary became very special to me; they meant that one could find a certain tranquility even in the city, but only if one opted not to be part of it." He stopped going to church around age eighteen, and rejected religion in the denominational, doctrinal sense. Nevertheless, he absorbed the conservative social and moral values of Ontario's Victorian Protestant culture, which cast a long shadow into the twentieth century. It was a self-assured and self-satisfied culture that saw moral questions in black-and-white, that valued reason more than passion, moral earnestness and rectitude more than beauty, that made a virtue of order in every respect – cosmic, social, intellectual. It was a culture that valued work, that thought idleness a sin. And it was puritanical, prudish about the body and especially about sex, insistent on modest appearance, chaste behaviour, and control of one's appetites and thoughts, fearful of the unguarded expression of instincts and emotions. "Acceptance of the full gamut of human experience, from high to low, is greatly feared by a substantial number of Canadians," Robertson Davies wrote, with handsome understatement. Gould was emotionally reticent even in infancy. He never cried, Bert recalled; he hummed instead. By all accounts, sex was a taboo subject in the Gould house, and his parents considered swearing evidence of ignorance. "Alone among all my male contemporaries, he never told dirty jokes, never speculated about the sexuality of girls, and never said 'fuck,'" Robert Fulford recalled. "Moreover, he was disturbed when other boys, such as my brother Wayne and I, used offensive language. He would ask us to stop and even threaten us ('You can't come to my cottage') if we failed to obey." Probably only half in jest, Gould would refer to a ball, in the ordinary sense, as "a censored," to avoid the connotation of testicles.

His English ancestors notwithstanding, Gould always identified his roots, upbringing, and temperament as Scottish and Presbyterian, and his mother's ancestry does seem to have powerfully influenced his development. Florence's family tree was solidly Scottish on both sides,* replete with names like Flett, Webb, Scott, Mackenzie, Ewing, and Durwood. At least three of her grandparents, and all earlier generations of her family, were born in Scotland. Gould claimed among his ancestors William Lyon Mackenzie – the controversial journalist, first mayor of Toronto, and leader of the Upper Canada Rebellion of 1837 – as well as the Norwegian composer Edvard Grieg, who, he wrote, "was a cousin of my maternal great-grandfather." (The Griegs do indeed trace back to a certain Alexander Greig of Scotland, who emigrated to Norway in the mid-eighteenth century and switched the vowels in his surname to best approximate *greg*, the correct pronunciation, on local tongues.) The Greigs descended from the famous Clan Gregor, which included the outlaw Rob Roy. When the surname MacGregor was banned by King James VI of Scotland (James I of England) in the early seventeenth century, some members of the clan adopted the name Greig as a pseudonym. Florence's branch of the family had settled in Ontario, at first mostly around Wellington County, at least as early

---

* Bert Gould, too, had Scottish ancestors: his mother's father, Andrew T. Horne (ca. 1830–1910), a storekeeper in the Uxbridge area, was born in Scotland.

as 1830. Her father, John Charles Holman Greig (1855–1927), was born in Hamilton and taught school around Ontario, and her mother, Mary Catherine Flett (1862–1939), was born in Mount Forest; they were married in 1888 and retired to Uxbridge in 1919.

From the mid-eighteenth century, Scots, though never a majority of the population, had an enormous influence on Canadian society and culture and on the Canadian character (it's one reason we say "oot and aboot"), nowhere more so than in Southern Ontario. Scottish propriety, Scottish sombreness, and the Scottish work ethic shaped much of Toronto's moral code in its early years, and was still at the core of city life in Gould's youth (Wyndham Lewis, in 1940, called Toronto "a mournful Scottish version of America"). Gould seems not to have chafed against his puritanical upbringing. As an adult, he became, if anything, an exaggeration of his parents' values: they were thrifty and unostentatious, but he was positively Spartan, even though he had more money; they were discreet, he reclusive; they orderly, he obsessive; they hard-working, he driven; they self-reliant, he iconoclastic. In fundamental ways he remained identifiably his parents' son. His private motto, which he loved to quote, was "Behind every silver lining there's a cloud," and he once said, "My ability to work varies inversely with the niceness of the weather." He identified himself as a Nordic man, and all things southern and Mediterranean were anathema to him: sunshine and blue skies, spicy food, physical exertion, easy sensuality, emotional openness, Italian opera. He hated bright colours, and equated red with violence; at the age of four or five he flew into a tantrum when someone gave him a red fire engine. His favourite colours were "battleship gray and midnight blue," and he loved black-and-white movies, including war movies, in which the prevailing images were cool and dark. (Among his surviving schoolwork are doodles of battleships and submarines.) When he was eight, his parents took him to see Walt Disney's *Fantasia* at Shea's Hippodrome, and he hated its "awful riot of color," as he recalled years later. "I went home depressed, feeling faintly nauseous, and with the first headache I can remember."

Whatever else he may have been, Gould was at heart a *good* person, like his parents. Bert and Florence, by all accounts, were quiet, serious people, pious and moral, sober and dignified, honest and responsible, but also friendly and warm, good neighbours and good citizens: decent people, about whom almost no one has ever had a bad word to say. Their only flaws, it would appear – emotional reticence, cultural provincialism – were native to their breeding. In any event, they made a comfortable and supportive home for their pampered only child. Most everyone who knew Gould as a child remembers him as happy and friendly, and Gould himself never referred to his childhood as anything but happy; the earliest photographs and documents of his life support this view. "Glenn's early life was that of any normal, healthy, fun-loving boy," Bert insisted; he was a "reasonably lusty" child, with "a very sunny disposition and a marvelous sense of humour." His appearance – though neat where, as in posed photographs, his parents took charge – was, it is true, often slovenly when he was left to his own devices, but for the most part he was a well-mannered, well-behaved boy, independent-minded but rarely rebellious and never delinquent.

In his parents' eyes, he was, as Bert said, "the answer to a prayer." Florence, ten years older than Bert, was forty when Glenn was born, and had suffered several miscarriages (the birth was not difficult, however). It is no surprise that she would coddle the boy, or that Gould would form an especially intimate bond with her. His relationship with his father seems to have been more distant. In fact, in the late fifties, Gould told a friend that he felt he was a disappointment to his father, not the kind of son his father would have wanted – a startling admission, since Bert's support for his son and pride in his accomplishments never wavered. Gould must have believed that his father would have preferred him to follow in his own footsteps and gain a wife, children, a respectable middle-class job, and manly pastimes. All three Goulds were devoted to each other, but the most intense relationship in the house was between Gould and his mother. As Fulford wrote, "there were just three Goulds and the lines of love and tension were tightly drawn. Glenn was the classic only

child, closely scrutinized and at the same time pampered and over-
indulged. He explained to me [around age twelve] that at the
cottage he would sleep with his mother one night and his father
would sleep with her the next, this arrangement having been worked
out some years before." Here is an Oedipal triangle so textbook as
to be almost comical, and we might properly wonder what sort of
tension it might have created in the Gould household. Gould's
conservatory friend Stuart Hamilton saw clear evidence of rivalry
between Glenn and Bert for Florence's attention. Florence clearly
had the stronger parental personality; certainly, she had the greater
impact on Gould's upbringing.

Strong love can provoke strong resentment, of course, and it is
no surprise that as Gould grew up, as his personality and ideas
inevitably conflicted at times with those of his parents, whatever
resentment he felt would be aimed mostly at his mother. His friend
John Roberts once recalled that Gould's relationship with his
mother, though never really endangered, was frequently "prickly":
he would tease her with comments intended to rouse her ire, and his
remarks could be barbed. To his record producer Andrew Kazdin,
he once related a revealing incident from his childhood.

Apparently he had committed some infraction of the family
rules and was engaged in an argument with his mother. He
revealed to me that at the height of his rage, he felt that he was
capable of inflicting serious bodily harm on this woman –
perhaps even committing murder. It was only a fleeting spark
of emotion, but the realization that he had, even for a split
second, entertained the notion frightened him profoundly. He
had suddenly come face to face with something within him that
he didn't know was there.

The experience caused him to retreat into serious introspection, and when he emerged, he swore to himself that he
would never let that inner rage reveal itself again. He was determined that he would live his life practicing self-control. Glenn
concluded by saying that he had been successful in this endeavor

and that he had never lost his temper since that first day so many years ago.

Gould himself, in a 1959 interview, noted that "I didn't have any brothers or sisters, which means I was a bit spoiled, in fact quite a bit spoiled, and it also means that I learned somewhat slowly to get along with people of my own age. I think there is no question of the fact that like most only children, I had things very much, too much, my own way. It took me quite a while to get over this. I recall that in my teens I had a violent temper, [which] was a very hard thing to overcome. I think it was largely attributable to the fact that I never had to share anything with anyone else." Clearly, he was disturbed by the power of his own emotions, and in the milieu in which he was raised he learned to deal with it through repression, which became a lifelong habit. When angry, he would grow quiet and withdraw. He disapproved of emotional displays in others, too, and counselled friends against them. He defended his own repression on moral and medical grounds, even when, in later life, it was clearly having a negative impact on his relationships, his psychology, and his physical health.

Physically, Gould was always fragile, and all his life his posture was terrible. "In the living room, year after year, on the plush chesterfield beside the piano, he slouched so much that his body was almost horizontal," Fulford recalled, and there were running battles on the subject: "Sit *up*, Glenn," his mother would implore him, "sit up straight, *please*." Herself somewhat frail and hypochondriacal – "her nerves were bad," an acquaintance recalls – Florence fussed over the state of her son's health. She worried constantly that he was too cold or overheated, that he was not eating right or not getting enough sleep, that his complexion was too pale, that he needed sunshine and fresh air and exercise. Sometimes she sent him mixed messages – wanting to send him outdoors yet protect him from the elements – and this can only have encouraged his own anxiety about his health. Her behaviour is in some ways understandable. She and Bert were old enough to remember the influenza epidemic that followed the First World War, for instance. Of course her own miscarriages likely encouraged her to be overprotective of Glenn, and she would have known that Thomas Gould's son by his first wife had died when he was barely a year old. In the Toronto of Gould's youth, moreover, "polio season" arrived each summer, and newspapers carried pictures of children in iron lungs, so Florence was not being absurd when she sought to keep Glenn away from the summer crowds at places like the Canadian National Exhibition (CNE), the world's largest annual event of its kind. Thomas, according to Bert, was also a hypochondriac, and carried a doctor's bag full of medications to work.

Before long, Gould was manifesting hypochondriacal tendencies of his own. As early as age six he had a fear of germs and of getting sick, and as a schoolboy he was already bundling himself up like the Glenn Gould of legend; even Florence came to believe that Glenn fretted too much about his health and overdressed on hot days. When he was eight, as he later told the journalist Pierre Berton, he witnessed his fellow-students staring at a child who had vomited in public, and was haunted by the image. "That afternoon," Berton wrote, "he returned to school with two soda mints in his pockets," determined never to suffer the humiliation of losing control in public, which he now dreaded. In his teens he was already a figure of fun among people who noticed that he seemed always to have a bottle of pills in his pocket. Fulford does not believe that Gould was ever seriously ill, though Ray Dudley recalled that "Glenn was quite prone to catching colds," and Florence would confine him to bed at the first sign of a sniffle. Bert was gruffer, less indulgent in this respect. "Use a little mental effort and you'd feel fine," he would say, and he insisted that his son "was never really sick a day in his life."

Gould was raised in secure and comfortable circumstances. Middle-class Toronto Methodists had long been reputed for business acumen, and Thomas and Bert Gould were no exceptions. Their business was located in the Manchester Building at 33 Melinda Street, off Yonge Street on the edge of the financial district (and next door to the *Telegram*). They advertised as "wholesale dealers in high-class furs" and offered a variety of services: design and creation of fur coats and wraps, special orders, repairs and restyling, cold storage. By the time Glenn was born, Bert was the assistant manager and effectively in charge. He worked hard, was organized and disciplined, ran the business honestly and profitably, and produced garments of high quality. The twenties was a decade of rapid growth for Canadian fur-goods manufacturers, and the Goulds were relatively wealthy by the standards of the largely lower-middle-class Beach. Gould was born in the middle of the worst years of the Depression, when it was difficult not to notice, on the streets or in the newspapers, the sometimes dire poverty and hunger of others, the soup kitchens and flophouses and public-works projects that sprang up all over town, the strikes and protest marches of the disaffected. But the family's prosperity, as well as his age, mostly shielded Glenn from such realities.

The Goulds could afford cars and radios and other material goods that required some affluence. They had a live-in housekeeper, Elsie, and, when necessary, nannies and tutors, but they did not live ostentatiously. At a time when lavish homes could already be seen at Lake Simcoe, the Goulds were content with a cottage of modest size and drab design, and nothing about their house in Toronto set it apart from its neighbours. In the Beach it was in bad taste to show off, to put on airs, and in the Goulds' tradition wealth was not incompatible with spiritual and moral well-being, as long as one acquired it honestly and used it to more honourable ends than personal display and social status. Glenn never wanted at any time in his life, and the security bred by his parents' prosperity had a marked effect on his character: he had none of the particular fears and neuroses that come from having known poverty, yet none of the snobbery that comes from revelling in privilege.

All things considered, he was lucky. A secure, happy childhood and devoted, protective, loving parents can destroy an artist (there's nothing like shame of your roots or hatred of your parents to get the creative juices flowing), but Gould, given his particular talent and temperament, *needed* a sheltered upbringing in which to thrive. Or at least, had he been brought up in different circumstances, he might have been a very different, and perhaps less interesting, artist than the one we know.

"By the time I was six I'd already made an important discovery: that I get along much better with animals than with humans."

Gould had a lifelong love of animals, and throughout his childhood he maintained an ever-fluctuating bestiary. In his Grade 9 class newspaper, the *9-D Bugle*, in a column loftily headed "PERSONAGES," Robert Fulford reported that "Glenn has had many pets, including two dogs, two rabbits, four goldfish (named Bach, Beethoven, Haydn, and Chopin), a budgie (Mozart), and, of all things, a skunk" – *not* a de-scented skunk, let it be said. "He brings home every stray pet in the neighborhood," his mother told a reporter when he was sixteen. He felt a special bond with animals, and they in turn trusted him. He sought out their company, even cycling into the farmland near the cottage to sing to the cows. ("Certainly I've never encountered so attentive an audience before.") When he was about eight or nine, he put out a single, pencil-scrawled edition of *The Daily Woof – The Animals Paper*, in which he reported news of local pets and wildlife – the neighbour dog's indiscretions, the larceny of a squirrel, Mozart's lice, and the sad death of Bach, from fungus. He loved dogs best of all. When he was an infant there was a big Newfoundland, Buddy, and a black Dane; later came Sir Nickolson of Garelocheed, better know as Nick or Nicky, who was a blue belton (white and black) English setter, his beloved companion through his teen years. When Nicky became old and infirm, there was a collie, Banquo, and later still a mixed-breed stray Gould rescued and named Sinbad. He repaid his dogs' affection. In May 1957, in the midst of a newsmaking tour of Russia, he found the time to write a charming postcard to Banquo, filled with news about the (grim) local pet situation. As an adult he could not properly keep a dog, but he continued to rescue lost or injured or mistreated ones, usually taking them to a shelter or a vet or finding them a home; once, he brought a stray into the CBC studios and fed it a hamburger. His library included, in additional to lofty tomes, books like *The Dog's Scrapbook* and *The Blue Book of Dogs*, some of which he had had since childhood, along with odd newspaper clippings ("Dog attempts to save birds in store fire").

With people he usually avoided physical contact, but with animals he was capable of open affection; he felt safe enough with them to roll around on the floor. Animals, he told John Roberts, "don't have words to waste and are more trustworthy than some humans I know." He seemed to *identify* with animals, with their vulnerability and decency and need for affection. About a dozen greeting cards he gave his parents (most often his mother) as a child still survive among his papers, and they are both sweet and curiously revealing. Sometimes he signed these cards on behalf of the pets ("Your Setter, Nicky"), but most often he numbered himself among them ("From your Two Puppies," "THE TWO DOGS," "from Puppy," "Love and Woofs From the Pup," "Your Puppy Dog GLENN"). Gould's cousin, Jessie Greig, remembered that "as a young teenager he demanded love and affection from both his parents and happily received it at his mother's knee, where, after long hours of practice he would lay his head and demand 'pats' as one would give to a dog. These pats were a reward for a day well spent and a fulfillment of his great need for love and acceptance." His nickname for his mother was "Mouse," for his father, "Possum."

His love of animals was tied up with his passionate pacifism and hatred of cruelty and violence. He "hated" the fur business, Bert recalled, because he connected it with mistreatment of animals. At Bert's place of business there were often dead animals and fresh pelts, to Gould's distress. (Did he know that his great-great-great-grandfather, John Gold (1773–1836), was a currier, someone who prepared tanned leather?) He hated to see or even think about anything being killed. He was upset when his mother wore a fur, or when his Uncle Grant, studying to become a doctor, dissected a frog. He once referred to Latins as "savages" because they countenanced bullfighting. Like one of his heroes, Albert Schweitzer, he had a reverence for life that extended to God's less lovable creatures. At one point in his life, he claimed, he walked with his head down to avoid stepping on insects (or was this just an excuse to avoid eye contact?), and his friend Paul Myers watched him spend ten minutes shooing a housefly out an open window.

Hunting and fishing were a regular part of cottage life, of course, and Gould fished with his father when he was very young, but in summer 1939, when he was six, he saw the light while fishing with a neighbour's family. He caught the first fish, but as it flopped about in the boat, he later recalled, "I suddenly saw this thing entirely from the fish's point of view." He tried to put the fish back, but his companions just laughed, and the father pushed him back down in his seat. He then kept up a "screaming tantrum" until the party returned to shore, and he refused to speak to those neighbours for the rest of the summer. After ten years of trying he finally convinced his father to give up fishing – "probably the greatest thing I have ever done" – and as an adult he liked to roar around in a boat in an effort to spook the fish, despite the hollers and curses of the fishermen. He called himself "The Scourge of Lake Simcoe."

Animals even figured in retirement plans he thought up as a child and was still entertaining at the end of his life. He often talked of leaving the city behind and retiring to some rural setting, where he would buy property that could become a refuge for unwanted pets, or for old cows and horses and other obsolete farm animals – the "Glenn Gould Puppy Farm" was one incarnation of the plan. It is a touching scenario, and for someone genuinely happier singing to cows than playing before ravening hordes in Carnegie Hall, it might have been a nice way to go out.

"I found going to school a most unhappy experience."

The idyll of Gould's early childhood came to an end when he had to go to school. As he told Joseph Roddy in a 1960 *New Yorker* profile, "When I was six, I managed to persuade my parents that mine was an uncommonly sensitive soul, which ought not to be exposed to the boorish vandalism I perceived among my contemporaries." As a result, he was tutored privately at home during the 1938–39 school year. ("By one school of my biographers it is considered that this was my undoing.") In the fall of 1939, he began Grade 2 at Williamson Road Public School, a large, sombre brick edifice that bordered the back of the Goulds' property. He passed Grade 2 with honours, and was permitted to skip ahead to Grade 4 in the fall of 1940. "He was interested in everything," Jessie Greig said. "And his desire to learn everything was just boundless." That is true, but he was mostly bored by the particular confines and curriculum of public school. His schoolwork was usually above the class average, but rarely stellar, often careless, always messy. His sloppy handwriting was the bane of his teachers.

Socially, he was ill at ease in school. He was already markedly eccentric, and his eccentricity was no put-on. Robert Fulford, who met Gould at Williamson Road after his family rented the house at 34 Southwood Drive, recalled, "He could act oddly, laugh good-naturedly at the oddness of his behaviour, and then act oddly again." "I got along miserably with most of my teachers and all of my fellow students," Gould said. "What the child psychologists would call the group spirit was found to be quite lacking in my personality." In fact, he hated the "organized relaxation" more than the schoolwork, for he had none of the athletic or social interests that bring young people together. He was mostly averse to exercise, and abhorred the rougher forms of sport. Hide-and-seek, sleighriding, quoits, horseshoes, and croquet were his games of choice (skipping Grade 3 would have made him younger and smaller than his fellow-students). He was a loner, happiest at home where he could pursue his own interests and control his environment.

Glenn's unusual intellectual and artistic gifts were apparent early on, and his schoolmates knew he was special, which did not help him fit in. Hugh Thomson was presumably acting on information from Gould when he reported, in a 1956 *Toronto Daily Star* profile, that Gould had been "tormented" by bullies, and he was known to go home from school in tears. Gould himself said, "Because I wouldn't fight back, the neighbourhood kids used to delight in beating me up. But it's an exaggeration to say they beat me up every day. It was only every other day." He told John Roberts that a bully once followed him home from school and even took a swing at him. "And Glenn just went for him. And hit him so hard that this kid wondered what had struck him. Then Glenn grabbed him by the lapels and shook him and said, 'If you ever come near me again, I will kill you.' And this kid was absolutely scared out of his mind, and the thing which also frightened Glenn was that he realized that it was true." The effect of such an incident on a child of Gould's sensitivity is easy to imagine; it made him only more anxious about keeping his feelings in check.

His anxieties about leaving the security of home and his emotional trials at school led to physical symptoms (headaches, stomach cramps), which gave Glenn an excuse to take time off and study in comfort at home. His Grade 2 records already reveal some impressive absenteeism: eleven and a half days in November 1939, eleven in March 1940, five or six in other months. It was the beginning of a pattern that persisted into adulthood: using real or imagined illness as an excuse to retreat from an uncomfortable situation.

When Glenn was thirteen, Jessie Greig, who was seven years older and lived in nearby Oshawa, moved into the Gould home while studying for a year at a Toronto teacher's college. "He had not experienced the give and take of brothers and sisters," she recalled. "At first there had been jealousy on his part. However, this 'meddlin' country cuzzin,' as I became known, soon became a friend and cohort with whom he could relax, tease, laugh, discuss, and rely on for support and encouragement. Many times he recounted the antics of that first year and said that it was the happiest one of his whole life." She would become his surrogate sister, and though she moved back to Oshawa to teach, they remained in contact for the rest of his life. She came to believe that he was unhappy as a boy, and certainly his school years were less idyllic than his early childhood. "I remember being in the sun porch and looking out at Williamson Road School," she said, "and seeing Glenn at recess standing up against the fence all by himself. That picture has always stayed with me, because he was lonely, even in those days." Fulford, she said, was the only real friend he had – at least, the only one he brought home – and she recalled seeing Glenn, around age eight, flee a Greig gathering in Uxbridge and take refuge at Grandmother Gould's to escape too large a gathering. Bert insisted that his son had "many friends," especially at the cottage, where Glenn was the ringleader of a group of boys who liked to frighten the cottagers by hiding in the woods and howling like wolves. But these were probably passing playmates more than real friends. The young Gould was already, by choice, a loner.

The whole of Gould's public-school career fell in the years of the Second World War, for which Toronto mobilized aggressively: by 1943 two-thirds of the city's labour force was involved in some kind of war work. Even a sheltered Beach boy would have noticed the air-raid sirens, searchlights, and air patrols, the blackouts and "dim-outs," the shortages of some consumer goods, the rationing of certain food staples and gasoline. Uniformed guards were posted at strategic locations, including a hydro installation and a water-filtration plant not far from Southwood Drive. The CNE was closed for five years, its buildings given over to the military, and many British children were moved to Toronto as "war guests." Much of the news on the radio and in the newspapers was devoted to the war; the CBC greatly increased its news and political coverage, and even classical-music programs contained a patriotic or propagandistic element.

The Gould family made their own contributions. Florence was one of legions of women who helped out through the church – Red Cross sewing circles, Christmas Boxes, Bundles for Britain. At Williamson Road, as at other Canadian schools, children studied war-related subjects, participated in events designed to boost patriotism and morale, collected recyclable scrap materials. Students raised funds through concerts, plays, and sales, saved money to buy bonds, and gave money to the Red Cross for war orphans. Williamson Road students were assigned a military rank according to how many War Saving Stamps they bought. (Glenn ranked high in his class.) In later life Gould said little about the war, though he was certainly aware of it. For one thing, he saw his Uncle Grant, and at least one cousin, in uniform. And one item in *The Daily Woof*, in fact, is prefaced with a note: "This item was released from censor." For a boy with Glenn's sensitivity and horror of violence, the war surely made an impact, even at a distance; his later pacifism and concern about international events suggest as much.

"I was not a prodigy."

The young Glenn Gould was more than just a smart, sensitive, polite, odd little boy: he would grow up to be one of the great musicians of the twentieth century, though when he was born there was relatively little professional musical life in Toronto, or anywhere else in Canada. Asked to describe the prevailing musical climate in Canada in the thirties, the composer John Weinzweig replied, "Cloudy and cool!" There were few orchestras, and only in Toronto and Montreal was there anything resembling a professional musical education. Music in Toronto had historically been amateur and domestic; public music-making was mostly confined to churches and choirs (Toronto was known as the choral-music capital of North America). There was some music in schools, bands, and theatres, but very little opera or symphonic music, not even much chamber or large-scale piano music, given a dearth of performance opportunities and public interest.

Toronto's musical life was, moreover, colonial. Most of the leading local musicians were British by birth or training or inclination, most musical organizations were based on British models, most local composers were grounded in the English church tradition and the idiom of late-Romantic English art music. There were many non-British piano and violin teachers, and the influx of European émigrés, beginning in the thirties, significantly changed the complexion of Toronto's musical life, but well into the fifties ambitious young musicians like the composer R. Murray Schafer were still calling for a less insular, more international perspective, lamenting "the dummy culture which then burdened this country, with a British organist in every cuckoo-nest." In Gould's formative years, young Canadian musicians were starved for contact with the larger musical world. They found inspiration in records and radio and musicians passing through from overseas, and dreamed of studying in Europe or New York. The composer Harry Somers compared Toronto's musical life, in those days, to "an enormous restaurant that serves only fish and chips."

Neither Methodism nor Presbyterianism, traditionally, had much encouraged the arts, and in rural Ontario, as Gould's grandmother Alma Horne once told him, "it was considered no asset at all to be an artist," because "to be an artist was to put oneself needlessly in the way of damnation." Nevertheless, both sides of Gould's family were musical. Alma Horne played piano and organ. Grant Gould, who earned his M.D. in 1942 and practised in Vancouver, also played piano, and Bert's other brother, Bruce, who ran an insurance agency in Uxbridge, and sold and repaired electrical supplies, played violin, saxophone, and several brass instruments, and led a dance band. Bert had played violin as a child until he injured his hand, and Florence gave piano and voice lessons; both sang, too, and according to a 1940 newspaper report Bert directed the Ensign Male Quartette, with Florence's piano accompaniment.

For the Goulds, music was inseparable from church, something Glenn stressed in his eulogy for his mother: "From the time she was a teenager, she devoted her life to classical music – and, in particular, to music for the sacred service – being active in church and young peoples' groups." Florence had studied piano and voice in Uxbridge and in Toronto, where she sang with several large choirs and was organist in a local Presbyterian church; she later served as choirmaster at Uxbridge United Church, and taught privately in Uxbridge, Bradford, and Toronto. It was through her choir work in

Uxbridge that she met Bert. After she married, she continued to do choral and solo work in churches in and around Toronto, and successfully reorganized the musical life of one troubled church in the east end. Music was a fixture of the Business Men's Bible Class, too, which had its own chorus and orchestra, for which Florence and Alma both played. Both of Gould's parents sang, separately and in duet, for Bible Class events. The couple also organized musical programs for churches in the Toronto area, and these, according to Bert, occasionally included recitations by Lucy Maud Montgomery, the author of *Anne of Green Gables*, who lived near Uxbridge in Leaskdale from 1911 to 1926.

In puritan cultures, as Gould once wrote, people tend to take "the view of art as an instrument of salvation, of the artist as missionary advocate," and in Toronto no less than in rural Ontario in his day, it was commonplace to view music less as a passion or a vocation than an adjunct to religion and morality. Music was undeniably a great force in his mother's life especially, though the Goulds, Robert Fulford recalled, "saw music as uplifting and educational, roughly on the level of saying grace at supper and attending the United Church. Once, after an extremely difficult concert of atonal music, I heard Mrs. Gould say that it should be put on for children in the schools. 'It's so *educational*,' she said. Clearly, she hadn't liked it, but felt it would be good for someone." (One of Gould's musical friends compares Florence's ideas on music to those of a Sunday-school teacher, and recalls her own playing as "embarrassing.") Gould would soar far above his family musically and intellectually, and in later life poked gentle fun at, for instance, his grandmother's love for "those indefatigable anthem composers of the English Victorian tradition, whose works she kept stacked on the console of her reed organ, and to the greater glories of whose Mendelssohnian euphony she would pump furiously at the bellows pedals, convinced that with each scrupulous avoidance of parallel fifths the devil was given his comeuppance." Yet he would become, in his own way, a passionate advocate for a moralistic – and, yes, puritanical – approach to music, and some of the music his family played, particularly hymns, made a profound impact on him long before he discovered composers like Bach and Schoenberg and continued to move and inspire him to the end of his life.

As a young woman, Florence told friends that she would one day marry and have a son named Glenn who would be musical. She played music to him when he was in the womb, and she surrounded him with music from the day he was born: she sang and played for him, played the radio and recordings, and generously exposed him to what music Toronto had to offer. He attended his first recital when he was about six – it was the pianist Josef Hofmann, and the event made a "staggering impression," he recalled – and he began attending concerts of the Toronto Symphony when he was seven. Florence had turned down what Gould called "a very interesting opportunity to pursue an operatic career" in order to marry Bert, and though she was not an aggressive stage mother her singular devotion to her son's musical development might have grown out of a feeling that he was her own second chance as a serious musician. (Did Gould sense this? Did he resent it?)

Glenn's gifts quickly became apparent. "As a baby a few days old," said Bert, he would reach his arms up and "flex his fingers almost as if playing a scale." His hands were naturally agile and flexible, and he instinctively guarded them. Even as an infant he would pull them away or turn his back if someone threw or rolled a ball at him. Once, when he was just seven or eight, Jessie Greig asked him to join in a game of marbles. He wanted to play, but when he put his hand down and found the ground cold, he withdrew it at once, and said, "I'm afraid I can't."

When he was three years old, Glenn's parents determined that he had perfect pitch when he correctly named a note being sung on a record. "As soon as he could talk he would call the notes by name and before long he would recognize every note struck in a four- or five-note chord," Bert recalled. Florence "used to play a game of note recognition with Glenn. He would go to a room at the far end of the house and his mother would strike a difficult chord on the piano in the living room. Invariably Glenn would call the correct answer." (The young Mozart used to impress people with the same trick.) When he was four, Florence began to give him piano lessons, and he took to the instrument instinctively. By the time he was five, he was picking out tunes and making up his own. Other gifts soon became apparent: a discerning ear, good ear-hand co-ordination, and a talent for improvising and musical mimicry, sight-reading, and transposing. Gould himself once said that the three most important aspects of his musical makeup were "the ability to concentrate, perfect pitch and an excellent musical memory." Florence was a nurturing but strict teacher. She never allowed her son to fudge a passage or play a wrong note, and it paid off: the adult Gould's precision and accuracy at the keyboard amazed everyone.

He was a pianist with a peculiarly intimate physical relationship with the instrument. Consider the familiar image of Gould at the piano: seated unusually low, hunched over with his face almost on top of the keyboard, his knees higher than his buttocks, stroking the keys as his body rocks and rotates – he appears at times to be *hugging* the instrument, maintaining a physical posture that is as close to a fetal position as is compatible with playing. And he sang while he played. He had a predisposition to sing from earliest infancy, and Florence actually taught him to sing everything that he played, instilling an unbreakable (and notorious) habit. The whole physical spectacle of Gould at the piano and his intimate attitude toward it may have had a great deal to do with his having studied under his mother – the association of playing with singing and of singing with Mother. Embracing the instrument as he played, he may instinctively have been recapturing the womblike shelter he always craved, and that special security he felt pressing down keys while sitting on his mother's lap. Paradoxically, this intensely physical relationship with the piano was probably one important source of his later idealistic, otherworldly view of music. The piano was always a refuge for Gould – a "Shangri-La," he said – a direct link with the idyll of his infancy, and he came to view music as (in his words) "a thing apart," unconnected to the real world.

His instruction began with simple pieces like folk songs and hymns, and baby-books that made a game of playing, but Glenn was a serious student from the start, and his progress was impressive. (According to Grant Gould, Florence often compared her son to Mozart.) By the time he was ten, he could play all of the preludes and fugues in the first book of Bach's *Well-Tempered Clavier*, as well as sonatas by Mozart, waltzes by Chopin and Liszt, and comparable works. His parents devoted themselves to his musical education. Florence took fewer pupils after Glenn came along, and he was excused from household chores in order to practise. He loved playing, and never needed to be encouraged to do so. He would practise for hours, and his parents eventually had to enforce daily time limits (Fulford remembered a four-hour limit being imposed at one point). Bert said that locking the piano was more effective than corporal punishment in enforcing discipline. The piano, Gould said, became a "means to isolation," helping him cope with the difficulties of school and schoolmates by allowing him to retreat into the world of his imagination.

As early as age five or six, definitely by nine or ten, Glenn had decided he would become a professional pianist. But his parents, though themselves in awe of the wonder they had produced, refused to push him into the life of a star prodigy. (There are advantages to having discreet parents who think it a sin to show off.) "The word *prodigy* was banned from the Gould household," Fulford wrote. "Prodigies were children of freakish talent, exploited by their parents and ruined by over-exposure; Mozart, in Gould family mythology, was a cautionary example." The Goulds did not want to put strain on their son's mental or physical health, and they were prosperous and unpretentious enough not to be tempted by the money and fame their son might earn. So they allowed him to develop at his own rate according to his own tastes, exposing him only very gradually and modestly to the public.

Still, there were conflicts. The Goulds were pleased that their son was an exceptional musician, but they also wanted him to be a normal boy with normal interests and normal friends and normal standards of propriety. As a child Gould already had a "free-ranging, almost wild, extremely irreverent" way of talking, according to Fulford;

long, excited monologues, of a sophistication far above his contemporaries, came streaming out of him whenever he had an audience. He had some of the pompousness and pretense of most prodigies, and did not hesitate to spout off on arcane subjects or offer outrageous opinions where he was hardly qualified to do so. He had a snobbish commitment to classical music. "Popular music is terrible," he said, at thirteen, to a local newspaper – to which his mother added, "He is still young, and may change his mind." (He didn't.) Florence "hated conflict, and she hated anything extreme or eccentric," Fulford wrote. "In my memory, she is always admonishing Glenn about something, calling him to account for a transgression of her rules." Fulford remembered seeing Florence upbraid Gould for calling Caruso a fraud and a "terrible" singer, saying that he had neither the insight nor the experience to make such bald judgements. She was right, of course, but then throughout his life Gould never feared making reckless generalizations on the basis of imperfect knowledge, even downright ignorance, especially when it came to his *bêtes noires*. "Florence Gould had a talent for exasperation and she was a much exasperated, much put-upon woman," Fulford wrote, adding that she could be "a bit of a dragon." But she wanted the impossible, a genius who was also a well-behaved boy who sat up straight and didn't espouse bratty, precocious ideas, a child who would stand out *and* fit in.

Gould's first documented public appearance as a musician was in Uxbridge, on the afternoon of Sunday, June 5, 1938, when he accompanied his parents in a vocal duet at a service celebrating the thirtieth anniversary of the Business Men's Bible Class. The next day, when he performed as part of the golden jubilee celebrations of the Trinity United Church building, the *Uxbridge Times-Journal* praised "the several numbers rendered by the little five year old son of Mr. and Mrs. Gold, Glenn, by name, who quickly impressed the audience that here was something of a musical genius in the making. All his numbers were splendid, but the two original compositions of the little chap were quite remarkable in one so young, and foreshadowed one of the country's talented composers in the not too distant future." At five, it was clear that Glenn's wide-ranging talent for music would not be confined to playing the piano. His mother encouraged him to write "my own little masterpieces," and some competent (though not exceptional) compositions from his childhood still survive. The earliest is *A Merry Thought*, a sprightly, twenty-nine-bar march for piano, set in a respectable ternary form, dated December 18, 1941, and dedicated "to my dear teacher, Miss Trott." When he was ten, Gould helped his school contribute to the war effort with a little patriotic song, also march-like and full of Edwardian pomp, called *Our Gifts*, for two vocal parts (boys and girls) with piano accompaniment. Copies of the music, dated March 25, 1943, were duplicated by Bert, with a dedication "to the Junior Red Cross throughout Canada." The first of the two wince-inducing stanzas of text (by Gould?) reads: "We are the boys,/We are the girls of all the Public Schools./We have a Red Cross job to do, to furnish all the tools./So many fathers, brothers too, may have a chance to live./When wounded on the battlefield, they'll live because we give."

Until he was a teenager most of Glenn's public appearances were in churches in Toronto and Uxbridge and nearby towns. Sometimes he played solo as part of a concert or service, sometimes he led or accompanied singers, occasionally he offered his own compositions. Jean Brown (formerly "Miss Trott") recalls that he would perform regularly at school assemblies, too. He played organ as well as piano. At eleven he was hired as organist by a local Anglican church, but tended to lose his place whenever the congregation sang. After one particularly embarrassing mistake, he was abruptly dismissed. Programs survive for about a dozen performances between 1938 and 1946, and we may assume there were others, perhaps many. The venues included the likes of the Annual Spring Tea and Concert of the Wanstead Women's Association, and Gould's memories of them included "the Lord Fauntleroy suit – the sort of garb with which I was usually decked out by my doting parents." The ladies loved him: one local woman recalled seeing him play in a white satin suit with short pants. It all sounds charmingly provincial and innocuous,

The first two pages from the original printing of *Our Gifts*, which Gould composed when he was ten years old. *(Estate of Glenn Gould.)*

revealing the admirable caution with which his parents marshalled and exposed his talent.

"I must have been a rather difficult student to handle."

In fall 1945, Gould began high school, with Grade 9, at Malvern Collegiate Institute, a large brick school on Malvern Avenue just north of Kingston Road, about a kilometre from his house. ("Collegiate Institute" was just a fancy name for a high school that was academically oriented, as distinct from, say, a technical school or a high school of commerce.) Malvern, in Robert Fulford's view, was "the Beach incarnate," a school that set great store by propriety and "school spirit," and prepared its students for life in a materialistic world. Documents survive for Gould's last few years of high school, and they reveal dense, highly structured, conventional courses of study, long on facts and rote learning, and there is nothing to suggest that Gould found it intellectually challenging or inspiring, though he remembered several teachers and principals with affection. By Grades 11 and 12 he was taking only four courses – English, French, history, and geography – and for Grade 13 he dropped geography. His surviving schoolwork suggests a want of application: his poorest marks were in those courses for which he had the least innate talent and really had to work. He fared worst in French, earning marks in the 50s and 60s. His history marks were not much better, and his English marks hovered mostly in the 70s and low 80s. Better marks were rare, lower (even failing) marks not unknown. Yet he was usually near the top of his class, substantiating Fulford's recollection of Malvern as a notoriously mediocre school.

Gould's schoolmates were nonetheless aware that he was exceptional. "Glenn's intelligence reached far beyond music," Fulford wrote. "In Grade Ten geometry he mastered the textbook by the end of October, while the rest of us were just getting started." (At Williamson Road, too, his math grades were always among his best.) He was showing signs of adult interests, too – already, for instance, launched on his lifelong habit of gathering news and gossip and analyzing world affairs. He could discourse on politics with grown-up insight; Fulford remembered him eagerly following the 1948 Republican National Convention, jotting down delegate counts the way most kids would track baseball stats. He liked to show off in his schoolwork, revealing a prodigy's contempt for the mundane. Bert once queried a teacher about a respectable-looking English-composition exam that had received a failing grade, and was told, "Mr. Gould, I am a busy teacher and have better things to do with my time than to read papers that require one to constantly have to refer to a dictionary for half of the words used." Asked to write on "My Plans for the School Year," at the start of Grade 13, Gould began:

> I am at something of a disadvantage in writing on this subject, for my adventures in the halls of learning are curtailed at the close of the fourth period each morning. The remainder of my day is spent in the pursuit of music, with the exclusion of an hour or so in the evening which I rather grudgingly bequeath to MacBeth, the Treaty of Ghent, and the subjunctive mood.
>
> It must not be assumed, however, that I have a complete disregard for higher education. On the contrary, I find it stimulating, enlightening, refreshing, and capable of tremendous influence on otherwise stagnant minds. (For this well defined phrase I am indebted to the preface of a Manitoba school textbook authorized and published in 1911, entitled, "Crop, Cricket and Tariff Control.")

"My plans for the school year," he concluded at length, "therefore are non-existent." ("Clever!" wrote his teacher, at the end.) Elements of Gould's adult writing can be seen here: the pompous, self-satisfied tone, the verbosity, the attempt at breezy humour and sophistication, the evident delight in writing that is plainly ghastly. He was not merely a bored genius, however. In most subjects he lacked the natural aptitude that he had for music, though he would not admit it. He thought he was smarter than his teachers and was loathe to take their advice, though they were often right. And anyway, by high school he knew he was headed for a career – probably a *great* career – in music, and was not motivated to take academic life seriously.

Many people remember Gould in these years as a sweet, funny, courteous, lovable boy, though he was clearly peculiar, which precluded intimacy with his less complicated schoolmates. And of course, his talent and intelligence and temperament set him apart, and he had no extracurricular activities at school besides music. Neighbours at the cottage recalled a "solitary child with strong opinions," and Father Joseph H. O'Neill, a clergyman in Orillia, remembered the twelve-year-old Gould as "a rather reserved kind of person," somewhat superior and antisocial. In summer 1945, in an effort to "normalize" him a little, F. O'Neill prevailed upon him to play some music at a weiner roast for teenage altar boys who were visiting from Toronto. Gould, whether naively or arrogantly or defiantly, insisted on playing Bach – and, as F. O'Neill noted, "it was a tough job keeping restless young people quiet during a recital of this kind." Some people saw him as standoffish, or at least impenetrably shy. Fragile and bundled up, his appearance said "Hands off" to some of his peers. Gould himself admitted, "At the age of 14, I was a spoiled brat, being an only child. Perhaps some of this is necessary for the supreme arrogance a concert artist requires."

He arrived at Malvern, at the age of thirteen, with a reputation as a local celebrity in the making, and among his classmates he was the subject of much rumour and speculation. He was an oddity, to be sure, conducting and singing to himself as he walked to and from school, the sort of school in which the arts were viewed as sissy stuff. Awkward in his gangly adolescent body and often dishevelled, he was not physically impressive, either. Other kids were not above laughing at him behind his back, though he seems not to have been bullied and tormented the way he had been at public school. Fulford, at least, recalled that he was not despised for being an oddity, because his gifts were "prodigious and mysterious" enough to inspire a kind of awe. As at Williamson Road, those gifts isolated him, and he made few real friends, but even at this age he was so committed to music that he willingly sacrificed friendship, however much he desired it.

Dubbed "The Ten Hottest Fingers in Malvern" in a 1946 school publication, *The Muse*, Gould was well known there as a pianist. He performed at assemblies, holiday concerts, and other school functions, sometimes with his own works, and in January 1948 he arranged for his friend Ray Dudley to play Beethoven's "Emperor" Concerto (Gould played the orchestral part on an organ). In February 1949, as an overture to a school production of *Twelfth Night*, he performed a fifteen-minute suite of his own composition – four short pieces in very different styles intended to reflect the different styles of writing in various scenes of the play. A private recording of him playing the suite, with his own spoken introduction, survives from around this time,* and reveals that the sixteen-year-old had developed real compositional skills, though all four pieces call for arch-Romantic virtuoso display of the sort that the adult Gould repudiated. The first piece, "Nocturne," is strange, rhapsodic, often impressionistic. "Whimsical Nonsense" is a mischievous, jig-like scherzo in a Romantic style (think Mendelssohn, or perhaps Victor Herbert), full of scampering figuration. "Elizabethan Gaiety" is a busy, jolly, Baroquish jig – an exercise in neo-Handelian pastiche. And the long finale, "Regal Atmosphere," begins funereally but builds to a grandiose and highly ornate march. Gould's longhair music bored some of his classmates, and he would occasionally oblige them with popular songs, but they seemed to know intuitively that he was destined to become a world-famous musician. "Already we knew he was special," Wayne Fulford said. "*He* knew it too."

---

* No score survives, however. According to a contemporary report on the subject published in the *Weekly Mail*, "Miss Joan Dobe, of London, England, a theatre critic and writer, has asked for Glen's [*sic*] composition for her own correlation of creative arts for children" – whatever that means.

"I didn't approve of my teacher."

Born into a bourgeois family with puritan roots, yet receiving nothing but support in his pursuit of an artistic career, the young Gould was a rare, fortunate creature indeed. Once his talent was apparent he became the focal point of his household; Florence in particular was always there to meet his needs. Of course he was spoiled – he later admitted to friends that getting his own way so much as a child had not necessarily been good for his development – but he was nourished, too, and we may credit much of his later confidence and originality as a performer to the support he received as a child. Bert's prosperity, Robert Fulford wrote, "made it possible for him to spend about $3,000 a year on Glenn's musical education, in 1940s money" – and Fulford was not exaggerating when he added that three thousand dollars "was roughly the sum that supported our entire family of seven, next door." In the late thirties the average yearly salary in Toronto was about half that amount, and a professor of music at the University of Toronto received a stipend of four thousand dollars. Even as a child Gould was never satisfied with any one piano for long, and Bert recalled having often to buy newer, better instruments, uprights at first and later grands, though he balked at tearing up the house to install a pipe organ, which Glenn innocently requested as a birthday gift around age twelve. In his teens he was already beginning to keep late hours, and sometimes wanted to practise long into the night. Bert eventually knocked down a back wall to build a studio, which Gould filled with his many books and musical scores, his recording equipment, and a *second* grand piano, for which Bert paid some six thousand dollars. Bert was buying new uprights almost annually for the cottage, too: the winter weather tended to ruin them after a year or two.

Gould quickly outgrew his mother as a musician. She took the logical next step, early in 1940, and sent him to the Toronto Conservatory of Music, which in those days was located downtown at College St. and University Ave. Though incorporated in 1886, it still did not offer the highest level of professional training; most of the pupils were children and amateurs. Not surprisingly, the basic orientation, structure, and curriculum of the conservatory, and much of the faculty, were British, and it conducted annual nationwide examinations modelled on the British system. Between February 1940 and June 1943, Gould passed piano examinations for Grades 3 through 9, with first-class honours, earning praise as early as age seven for his finger-work, his rhythm and tone, and his "remarkable" ear, and usually receiving a silver medal for having the highest marks in Ontario. He later took theory classes from one of the pillars of Toronto's musical establishment, the English-born cellist, composer, and writer Leo Smith (1881–1952), who joined the conservatory in 1911. A "sweet, dreamy character," according to the composer Murray Adaskin, Smith composed in a turn-of-the-century English-Romantic style, and took a conservative approach to theory. Surviving documents show Gould passing theory exams for Grades 2 through 5 between February 1942 and June 1946, in subjects including harmony, counterpoint, form, and history,* as well as earning perfect scores in singing and sight-singing. (He had "a beautiful boy soprano voice," Bert recalled, "but as he grew older it just deteriorated into a squawk.")

More significant were lessons with the English-born organist and choir conductor Frederick Silvester (1901–66), who became a friend of the family. Gould began organ lessons in 1942, and made rapid progress toward a professional technique, earning first-class honours, several medals, and glowing adjudications from resident experts like the English-born organist, composer, and choir conductor Healey Willan: "He possesses a real organ sense," Willan noted in 1944. The organ, Gould later said, gave him a taste for Bach and other early music, and had a profound influence on his piano style. It taught him to "think with his feet," which led to a fondness for bringing out basslines (he was also left-handed, incidentally); it taught him to "think of music as being played by three hands – the feet acting as the third hand," which led to a passion for

---

* Those already familiar with Gould's adult proclivities will be amused to note that his worst marks – bare passes – were in counterpoint and form.

counterpoint unusual among pianists; and it taught him not to pound the keys but to develop a technique based on "the tips of the fingers," and to make expressive nuances through slight shifts of tempo instead of dynamics, both of which encouraged his clean, "upright," clearly articulated piano playing.

When Gould was ten, Florence knew it was time for him to find another piano teacher, of which there were many at the conservatory, where the vast majority of students were pianists. After seeking the advice of Smith, Willan, and the organist, composer, and conductor Sir Ernest MacMillan, the conservatory's principal from 1926 to 1942, the Goulds placed their son, in the fall of 1943, in the class of Alberto Guerrero, with whom he would study for the next nine years. Guerrero rarely accepted very young pupils, but he recognized that he had something special in Glenn, who became the golden boy of his class; he considered Glenn a genius, in fact (though Gould himself would always regard that word "with great suspicion"). They would have one or two lessons a week – Guerrero was always generous with lesson time – at Guerrero's studio in his penthouse at 51 Grosvenor Street, a few blocks from the conservatory. The teacher maintained both an artistic and a physical distance from the mainstream of local musical life: "Guerrero never taught in the Conservatory building, and only rarely appeared there," the composer John Beckwith, another former pupil, recalled. The Gould and Guerrero families became close. Gould would attend parties at his teacher's home, and the families would see each other at Lake Simcoe, where Guerrero had a cottage Bert had helped him find.

Alberto Antonio García Guerrero was born in 1886, in La Serena, Chile, about four hundred kilometres north of Santiago, into a wealthy, cultured, liberal family that traced its origins back to Catalonia, in northeastern Spain. He was a privileged child who was bred with the manners of an aristocrat, and he received a broad education at home from tutors. He studied dentistry briefly, before deciding to devote his life to music. His mother was an accomplished pianist, as were his sisters, his brother Daniel (who became a doctor), and his brother Eduardo (who became a law professor, was well-read in literature, philosophy, and music, and became an important critic and lecturer in music). Guerrero's early musical training seems to have been entirely *en famille*; he had a better claim to being self-taught and *sui generis* than his most famous pupil ever did. In 1912 the Guerrero family moved to Santiago, where it became a respected and influential force in the development of a modern classical-music culture in Chile. Alberto, before he was even thirty, was renowned as a pianist and critic; as the composer of piano pieces, songs, chamber music, and several theatrical works; as the author of a textbook on modern harmony; as a teacher and mentor to some of the most important musicians in the country; and as a driving force behind local performing groups and musical organizations. Fellow-musicians admired his grasp of piano technique and musical analysis, his wide repertoire, his familiarity with the latest European literature on music theory and aesthetics. He championed modern music, and composers sought his input. According to the composer Alfonso Leng, "His superior intelligence and exceptional talent changed the course of Chilean musical history."

By the time of the First World War, Guerrero had performed throughout South and Central America. He married in 1915, and his honeymoon doubled as an extensive concert tour that included, in 1916, his debut in New York, where he worked as a pianist and vocal coach. In August 1918 he moved to Toronto to teach at the Hambourg Conservatory, and in 1922 he transferred to the Toronto Conservatory, where he taught for the rest of his life. (He, too, liked Toronto because "they leave you alone.") He quickly established a reputation through concerts and high-profile appearances on Canadian and American radio, and was the most active and versatile performer among Toronto's piano teachers. In the twenties and thirties he played frequently and successfully in recitals, with orchestras, and in chamber music, but he was too self-effacing and too wide-ranging a musician to be content with a career as a virtuoso, and he gradually performed less often. He did play in major halls, even in Maple Leaf Gardens at least once, but he preferred more intimate venues like Malloney's Gallery, the Art Gallery of Toronto, and Hart House, a cultural centre at the

University of Toronto, and he gave concerts in at least one private home in town. He found small settings and connoisseur audiences more congenial to his tastes and temperament, and did not encourage his pupils to pursue a conventional concert career – "That's no way to live," he told his pupil Ray Dudley. (In this he may well have influenced Gould.) Between the wars he became increasingly devoted to teaching, and by the time the Goulds approached him his reputation was such that even his colleagues came to him for advice.

Robertson Davies' last novel, *The Cunning Man*, which offers a colourful portrait of early-twentieth-century Toronto, includes a reference to Guerrero, thinly disguised as "Augusto DaChiesa, a Chilean who is not in the little brotherhood that runs the local Conservatory, and who plays Scarlatti like an angel. DaChiesa is said to have a pupil who will make them all sit up and take notice in a few years. But we can't get him to our Sundays; stomach is bad and he seems to live on milk and crackers – and Scarlatti, of course. Has a mistress – would you believe it?" The "mistress" was Myrtle Rose, a former pupil, twenty years his junior, whom he met in 1931 and lived with openly; she became his second wife in 1947.

Guerrero's intellect and musical gifts were impressive. He told one of his pupils, Stuart Hamilton, that after hearing Saint-Saëns's opera *Samson et Dalila* for the first time, in Chile, he rushed home and began playing through the music from memory. Hamilton was skeptical, so Guerrero, though he had not glanced at the score in decades, sat down at the piano and played the whole first act. Another pupil, Sylvia Hunter, remembers a lesson in which she was to play Khachaturian's difficult and then rarely played piano concerto. Guerrero, who was to accompany her on a second piano, could not find his own copy of the score, so he simply played the whole orchestral part from memory, even though he had not played or thought about the piece for many years (he did not even like it much). His most popular published composition, *Tango* (1937), was something he had improvised at a party. But he was not a music machine: he had a breadth of culture that distinguished him from his colleagues. He had many musical interests beyond the piano, particularly opera, and he had a large library of scores, including such works as Mahler's symphonies, from which Gould benefited.

And he had many cultural interests outside music. He spoke several languages, including Esperanto, was well-read in literature, philosophy, and much else, was a connoisseur and amateur practitioner of painting, loved good food and wine (not just milk and crackers). He was a worldly, civilized man, "an extremely cultured and courteous gentleman," as the conductor Boyd Neel put it. "An evening at Guerrero's home took one back into the atmosphere of the Proustian salons of the turn of the century." Beckwith compared him to "a latter-day eighteenth-century French rationalist," and the composer R. Murray Schafer, who studied with him in 1954, wrote that "our lessons usually consisted of talks about philosophy (I recall discussing Comte, Husserl and Sartre with him) or the modern painters and poets, of which he was particularly fond of the French. He was one of the few musicians from whom a student could get ideas beyond music." He told his pupil Margaret Privitello, "Don't spend your whole day at the piano."

Always open-minded, Guerrero was sympathetic to the individual tastes and ambitions of his pupils. In Toronto, as in Chile, his pupils included many who would pursue musical careers away from the piano – as musicologists, theorists, broadcasters – and some notable composers, such as Beckwith, Schafer, Ruth Watson-Henderson, Edward Laufer, Bruce Mather, and Oskar Morawetz. Even the professional pianists among his pupils ranged widely: virtuosos like William Aide, Arthur Ozolins, and Malcolm Troup;*

---

* "One of the students Glenn talked about all the time was Malcolm Troup," Ray Dudley, another Guerrero pupil, recalled. "You see, Troup was a kind of character in the class. He was about three years older than Glenn, and I think he had a tremendous influence on him. Troup was radical in everything he did – in the way he dressed, the way he spoke, even the way he wrote. He'd write long, involved essays on some esoteric subject and then read them to the class. Well, I think Glenn would just sit there, fascinated. And Troup usually came into class with holes in his socks or wearing clothes that were rather dirty-looking. He was always trying to create a sensation with his appearance."

contemporary-music specialists like Mather and his wife, Pierrette LePage; polymaths like Ray Dudley, who played conventional piano repertoire while pursuing an interest in early music on the forte-piano; and the accompanists Gerald Moore and Stuart Hamilton, the latter also a vocal coach and the founder of Opera in Concert. All of his pupils, it appears, remember his teaching fondly, and praise his ability to serve their particular needs. He was a gentle, subtle, quietly confident man with a good sense of humour, though emotionally reserved, and he taught through suggestion and persuasion, not domination. Aide compared him to a "Virgilian guide," but added that he could be "as hard as nails." While never cruel, he was realistic and could be blunt, occasionally mildly sarcastic. His own unconventional musical training made him refreshingly skeptical about inherited traditions. "As a teacher," Beckwith wrote, "he had exceptional resources, but no 'method.'" He took a relaxed, flexible, improvisational approach to teaching.

He was, in short, the ideal teacher for the young Glenn Gould, who was already a stubborn and independent-minded musician. "I couldn't teach him the way I did others," Guerrero told the journalist Gladys Shenner in 1956. "Glenn resented it if I told him, 'That's not right.' Even at 11 he had a perfectly good idea of his powers and he hasn't changed much." Glenn, he added, "won't take anyone's word for anything. And it's better this way, because he keeps his originality." Gould was eager to absorb whatever came his way, and Guerrero saw his task as suggesting and proposing but always encouraging Gould to find his own way. As he told Myrtle, "The whole secret of teaching Glenn is to let him discover things for himself" – or at least, let him *think* he was discovering them for himself.

Under the cosmopolitan Guerrero, Gould's musicianship developed new sophistication. Guerrero's repertoire was unusually broad and conspicuously light on fluff, as Gould's would be, though Guerrero had a taste for many musical idioms that Gould would reject. He played a wide range of Classical and Romantic works, and though he tackled some of the most virtuosic music in the repertoire – Weber and Liszt, the Tchaikovsky concerto, even showpieces like Adolf Schulz-Evler's paraphrases on themes from the *Blue Danube* waltz – Guerrero was not a seeker after sensationalistic effects. His Romantic repertoire favoured substantial works: big sonatas by Beethoven, Schubert, and Chopin, major works by Schumann and Brahms.

In his first few years of lessons, Gould made rapid progress technically, and as a young teenager he commanded a wide range of conventional repertoire: sonatas by Mozart and Haydn; concertos by Mozart and Beethoven; difficult early sonatas by Beethoven (including Op. 2/No. 3, Op. 10/No. 3, and the "Tempest," Op. 31/No. 2), shorter works by the likes of Schubert, Chopin, Mendelssohn, Liszt, Brahms, and Paderewski. But it was Guerrero's unusual fondness for early music and modern music that had the greatest impact. Bach and Schoenberg were the axes of Gould's adult repertoire and aesthetic of music, and he developed his appreciation for both composers under Guerrero.

"I wasn't much attracted to multi-voiced things until I was a teenager," Gould recalled in 1970. "I was definitely homophonically inclined until the age of about 10, and then I suddenly got the message. Bach began to emerge into my world then and has never altogether left it. It was one of the great moments of my life." He played music by Bach under his mother, but his "first great contrapuntal awakening" actually came about through Mozart's C-major fugue, K. 394, which he was practising one day as the housekeeper, with whom he was feuding, ran the vacuum cleaner near the piano. Unable to hear the music properly but *feeling* it under his fingers, he received an idealized sense of the music that permitted deeper insight into its contrapuntal structure, and with Guerrero's guidance he developed this new sense into a fuller initiation in the world of counterpoint at the piano, Bach's in particular.

Bach's music was not a staple of the repertoire in the Toronto of Gould's youth – it was positively avoided by many musicians and listeners – though it did have some influential champions in what was, after all, an organ-and-choir town. Ernest MacMillan gave a ground-breaking series of all-Bach organ recitals in the early twenties, programmed Bach in his capacity as conductor of the Toronto Symphony, and led legendary annual performances of the St. Matthew Passion for more than three decades, beginning in 1923. ("No one has done more to make Canadians Bach listeners than Sir Ernest," noted the *Financial Post*, in 1948.) Reginald Stewart's Bach Society gave annual performances of the St. John Passion in the thirties, and the Toronto Mendelssohn Choir, too, performed Bach's music. Guerrero had always been a champion of Bach – in 1917, in Santiago, he and his brothers had spearheaded the organization of the Sociedad Bach – and in Toronto he performed works including the Two- and Three-Part Inventions, the Italian Concerto, the suites, and the Goldberg Variations, all of which would figure prominently in Gould's repertoire.

Guerrero, in fact, was a champion of all sorts of early music originally written for the harpsichord, clavichord, and fortepiano, by such composers as Anglés, J. S. Bach's sons, Cantallos, Couperin, Durante, Gluck, Soler, and above all Scarlatti, as well as the English Tudor composers. (The Tudors had other local champions, including Healey Willan, who led a madrigal choir in the thirties, and Leo Smith, who played the viola da gamba and published the widely used textbook *Music of the Seventeenth and Eighteenth Centuries* in 1931. Toronto was familiar with English Protestant church music, and the four-hundredth anniversary of the birth of the composer William Byrd was celebrated locally in 1943.) Guerrero's championship of early music won him a devoted following among local connoisseurs, and made a deep impression on Gould: "Ever since my teen-age years," Gould wrote, "the composers of the English Tudor School have elicited a very precise – and yet impossible to define – spiritual response from me." In 1949, as a Christmas present, Guerrero gave Gould the first volume of Harvard University Press's *Historical Anthology of Music*, which included Orlando Gibbons's "Lord of Salisbury" pavan and galliard, a staple of Gould's repertoire. Later, Gould discovered *The Fitzwilliam Virginal Book*, which included a Sweelinck fantasia he would play for decades, and he read books on Medieval and Renaissance music.

Guerrero owned a fortepiano, played the harpsichord at least once in public, and was an admirer and acquaintance of the pioneering harpsichordist Wanda Landowska. He attended some of her classes in Europe in the mid-thirties, and played her records for his pupils, including Gould (who didn't like her playing much). When Landowska came to Canada in spring 1943 to make a major series of CBC broadcasts, she stayed in Mélisande Irvine's apartment and would permit no one but her father to attend her recording sessions. "Guerrero was completely in awe of her," Margaret Privitello said. "He acted like an embarrassed schoolboy in the presence of his idol." Like his idol, Guerrero advocated the study of historical performance practices, and was unusually literate in matters like Baroque ornamentation. He introduced his pupils to Arnold Dolmetsch's watershed book *The Interpretation of the Music of the XVII and XVIII Centuries*, and to eighteenth-century treatises on performance by the likes of C. P. E. Bach, François Couperin, Leopold Mozart, and Johann Joachim Quantz, which were becoming available in English when Gould was in his teens. Thanks to Guerrero, Gould developed something of a reputation (in the early part of his career, at least) as an informed, even "scholarly" performer of early music.

As for modern music, Gould recalled that he was "a complete reactionary" until the age of fifteen, when he "flipped completely" over a recording of Hindemith conducting his *Mathis der Maler*.* With this work, he said, and Berg's Violin Concerto, he first "came alive to contemporary music." But for the most part, in Toronto, appreciation for modern music developed erratically in the first half of the twentieth century, and the city was slow to accept many of the musical developments coming out of Europe and America. At the conservatory and the University of Toronto, there was little

---

* In January 1946, Hindemith made his only visit to Toronto and lectured at the conservatory. It is difficult to imagine that Gould missed such a momentous event, but there is no mention of it among his writings and interviews and unpublished papers. He was just thirteen at the time, and so still "a complete reactionary"; perhaps he simply could not rouse enough enthusiasm to attend.

instruction in composition of any kind, and little support for budding modernists, especially among the British contingent. Between the wars there were a few performers receptive to modern music, like the Hart House Quartet (1924–46) and the Vogt Society (1936–45), and MacMillan programmed some modern music with the Toronto Symphony, particularly that of English composers. But symphonies by Walton, Bartók's *Concerto for Orchestra*, decades-old works by Stravinsky and Sibelius, even some works by the conservative Richard Strauss were too modern for many Toronto patrons – never mind Shostakovich or Prokofiev, Britten or Hindemith, the neo-classical Stravinsky or the Second Viennese School. Music by contemporary Canadians was no more welcome; to program it was brave and financially reckless. (Quebec was further ahead than English Canada when it came to musical modernism.) Still, Gould's particular tastes in modern music had some encouragement in his hometown – Ernest MacMillan's passion for Sibelius's symphonies, for instance, and the soprano Frances James's championship, from the early forties, of what would become Gould's favourite song cycle, Hindemith's *Das Marienleben*.

Gould was fudging the truth when he claimed, in a 1980 interview, that he was first attracted to modern music "because some of my teachers hated it." That was true enough of the British contingent but not of Guerrero, who had impressive credentials as a champion of modern music. In Chile the Guerrero home had been a salon for modernist artists, and Alberto had belonged to the Grupo de "Los Diez," a society of avant-garde poets, novelists, painters, and musicians, with its own journal (1915–16). He was a champion of Debussy and Ravel, of Berg and the atonal Schoenberg, long before he arrived in Toronto, when that music was new. In the thirties, he introduced Toronto to major works by these composers, and by Bartók, Hindemith, Milhaud, Stravinsky, and others. His modern repertoire included many Russian, French, Spanish, and Italian composers, major figures (Albéniz, Casella, Fauré, Granados, Prokofiev, Satie, Villa-Lobos) as well as obscure ones (Allende, Auric, Chávez, Cras, Hahn, Polovinkin, Shebalin, Tailleferre). "His personal support of 20th century music was almost in the nature of an underground movement," the Canadian-music scholar Carl Morey wrote, and his performances had a great influence within a select circle.

Crucially, it was Guerrero who introduced Gould to Schoenberg. As Beckwith remembered the story, Guerrero, at a lesson sometime around 1948, "was amazed at Gould's reaction" when he showed him Schoenberg's Op. 11 and Op. 19 pieces, which he had performed in Toronto on several occasions. "The first response was rejection. Strong arguments against Schoenberg and atonality were raised, Guerrero being put on the defensive. But, a few weeks later, Gould showed up with some pieces of his own in the same style, for which Guerrero was full of praise." Gould took up this repertoire as a new cause: he read about Schoenberg and his school, absorbed other modern music in Guerrero's repertoire, moved on to the twelve-tone idiom as practised by Schoenberg and his disciples, particularly Anton Webern and Ernst Krenek, and finally explored some music by the post-war serialists.

Guerrero's musicianship was informed by his wider culture. He was, as Beckwith put it, "not so much a teacher of piano as a teacher of *music*." For the young Gould, already expressing musical interests outside the piano, Guerrero was a vital intellectual catalyst, nurturing some of his most characteristic predilections and aesthetic positions, though ultimately his thinking would also depart in many ways from his teacher's. Gould absorbed Guerrero's seriousness and commitment toward music, his insistence on being a well-rounded musician; indeed, *pianist* would become a dirty word in Gould's vocabulary. In later life he sometimes dismissed Guerrero as a Romantic: "Our outlooks on music were diametrically opposed," he told Joseph Roddy. "He was a 'heart' man and I wanted to be a 'head' kid." Yet it was Guerrero who helped nourish the young Gould's increasingly idealistic, intellectual, and structural approach to music. When the adult Gould insisted that structure was the most important criterion for a performer, he was paraphrasing Guerrero, one of whose premises was that music "must be architecturally conceived." And when, in his last interview, he offered up his most basic premise – "One does not play the piano with one's fingers, one plays the piano with one's mind" – he was all but quoting, more than thirty years after his last lesson, a cherished maxim that Guerrero had borrowed from a French doctor: "Our hand is part of our mind."

Gould was indebted as well to his teacher's analytical approach to preparing an interpretation. Ray Dudley recalled that Gould had been devastated by a minor memory lapse in an early conservatory concert, so Guerrero taught him to learn scores away from the piano, which became a lifelong habit abetted by his astonishing memory. (Bert once saw his son go into his bedroom with the score of a Beethoven concerto and emerge a little while later able to play the piece entirely from memory.) Gould told an interviewer, in 1981, "From the time I was about 12, I was forced to do a complete analysis and to memorize any work I was going to play before actually going to the piano and playing it. When you are compelled to do that, you get a kind of X-ray view of the score, much stronger than any tactile imagery the piano might create for you." By his late teens, he said, he was spending more time studying scores than practising them.

A few private recordings of Guerrero survive – he made no commercial recordings – but his radio broadcasts appear lost, and among the private recordings Gould made in his teens Guerrero is present only as an accompanist in concertos. On the basis of the recordings that do survive, however, as well as reviews and first-hand testimony, there is no question of Guerrero's influence on Gould's distinctive piano style. He was certainly a "heart man" in terms of the warmth and expressive power of his playing and his Romantic temperament. He had a commanding though not self-aggrandizing technique, and his interpretations were at once intellectually insightful and emotionally profound. The beauty of his tone was renowned, and it was something he stressed in his pupils. Like pedagogues since the nineteenth century, he encouraged pupils to get beyond the abstract, monochromatic, percussive nature of the piano by thinking orchestrally, trying to evoke other instruments ("in a passage in thirds," Beckwith recalled, "he would ask for 'more second oboe'"), and the adult Gould would often defend his choices of colour and phrasing by invoking string instruments, woodwinds, lutes, harpsichords, and even the human voice. Guerrero's playing was dynamic and clearly articulated (unlike many piano teachers he warned his students against overuse of legato phrasing); it was contrapuntally transparent, in all repertoire; and it was subtly nuanced, with particular refinement at the lower end of the dynamic spectrum (Dudley recalled, "He was always telling me to play pianissimo!"). Particularly noted was Guerrero's harpsichord-like approach to Bach. And if all of this reads like a précis of Gould's own playing it is hardly surprising: as many observed, Gould was the Guerrero pupil whose playing most closely approximated the teacher's.

A private recording survives of Guerrero playing Bach's Italian Concerto, perhaps taken from a recital or broadcast from 1952. It is a performance that Gould himself praised, and it is revealing to compare it with Gould's own CBC broadcast of the same piece the same year. A family resemblance between the performances, in terms of general style and specific interpretation, is unmistakable. Gould's tempos are almost exactly the same as Guerrero's, and the timings for all three movements differ only by a few seconds. There is more rhythmic flexibility in Guerrero's performance; Gould maintains tempos more strictly, though his playing is no less dynamic as a result. Gould's playing *seems* faster because it is so clearly and precisely articulated, though one can hear that his technique is founded on the sort of fleet fingerwork audible in Guerrero's recording, even if there is more *cantabile* phrasing in the latter's. Moreover, there are specific details in common that suggest that Gould was convinced by Guerrero's interpretation – choices in phrasing, rendering of ornaments, little expressive nuances, and so on (both add left-hand octaves at the end of the first movement, for instance). Technically the pupil had already surpassed the master (Guerrero was nearing seventy by then), and neither technically nor interpretively could he be called a mere copy of his teacher, but in many ways, as these recordings show, his playing was an extension of Guerrero's. In fact, much of what was characteristic of Gould's playing can be heard as an intensification, a refinement, a focusing of Guerrero's. Even his singing, perhaps: Mélisande Irvine says that her father used to hum very quietly as he played.

At the piano Gould *looked* like Guerrero, too, even gave the impression of aping him. "As a child he sat at the piano exactly as Guerrero did," Margaret Privitello said. "We all laughed about this." (He sometimes did wicked parodies of his teacher.) The low, hunched seating posture for which Gould was famous grew out of Guerrero's idiosyncratic method for playing in a relaxed manner with a technique founded as much as possible on the fingers alone. Unlike most pianists, Guerrero believed that the power and support for the playing mechanism should come not from the upper arms and shoulders but from the back. (To feel something of the intended effect, imagine pushing your back against a wall while trying to push a heavy object forward.) The aim of back support was to create a posture that would allow the forearm to seem suspended, weightless, and for the hands and fingers to be perfectly relaxed. Relaxation and ease of technique were hallmarks of Guerrero's technique, and crucial to his teaching. It was not a technique that made a priority of generating the sort of power required to play concertos by Liszt and Rachmaninov; the aim, rather, was to enhance the strength and independence of the fingers, permitting clear articulation at even the fastest tempos, as well as a control over tone and nuance that permitted fine discrimination of colour, dynamics, and phrasing. Gould, like his teacher, was not particularly interested in concertos by Liszt and Rachmaninov, and willingly sacrificed his ability to play a volcanic *fortissimo* in favour of the control he demanded in his preferred repertoire. Guerrero's method was the way to get it. Seated low, with the elbows dangling below the keyboard or out from the sides, one could get in close to the keyboard and come at the keys from below – for Gould the ideal position for exploring the subtleties of refined, structurally complex music.*

---

* Many other pianists renowned for discrimination of nuance and disdain for virtuoso fireworks also sat unusually low, including two of Gould's pianistic heroes, Artur Schnabel and Rosalyn Tureck.

Guerrero pupils including Gould have recalled that, as they played in lessons, Guerrero would press down on their shoulders and they would resist by pushing up; the intention was to develop the muscles of the back, and to feel what it is like to draw one's power from the back rather than the triceps or shoulders while leaving the arm and hand relaxed and letting the fingers do as much of the work as possible.* Hunching as such was not the goal, but it was an almost inevitable consequence, especially for Gould, whose torso was unusually long relative to his legs. He once said, "My teacher's the biggest hunchback in Canada."

Guerrero was fascinated by the *science* of piano playing. He was a keen student of books like Otto Ortmann's *The Physiological Mechanics of Piano Technique* (1929) and Arnold Schultz's *The Riddle of the Pianist's Finger and Its Relationship to a Touch-Scheme* (1936), and he studied the methods of the great pedagogues of the nineteenth century and of Landowska; with Myrtle Rose, he wrote a two-volume primer for beginners, *The New Approach to the Piano* (1935–36). William Aide recalled the "uncanny effect" of Guerrero's "eccentric insights into that astonishing circuitry between mind and hand. He knew the tricks of the trade as no-one else." He avoided assigning scales and other generic exercises; as Ray Dudley wrote, "Guerrero never taught with any particular method except to develop each of his students individually with special exercises designed for each student." Most of these exercises he developed himself, intuitively, and most of them had the aim of encouraging relaxation and strengthening the fingers (both essential to his up-from-below approach to the keys), and of enhancing the independence of the fingers. Lessons with Guerrero often began with arm

---

* As an adult, Gould turned to technology in an effort to enhance the physical system that Guerrero advocated. He often used an ultrasound-therapy unit on his shoulders and upper arms, with the avowed aim of "breaking down" or "thinning" the "hypertrophied" muscle tissue in those areas, and thus helping to maintain the back alone as the locus of support and power. Gould's biographer Peter Ostwald, a psychiatrist specializing in the physical and mental problems of performing artists, dismissed his theories on ultrasound as "highly improbable, if not actually dangerous."

massage, sometimes with hand vibrators, and he recommended soaking the arms in warm water – later one of Gould's legendary habits. Dudley described many exercises he and Gould and other pupils were encouraged to practise: gripping a vase as it is pulled away; squeezing a rubber ball; "clapping" firmly with one hand (imagine catching a fly with one hand); rotating the wrist or elbow while keeping the hand loose; practising with one hand while holding it with the other; playing scales as smoothly as possible with just one finger, moving it with the upper arm only; practising on a table or using silently depressed keys in order to find the correct weight and voicing of chords. To improve rapid octave passages, Guerrero developed an exercise whereby one pushed down into a pillow on a chair with the upper arm. Then there was the "high-finger down-up stroke": pushing down quickly and forcefully with fingers held outstretched several inches off the keys, the arm relaxed. Guerrero even convinced Gould to help his father saw fire-wood at the cottage by showing him it was good exercise for the hands and arms.

The most curious of the exercises was "tapping," which helped to develop what Ortmann had called "pure finger-technique" and enhance the ease, evenness, and clarity of touch. As Beckwith described it, tapping "consisted of playing the music for each hand separately, very slowly, but making the sound by tapping each finger with the non-playing hand. One learned from this how very precise and economical the muscle-movements needed for fast playing really could be."* (The fingers being tapped are placed in the correct position at the keyboard, resting on but not depressing the keys, and the fingers are tapped at the tips.) This would be followed by slow,

---

* Guerrero developed the method in Chile. As William Aide wrote, "Guerrero attended a travelling circus and saw a three-year-old Chinese boy do an astounding dance full of breath-taking intricacies. Guerrero went backstage to meet the child and asked his trainer for the secret. The teacher-trainer demonstrated how he placed his hands on the child and moved his limbs, while the child remained still and relaxed. Then the child was asked to repeat the movements by himself." The child thus learned to make the movements in an instinctive and relaxed manner.

staccato practice before the piece was brought up to tempo. As a result, the brain learned what was required in order to play in a relaxed manner with the fingers alone doing the work. According to Dudley, Gould "had been tapping everything" under Guerrero, and Gould admitted that, when making his famous 1955 recording of the Goldberg Variations, he tapped each variation before recording it – a process that took altogether about thirty-two hours. It is true, as he claimed, that he practised little as an adult, but in his youth he practised for hours on end, with endless patience and concentration, beyond even Guerrero's standard of perfectionism. The secure, preternaturally refined, and almost infallible technique for which he was so justly revered, though based on innate gifts, was thus built up the hard way, under his resourceful teacher.

Clearly, the commonplace notion, abetted by Gould, that his piano lessons amounted only to exercises in argument – Gould's individualism and modernism at war with Guerrero's conservatism and Romanticism – is too simplistic, but so too is the notion that he was ever merely a Guerrero clone. Strong-willed and idiosyncratic even as a child, he departed from his teacher's ideas and practices increasingly as he passed through his teens, and there certainly *were* arguments – or at least heated differences of opinion on musical matters. The differences in their upbringings and temperaments became clear: the puritanical Gould lacked Guerrero's generosity and inclusiveness as a musician. Gould took much from Guerrero's repertoire and playing style and premises, but more and more selectively, developing a narrower, more focused, more fiercely maintained aesthetic, and rejecting much that Guerrero loved. Guerrero disapproved of Gould's mannerisms at the keyboard, and Gould would notoriously reject his teacher's insistence on respecting the directions in a composer's score. He never rebelled, really, but increasingly he went his own way, and in his later teens he took less seriously what Guerrero had to say, though he never stopped recommending Guerrero to other piano students.

Eventually, Gould began to forget that he had learned *anything* from Guerrero, let alone anything fundamental. By the time he was internationally famous, in the mid-fifties, he encouraged people to think of him as self-taught. (Guerrero always told people that *he* was self-taught. Was Gould aping his teacher in this respect, too?) He did not literally write Guerrero out of his formative years, but he rarely credited him with anything beyond "some novel ideas on technique," and he claimed that everything that really mattered he had learned on his own, when his piano lessons ended. He told an interviewer in 1980 that "Guerrero was a very interesting man in many respects and had some interesting thoughts about playing the piano" – which must count as some kind of record for faintness of praise. He sometimes belittled Guerrero's playing as overpedalled or otherwise unpleasantly Romantic, as when he complained of Guerrero's "extraordinarily whimsical" ideas about phrasing (look who's talking!). Yet he could tell an interviewer, in a discussion of his own playing, that Guerrero was "the only other person I know who plays this way" without realizing how extraordinarily revealing was this admission.

Gould would say that one learned best through private observation and contemplation, that the best teacher was the one who stood aside and, at best, posed questions; once, notoriously, he claimed in front of some music teachers that "everything there is to know about playing the piano can be taught in half an hour" – everything *physical*, anyway. These denials of the value of most teaching came from his having had a teacher who preferred to guide than to dictate. Guerrero was constitutionally modest, and not much concerned about receiving credit, and so his influence on Toronto's musical life, though significant, was quiet, and forgotten after his death. He did not like his career to be celebrated or even documented. "I have no story," he told John Beckwith, and this modesty certainly harmed his posthumous reputation, abetting Gould's effort to downplay his influence. There is nothing surprising or nefarious here: it is standard-issue "killing of the father," and it does not require Freud's Oedipus complex or Harold Bloom's "anxiety of influence" to make sense of it. Guerrero certainly was a father figure to Gould through his most formative years, perhaps not only musically (recall Glenn's distant relationship with Bert); indeed, Margaret Privitello called

Gould "the son that Guerrero never had." But Gould's adult image as a pianist and a thinker was founded on his uniqueness and independence and iconoclasm, and this image would have been compromised had he acknowledged influences too willingly. He absorbed everything around him and made it his own, and in the end came to think that he had *thought* of it all on his own, too, conveniently forgetting how much of his piano playing and thinking were built on Guerrero's foundation. He felt, apparently, that nothing was less helpful to his image than to give credit to something as banal as a childhood music teacher in his own hometown.

Some have reported (perhaps assumed) that Guerrero was hurt by Gould's lack of gratitude, yet he once told Myrtle, "If Glenn feels he hasn't learned anything from me as a teacher, it's the greatest compliment anyone could give me." He meant that he had done his duty by helping Gould to realize his innate potential and bring out his native proclivities. ("Glenn would have found his way no matter who he studied with," he told Stuart Hamilton.) He recognized Gould's independence and, far from trying to crush it, built his teaching around that fact, though it meant creating precisely the sort of pupil most likely to deny his influence. Guerrero showed more insight and more grace on the subject than Gould ever did. Not long before he died, in 1959, from complications following a routine hernia operation, his daughter Mélisande showed him a published article in which Gould had made some deprecating remarks about his teacher. She was angry, but Guerrero was sanguine: that was just as it should be. "*Al maestro cuchillada*," he said to her – "To the teacher goes the knife."

"Performing before an audience gave me a glorious sense of power at fifteen."

When Gould entered the Toronto Conservatory, his schooling – and everything else in his life – already took a back seat to music. As early as January 1943, the Conservatory was in contact with his school to ask for special consideration in accommodating his musical studies. Bert eventually made arrangements with Malvern's principal and the board of education for the boy to attend school only in the morning and to devote the afternoon to music, either taking lessons or practising at home, and to work with tutors in the evening to catch up on the schoolwork he missed. He maintained this split schedule to the end of high school, and later remembered the "enormous goodwill and generosity of the staff" at Malvern, where, he knew, some regarded him as a nuisance. Though he was often absent in high school, he never dropped out; he was enrolled and studying to the spring of 1951 – that is, to the end of Grade 13, then the final year of high school in Ontario. He did not, however, complete the requirements for formal graduation, because, he later told a friend, he refused to take P.E. In fact, Gould spent more time in high school than most. Though he skipped Grade 3, he did not finish Grade 13 until he was almost nineteen. He took six school years to complete Grades 9 through 13 – which is to say he required two years to finish one of those grades (probably Grade 11, in which year his professional career began).

At the conservatory, his progress was swifter and more exceptional. On June 15, 1945, at the age of twelve, he passed, with the highest marks of any candidate, his examination in piano for the ATCM diploma (Associate, Toronto Conservatory of Music). He passed his written theory exams a year later, and was awarded the Associate diploma, with highest honours, at a ceremony on October 28, 1946. Thus it is not literally correct, as is always reported, that Gould became an Associate at the age of twelve, but we can at least say that the conservatory considered him, at twelve, to have reached professional standing as a pianist – which is impressive enough. On November 29, 1945, in a conservatory recital, he played the first movement of Beethoven's Fourth Piano Concerto, with Guerrero accompanying, and he played the movement again, on May 8, 1946, at one of the conservatory's Annual Closing Concerts in Massey Hall, this time with the Conservatory Symphony Orchestra, conducted by the principal, Ettore Mazzoleni – his first performance with an orchestra. He "had to keep the conductor waiting while he fumbled with a bothersome button on his doublebreasted coat," Fulford reported in the *9-D Bugle*, but the local critics were mostly impressed. One pronounced him a genius and compared his singing tone to that of de Pachmann; another noted a narrow dynamic range and phrasing that was "a little choppy" – all of which sounds like the pianist we know.

Gould first appeared in a music competition as a five-year-old, on August 30, 1938, at the CNE (he won no prizes); otherwise, his experience in competitions was limited to appearances in the first three annual Kiwanis Music Festivals. Events of this kind, involving thousands of children, had been fixtures on the English-Canadian music scene from the beginning of the twentieth century, and many people perceived them as a healthy force for cultural betterment (they encouraged young people to play "the right kind of music in the right way," Ernest MacMillan said). The model, once again, was imported. "The music festival is a peculiarly British institution," Geoffrey Payzant wrote in 1960; "in our time only the British could make a virtue out of music-making in public under the conditions of an athletic contest. Love of competition and the fair-play tradition are components of the image we all have of the typical Briton." As in the annual Dominion Drama Festival, most of the adjudicators were imported from England, and their condescension was sometimes palpable. (As Payzant wrote, "There is one detestable type of British adjudicator that has become a stock figure in this country" – namely, the colonialist who "arrives with the intention of being a light unto the Gentiles.") The goal of such events was reinforcement not just of British ideals of music, but of British manners and values. Deportment was a priority. In the 1966 article "We Who Are About to Be Disqualified Salute You!" Gould parodied the "superannuated British academicians" he had encountered at the festivals, with their "aura of charity and good fellowship": "I say, that's jolly good, Number 67 – smashing spirit and all that. Have to dock you just a point for getting tangled at the double bars, though. Four times through the old exposition is a bit of a good thing, what?"

Bert was a member of the Kiwanis Club and helped to run the festival, so it was inevitable that Glenn would enter. In February 1944, at the inaugural festival, which attracted about seven thousand children, he won three first prizes, one of them in a large Bach-prelude-and-fugue class; won a silver cup in a runoff against other first-prize winners (most of them older); and won a two-hundred-dollar scholarship to continue his studies with Guerrero. A year later, he won a third prize and two more first prizes, in classes devoted to Bach and Beethoven, and a hundred-dollar scholarship. In 1946, he won two more first prizes, in classes devoted to Bach and to the piano concerto (he played the first movement of the Beethoven's Fourth, again with Guerrero), and was pronounced a "wonder child." Ray Dudley, who met Gould at the 1945 festival and entered Guerrero's class a few years later, remembered the "fluidity," "clarity and brilliance," and "great depth of expression" of Gould's playing at this time. He was already attracting attention for technique and musicianship, and for subtlety and understanding beyond his years. Beckwith recalled "the extraordinary clarity of the lines and the singing tone" in his playing of a Bach prelude, his "insight and poetry" in the Beethoven concerto, and, more generally, his "eloquence" and "elevated seriousness." His appearances in public concerts of festival prize-winners were some of his earliest performances to earn attention from Toronto's music critics.

Gould never participated in competitions as an adult, but the Kiwanis Music Festivals, modest and provincial as they were, sufficed to instill in him a lifelong antipathy toward competition in every facet of life. By the age of fifteen, he recalled in a 1978 interview, "I was appalled at the idea of competing, wrapped up with violence, and despite the urging of my teacher I entered nothing." (He conveniently forgot about his tenacity at games like croquet.) "I happen to believe," he said in 1976, "that competition rather than money is the root of all evil." It was a subject he wrote and spoke passionately about on many occasions, and a linchpin of his ethics and aesthetics. He opposed all musical activities in which he perceived some manifestation of the competitive instinct – the concert hall, concerto form, the pamphlet wars of avant-garde factions – but contests especially, he thought, enforced standards of conformity and compromise that crushed individual creativity. Adjudicators, he wrote, tend "to decry the unaccountable mysteries of personality, to downgrade those virtues of temperamental independence which signal the genuine re-creative fire. . . . The menace of the competitive idea is that through its emphasis upon consensus, it extracts that mean, indisputable, readily certifiable core of competence and leaves its eager, ill-advised supplicants forever stunted, victims of a spiritual lobotomy."

In his teens Gould was too far advanced to be confined to amateur performances in church and at school. And so, on December 12, 1945, he made his professional debut as a performer – on the organ, as it turned out: he joined two other young organists, and the Malvern Collegiate Choir, in a Christmas concert in Eaton Auditorium. (He earned fifteen dollars.) He was just thirteen years old but looked younger; his feet barely reached the pedals, and one reviewer noted that he announced his encore (a Bach prelude) "in a voice which has not yet changed." He played movements from a sonata by Mendelssohn and a concerto by Dupuis, as well as the "Little" G-minor fugue by Bach, and astonished everyone with his dexterity and musicianship and his command of the big Casavant organ. Edward W. Wodson, in the *Evening Telegram*, called him a genius: "From start to finish and in every detail his playing had the fearless authority and finesse of a master."

For a time Gould envisioned a dual performing career, and in the mid-forties he gave a handful of organ recitals at local churches and in conservatory events. But his performance at a Malvern Memorial Day service in 1948, when he was sixteen, seems to have been his last on the organ. On January 14 and 15, 1947, in Secondary School Concerts of the Toronto Symphony, he made his professional concerto debut, again in Beethoven's Fourth, under the baton of the visiting Australian conductor Bernard Heinze. The critics were suitably impressed; even the orchestra and conductor were taken aback by the performance. (His own recollections of the event were not musical, however. His dog, Nicky, greeted him effusively before the concert, leaving clumps of hair on his suit. Trying to clean himself during orchestral passages, he almost lost his place in the finale.) On April 10, 1947, he gave his first full solo recital as a pianist, at the conservatory, in a program of major works by Haydn, Bach, Beethoven, Chopin, and Mendelssohn, and tentatively he began to perform around town – on the ninth-floor mezzanine of the Simpson's department store, where he followed a puppet show, "Tubby the Tuba"; at a luncheon of the Empire Club of Canada, in the posh Royal York Hotel. Through the conservatory's Concert and Placement Bureau, he began to make forays outside Toronto, including several Sunday-afternoon musicales at Pickering College, in Newmarket, in the mid-forties. In those days, he enjoyed giving concerts; in 1962 he called his Toronto Symphony debut "perhaps the one most exciting moment in my entire life."

On October 20, 1947, at Eaton Auditorium, Gould made his official recital debut as a professional pianist, in a program characteristic of his student years: five sonatas by Scarlatti; Beethoven's "Tempest" Sonata; Couperin's Passacaille in B Minor (arranged by Guerrero in imitation of Landowska's 1934 recording); Chopin's Waltz in A-flat Major, Op. 42, and Impromptu in F-sharp Major; Liszt's *Au bord d'une source*; and Mendelssohn's *Rondo capriccioso*. Ticket prices ranged from $1.50 to $3.00, though the concert was poorly attended ("a mere handful of self-conscious if enthusiastic cognoscenti," by one account); Gould made $250. Artistically, it was a triumph. Dudley remembered Gould's performance as "polished and poetic," and though not all the critics were convinced that his playing had attained adult depth, there was much praise for his virtuosity, his phrasing, his delicate tone, for his emotional and intellectual maturity, and for the precocious authority and cultivation of his interpretations. He was, one of them wrote, "uncanny."

Mixed with the praise was some early evidence of one of the Gould legends. A conservatory adjudication as early as 1941 noted that the eight-year-old used "too much arm movement in finger passages," and after his Kiwanis and conservatory concerts there would be much tut-tutting about his self-discipline ("all sensitive young players have to guard against mannerisms of the arms which look odd in public"). Alas, he was already singing audibly as he played, too, just as he had done in the comfort of home. He once claimed, indeed, that his mannerisms had begun naturally, in the sheltered surroundings of home, and he had discovered only too late that they disturbed some people. At any rate, the early dates of these first reviews contradict those who assume that the adult Gould's mannerisms were put on and that he could easily have stopped them. Of his professional concerto debut in 1947, Augustus Bridle, in the *Toronto Daily Star*, noted some byplay with hankie and tux-collar, and Pearl McCarthy, in the *Globe and Mail*, observed what would become another ingrained habit: the inability to sit still during orchestral passages. "As he approaches adult status," she wrote, "he will undoubtedly learn to suppress this disturbing fidgeting while his collaborators are at work." That fall, at Gould's debut recital, McCarthy confidently wrote that his mannerisms "will disappear in time."

Gould's conservatory achievements, his Kiwanis victories, and his early concerts received enough press coverage that by age thirteen he was a bona fide local celebrity, occasionally the subject of published profiles ("Brilliant 13-Year-Old Pianist Names Goldfish After Masters"), some of which were reprinted outside Toronto. On November 16, 1947, he repeated his debut-recital program (minus the "Tempest") at the Art Gallery of Toronto, and on December 3 he played Beethoven's First Piano Concerto, in Hamilton, with the Toronto Symphony, this time with MacMillan conducting. Audiences and critics continued to be astonished; in Hamilton he had to play two encores (Chopin waltzes). There were no longer any "excuses" for his performances – no more debuts, no more school or conservatory events, no more festivals. He was simply appearing on the concert circuit, in recital and with the most important orchestra in Canada, as a full-fledged professional pianist. He was fifteen years old.

Opposite: Gould in the early 1950s. *(Photograph by Donald McKague.)*

PART TWO

NATIONAL TREASURE

The Young Professional, 1947–54

**"Once I turned pro, so to speak,
I put away childish things forever."**

In his last years with Alberto Guerrero, Gould, as both performer and thinker, gained quickly in maturity, self-confidence, and independence. He was voraciously curious, eager to absorb everything around him, and his late teens were a ferment of musical passions. He would discover some new repertoire or idea and drink up all he could of it – Bach and Schoenberg were just two of many examples. He had his "first Haydn period" at eleven, when he studied many of the piano sonatas, his "second Haydn period" at nineteen, when he discovered the string quartets; he seems to have tackled Beethoven's piano music in a similar fit of enthusiasm. He told John Beckwith, in a 1951 letter, that he was exploring Purcell's keyboard music ("really great stuff"), though he never played any of it in public. His conservatory friend Peter Yazbeck remembers him studying, of all things, the choral music of Buxtehude. Yet he did not accept everything he took in. "When I was in my teens," he recalled in 1962, "I hated about ninety-five per cent of all music, of all periods. I had *very* strong opinions, much stronger than I would dare to have today." He was judgemental and defensive in his thinking, not worldly or catholic, and his curiosity was balanced by a powerful filtering mechanism: he

retained only what suited his highly constrained aesthetic. The combination of powerful curiosity and powerful constraint is hardly surprising in an excitable adolescent, though in this respect Gould's
mind retained a streak of adolescence throughout his life.

The outrageous opinions for which he became notorious were
already in place in his teens, and he would defend them passionately
to all who would listen. He would hold court in the conservatory cafeteria, discoursing and debating about his latest enthusiasms and *bêtes
noires*, musical and otherwise, and Yazbeck remembers him startling
one tableful by explaining that Mozart couldn't really write a piano
concerto. "He was a sweet guy, really the nicest kid you'd ever want
to meet – a gentlemanly kind of kid – but you just talked mainly about
musical things with him, and he had his strong opinions at a young
age," Yazbeck says. "He was not a snob in any sense. I never heard him
say a bad thing about anyone. He was just always very opinionated,
and yet not in an obnoxious way. He would just make statements
about things, and that was it." Robert Fulford saw in his young friend
"the most breathtaking confidence I've ever known": in his early teens
Gould was already thinking of himself as part of the larger musical
world. Ruth Watson-Henderson, a former Guerrero pupil, recalled
that "he always seemed to be at the centre of any discussion" – even
when he was with adults. Fellow-students were shocked, amused,
intimidated, but always intrigued. Gould was already a curmudgeon,
a young fogey, cultivating a serious, all-masterpiece diet of classical
music and harbouring little patience for anything less. He liked *some*
popular music (Cole Porter, Ella Fitzgerald, *Porgy and Bess*), later
thought Leonard Bernstein's score for *West Side Story* "a masterpiece,"
confessed to being "rather fond of Gilbert and Sullivan in small
doses," and even acknowledged an interest in Dixieland, but mostly
his taste did not stray beyond the usual classical canon. He hated simplistic, repetitive music – minimalism ("boring as hell"), rock ("offensive"), folk music ("I can be charmed by the peasant wrongheadedness
of it all") – and had no apparent interest in non-Western musics.

Even within his own field, his taste was already highly selective.
"I've often said that I have something like a century-long blind spot

with regard to music," he told an interviewer in 1980. "It's roughly demarcated by *The Art of the Fugue* on one side and *Tristan* on the other, and almost everything in between is, at best, the subject of admiration rather than love." For a pianist that's quite an admission: it means, in effect, rejecting the core of the conventional piano repertoire – and, by implication, the conventional approach to the tonal resources of the piano. Gould came to deplore middle-period Beethoven (too belligerent), Schubert (too repetitive),* almost all of the "super-sensual," virtuosic piano music of the early Romantics (Schumann, Mendelssohn, Chopin, Liszt, and their contemporaries), and twentieth-century music in a similar vein: Rachmaninov, for instance, was "absolutely intolerable," except for a couple of late works like the *Rhapsody on a Theme of Paganini*, which he considered performing in the fifties. Music outside the Austro-German canon and its satellites was suspect; he dismissed whole repertoires from France, Italy, Spain, and almost all points south. His friend Barbara Little remembers him, as early as fourteen, berating her for singing "junk" like Fauré. He did not like the ballet, and considered opera, especially Italian opera, to be "rather less than music." "I don't go to the opera house very much," he confessed, in a 1959 profile. "And when I do, I'm more interested in the actual music I hear than in what I see on the stage – in fact, quite often, when I do go to opera, I shut my eyes and just listen." Often he barely knew the words or plot of the operatic music he listened to. In a diary entry from 1980, he admitted, after listening to *Tannhäuser* on the radio, that "I'd never even known what it was about (I'm ashamed to say)" – a surprising gap for a self-described Wagnerite. He was squeamish about the sensuousness and melodiousness and violent emotions of Italian opera; the music of Verdi and Puccini, he admitted, made him "intensely uncomfortable" – a revealing choice of words.

---

* Gould deplored the "interminable ostinatos" in Schubert, yet admired "the unself-conscious use of ostinato" in Schoenberg – the sort of contradiction typical of his highly prejudiced aesthetic.

Gould's studiously blinkered view of music was a by-product of his puritanism. Randiness or delinquency are not the only extreme reactions a boy can have to puberty; no less a cliché is the teenage puritan, in whom the physical and emotional upheavals of adolescence induce a powerful repressive reaction. Gould was precisely the sort to use repression and rationalization to deal with what he called "the harrowing business of being a teenager." As his teen years progressed, his puritanism yielded an increasingly rational and idealistic approach to music. Fulford noticed the change: "In Glenn's mind, music was becoming refined and bodiless, almost entirely separated from the physical. Sometimes he spoke of music as if it existed in some distant and abstract sphere, beyond physicality." If, during his school years, Gould turned to the piano as a kind of refuge, it is hardly surprising that he should have been drawn to the music least wrapped up with worldly things. In a letter to John Roberts in 1971, he wrote of the "therapeutic and remedial" value of art: "for me all music which lacks that ability to isolate its listeners from the world in which they live is intrinsically less valuable than that which manages the feat." He liked to talk about "ecstasy" as the highest goal of playing or listening to music, and he meant not exultation but the sense of standing outside oneself, of stopping time, of being in touch with an otherworldly realm.

There was a moral basis to his artistic views. Like his parents, though in a more sophisticated sense, and like countless musicians and thinkers since the ancient Greeks, he was devoted to the idea that music can and should, finally, be judged on moral rather than aesthetic grounds. The music that he admired aesthetically, from Byrd to Krenek, was music that he also considered morally uplifting, because it was rational, abstract, introspective, and encouraged contemplation and repose. *This* was the "therapeutic" music that could "isolate its listeners from the world in which they live," could offer "the peace the earth cannot give." The music that he criticized aesthetically, from Scarlatti to Bartók, was music that he also considered downright sinful, because it was sensual, self-aggrandizing, and encouraged excitation, competition, hysteria – music stained with "worldly grime" (as he once said of Scarlatti). Like a Methodist of old, he thought all the performing arts disreputable – he thought it immoral to test people in live situations – and he was disturbed by all of the musical corollaries of "live-ness": staged opera, the concert hall, audience-grabbing concertos, improvisation, chance music. He never attended a jazz concert, and was, by his own admission, "a complete flop" as a performer of jazz. He took a stab at enjoying Charlie Parker and other bebop performers in his teens, "but it was a very passing fancy"; despite occasional praise for, say, Lennie Tristano or Bill Evans,* he admitted that jazz appealed to him only in "very small doses." He pompously dismissed jazz as "a minor and transitory offshoot of the romantic movement" – and besides, he said, "no one ever swung more than Bach." (Jazz musicians have always been fond of *Gould*, by the way, usually because of the drive and "swing" of his rhythm.)

Gould's debut recital program, in 1947, marked the beginning of the end for the student phase of his musical life. In his earliest professional recitals, given while he was still a conservatory student, he played Scarlatti and Couperin, Czerny and Mendelssohn, Chopin and Liszt, and enjoyed doing so. But by the time he was nineteen and had stopped taking lessons, he quickly phased out most such repertoire in favour of his adult preferences, which were focusing increasingly on early and modern music. He retained a few sonatas by Haydn and Mozart and a few (mostly late) sonatas and variation sets by Beethoven, but his repertoire of solo works in the Romantic

---

* Gould and Evans were mutual admirers and friends. (Gould called Evans "the Scriabin of jazz.") In the early sixties, the Canadian jazz musician and writer Gene Lees suggested that the two pianists review each other's recordings in *High Fidelity*, and they agreed, though in the end Evans backed out. Lees introduced them (by telephone) around 1970, and they spoke often after that. According to Evans's biographer, Peter Pettinger, Evans recorded *Conversations with Myself*, in 1963, on Gould's own Steinway.

style was limited almost exclusively to a few intermezzi by Brahms. Early music figured rarely in his earliest programs, but around 1950 he began to perform, in concert and on the radio, substantial works of Bach's like the Italian Concerto (which he added to his public repertoire in 1950), the Partita No. 5 in G Major (1951), some preludes and fugues (1952), the three-part Sinfonias (1953), and the Goldberg Variations (1954), as well as Gibbons's "Earl of Salisbury" Pavan and Galliard (1951) and Sweelinck's "Fitzwilliam" Fantasia in G (1952) – all of which were staples of his repertoire in his concert years. His twentieth-century repertoire began with the Seventh Sonata of Prokofiev, whom he considered the only post-Revolutionary Russian composer of genius. He performed the sonata for the first time in 1949, and soon added other modern works to his concert and broadcast programs: Hindemith's Third Sonata (1950); Krenek's Third Sonata and Morawetz's *Fantasy in D* (1951); Berg's Sonata and Schoenberg's songs and Opp. 11 and 25 piano pieces (1952); and Webern's *Variations* (1953).

When he performed at Hart House on February 12, 1950, at age seventeen, he offered what we may call the first truly characteristic Gould program: Bach's Italian Concerto, Beethoven's "Eroica" Variations, and Hindemith's Third Sonata. But it was his program for the Ladies' Morning Musical Club, in Montreal, on November 6, 1952 – Gibbons, Bach, late Beethoven, Brahms, Berg – that really set a pattern. A smattering of sixteenth- and seventeenth-century pieces, a generous helping of Bach and of (mostly) Austro-German twentieth-century music, a *very* select handful of Classical works, a little Brahms – that, with few exceptions, was Gould's recital repertoire for the next dozen years.

His concerto repertoire was no more catholic: it would always focus largely on the Beethoven concertos he had played since his early teens (his specialty was the Second, his least favourite the popular "Emperor"). In the early fifties he added Schoenberg's concerto and a few by Bach, in 1955 Strauss's early, rarely played *Burleske* (which he once said was "not a very good piece"), in the late fifties one concerto each by Mozart and Brahms. And that was it – not one of the popular Romantic concertos. He played Weber's glittering, virtuosic *Konzertstück* in F minor – an early monument of the Romantic solo concerto – exactly once, with the Toronto Symphony, in 1951, and only because Guerrero had insisted. Gould was so adamant about not making concessions to contemporary tastes that he would play bits of Gibbons or Bach or Schoenberg, even whole works by Berg or Webern, as encores after the most challenging programs. Surprisingly, he did not encounter a lot of resistance. A reviewer in 1953, for instance, praised him for playing Sweelinck as an encore, rather than betraying his program by offering, say, Chopin's "Minute" Waltz.

"The question which governs all art is to what degree is it entirely logical."

It is with Bach that Gould has always been most closely associated, yet it was the music and thought of Schoenberg and his school – the twelve-tone idiom especially – that most crucially influenced his view of music in his formative years. He recognized that there was something arbitrary about the whole premise of twelve-tone music, and he willingly admitted that he found some of Schoenberg's works "cold" and "relentless" and "austere," but the passion for reason and order, economy and unity in this music could only appeal to a puritan like Gould. A twelve-tone piece is inherently *organized*: every pitch is accounted for, and the melodies, harmonies, and forms are (usually) logically derived from the piece's tone row. Twelve-tone music, in effect, involves the constant variation of a single given idea, and as such is a model of music that unfolds organically – precisely what Gould admired. He said in 1952 that he admired the music of Webern, one of Schoenberg's star pupils, because it represented "an approach which eliminates all but what can be felt as absolutely essential, which calls for the greatest economy of means." Moreover, in the music of the Schoenberg school he, like the Schoenbergians themselves, saw an idealistic and moralistic aesthetic that suited his emerging adult personality.

Gould was particularly influenced by the French composer and musicologist René Leibowitz, who studied with Schoenberg and Webern and was an influential teacher, conductor, and advocate of twelve-tone music. His ground-breaking book *Schoenberg et son école*, published in 1947, appeared in English in 1949, and Gould devoured it, discussing it eagerly with friends like John Beckwith. The book became, as the composer Oskar Morawetz recalls, a kind of Bible for Gould, who could quote it by heart. His later writings on Schoenberg, Berg, and Webern, including his most important, are indebted to Leibowitz in fundamental ways, and are peppered with terms and phrases picked up from Leibowitz ("*Spiegelbild*," "new world of sound").

He did not absorb *every* aspect of the Schoenberg aesthetic. The Schoenbergians, for instance, propounded the notion of musical progress: they insisted that Schoenberg's revolution was an inevitable, necessary step in the history of music, in comparison to which the music of his contemporaries was not "genuine." But Gould rejected the teleological approach to music history – what he called "the curse of the zeitgeist" – and the competitive factionalism that goes along with it. In this respect he was a postmodernist *avant la lettre*, who insisted that one could love the "revolutionary" music of Schoenberg without rejecting, say, the "reactionary" music of Strauss, and he deplored the propagandizing of the young Pierre Boulez, an ardent serialist who insisted that "history is much like the guillotine," and that any composer "who is not moving in the right direction" – that is, writing twelve-tone music – "will be killed, metaphorically speaking." Still, Gould did take up many of the prejudices of the Schoenberg school, principally the belief that their highly rational approach to music should apply to *all* music, of whatever period or orientation, and that whatever stubborn, wicked composers of the past and present choose not to partake of such rationalism were to be banned from serious consideration. Gould never could see the values he picked up from Schoenberg as embedded in their time; he insisted that they were permanently valid. He admitted that in adolescence he had been influenced by Schoenberg's "type of molecular analysis in which every facet of a work has to prove itself of structural necessity" and then "applied this kind of analysis to the music of all earlier times as well." Naturally, he was drawn to the earlier music that most repaid such anachronistic analysis – which meant fugues rather than nocturnes, which meant Bach.

Like the Schoenbergians, Gould viewed Bach as the fountainhead of the Austro-German canon and an early exponent of rational, modern musical values. Schoenberg once described Bach's art as that of "producing everything from one thing," and, with Bach in mind, defined fugue as "a composition with maximum self-sufficiency of content." For Gould, too, Bach was a paragon of order, logic, and structural integrity, and he conveniently ignored those aspects of Bach's music that did not support this view. He had little to say about Bach as a rhetorician, a Lutheran, a tone-painter, a man of the theatre, a keyboard performer; his Bach was an architect, a "contrapuntal craftsman," an idealist whose music stood apart from mundane matters like instrumental realization, and his preferences among Bach's works (fugues rather than toccatas, suites rather than fantasias) were of a piece with this view. With Bach and Schoenberg – and Schoenberg's Bach – as his models, it is no wonder Gould was enthralled with counterpoint, particularly the strict forms of counterpoint like canon and fugue that most lent themselves to rigorous analysis. (The flexible, "poetic" counterpoint of, say, Chopin or Schumann, he, like Leibowitz, did not even recognize as counterpoint.) "I've always been attracted to music that is in one way or another contrapuntal, whereas I'm essentially bored by homophonic music," he said in 1980. Whatever composer he championed, from whatever century, had a pronounced contrapuntal bent, and with composers about whom he was ambivalent he gravitated to their most contrapuntal essays – Mozart's K. 394 fugue, Beethoven's *Große Fuge*. Even Verdi's *Falstaff* was tolerable because it has a fugue at the end.

Gould took up not just enthusiasms of the Schoenbergians but prejudices, too. For instance, he was never interested in Handel the way he was in Bach.* Schoenberg derided Handel's music as full of "empty, meaningless" figuration, even "trash," and it is significant that when Gould recorded Handel's A-major harpsichord suite, in 1972, he did not improvise his way through the sketchily notated Prelude, as Handel had intended, but instead composed an arrangement of the piece, creating a tightly unified, Schoenbergian network of recurring motifs. Gould always preferred Haydn to Mozart, for the commonplace reason that Haydn's music was better "developed"; he shared the Schoenbergians' discomfort with sensuous and heterogeneous music, even when it was by Mozart. He also shared their disdain for Italian music (not just opera), which Schoenberg derided for "the poverty of its ideas and development." (In Gould's words, "the Italians are always churning out the top line.") And Gould had little patience for the music of most of Schoenberg's contemporaries. He derided "bloated Slavic tone poems" like Shostakovich's Seventh Symphony, and was skeptical of Ives. Stravinsky, above all, was the enemy, and all his life Gould regurgitated the anti-Stravinsky polemics of Schoenberg, Leibowitz, Theodor W. Adorno, and others. He found Stravinsky's *Rite of Spring* a "very offensive work," his *Soldier's Tale* a "piece of trash," and he heaped scorn on Stravinsky's neo-Classicism as cold, mechanistic, barren, shallow, trivial, mere pastiche, technique for technique's sake – as the work of a "nose-thumbing enfant terrible" (his comments on this subject rarely were more subtle than that). Predictably, he had kind words only for Stravinsky's late twelve-tone works, like the ballet *Agon* and the *Movements* for piano and orchestra, which he once considered playing.

Gould's characteristic piano style, in all music, was decisively influenced by Schoenbergian values, too. Schoenberg advocated performances in which architectural and thematic relationships were

---

* Though often called a champion of "Baroque music," Gould played little from that period besides Bach – just some Scarlatti and Handel and the Couperin-Guerrero Passacaille. He admired some other Baroque composers, including Purcell and Rameau, but never performed their music.

made explicit to the listener: "The highest principle for all repro-
duction of music would have to be that what the composer has
written is made to sound in such a way that every note is really
heard, and that all the sounds, whether successive or simultaneous,
are in such relationship to each other that no part at any moment
obscures another, but, on the contrary, makes its contribution
towards ensuring that they all stand out clearly from one another."
That could stand as a motto for Gould's own immaculate and analytical playing. Robert Fulford recalled that Gould once described
his approach to music as "architectonic," by which he meant seeing
a piece "three-dimensionally," in all its facets simultaneously, so it is
hardly surprising that transparency of counterpoint would become
perhaps the most lauded aspect of the Gould style.

The young Gould pointedly rejected the Romantic approach to
Bach that he associated with venerable (though still living) performers like Wanda Landowska, the pianist Edwin Fischer, the
cellist Pablo Casals, and, closer to home, Ernest MacMillan, who
took a devotional approach to Bach, with slow tempos that earned
him the nickname "Lord Largo." Gould was listening to the more
cutting-edge performers then advocating clear, strict readings of
Bach with some attention to historical performance practices, particularly the American pianist Rosalyn Tureck, who had had a reputation as a Bach specialist since the mid-thirties. The fifteen-year-old
Gould was in the audience when she made her Toronto debut in
1948, and he studied her early recordings, which came out in the
late forties and early fifties. "Back in the forties, when I was a
teenager, she was the first person who played Bach in what seemed
to me a sensible way," he said in a 1974 interview; "her records were
the first evidence that one did not fight alone. It was playing of such
uprightness, to put it into the moral sphere. There was such a sense
of repose that had nothing to do with languor, but rather with moral
rectitude in the liturgical sense." Tureck's style – cleanly articulated,
sparsely pedalled, contrapuntally transparent, at once analytical and
historically informed – reinforced his own evolving ideas about
Bach performance. Though he differed with her in some ways, his

Bach being more dynamic, with a greater preponderance of fast tempos, he also clearly took much inspiration, and even some details like ornamentation, from Tureck.*

Gould was composing throughout these heady years, and his various musical discoveries inevitably found voice in original works. "The manuscripts of junior masterpieces occupy many drawers in my home," he once wrote. "They are tokens of that swift-moving parade of enthusiasms which is the student life, and they exhibit attempts at every style from Palestrina (which was done to please my teachers) to Schoenberg (which was done to annoy them)." His music was not always secure technically, or of high quality, but he nonetheless learned to move with confidence in a variety of idioms. It was generally contrapuntal, full of canons and fugues, though only once, apparently, did he actually emulate his beloved Bach, in *Prelude, Cantilena and Gigue*, a little suite for clarinet and bassoon in the texture of a two-part invention, composed in 1951 for two conservatory friends, the clarinetist Norman Glick and the bassoonist Nicholas Kilburn, who performed it once, probably at a private musicale. It is a slight work, perhaps written in haste. Two other early works reflect the eighteenth- and nineteenth-century tonal idioms that Gould absorbed through the conventional piano repertoire. The loquacious *Rondo in D Major* (1948), set in a well-behaved sonata-rondo form, sounds like an early-Romantic takeoff on Mozart, while *Variations in G Minor* (1949), prefaced with an unexplained heading – "And so, from the light of Fantasy, we enter the dark of reality" – consists of a banal chorale-like theme and sketches for six mildly virtuosic variations.

Once he became more familiar with twentieth-century music, Gould tried his hand at more chromatic tonal styles – for instance,

---

* "He took a great, *great* deal from me," said Tureck in a 1985 interview. "Playing his records I hear myself playing, because I was the only one in the world who did these embellishments." Fulford recalled hearing Gould, around age twenty, demonstrating why his interpretation of a Bach partita was superior to that in a recording "by one of the greatest Bach interpreters of the age." Was it Tureck? A case, perhaps, of symbolically killing the *mother*?

in *3 Fugues on one Subject* (1952), of which only No. 2 survives, a work on three staves with no indications for instrumentation (it is clearly not for organ). More ambitious was the *Sonata for Piano*, composed sometime before spring 1950, perhaps as early as 1948. Just over four hundred bars, headed "Movement I," survive for this angular, brooding work, in which the combination of post-Romantic tonality, formal counterpoint, motivic development, and heavy late-Romantic piano textures says much about Gould's various musical preoccupations at the time. He told a newspaper reporter that the sonata was written in the style of Hindemith, and in fact one of the themes alludes to the fugue subject from the finale of Hindemith's Third Sonata.

In early 1950, not long after Guerrero introduced him to the music of Schoenberg, Gould composed his earliest surviving work in that style: *5 Short Piano Pieces*, influenced by Webern's Op. 5 miniatures for string quartet and by Schoenberg's Op. 19 miniatures for piano (the ethereal last piece pays homage to the last piece of Op. 19). All five pieces are atonal, though only the first two feature some twelve-tone writing. (Gould felt confident enough to send the newly completed pieces to the CBC, apparently without result; his own brilliant, impetuous private recording of them survives, however.) In a three-movement *Sonata for Bassoon and Piano* (1950), he attempted a stricter twelve-tone style, without relinquishing his usual priorities: there is an extended fugue in the second movement. (A private recording of this piece, too, with Nicholas Kilburn, survives.) Other twelve-tone works quickly followed: *2 Pieces for Organ* (1950), his only known composition for the organ, of which just fifteen bars survive, laid out for a large English-style church organ with pedals; a *String Trio* (1950), his first work for strings, of which just a few pages survive; and *2 Pieces*, for piano (1951–52).

"Actually, I am very much a romantic."

Among pianists, the hero of Gould's youth was Artur Schnabel, whom he, like many others, considered the greatest of all Beethoven interpreters, and indeed "the greatest pianist of his generation." Schnabel's records, Gould said, were "Biblical" to him when he was young. In 1969, for a CBC radio program, Gould gave an entertaining account of his Schnabel-worship. While preparing for his orchestral debut with Beethoven's Fourth Piano Concerto, he listened almost every day to his 78-r.p.m. discs of Schnabel's 1942 RCA Victor recording of the work and copied all of Schnabel's nuances, sometimes going so far as to practise while the record played; he claimed even to have allowed the breaks required to change discs to influence his conception of the music's structure. Finally, he said, Guerrero compelled him to hand over the Schnabel album and to give a more streamlined performance, though he claimed to have resorted to Schnabel's interpretation when it came time for the public performance. It is a tall tale, but there is no doubt that Schnabel had a huge impact on Gould.

Schnabel was a serious, intellectual musician of great integrity, and a true polymath – a composer, editor, writer, and teacher, as well as a pianist. (Gould studied his 1935 edition of Beethoven's sonatas.) Schnabel's own teacher, Theodor Leschetizky, had famously told him, "You will never be a pianist; you are a musician," a distinction Gould always held dear. As a pianist Schnabel had no patience for crowd-pleasing virtuosity or sensuality; his repertoire was chaste and substantial, focused on the Austro-German canon, and his playing revealed a strong grasp of musical architecture and a command of counterpoint. The performer's task, in Schnabel's view, was to serve great music, not merely to display himself and ingratiate himself with the audience; as he once said, applause is the receipt, not the bill. From Schnabel's recordings the young Gould took away the image of a fellow-idealist, a pianist who transcended the piano and cared only about "the structural concept behind the music." But this is not the whole story. Schnabel was also a highly individual and profoundly Romantic pianist. His famous recordings of Beethoven's sonatas from the 1930s, for all their intellectual insight, are impulsive and passionate, rhythmically flexible and dynamic, often extreme in tempo, rich in tone, and insistently contrapuntal. Moreover, his interpretive insights were often eccentric, for he was a truly creative performer, never a literalist. In Gould's brash, gripping, caution-to-the-winds early concert performances and broadcasts of Beethoven, even his commercial recordings well into the 1960s, one often hears almost an imitation and sometimes an exaggeration of Schnabel.

This is not so surprising. Notwithstanding many of his published remarks, Gould owed far more to the Romantic view of music, even in the days of his twelve-tone kick, than he was willing to admit. He was a person of deep feelings and great sensitivity, but uncomfortable with the overt expression of emotion, and in his music he needed always to rationalize his Romantic tendencies through high-modernist rhetoric about structure. But to rationalize one's passions is not to suppress them: he was a Romantic at heart. In his teens his absorption of the Schoenberg aesthetic was balanced by the powerful impact of late-Romantic music. He would come to describe himself as "a total Wagnerite – hopelessly addicted to the later things especially." He once wrote, "I love *Tristan*. I was fifteen when I first heard it, and wept" – hardly the words of a dry rationalist. Around the same time, he was drawn to the music of Richard Strauss – the tone poem *Ein Heldenleben*, the *Burleske*, and especially such late (and then rarely heard) works as *Metamorphosen*, the Oboe Concerto, and the *Duett-Concertino*, which he discovered on the radio. By his late teens he was a confirmed admirer of other late-Romantic figures like Bruckner, Mahler, Reger, and even (surprisingly) Saint-Saëns and Tchaikovsky, though the early post-war years were precisely those when overt Romanticism was very much out of fashion. A few months before he died, he told a friend that his favourite opera was Humperdinck's *Hänsel und Gretel*.

It was only early-Romantic piano music that he really rejected; in fact, he regretted that late-Romantic composers like Mahler and Strauss wrote almost nothing of consequence for the piano. Even from the early-Romantic period there was much music, mostly orchestral and vocal, that he admired – Cherubini, Berlioz, Bizet, Mendelssohn. When he played transcriptions on the piano, as he loved to do, it was usually the most luxuriant late-Romantic scores:

operas by Wagner and Strauss (some of which he apparently knew by heart in their entirety), symphonies by Bruckner and Mahler, tone poems by Strauss and Elgar and Schoenberg. Of course he had his rationalizations. Strauss, for instance, he could safely admire for his dense counterpoint, his harmonic control, a degree of "abstraction." In truth, though, he loved a good wallow in Romantic excess: it was the "contrapuntally bombastic" Mahler of the Second and Eighth symphonies he admired, not the "thinness" of Mahler in, say, the more neo-classical Fourth.

Significantly, his early heroes among performers tended to be mystical or flamboyant figures of previous generations, particularly conductors like Wilhelm Furtwängler, Willem Mengelberg, Leopold Stokowski, and Felix Weingartner, and he was practically alone among his contemporaries in refusing to be won over by the more literal, "objective" style of Toscanini, whom he once dubbed "a good Xeroxer." Gould did not necessarily *play* in the style of his heroes; what he called "the Furtwängler tradition of legato-at-all-costs-and-the-counterpoint-be-damned" hardly sounds like him. But he did admire the tradition of "Romantic self revelation," he said, "the tradition of intense personal involvement, possibly even self-indulgence." He admired "ecstatic" performers whose idiosyncratic engagement with the music yielded "transcendent" and "spiritual" performances – again, hardly the words of a dry rationalist. Gould may not have *sounded* like a Romantic with his transparent, articulated readings of Sweelinck and Bach and Webern, yet he advocated the Romantic notion that the performer should creatively impose his own personality on the music he plays, a notion that, in the years after the Second World War, was unfashionable and almost universally discredited. He was a rare, fascinating case of a performer who combined high-modernist traits as a performer with an utterly Romantic approach to interpretation.

Moreover, Romanticism had a profound impact on his advocacy of modern music. Schoenberg, after all, was a product of German Romanticism and never abandoned its tenets. It is certainly revealing that Gould was attracted to Schoenberg and not to those modern

composers whose music might be called anti-Romantic in spirit, like
Stravinsky and Bartók, whom he dubbed the "most over-estimated
modern composers" as early as 1952. Gould always took the view that
Schoenberg remained a Romantic at heart, and he liked to stress the
forces of "conciliation" rather than revolution in Schoenberg's development. His first surviving writing on Schoenberg, a 1953 lecture,
notes "contradictory influences" in Schoenberg's music – that is,
forms and procedures of tonal music persisting in twelve-tone con-
texts – and includes the startling suggestion that Schoenberg's spirit
"was, in many respects, incompatible with the twelve tone technique." Young modernists like Pierre Boulez, in those days, were
already arguing that Schoenberg's lingering Romanticism was a
betrayal of his own twelve-tone innovations, yet here was Gould suggesting precisely the opposite, and *approving* of it.

Besides Schoenberg, the modern music in Gould's repertoire was
often overtly Romantic in its rhetoric and piano textures – works like
Berg's Sonata, Morawetz's *Fantasy in D*, and even twelve-tone pieces
like Krenek's Third Sonata and István Anhalt's *Fantasia*. And he preferred the approachable, neo-classical Hindemith of the thirties and
forties to the more pungent Hindemith of the twenties. A Romantic
sensibility lurks behind Gould's own twelve-tone compositions, in
which a yearning lyricism is generally present, and which often
sound suspiciously like turn-of-the-century, pre-twelve-tone music.
Significantly, he never composed in the more pristine style of
Webern, much as he admired it, nor did he ever play or compose or
profess to admire music in the post-Webern, total-serialist style,
which was all the rage after the war. It is revealing that, though a
professed advocate of musical logic, he was skeptical about the most
logical, most organized music of all.

Gould was certainly influenced by some of the older pianists
active in his youth, his own comments notwithstanding. Most of the
leading performers of the day passed through Toronto: Clifford
Curzon, Walter Gieseking, Myra Hess, William Kapell, Arturo
Benedetti Michelangeli, Benno Moiseiwitsch, Arthur Rubinstein,

and many others, including the Chilean-born Claudio Arrau, who visited his friend Alberto Guerrero whenever he was in town. Gould especially admired some of these pianists, notably Rudolf Serkin and Robert Casadesus, but he heard them all. In those days, the one pianist whom all the students talked about and tried to emulate was Vladimir Horowitz, and the teenage Gould was not immune to his spell. Horowitz gave four recitals in Toronto between 1940 and 1950, usually advertised as an appearance by "the world's greatest pianist," always drawing huge crowds and glowing reviews. Gould attended at least two of these recitals, in 1947 and 1949, and he listened to Horowitz's recordings.

Horowitz was in many ways Gould's antithesis as a pianist, and to Gould he represented everything that was wrong with the standard piano repertoire, with Romantic pianism, with concert life. Gould rarely had a bad word to say (out loud) about a colleague, but Horowitz was an exception. On that subject he was grudging, petulant: about Horowitz's famed octave technique, for instance, he once said, "He *fakes* them." But he protested too much. He was entranced enough by Horowitz to take up some of his repertoire. In his debut recital, six months after Horowitz's 1947 appearance in Toronto, Gould adopted the older pianist's practice of opening with a group of Scarlatti sonatas, and did so in other early recitals. The debut recital included another Horowitz specialty, Liszt's *Au bord d'une source*, which he had recorded in May of that year. Gould added two more pieces that Horowitz recorded in the mid-forties to his early concert programs: a set of variations, by Carl Czerny, on Rode's aria "La Ricordanza"; and Mendelssohn's virtuosic *Variations sérieuses*, which he greatly admired. (Guerrero had suggested both works.) A sometimes stunning private recording survives of the young Gould practising the latter work, and another early recording survives of a Clementi sonata – music that, in those days, no one but Horowitz played. Ray Dudley recalls that Gould enthusiastically took up Prokofiev's Seventh Sonata, in 1949, after hearing Horowitz's recording, released four years earlier.

Gould seems to have acknowledged a debt to Horowitz only once, in an unpublished interview in 1979,* and he took pains on that occasion to minimize the debts. "There was only one period in my life – very brief period – when I was influenced by Horowitz," he said, a "brief, slightly giddy period when I was around fifteen . . . one strange, quirky, utterly odd year in my life in which I imitated Horowitz like mad, and after that I stopped doing it – as far as I know." After he sobered up and turned sixteen, that was all past, and he dropped "utterly banal music" like Czerny's from his repertoire. It is revealing that he did not mention Prokofiev's sonata: he was willing to acknowledge Horowitz's impact only in repertoire that he could point to as a trivial youthful indiscretion quickly set right.

The influence was deeper and more lasting than Gould would admit. "I think I was probably attracted by the sense of space that very often infiltrated his playing," he said, "the way in which, sometimes very unexpectedly, an alto voice or a tenor voice would appear that you weren't aware of. . . . It suddenly gave a sense of a three-dimensional aspect to the playing." He is talking about Horowitz's counterpoint, his astonishing command of simultaneous lines and colours – that "may have had some small influence, perhaps." Not small, and not perhaps: Gould's rendering of counterpoint was often precisely of the Romantic variety, the revelation of unexpected but colourful details. For all his structural rationales, his counterpoint was not as consistently analytical and calculated as, say, Tureck's, but more spontaneous, dynamic, expressive. He may well have learned from other performers whom he claimed to reject. In his Bach, for instance, one sometimes hears the dynamic rhythm and phrasing of Landowska, even some of her idiosyncracies (like the occasional staccato ornament).

The earliest professional judges of Gould's playing, conservatory

---

* Glenn Plaskin interviewed Gould as research for his biography *Horowitz* (1983). The interview, conducted by telephone and never intended to be published, turned out to be more about Gould than about Horowitz, and in the end Plaskin did not quote Gould in his book.

and festival adjudicators in the early and mid-forties, already praised his rhythmic vitality, clear phrasing, and part-playing, and his maturity and command of musical architecture. But they also complained, at times, about Romantic excesses: too much pedal and too much legato (even in early music), overly fast tempos and too much fluctuation of tempo, a tone that could be too brilliant or violently nuanced. An adjudicator at the 1945 Kiwanis festival wrote, "'Sings' well at the piano, left hand rubato a trifle overdone, but a poetical idea of the piece," which sounds more like Paderewski than Glenn Gould. The adjudicator also noted "too much left-hand anticipation," referring to the Romantic practice – a favourite of Paderewski's – of not playing the two hands precisely together, usually with the bass part slightly anticipating the melody, to get an expressive effect resembling the portamento of a string instrument or human voice. The practice was almost universally dismissed as sloppiness in the later twentieth century, and Gould was just about the only major pianist of his generation to make use of it pervasively. These adjudications, and the early private recordings, reveal that the old Romantic style of playing was very much in his bones as a young musician. His teenage recording of Mendelssohn's *Rondo capriccioso*, for instance, so teases the listener with its little rhythmic pushes and pulls that it might almost pass for a turn-of-the-century performance by, say, de Pachmann or Godowsky or Hofmann. In many of his professional concerts, especially his early ones, he was criticized for overly effusive Romantic playing, and in fact one hears more of this sort of thing in his later recordings than his avowed theories on the matter would lead one to expect.

The private recordings reveal another surprising fact: Gould was never a pianistic prodigy of the highest order, even leaving aside the likes of Mozart, Mendelssohn, Saint-Saëns, and Strauss. He was not nearly as advanced as such past prodigies as Josef Hofmann, Erich Wolfgang Korngold, Claudio Arrau, and Ervin Nyiregyházi, and there were few top pianists of his own generation who could not boast of childhood musical gifts at least as impressive as his. Van Cliburn, for instance, showed no less precocity than Gould at age three, gave adult recitals before age ten, first played his signature piece, the Tchaikovsky concerto, at twelve, and made his Carnegie Hall debut at thirteen. Daniel Barenboim made his debut at seven, was taking Europe by storm at ten, and recorded all of Mozart's sonatas at twelve. The list can easily be extended, and it is not necessary to look outside Canada. Torontonians had marvelled at the precocity of Ernest MacMillan a generation before Gould (at nine he was composing an oratorio based on the Resurrection, and at ten he made his debut as an organist), and in 1940, the ten-year-old André Mathieu, from Montreal, played at Town Hall in New York, including a series of études he had composed at age four. Gould's concerto debut in January 1947 was in fact upstaged two months later by that of another local pianist, nine-year-old Patsy Parr, who played several short works (some of her own composition) with the Toronto Symphony, and, the following year, made her recital and Philharmonic debuts in New York. Admittedly, the Beethoven Fourth is no walk in the park for most thirteen-year-olds, but the evidence at our disposal suggests that Gould did not have the technical skill, at comparable ages, of the greatest prodigies. The private recordings from around the late forties reveal, for instance, his struggles with Romantic showpieces like Mendelssohn's *Rondo capriccioso* and "The Bee's Wedding," and include a dry, lumpy performance of Chopin's A-flat-major impromptu.

This is not to belittle Gould, but to stress that his proclivities were never those of a typical prodigy. It was interpretive wisdom beyond his years that most impressed his listeners as a child, not bravura technique. The private recordings sometimes reveal mature musical insights even where the technique is less secure. The recording of Chopin's F-sharp-major impromptu, one of the pieces in his 1947 debut, offers a subtle, poetic, beautifully nuanced performance that weaves a real emotional spell, despite some clinkers and a tubby piano, and reveals a true command of the Romantic style. In any event, Gould's progress, both technically and interpretively, was rapid through his teens, especially when he began devoting more time to practising than to schoolwork. If Gould at twelve or fifteen had his betters in the prodigy department, Gould at sixteen and seventeen was something else altogether: his recording of his *Twelfth Night* suite, from (presumably) 1949, reveals a fluent and brilliant technique, superb control of counterpoint and tone colour, great range and depth of expression. And Gould at eighteen and nineteen and twenty was one of the most impressive and original pianists in the world; his live and broadcast recordings from those years are sometimes breathtaking. His dazzling concert performance of Weber's *Konzertstück* from 1951, for instance, leaves no doubt that he could have commanded more such bravura repertoire had he wanted to do so. "It went extremely well," he wrote to John Beckwith of that concert, "to the surprise of everybody (including me)."

"Throughout my teens I rather resisted the idea of a career as a concert pianist."

Between the wars there was no national concert-management business in Canada, and New York–based organizations like the Community Concert Service and the Civic Concert Service had a virtual stranglehold on Canadian concert life, hampering the efforts of native musicians to control and profit from their concerts. In the late forties there were still only a few professional managers in Canada, and it was the teenage Gould's great good fortune to attract the attention of one of them: Walter Homburger. "As Gould's manager," the *Toronto Daily Star* reported in 1962, Homburger "became the first person to handle the world-wide career of a concert artist from Canada, something experienced New Yorkers told him was impossible." Born in Germany in 1924 into a banking family, Homburger went to England as a "friendly enemy alien" before the Second World War, but in 1940 he was sent to Canada, where he spent time in internment camps – not the only important figure in Canadian music to have been introduced to his adopted country that way. In 1947, after having organized a few concerts in Toronto, he founded his own concert agency, International Artists, through which he would present annual concert series featuring the best local and international musicians. He immediately offered to manage the fourteen-year-old Gould, whom he had heard play Beethoven's G-major concerto at the 1946 Kiwanis festival ("I thought it was phenomenal"), and the boy's parents agreed, with the understanding that he never be exploited as a prodigy. On March 13, 1947, Homburger signed Gould for a single concert, his October 20 debut, and the experience was obviously mutually satisfying: for the remainder of his concert career, Gould never had another manager.

Homburger was a canny and resourceful manager, and a sympathetic shepherd of Gould's career. He had a maverick on his hands, a performer who refused to play the expected repertoire and loathed most of the trappings of concert life, fame, and the music business. "Walter and I never disagree about anything," Gould once said, "except money, pianos, programming, concert dates, my relations with the press and the way I dress." Homburger did occasionally try to convince Gould to moderate some of his more radical ideas and more eccentric behaviours, but "Glenn in those days already knew what he wanted," he said. For the most part, he weathered his star client's idiosyncrasies with patience and good humour, and helped to protect his fragile constitution, and Gould, despite the odd barbed wisecrack, appreciated the support. Homburger, as an independent manager, was not beholden to the American concert organizations, and Gould, as the son of prosperous parents, was not wanting for money; as a result, he did not, like many Canadian classical musicians, have to scramble to earn a living in a country with then only four major orchestras and a concert circuit that could be remarkably provincial. (The contralto Maureen Forrester recalled singing, as a young artist, in church basements and in high-school gyms pervaded by "the smell of over-ripe socks.") Besides, Gould's talent was so great that it effectively sold itself.

As a teenager the serious-minded Gould already considered a concert career "a kind of superficial thing, some sort of pleasant adjunct to a scholastic interest in music," as he told an interviewer in 1962. "I imagined that only a career that was musicologically motivated was worthy and that everything else was a little bit frivolous." A concert career was necessary if he wanted to make a name for himself, of course, but he was not willing to expose himself publicly more than was necessary. Between 1947 and 1954 he sometimes gave only a few major concerts in a single season, and never more than seven or eight. He was still playing from time to time at Malvern, at the conservatory, in local churches, still appearing occasionally as an "assisting artist" or accompanist, and in benefit concerts. He performed at the CNE, too, when it reopened after the war. His last appearance there was in the summer of 1952, on which occasion he finished with Prokofiev's Seventh Sonata. He was supposed to stop by 6:00 p.m., but his performance ran two minutes long. The CNE, he recalled years later, ran on a tight schedule, and a dive-bombing demonstration had been scheduled for 6:01, so as he stormed to the end of the noisy, hard-driving finale of the Seventh – appropriately, one of Prokofiev's "War Sonatas" – he was drowned out by planes overhead. That performance, he said, "would have warmed the cockles of P. T. Barnum's heart."

But Gould was also, by this time, making high-profile appearances in more prestigious venues, including several Ontario universities, the Art Gallery of Toronto (now the AGO), Eaton Auditorium, and Massey Hall, which he, like musicians from Stravinsky to Dizzy Gillespie, considered "one of the great acoustical properties of the continent." Like Guerrero, he had a special fondness for the more intimate surroundings of Hart House, where he gave three recitals between 1949 and 1952. He also gave recitals under the auspices of women's musical societies, then among the most active sponsors of classical recitals, in cities large and small. In Toronto he played for the Heliconian Club in 1948, and for the Women's Musical Club in 1953, and he was sponsored by women's groups in Ottawa, Montreal, Winnipeg, Calgary, and other cities.

In the 1950–51 season he began to appear regularly in other major Ontario cities, and in fall 1951 he undertook his first western tour, appearing in Vancouver and Calgary. His mother went with him – it was the first time in the West for both of them – though she was now past sixty and admitted that the trip exhausted her. (According to Ray Dudley, she was upset that she could no longer control Glenn, and refused to tour with him again.) Gould's reputation was growing quickly. By the time he was twenty he had performed with the Toronto Symphony five times – "I'm generally regarded as a brat in those circles," he once said – usually under Ernest MacMillan, who led the orchestra from 1931 to 1956. He appeared in Montreal for the first time in 1952, the Maritimes (Saint John, New Brunswick) in 1953, and Winnipeg in 1954. He was not yet making a lot of money. Recital fees of a few hundred dollars were typical, and at Hart House he played for an honorarium of $25 in 1950, $50 in 1952. But his reception among audiences was often tumultuous – for instance, five curtain calls from a crowd of two thousand in Vancouver.

As early as 1950, Gould was subscribing to a press-clipping service, and needing one: he already had a national reputation, and some critics were ranking him with the greatest pianists in Canada and abroad. He was also being recognized for his exciting musical personality and flamboyant platform manner – the rumpled appearance, the simian crouch over the keyboard, the flailing arms and gyrating torso and bobbing head, the glass of water to his side and the little Oriental rug beneath his stomping feet, and of course the singing, which could sometimes be heard at the back of the largest halls. His mother begged him to tone down his mannerisms, and even the Governor General of Canada, Vincent Massey, weighed in on the subject: "You *must* tell him to stop it!" he said to Maureen Forrester. Homburger, too, told Gould forthrightly to improve his onstage appearance, and Gould once tried sincerely to do so for a couple of weeks, but his musical concentration was compromised, and he gave up. "I'm incapable of changing the way I play the piano," he concluded. "People will have to accept or reject me as I am."

Then there was the most enduring symbol of Gould's eccentricity: his chair. He wanted an unusually low chair, one that had the "give" he needed, both front-to-back and diagonally, in order to accommodate his movements while he played. It required a seat that sloped forward ("I have to sit on the edge") and a backrest at a greater than ninety-degree pitch to accommodate the "leisurely angle" at which he liked to sit. No conventional piano bench met his needs, so in 1953 his father customized a light, high-backed, wooden folding chair. "I had to saw about four inches off each leg," he told Otto Friedrich, "and I made a brass bracket to go around each leg and screw into it, and then welded the half of a turnbuckle to the brass bracket so that each leg could be adjusted individually." The chair placed Gould about fourteen inches off the ground, which was still not low enough, but since his knees were already higher than his buttocks it was not practical to lower the seat any more. So he fabricated a set of black wooden blocks that allowed him to raise the piano up about an inch and a quarter – in effect, placing him barely a foot from the floor.

Bert's chair was perfect, and Gould would use it for every concert and recording, every rehearsal and practice session, for the rest of his life. He carried and shipped it around, as required, in a special case, often at considerable expense, and it was occasionally lost or damaged in transit. By the later fifties the chair was already so well worn that his audiences sometimes feared its collapse. Oiling it became one of his pre-performance rituals, though it still squeaked in concerts, and some of its squeaks are permanently enshrined in his recordings. The frame had eventually to be taped and wired together, and the seat deteriorated with use: the padding oozed gradually out of the green leatherette cover, which itself fell apart – one can almost date Gould's photographs and films by the condition of the seat. By the mid-seventies he was sitting on a bare frame only, with one wooden support running front-to-back along his crotch, yet he was never heard to complain about it. Over the years he made sincere efforts to find (or have made) a new, sturdier wood or metal chair, but no substitute was ever right. Bert's chair became a talisman for Gould – a security blanket upon which he depended.

"I thought of myself as a valiant defender of twelve-tone music and of its leading exponents."

Gould became a passionate proselytizer on behalf of the Schoenberg school, and he spread the word to all who would listen. In a Grade 13 English essay, "My Pet Antipathy," he produced a polemic against the general public's resistance to contemporary music, and when asked to say a few words about his musical tastes in 1952 on a personnel questionnaire for the CBC, he responded with a four-hundred-word defence of the Schoenberg school and its place in music history. His first public lecture was delivered at the conservatory in 1951, in observance of the death of Schoenberg that summer (the text has not survived), and on December 17, 1953, also for the conservatory, he delivered a long, densely analytical lecture on Schoenberg's Piano Concerto,* of which he gave the Canadian premiere a few days later.

His efforts to educate himself about modern music were impressive. There are letters from early 1952 in which he solicits Oskar Morawetz, then in Europe, to find him scores of twentieth-century piano music and of works like Hindemith's *Kammermusik*, Schoenberg's Chamber Symphony No. 1 and Op. 10 string quartet, Webern's songs and Op. 24 concerto – hardly standard fare for a young Canadian pianist in the early fifties. He read books and articles on twentieth-century music, and studied many scores, including those of his Canadian contemporaries. One never knew what modern repertoire he would poke his fingers into next: operas by

---

* "On that famous occasion," Gould wrote in a 1959 letter, "I was a guest lecturer on a series at the University here and was asked to prepare a 50-minute talk. Somehow or other" – the *thirty* musical examples, perhaps? – "it extended into one hour and 35 minutes and the Assistant Principal of the Royal Conservatory finally strode on stage and informed me that I was infringing on the time of the annual Christmas party and even if I hadn't got around to discussing the inversions in the last movement, would I please shut up and go home!" Sylvia Hunter, a former Guerrero pupil, recalls, "I don't think anybody in the room had a clue what he was talking about."

Alban Berg or William Walton, symphonies by Aulis Sallinen or
Wilhelm Furtwängler, sonatas by Charles Ives or Fartein Valen or
Leon Kirchner, piano concertos by Ernst Krenek or Wolfgang
Fortner, music by Frank Martin (which he greatly admired) or Alfredo
Casella. Over the years, some composers (like Krenek, whom he came
to know personally in the fifties, and Vincent Persichetti) tried to get
him to perform their music, and in modern-music circles he acquired
a reputation as a mainstream performer sympathetic to their cause.

Yet, Gould was never really a new-music specialist. The music
he actually incorporated into his active repertoire, and his personal
canon, rarely extended beyond that which was new in his teens, most
of it Austro-German. He kept informed about what was going on
in the musical world, but had little sympathy for most of the post-
war trends in composition: serialism, electronics, *musique concrète*,
aleatory music, minimalism, the fusion of classical and jazz idioms
in a "third stream," and so on. And he had almost no direct contact
with the more adventurous young Toronto composers like Harry
Freedman, Harry Somers, and John Weinzweig, who, in his Suite
for Piano No. 1 (1939), had been the first Canadian composer to
make use of twelve-tone principles. Still, Schoenberg and Berg and
Webern were plenty dissonant enough for most Torontonians even
long after the war, and to the general public, anyway, Gould had a
reputation as a champion of modern music, and as a performer was
widely admired for his ability to make difficult twentieth-century
music comprehensible, to communicate its lyricism, tonal beauty,
and passion. He first attracted notice as a modernist by organizing
an ambitious Recital of Contemporary Music at the conservatory on
January 4, 1951. The program – all of the music was composed
between 1936 and 1950 – was astonishing for its time and place:
Hindemith's Third Sonata, Krenek's Third Sonata, the premiere of
Morawetz's *Fantasy in D*, and two of Gould's own atonal works: the
5 *Short Piano Pieces* and the Bassoon Sonata. For an eighteen-year-
old high-school student, the evening was a tour de force.

In spring 1952, Gould joined forces with his old classmate
Robert Fulford, by then a sports writer for the *Globe and Mail*, to

form a legally registered company: New Music Associates. The official mandate was to present concerts of twentieth-century music; the more immediate motivation was to commemorate the death of Arnold Schoenberg. Gould looked after all matters musical, while Fulford rented the hall, sold the tickets, did the publicity, found the ushers, and kept the books. In all, New Music Associates sponsored three concerts in the conservatory's concert hall, the first two of which consisted almost entirely of Canadian premieres. The Schoenberg Memorial Concert, on October 4, 1952, included six early songs, with soprano Elizabeth Benson Guy; two piano works, Opp. 11 and 25; and the *Ode to Napoleon*, Op. 41, for string quartet, piano, and reciter, with Victor Feldbrill conducting. By this time Gould had already developed a fondness for making impromptu speeches from the stage in order to introduce the modern music on his programs, though at the Memorial Concert, strangely, he was more reticent. His specially written essay on Schoenberg's development was read to the audience by the CBC announcer Frank Herbert, who later admitted that he had understood almost nothing of what he had been reading. On January 9, 1954, Gould presented an even more ambitious program exploring the whole Second Viennese School: Schoenberg's song cycle *The Book of the Hanging Gardens*, with soprano Roma Butler; Webern's *Five Movements* for string quartet, Op. 5; Webern's Saxophone Quartet, Op. 22, conducted by Feldbrill; and two piano works, Webern's *Variations* and Berg's Sonata. Gould's printed program note was a dense, verbose essay, "An Appreciation of Anton Webern."

Neither concert sold out, and Gould's programs challenged local audiences; he did not make things easier by insisting that Webern's Opp. 22 and 27, because of their difficulty, both be played twice. Some reviewers were not impressed. "Babies' Rhythm Practice Sounds Better Than This" was the headline in the conservative *Telegram* after the second concert. But the more sophisticated critics and listeners, and fellow-musicians, recognized the importance of Gould's modern-music concerts, and remembered them for years.

The third New Music Associates concert, on October 16, 1954, was devoted to Bach. (Fulford: "Why Bach?" Gould, loftily: "Bach is ever new.") Maureen Forrester, making her Toronto debut, sang arias, and Gould joined in performances of the trio sonata from the *Musical Offering* and the C-minor violin sonata, with Morry Kernerman, and gave his first live performance of the Goldberg Variations.* The concert was poorly attended because of the deadly flooding and devastation caused the night before by Hurricane Hazel, the worst natural disaster in Toronto's history. Those who did attend included critics as well as luminaries like Ernest MacMillan, and all were dazzled by Gould's bold performance of the Goldberg Variations, then still widely considered to be an academic, even unplayable work. The musicologist Harvey Olnick was stunned, and the following month, in Gould's first American notice, in the *Musical Courier*, pronounced him the equal of Landowska and Serkin. The concert made a big impact musically, and the small financial loss was easily covered; Forrester earned the stately sum of $50. But that was the last hurrah for New Music Associates. Gould and Fulford were beginning to drift apart, and soon Gould, even in Baroque and modern repertoire, would no longer need to create his own opportunities; they would come to him.

"The Stratford Music Festival is an adventure for us."

Stratford, Ontario, about 140 kilometres west of Toronto, was a small industrial town and railway stop in the middle of the countryside,

---

* "I began to study the Goldberg Variations much earlier than when I recorded it – it was perhaps in 1950," Gould said, in a 1959 interview. "This was a work which I learned entirely on my own. I never really had a lesson with anyone on it and in fact it was one of the first works that I did learn entirely without my teacher. It was a work which I made up my mind about relatively [early], much more so and much more decidedly than was the case with most works in my repertoire at that time. And therefore I think that it's a work that I probably have changed less about in the last few years than most others."

with no history as a cultural centre, when a local businessman decided to create an annual drama festival focused on the plays of Shakespeare. In July 1953, the Stratford Festival was officially launched, with a six-week season of two Shakespeare plays held in a specially constructed tent seating just over eleven hundred. The festival, which received national and international recognition, proved to be crucial to the development of professional theatre in Canada, but from the beginning there was music, too. The Canadian composer Louis Applebaum organized a series of sixteen hour-long afternoon concerts for the 1953 season, with help from Walter Homburger, the CBC, and others. Soon the festival was attracting some of the best musicians in Canada and the world, and with them visitors who came more for the music than the theatre.

Gould performed in three concerts in 1953, making his debut in a chamber-music setting on July 31, in the first and only concert of the Festival Trio: he joined the violinist Albert Pratz and the cellist Isaac Mamott in works by Beethoven and Brahms.* He gave two recitals, too, on August 4 and 14, offering characteristic programs of works by Bach, Beethoven, Berg, and Morawetz – he was not about to compromise even for afternoon crowds of summer tourists in a relatively informal venue. He had to endure "leaky dressing rooms, a prevailing humidity to which even I responded by playing in shirt sleeves, a miserable instrument and no organization whatsoever," as he recalled a decade later – and he left out the acoustically poor theatre, the haphazard publicity, the very poor attendance, the thunderstorm that drowned him out in one of his concerts, and earnings of just $127 for the season. Yet he enjoyed that chaotic first summer, because he saw the festival as a forum in which he could explore repertoire and ideas and approaches to performance that had no place in his regular concert season.

There were only a few informal performances in the summer

---

* The Festival Trio later appeared at least once on CBC radio, on June 15, 1954, in a performance of Schubert's Piano Trio in B-flat Major for *CBC Concert Hall* (no recording survives).

of 1954;* it was the ambitious series of concerts in the summer of 1955 that was officially designated the "inaugural season of music" at Stratford. Applebaum had little money to spend but enticed musicians like Gould by offering almost unlimited creative freedom. He attracted soloists including Maureen Forrester, Lois Marshall, Elisabeth Schwarzkopf, and Isaac Stern, and mounted a legendary production of Stravinsky's *Soldier's Tale*, in which the French mime Marcel Marceau made his North American debut. On July 12, Gould played Beethoven's Second Piano Concerto with the Hart House Orchestra, a chamber orchestra under the direction of Boyd Neel, and on July 29, he gave a performance of the Goldberg Variations that Jacob Siskind, the *Montreal Star* critic, compared "with those by a Landowska, a Kirkpatrick, or a Tureck." His eccentricities, onstage and off, caused some comment, too. Summers in Stratford are hot and humid at the best of times, but in 1955 temperatures reached 41°C (105°F), and the afternoon concerts were moved from the scorching tent to the Casino, a barnlike building that originally served as a badminton hall. That didn't stop Gould from living up to his own publicity, walking around town dressed in a coat, scarf, cap, and gloves, and demanding that windows be closed before he could rehearse. The bundled-up Gould, a strange but lovable figure, became a fixture on the Stratford scene for most of the next decade.

The 1956 music season was even more ambitious, with stellar talent and adventurous programming. Half of the concerts were devoted to high-profile jazz performers, while the classical concerts included piano recitals by Claudio Arrau and Rudolf Serkin, and a variety of vocal, chamber, orchestral, and choral music, with works drawn from the Renaissance through the twentieth century,

---

* On July 18, according to CBC records, Gould joined the violinist Alexander Schneider and the cellist Zara Nelsova in the Festival Theatre performing chamber music by Bach, Beethoven, and Brahms. The performance was broadcast (presumably live) on CBC television in Toronto, Ottawa, and Montreal, in the series *Summer Festival* (and on the radio, too?); no visual record survives, though recordings of Beethoven's "Ghost" Trio and *Allegretto* in B-flat Major, WoO 39, do survive, and they do not sound as though they had been made in the presence of an audience.

including several specially commissioned new works, and a production of Britten's chamber opera *The Rape of Lucretia*. In the busy year since his last visit to Stratford, Gould had become a concert and recording artist of international renown, and he took the whole summer of 1956 off except for one concert at the festival, on July 9. It was a tour de force before a packed house. He dazzled his audience with his versatility, appearing in the roles of pianist, conductor, composer, and writer, in an unusual program: solo works by Sweelinck, Krenek, and Berg; the premiere of his own String Quartet (more on that later); and Schoenberg's *Ode to Napoleon*, with the soprano Bethany Beardslee. Gould directed the proceedings from the piano and wrote the program notes. The critics, including visitors from New York (*Time, Musical America*) were impressed by his virtuosity and versatility. "On paper it looked awful," wrote Ross Parmenter, in the *New York Times*. "But it turned out to be an absorbing evening, largely because Mr. Gould is as gifted as a musical thinker as he is as a pianist."

"Canada's been terribly good to me."

Gould longed to do more than give concerts. He wanted to record and broadcast, to write and compose and conduct, and in his early years as a professional performer he would produce work in all of these fields, and earn a national reputation as a musician of unusual breadth. But talent and ambition are useless where opportunity is wanting, and he was lucky to have been in the right place at the right time. The beginning of his professional career coincided with a period of great artistic ferment in Canada and the burgeoning of cultural institutions in which he found venues and support for his increasingly multifarious work. Economic prosperity and newly invigorated nationalistic sentiments combined to create widespread optimism about Canada's future as an independent nation of enormous potential rather than a colony – look no further than the spate of books published after the war with titles like *Canada on the March, Canada*

Looks Ahead, Canada in the Making, Canada's Tomorrow, Prospect of Canada, Colony to Nation . . . These were fertile conditions for Canadian culture. The years from the Second World War to about 1960 were a heady time for the younger Canadian artists who sought to move beyond the parochialism of the past toward a more personal and professional brand of art that was both distinctly Canadian and in touch with international movements. It showed in a flowering of sophisticated, adventurous Canadian fiction and poetry – in the fifties, as one poet wrote, Canada was a veritable "nest of singing birds" – in which there was unprecedented public, commercial, and academic interest. It showed in the growth and the innovations of the Canadian film industry, in features, documentaries, and animation. It showed in the acceptance of radical modern developments in the visual arts – Expressionism, Surrealism, Abstractionism, "automatic painting" – by, for instance, the Plasticiens and Automatistes of Montreal, and, later, non-objective Toronto artists like the Painters Eleven.

And it showed in music, for which the forties and fifties are now remembered as a coming of age. The generation of composers then finishing their formal studies were belatedly but enthusiastically absorbing modern idioms – Impressionism, Expressionism, neo-Classicism, twelve-tone music, and later serialism, electronics, aleatory music, and so on – despite the hostility of older colleagues and audiences, and were working prolifically in genres like orchestral and chamber and large-scale keyboard music that had previously been relatively neglected. "We are actually the first generation of Canadian composers," the thirty-eight-year-old Barbara Pentland wrote in 1950, by which she meant the first generation to have received most of its training, and to have begun earning serious national and international recognition, without leaving Canada. She could have included performers like Lois Marshall and Maureen Forrester and Gould, too. True, many composers and performers at that time were still going to Europe or the United States to finish their professional educations and to nourish their avant-garde ambitions, but through the post-war period a career in classical music based in Canada became increasingly possible.

New institutional support was crucial in helping all this talent to flower. When Gould was a child, the sort of sustained, co-ordinated government support of the arts taken for granted after the war scarcely existed, and corporate and private patronage was neither widespread nor systematic. But the war, which itself inspired much art, some with government funding, helped to reinforce the notion that culture had a social role that made it worthy of state support and aroused widespread support for a sort of "New Deal" for the arts in the form of state-sponsored cultural institutions or even a sort of "ministry of culture." After a decade of fierce debate and passionate lobbying on cultural policy, a Royal Commission on National Development in the Arts, Letters, and Sciences (the Massey Commission) was appointed, in 1949, to examine cultural, educational, and scientific institutions and make recommendations for their future. The Commission became a kind of crusade for cultural nationalism. Its report, delivered in May 1951, documented the increased cultural activity since the war, but still noted a "lack of nourishment" for Canadian art and artists, and underscored the importance of government-funded organization in a vast but sparsely populated country besieged by the "menace" of American popular culture, American economic control of arts, and its own legacy of colonialism. As one brief to the Commission reported,

> No novelist, poet, short story writer, historian, biographer, or other writer of non-technical books can make even a modestly comfortable living by selling his work in Canada.
>
> No composer of music can live at all on what Canada pays him for his compositions.
>
> Apart from radio drama, no playwright, and only a few actors and producers, can live by working in the theatre in Canada.
>
> Few painters and sculptors, outside the fields of commercial art and teaching, can live by sale of their work in Canada.

But the situation was improving, precisely because all of that cultural lobbying in the forties spurred an extraordinary development of cultural organizations. A striking number of the most important arts institutions came into being in the forties and fifties, from the Canadian Arts Council (1945) to the Canada Council (1957), the latter the centrepiece of the Massey Commission's recommendations, or, in music, from the Canadian Music Council (1944) to the Canadian Music Centre (1959). Other organizations created new opportunities for performers and composers in these years: the Canadian League of Composers (1951), which organized its own concerts for fifteen years; the National Ballet of Canada (1951) and other major dance companies; the CBC Symphony Orchestra (1952); the Royal Conservatory Opera School (1946); the CBC Opera Company (1948); and the Opera Festival Association of Toronto (1950), which evolved into the Canadian Opera Company. Hugh Le Caine did innovative work in electronic music after the war, in his own studio and later for the National Research Council, and Canada's first electronic-music studio was established at the University of Toronto in 1959. In academia, younger Canadian composers, and many post-war immigrants, began to assume positions of authority and create forums for their work. Standards of music education improved at all levels, including the professional. In 1952, at the University of Toronto, the music faculty and the Royal Conservatory were enlarged and reorganized, and among the consequences were advanced degree programs and the introduction of proper courses in composition and musicology. The First Symposium of Canadian Music was held in Vancouver in 1950, and an International Conference of Composers was held at the Stratford Festival in 1960. The *business* of classical music expanded significantly after the war – particularly publishing. Important periodicals appeared, albeit briefly: the *Canadian Review of Music and Art* (1942–48) and the more substantial *Canadian Music Journal* (1956–62). The first major catalogues of Canadian composers and their works appeared at this time, as did retrospective surveys like the 1955 collection *Music in Canada*, edited by Ernest MacMillan. The first comprehensive history of Canadian music was published in 1960.

And it was precisely in these years that Glenn Gould went from being a local to an international phenomenon. He was, indeed, one of the great success stories of mid-twentieth-century Canadian culture, and though he was talented enough to have found success anywhere at any time, his career might have taken another path, perhaps less congenial, had he not had the opportunities that arose at home during his early professional career – above all, opportunities in broadcasting.

"My career was spawned in a radio studio."

Canada was a pioneer in the field of radio broadcasting and other electronic media. The Marconi company's station XWA in Montreal (later CFCF) became North America's (and perhaps the world's) first regular broadcaster in 1919, and Toronto's first radio station, CFCA, began broadcasting in 1922 from the offices of the *Daily Star*. Interest in radio exploded through the twenties, and network radio first appeared in the form of stations operated by the major Canadian railways, whose programming included a good deal of classical music. But like so much of Canadian culture in those days, early radio was monopolized by American commercial interests. In many quarters there was fierce lobbying against the influx of American popular culture over the airwaves, and in favour of a more unifying and edifying Canadian system modelled on the BBC, which was founded in 1922. The result was the establishment, in 1932, of the ambitious though controversial Canadian Radio Broadcasting Commission, and, in 1936, of the Canadian Broadcasting Corporation. Before long, the CBC was widely perceived as Canada's greatest cultural asset.

Of course, Canadians already had access to British and American music programs, and, according to Jessie Greig, Gould, like many Canadians, listened to the New York Philharmonic, Toscanini and the NBC Symphony, the Metropolitan Opera, and other American offerings. But he was listening avidly to the CBC, too, and it is difficult to overstate how vital a resource the early CBC was for Canadian musicians. It greatly increased public appreciation of serious music and awareness of Canadian music, musicians, and musical life. Gould gleaned much of his understanding of the larger world of music from the CBC, which supported experimental ventures of little appeal. The CBC was a vital source of revenue and promotion and artistic inspiration for Canadian musicians. It commissioned and premiered many new works by Canadian composers, offered countless opportunities for Canadian performers, even maintained its own orchestras. More than one Canadian musical career was literally saved, or at least kept in Canada, because of the CBC. Moreover, through its International Service, established in Montreal in 1944, the CBC brought Canadian music to other countries, where it was practically unknown. The resources, programming, and artistic range of the corporation expanded rapidly through the late thirties and during the war, and spectacularly after the war; between 1944 and 1962 there were *two* English-language networks, the Trans-Canada and the Dominion, the latter reserved for lighter fare, in addition to the French-language network, Radio-Canada. By 1948, half of the music on the CBC was classical, much of it live and Canadian; a decade later, Canadian content accounted for about 95 per cent of music programming. Moreover, the music department was largely controlled by creative people rather than businessmen; Geoffrey Waddington, a violinist and conductor sympathetic to Canadian music, became music adviser for the English networks in 1947, and director of music in 1952.

Gould made his CBC debut at the age of eighteen, and recalled the event in 1974 in his article "Music and Technology":

One Sunday morning in December 1950, I wandered into a living-room-sized radio-studio, placed my services at the disposal of a single microphone belonging to the Canadian Broadcasting Corporation, and proceeded to broadcast "live" – tape was already a fact of life in the recording industry but, in those days, radio broadcasting still observed the first-note-to-last-and-damn-the-consequences syndrome of the concert-hall – two sonatas, one by Mozart [K. 281], one by Hindemith [No. 3]. It was my first network broadcast . . . a memorable one . . . that moment in my life when I first caught a vague impression of the direction it would take, when I realised that the collected wisdom of my peers and elders to the effect that technology represented a compromising, dehumanising intrusion into art was nonsense, when my love affair with the microphone began.

It was not literally Gould's radio debut, incidentally. On the afternoon of Sunday, December 4, 1938, six-year-old "Master Glen Gold" appeared at a local theatre in the Reliable Doll All-Star Revue "Today's Children," which was sponsored by a toy company and broadcast on CFRB. He played several pieces, and took a pitch test, which he passed with what one newspaper called "flying honors." On March 10, 1945, he appeared on CFRB again in a concert of Kiwanis Festival winners, for which he received $10, and we may assume there were other childhood broadcasts on local radio. But it was the CBC, more than concert appearances, that first made him a national figure, and he himself acknowledged the enormous impact of the broadcaster on his musical development in the early fifties. Moreover, through his early CBC experiences he became an eager convert to the electronic media before he had even given a concert outside Canada, and came to view his broadcasting (and later recording) as his *real* career. He viewed his concert schedule as an adjunct to his media work, not the reverse, and in this light his ultimate rejection of concert life seems less an aberration than an inevitability.

From 1950 through 1955, Gould appeared almost thirty times on CBC radio, in studio recitals, which were then still broadcast live, as well as live relays of concert appearances with various orchestras, on both networks and often in prestige series like *Distinguished Artists* and *CBC Wednesday Night*, an innovative mélange of music, drama, news, documentaries, panels, and much else. At first his broadcasting repertoire was largely the same as his concert repertoire, plus a little chamber music, and the network had no qualms about giving him a forum for early and modern music. Indeed, his first public performances of some of the staples of his repertoire – Sweelinck's "Fitzwilliam" Fantasia, Bach's Partita No. 5, Berg's Sonata – were on the radio, and he gave the Canadian premiere of Schoenberg's Piano Concerto on the air, with the CBC's own orchestra. His first public performance of the Goldberg Variations, too, was in a CBC studio, on June 21, 1954.

Television came late to Canada. The BBC established the world's first regular television service in 1936 and it was more than fifteen years before Canada caught up: for an immense country covering six time zones with a sparse population and two official languages, television was an expensive and technologically complicated business. The CBC finally presented Canada's first telecast, from Montreal, on Saturday, September 6, 1952. The first telecast from Toronto's station, CBLT, followed two days later – a live, three-hour extravaganza of speeches, news, music, drama, and more, featuring some of Canada's best musical and dramatic performers, including Gould, who provided some unintended comedy. After performing part of a Beethoven concerto with orchestra, he became so absorbed backstage watching the next act, a brass sextet, that he set a decorative fake-marble column to tottering and had to wrestle with it to keep it from collapsing, while the brass players struggled to contain their laughter. ("Extremely unprofessional to say the least," snarled the conductor, Geoffrey Waddington.)

There followed a craze for TV in the fifties that rivalled the craze for radio in the twenties, and as in radio the CBC proved to be dedicated and innovative and financially generous when it came to music-related programming. Ambitious, too: in its second year CBC television was already broadcasting full-length operas, operettas, ballets, orchestral and concerto concerts, and solo recitals, including modern works (sometimes North American or world television premieres) as well as classics, along with music documentaries, children's and educational music shows, and more. Gould appeared on television in a variety of CBC series in his twenties – *Chrysler Festival, Folio,*

Ford Startime, Graphic, Scope – and, several times, in the Radio-Canada series *L'Heure du concert*. Already he had innovative producers to work with, though it would be almost a decade before he began to experiment with television formats other than the conventional filmed concert. The first visual document of Gould performing dates from December 16, 1954, his second appearance in the inaugural season of *L'Heure du concert*: he gave a dashing performance of the first movement of Beethoven's First Piano Concerto with the CBC Symphony, featuring his own new cadenza. He had composed cadenzas for the first *and* last movements, and performed them for the first time two days earlier with the Montreal Symphony. Both cadenzas are openly anachronistic: the first, Gould wrote, is "a rather Regerian fugue" based on the themes of the first movement, the other, a "rhapsody" in a highly chromatic idiom. Both, he claimed, were intended to subvert "the original purpose of cadenza writing as a virtuosic display." Yet the cadenzas are so eccentric that they call far more attention to themselves than would Beethoven's own cadenzas or any more conventional specimens.

"I've always been a record-buff."

Like many children, Gould and Robert Fulford created a tin-cans-and-string system connecting their two houses. Later, when they were about twelve, Fulford recalled, Gould "organized more sophisticated equipment, microphones and little speakers, so that we could make radio broadcasts, from our house to his and vice versa. This time the equipment worked fine, but our problem was content; after he did a brief concert and my brother Wayne and I did a newscast, we had trouble figuring what to put on the air." Gould was comfortable from an early age with more professional communications technologies, too, and he came by his technophilia honestly: his father enjoyed mechanical gadgets. On June 15, 1922, the *North Ontario Times* in Uxbridge reported, "Thursday evening last, Mr. Bert Gold managed to get in communication with the Star Radio

Concert [in Toronto] at 7 o'clock. This is the first time that radio has been heard in town and it is due to the active efforts of Mr. Gold that the new entertainment has arrived." Bert installed radio sets and phonograph speakers for the Gold Medal Radio & Phonograph Company for a time in the early twenties, and he was shooting eight-millimetre film footage of the family at the cottage as early as the summer of 1948.

The revolution of magnetic tape was introduced to radio and recording in the late forties, and the Goulds were among the first people in Toronto to acquire a recorder for use at home, despite the high cost; friends' recollections and the surviving recordings suggest that Glenn was using one as early as 1947 or 1948. He immediately recognized the value of recording, not only for preserving his repertoire and interpretations for posterity, but for analyzing his own playing. Recording, for him, became a practice technique. He also documented some of his compositions and the occasional improvisation, made recordings with Guerrero, including concertos on two pianos, taped some of his early concerts, and recorded performances and compositions by some of his friends. Among these private recordings are pieces of which no other Gould performance survives: Mozart's K. 488 concerto, études and impromptus by Chopin, short works by Scarlatti, Mendelssohn, Debussy, and others. Some of the them include Gould's spoken introductions. The Couperin-Guerrero Passacaille, recorded when Gould was about fifteen, is preceded by a hilariously pompous little speech that says much about his attitude toward Romantic piano playing in his mid-teens – and toward his teacher:

> Glenn Gould: I would like to record now Couperin's Passacaille in B Minor. Now, a great many people, when they hear that someone is going to play a work of this age and of this type, they'll say, "Now, my boy, the first thing to do is to play it very dully, and of course without any pedals." Now, there are two mistakes. For we must remember that we are not trying to sacrifice in the piano what the harpsichord did *not* have, but

rather to create an impressionistic effect of what the harpsichord *did* have. I shall try and do that for you now. Here is Couperin's Passacaille in B Minor.

Male voice in the background (Bert Gould?): As arranged by – Glenn Gould: As arranged by Mr. Alberto Guerrero.

As soon as he began to work for the CBC he was purchasing acetate discs of his broadcasts from local companies. Some of these, still in his possession when he died, preserved the only known recordings of certain performances.

Gould began to make commercial recordings as soon as the opportunity arose – first for the CBC. The network's International Service began a Transcription Service in 1947, and by Gould's time it had captured young Canadian musicians like Lois Marshall and Oscar Peterson on high-quality records, pressed in small quantities for use by the CBC itself and distributed to Canada's embassies abroad and to foreign radio stations. Gould made three recordings for the International Service, the first in 1954, featuring a vibrant and fully mature reading of Bach's Partita No. 5, coupled with Morawetz's *Fantasy in D*. Even though records had been produced in Canada since at least 1900, only a few companies were making classical recordings when Gould was a teenager – Quality Records and Beaver, for instance, both founded in 1950, and Hallmark Recordings, which claimed to be "the only Canadian recording company producing and cutting its own high-grade long-playing records." In November 1952, Keith MacMillan, the son of Ernest MacMillan and a producer of music programs for CBC radio, joined four friends to found Hallmark and set up a studio and lab in downtown Toronto. The company folded in 1959, but in the interim it amassed a small yet adventurous catalogue that included Canadian performers and composers in sometimes offbeat repertoire, and it even had some foreign distribution through Decca.

Ernest MacMillan had already tipped Keith off about Gould, so Keith was receptive when, in fall 1953, Albert Pratz, having played with Gould at Stratford that summer, approached Hallmark to suggest a duo recording with him.* On November 3, at the age of twenty-one, Gould taped his first commercial recording, a magnificent reading of Berg's Sonata, at the Bloor Street United Church in downtown Toronto; later that week, he and Pratz recorded transcriptions of light pieces by Prokofiev, Shostakovich, and Taneyev. "He wasn't too eager to record the Russian pieces," Pratz recalled shortly after Gould's death, "but he was very gracious about it, and even seemed to enjoy himself at the time. He did a wonderful job, too." When the album was released, John Beckwith wrote that those Russian pieces were "the only really cheap music he has ever been associated with professionally," and Gould himself, in 1958, sent the album to a friend with the admonition, "Please remember your promise about never listening to the second side!"

The Hallmark album brought Gould less than $150 in 1953, but it gave him his first opportunity to publish his writing, in the form of liner notes on the Berg Sonata. Even in school he had demonstrated, if not much literary talent, at least literary ambition and eagerness to express himself. Jessie Greig recalled that he used to write little plays for family and friends to perform in – "Always he was the star." His earliest professional writings took the form of championing the Schoenberg school – the Berg liner notes, the lectures and program notes on Schoenberg and Webern in the early fifties – though he branched out into Bach in November 1955 with a program essay on the Goldberg Variations for a concert in Montreal. His first published article, a wide-ranging look at the

---

* Gould had first met – or at least *sighted* – Keith MacMillan when he was seven and saw the Toronto Symphony for the first time. In a reminiscence from the mid-seventies, he wrote: "I was sitting with my parents directly back of two young Upper Canada College types a few years older than myself whom my mother pronounced to be Sir Ernest's sons. I have no idea what her sources were but mother had a habit of gathering information like that especially when it could he turned to a propaganda purpose. They were, of course, immaculately turned out (that was the propaganda purpose, since in those days I was hardly the style-leader of my social set), mother pronounced them the very model of decorum to which I should aspire, and I hated them on sight."

current state of the twelve-tone idiom with special emphasis on Boulez and his generation, appeared in fall 1956, in the inaugural issue of the *Canadian Music Journal*, in itself evidence of his position by then within Canadian music. Informed, provocative, and deeply personal, the article was a harbinger of things to come, as was (alas) its lamely punning title, "The Dodecacophonist's Dilemma." At its best, Gould's early writing was engaging and fresh, as well as thoughtful, but often it was awkward, pretentious, and verbose (or, more politely, baroque) – he made the prodigy's error of mistaking pomposity for sophistication – and his train of thought was often difficult to follow, especially where intricate musical analysis was involved. Still, his early writing heralded the emergence of a *thinking* performer who was likely to become something more than just a piano player.

"I decided it was time for me to set out on my own showshoes."

The Beach, Robert Fulford wrote, was

> the best place in the world to spend childhood, the worst place in the world to spend adolescence. For a child the Beach was a richness of grass and sand and water, of hockey "cushions" (as we called them then) and tennis courts and softball diamonds. For an adolescent it was a closed, deadening Wasp world, a suspicious and narrow and clique-ish little compartment in which we all worked hard to avoid knowing both ourselves and our neighbours. A Beach boy was emotionally fixated at age sixteen or less, bound to a code of athletic good-guyism that admitted the existence of no emotional, spiritual, or intellectual ambiguities.

Yet even as he was becoming a mature and unconventional artist, Gould continued to live at home, with his parents, and showed no inclination to move out. (Ray Dudley remembers the amusement of their peers when Gould appeared at a party, around age nineteen, in a car driven by his mother.) He had outgrown his parents artistically and intellectually, and was sometimes prodded to sarcasm and anger by their limitations. His real life now was in his head, in his music, where his parents no longer had any real input; he was independent where it mattered, and had no need to fly the nest to prove the point. Still, he remained close to his parents, and the house was hardly a hotbed of animosity. His parents continued to support him financially and emotionally, and he was content to let his mother look after his day-to-day needs (he would never become independent in that respect). He was asserting his independence in some ways, though. He stopped going to church around age eighteen, which must have disappointed his devout parents, and he grew increasingly cavalier about his studies, as the records for his last few school years show. His parents insisted that he finish high school, but after some discussion of college he decided against it.

In 1952, when he was nineteen, he ended his lessons with Alberto Guerrero, and Jessie Greig recalled seeing tears of anger and frustration in Gould's eyes when his parents objected. He felt he had outgrown his teacher, and Guerrero himself once admitted to Sylvia Hunter that he had nothing more to offer Gould. While the notion that Gould and Guerrero did nothing but argue is pure legend, it is true that in his later teens Gould's ideas about repertoire, interpretation, piano style, and much else diverged increasingly from Guerrero's, making artistic clashes between the two inevitable. Guerrero was dismayed by some of Gould's ideas, and by the onstage shenanigans that were increasingly part of his act; he refused to attend Gould's triumphant Massey Hall recital in April 1956 because he could no longer stand to watch him on stage. But Gould remained friendly with Guerrero until his death in 1959, and their two families continued to socialize. From time to time Gould still sought his counsel (and approval?) about his career and ideas and interpretations, even after he had achieved international fame. "*Never* was there a sign of a split between them," Ray Dudley insists, though rumours to that effect circulated even at the time. But as

Gould wrote to the photographer Yousuf Karsh in 1958, "I felt that at a certain point I was equipped with everything, except the kind of solidarity of the ego which is, in the last analysis, the one important part of an artist's equipment." When he had developed the "insufferable amount of self-confidence" needed for the task, he decided to continue his education on his own.

Though the newspaper profiles called him "a healthy, happy boy" as well as a prodigy, Gould in his later teens was already an eccentric character, especially by his parents' standards. It was clear that he was never going to sit up straight, dress properly, eat right, or keep his outrageous opinions to himself. His hypochondria, his overdressing, his night-owl proclivities – all were evident. "In those days," he once said, "I was really a character." He became increasingly uncomfortable with normal social life. He hated parties, particularly when it was musicians who gathered, and attended them only rarely. When he did, his puritanical personality – he couldn't abide smoking, drinking, swearing, flirting – tended to constrain those around him. Though serious, in some ways old before his time, he was funny, too, always polite and usually friendly, and challenging and interesting to listen to even when unconventional, so he did not lack for people who wanted to be with him. Nevertheless, he resisted close friendships. "He is a confirmed bachelor at 13," Fulford reported in the *9-D Bugle*, and there is not a wisp of evidence to suggest that he took an active interest in sex at precisely that time when boys are most curious about it. When Florence was asked, by a reporter in Calgary, if her nineteen-year-old son was "interested in girls," she replied, with a smile, "No, he hasn't time for them yet, and I'm glad he hasn't right now." (He had girls as friends, however.) He was already convinced of the creative necessity of solitude. "I'm not anti-social," he told the photojournalist Jock Carroll in 1956, "but if an artist wants to use his mind for creative work then self-discipline, in the form of cutting oneself off from society, is a necessary thing."

He found that solitude at the cottage, where he was free to lead a tranquil, contemplative life. He had no desire to leave home completely, but his interests and his schedule were conflicting more and more with those of Bert and Florence, and even with his own studio at the back of the house he was becoming a burden to his devoted parents. He would stay up all night, sometimes in the company of others, laughing and talking or playing the piano or running the stereo at full volume without regard for his parents' need to sleep. Finally, after leaving church and school and piano lessons behind, he retreated to the cottage more or less permanently. Dudley recalls that Gould would return to the house in Toronto when his parents wanted to use the cottage, and then switch back when they returned home, though he still saw them, and still had concerts and broadcasts and other work to draw him out of his retreat from time to time. He was becoming an incurable insomniac by his later teens, staying up most of the night reading or practising or listening to music, turning in at four or five in the morning and perhaps still having trouble falling asleep, getting up at noon. A neighbour, Doris Milligan, whose bedroom faced the Gould cottage, fondly remembered falling asleep with the sound of Gould's piano drifting through her open window.

Gould felt at ease at the cottage and in the surrounding towns, away from the pressures of stardom, which he was beginning to feel before he ever left Canada, and he felt nourished physically, emotionally, and creatively by the close contact with nature. For years, between concert tours and recording sessions, he would spend as much time as possible at the cottage, which his parents effectively ceded to him. It was his sanctuary. Besides his parents, the odd local, the postman, and a few friends, he saw almost no one but his dog, with whom he took long walks and ventured out in his motorboats, the *Arnold S.* and the *Alban B.* He appreciated the unpretentious nature of rural people, whom he treated without condescension, and to whom, on his walks or his forays into town, he would talk with genuine interest about anything but classical music: movies, books, world affairs, nature, local news. He told a reporter about Mrs. Isabel Doolittle, "a farm lady who comes in once a day and gives me the gossip and tells me whose dog ate whose hen," and Charles

Amsden, proprietor of the Champlain Grill in Orillia, remembered Gould dropping in often just to have coffee and chat. He was open, friendly, and even playful with such people; their company seemed to relax him. Those locals who viewed his solitude as snobbery, he told Jock Carroll, "lost some of that feeling after I sat down with the local fife and drum band, played the autoharp and worked out some musical arrangements for them. Later we tape-recorded some pieces together. I'm afraid it was a bit of a shock to my music teacher, Alberto Guerrero, when he walked in on one of these recording sessions and heard me banging away in a slightly risque ballad, 'The Hired Man's Saturday Night.'" He enjoyed the company of children – that was true all his life – and he let them join in his walks or in experiments with his tape recorder. Everyone in the cottage country knew of his musical success and recognized that he was "different," but they declined to fuss over him; they treated him as a friend, or at least a pleasant neighbour, rather than a great artist. Bill Seto, who ran a Chinese restaurant in Orillia, the Shangri-La Gardens, once chided Gould for cancelling a concert. Gould said he had felt ill on the train so decided to cancel and return home, but Seto felt that Gould's integrity was at stake – he had promised to play, he had given his word – and Gould accepted the reproof with grace. That says something about his distance from the prima donna personality.

Gould was no homemaker. All his life he lived and worked contentedly in cluttered, chaotic spaces. At the cottage, his mother occasionally stocked the fridge; otherwise there was almost no food, except for tea. He appeared gaunt and gangly in those days, already into his lifelong habit of nibbling and sipping but eating only when ravenous, and then with reluctance. Mrs. Doolittle sometimes cooked and cleaned for him, though for most meals he would drive into Orillia. For almost twenty years, until the late sixties, Bill Seto served Gould at the Shangri-La Gardens. "He came into 'The Shang' at 5 o'clock, three or four times a week with the *Toronto Star* tucked under his arm," Seto recalled. "I always seated him at the back of the room where he would be undisturbed by other diners and where, his meal finished, he could relax and watch television.

He stayed until 10:30 or so and I could tell if he wanted to talk or not." Seto stocked bottled Poland Water for Gould, who could not abide tap water, and played Gould's recordings (even Krenek) on the jukebox as a sign of respect, though he would turn them off when Gould left. Gould disliked Chinese food, or anything fancy. "He was a steak and potatoes man," Seto recalled, but he only appeared to be a hearty eater: what Seto saw was the only real meal he would eat in a day.

Between about 1952 and early 1955 Gould was not exactly in hiding but he was spending as much time as he could alone at the cottage, studying scores, practising on the battered upright, listening to records, experimenting with his recording equipment: "The greatest of all teachers is the tape recorder," he told a friend. "I would be lost without it." (Angela Addison recalls seeing wires strung treacherously throughout the cottage.)

He was surrounded by stacks of books. "I read in great splurges," he said, and one of his self-appointed tasks at the cottage seems to have been to educate himself in those subjects besides music that interested him: literature, poetry, drama, history, philosophy, theology, aesthetics. He read classics of every denomination, from Plato to Thoreau, with a particular fondness for the Russians – Tolstoy and Dostoevsky in particular, but also Gogol, Goncharov, Turgenev. He was widely read in modern literature. His professed favourites included T. S. Eliot, Christopher Fry, and Franz Kafka, though he gave time to Borges, Camus, Capek, Gide, Hesse, Ionesco, Joyce, Malraux, Mishima, Santayana, Soseki, Strindberg, and much else. His friend Ben Sonnenberg, thinking back to 1959, gave a more recherché list of Gould's then favourite writers: W. H. Hudson, R. B. Cunninghame-Graham, and John Cowper Powys. And at the head of the pack was Thomas Mann,* especially *Buddenbrooks*, *The*

---

* On October 19, 1955, Gould appeared in a CBC radio tribute to the recently deceased Mann, giving a full-throttle performance of Beethoven's Op. 111 sonata, which is discussed in *Dr. Faustus*. In the early sixties, he talked about making a radio documentary on Mann.

Magic Mountain, *Doctor Faustus*, and the early story "Tonio Kröger," which he read around age eighteen and with whose title character, a passionate and excitable young aesthete described as "foreign and queer," he identified throughout his life. Just as his repertoire included no fluff, his concert tours no pops, Gould's reading included no murder mysteries or adventure stories. He liked books with a strong message, books that dealt with weighty ethical or theological or aesthetic ideas or espoused a philosophy of life with which he could engage intellectually. And he was disapproving of books in which ideas were sacrificed to aesthetics or ironic detachment. Among the Russians, for instance, he did not like Chekhov, or the dazzling Nabokov, whom he thought immoral. He read a little Truman Capote on the advice of friends, but could admire only his technique, not his ethics. He found Henry Miller's writings "ponderous," Jack Kerouac's "flaccid."

The same German Romanticism that had fed into the aesthetics of Wagner, Strauss, the Schoenberg school, and other music Gould loved also fed into much of the literature and philosophy he read – Mann, for instance, whose ideas about the relationship of the artist to society he liked to steal – and his idealistic, moralistic approach owed a lot to his reading in this tradition. He loved all things German, it seemed, and though he never learned more than a few words of the language he could not resist putting on the accent whenever he discussed a German subject. "The year he discovered Nietzsche's *Also sprach Zarathustra*," Fulford wrote, "the accent grew almost impenetrably thick." One can imagine the appeal of Nietzsche's individualism to a strong-willed young artist living in a tradition-minded town, but Schopenhauer, too, seems to have made a big impact. John Beckwith recalls that Gould, in the early fifties, discussed (admittedly vaguely) writing an opera based in some way on Schopenhauer. It was Schopenhauer, for instance, who advocated a disengagement from worldly matters and conventional values and a sublimation of the baser instincts in favour of a life devoted to art, and who insisted that the significance of art stood outside the empirical world in another, immaterial sphere. "The composer," he wrote, "reveals the innermost nature of the world, and expresses the profoundest wisdom, in a language that his reasoning faculty does not understand." Gould likely did not share Schopenhauer's tragic, pessimistic, misanthropic view of life, but he certainly shared the idealistic thrust of the philosopher's aesthetics – Schopenhauer has always had a special appeal to artists – and he shared Schopenhauer's view of the redemptive power of art, of art as solace for an imperfect world. His Romantic notion of "ecstasy," in fact, sounds suspiciously like the very union with that immaterial sphere that Schopenhauer advocated.

This, above all, is what Gould was engaged in at the cottage in the years after he left Guerrero's studio: he was *thinking*, about matters theoretical and practical, about morals and aesthetics, about music and interpretation, about the piano and performance practice, about the future direction of his career and his adult relationship to the world of music. During these years of retreat, Gould was not in crisis; he was patiently laying the groundwork for a mature professional career. "He was just practising," said Bert, "and preparing himself." He was becoming Glenn Gould.

"I always thought of myself as a composer."

By his mid-teens Gould had determined that his ultimate goal was to compose, not merely to write some music as a sideline to a concert career but really to be a *composer* in the fullest sense of the word. He considered his concert and recording careers as means of providing him with enough money and enough of a reputation to devote himself to composition, and he envisioned leaving performing behind altogether in favour of composing. His steady output of music during his mid-teens does suggest that he considered composing more than a hobby, even if none of that music hinted at a first-rate talent. After his flurry of twelve-tone pieces in the early fifties – all of which he later disowned – he composed nothing until he was settled into his retreat at the cottage, at which point he determined to make a proper case for himself as a composer, once and for all. And so, between April 1953 and October 1955, he devoted a large proportion of his time to composing a string quartet in F minor.

He attacked the project enthusiastically, often neglecting the piano for long periods, though his lack of experience as a composer showed. His progress was slow – often just a few bars a day, as his dated sketches confirm. Being a pianist, even a great pianist, does not make one a composer, any more than being a waiter makes one a chef. Gould had evident talent and the right temperament to be a composer, but no training. He was fudging when he claimed, in an interview, that he had studied composition at the Toronto Conservatory: in his day, "studying composition" there meant at best learning a few rudiments as part of a music-theory class. And he was too proud to seek help from those more qualified than he. As he composed he often talked to musical friends about his work and played them excerpts, but he was not really seeking counsel, only approval; the advice he sought was on technical matters like bowing.

The end result was, to say the least, a curious piece. It shocked colleagues who knew Gould as one of Canada's most passionate champions of the Schoenberg school. John Weinzweig had written a twelve-tone quartet in Toronto as early as 1946, and most people expected the same from Gould. But the music is resolutely tonal, in fact unapologetically Romantic. Its lush, sideslipping harmonies, and some of its wide-spaced themes and developmental strategies, recall Richard Strauss – and there was no composer less fashionable in the early fifties. Gould freely admitted the influence of Strauss, but in various sources acknowledged other late-Romantic models, too: Wagner, Mahler, Reger, Franck, and the String Quintet in F Major by Bruckner, which he had just recently come to know. ("This is the most wonderful thing he ever wrote, I think – the only thing in which you can't have the tubas blasting out every climax.") But

A page from Gould's String Quartet, from the German music publisher
Schott's 1999 edition. This excerpt, from a self-contained fugue in B minor
in the first half of the quartet, shows the verbose, tangled part-writing characteristic of Gould's style, but also his cleverness in developing ideas in
counterpoint. In bars 247–49, one of the main themes of the quartet enters
in stretto (viola, then cello, then first violin), and beginning in bar 254, a
variant of this theme (second violin) accompanies the principal subject of
the fugue (first violin). Both themes, moreover, incorporate the chromatic
four-note motto on which the whole quartet is based – for instance, the
first notes of the fugue subject (C-sharp–D–G-sharp–A), in bars 254–55.
*(Gould STRING QUARTET © 1999 Schott Musik International. All Rights
Reserved. Used by permission of European American Music Distributors LLC, sole
U.S. and Canadian agent for Schott Musik International.)*

late Romanticism is only one of many sides to this piece, which draws on three centuries' worth of musical styles. Everything that interested the young Gould is here: late-Romantic harmony; Classical and Romantic sonata forms; fugue and other idioms of counterpoint drawn from the Renaissance through to the twentieth century; and, often, the near-atonal idiom of such early-twentieth-century works as Berg's Sonata and Schoenberg's Opp. 7 and 10 quartets (which Gould acknowledged as models).

"I've always had a sweet tooth for *fin de siècle* characters," Gould said on CBC radio in 1967, "for artists who sit perched at the very end of an epoch and who manage to reconcile two opposing tendencies within their work." He thought of himself as one of those characters, and his stated main goal in the quartet was to mate the self-indulgence of late-Romantic harmony with the unifying constructive techniques of the twelve-tone school. He admitted that the work was a kind of an exercise in which he sought to take a single, unassuming, rising four-note motif (C–D-flat–G–A-flat)* and make it the generating idea for all of the melodies, harmonies, and formal procedures in the piece. (Such thematic parsimony, what Schoenberg called "developing variation," was prized by the composers of his school.) The quartet is set out as a single unbroken movement of just over eight hundred bars, taking about thirty-five minutes to play. It (loosely) conforms to the usual sonata-form divisions – exposition, development, recapitulation – though a coda of some three hundreds bars, the longest single section, upsets the Classical proportions. Gould was clearly influenced by those

---

* Such four-note motifs have been commonplace in contrapuntal music since the Renaissance, and when (as here) they are cast in a minor key the resulting melodic shapes tend to give the music a "pathetic" cast, as in fugal works ranging from the chorus "And with his stripes" in Handel's *Messiah* to "Cool" from *West Side Story*. A "pathetic" four-note motif is common to Beethoven's late Opp. 131 and 132 quartets and *Große Fuge*, Op. 133, the latter introduced to Gould by Morry Kernerman around the early fifties. Gould never mentioned late Beethoven among the influences on his quartet, yet his permutations of his motif often yield striking resemblances to, especially, the slow introduction of Op. 132 and the *Große Fuge*.

several-movements-in-one forms taken up by many nineteenth- and twentieth-century composers, including Schoenberg in his Chamber Symphony No. 1 and Op. 7 quartet. In short, he wrote a string quartet that was as pointedly eclectic as he was, and as such the work can stand as an early salvo in his lifelong campaign against the ideas of fashion and progress in music. As he put it, "I sought to challenge the zeitgeist," to prove that one could love both Strauss and Schoenberg at the same time and even effect a rapprochement between them. But the work was autobiographical, too. At that time, he wrote, he felt "the urge to sum up in a composition all the influences in my adolescence [that] had most deeply affected me," and in this sense the quartet is a revealing document – an essay on the state of the artist.

All of which makes Gould's String Quartet a unique and fascinating piece, though not necessarily a great one. It has many merits, not least its very premise, to revisit Strauss in light of Schoenberg, which is indeed provocative and full of possibility. Notwithstanding what one reviewer (correctly) identified as "momentary tangles of ineptly-handled dissonance," Gould manipulates his complicated, chromatic harmonic idiom with impressive assurance, and the tension between pungent Schoenbergian dissonance and glowing Straussian resolution is often genuinely touching. He demonstrates a real insight into counterpoint in the Baroque, Romantic, and modern manners, and a certain cleverness in developing ideas in counterpoint. And the lyricism of the music is affecting, even though the melodies are often angular and tortured.

But the piece has serious problems, too, and the impressiveness of Gould's stylistic synthesis is sometimes undercut by his deficiencies of technique. His rhythms and counterpoint are often muddled. He had no experience writing for strings, as he admitted, and did not know how to dispose the instruments so as to put his material in its best light. (He hid behind the claim that he thought of the music as "abstract," indifferent to instrumentation.) The four instruments tend to be cramped within a relatively narrow range, as though Gould wanted subconsciously to make the music playable on the piano,* and the dense, knotty textures can be made clear to a listener only with difficulty, especially as Gould calls for almost continuous legato phrasing. His few stabs at string effects – pizzicato, *sul ponticello* – seem half-hearted, and there are some amateurish moments where one instrument runs out of notes and a musical line must be taken up, through double stopping, by another instrument. And there is not much relief from the four-part texture: everyone seems to be playing all the time. The work *sounds* as though it had been stitched together a few bars a day: it has an additive structure that, for all its complexity, lacks direction and drama, and for this reason its admittedly clever developments of the four-note motif can eventually become tiresome. The second half is particularly unconvincing, consisting of page after page of seemingly endless machinations of the main motif. It is the Pompidou Centre of string quartets – the guts are on the outside. Gould the composer had the same flaw as Gould the speaker and writer: reluctance to apply the blue pencil. Hence the loquaciousness and formal sprawl of the quartet, which lacks the grasp of large-scale architecture that was so infallible in Gould the performer. The composer Otto Joachim, who played viola in the Montreal String Quartet and composed an elegant, richly contrapuntal, and beautifully idiomatic twelve-tone quartet (which Gould knew) in 1956, said that Gould "made all the mistakes a young composer can make. He did not know when and how to bring his work to an end." And it is true that the enormous coda, more than anything else, reflects Gould's inexperience and insecurity. "In the end," wrote Ken Winters, in the *Canadian Music Journal*, "the panorama of the piece is not grand, only extensive; not lively, only industrious; not rich, only thick; not fascinating, only complex."

Apprentice work of mixed success, in short. But then, six months after completing the quartet, Gould suddenly became a world-famous

---

* "I can play the whole thing on the piano," Gould once said, "except that, in a few spots, I need another piano player to handle the cello part. It's so exhausting, though, that I have to go to bed for two days after I do it." He can be heard playing an excerpt from his quartet in the 1959 CBC radio interview *At Home with Glenn Gould*.

recording artist, and so was able to get support for the piece out of proportion to its merits. The first performance was given on the CBC's French radio network, by the Montreal String Quartet, on May 21, 1956, in the series *Premières*, and the first public perform-ance soon followed, at Stratford, on July 9. Later that year the Montreal quartet recorded the piece for the CBC's International Service, and in October Gould signed a contract for it with AM–CA Publishing Co., of Great Neck, New York, a small, enterprising company run by William C. Barger, a psychiatrist, and Robert L. Barclay, a Canadian-born composer. (A year later, the company changed its name to Barger and Barclay.) Several editions of the score and parts appeared beginning in the fall of 1956, and the same company also published Gould's Beethoven cadenzas, in 1958. The quartet had its American premiere in November 1959 on a program of the Cleveland Orchestra Woman's Committee, performed by the Symphonia Quartet, made up of members of the orchestra. Gould gave a lecture-recital on Schoenberg in the same program, and was so impressed by the Symphonia's interpretation that he convinced Columbia Records to allow them to record it. He was present at the recording session, in Cleveland, on March 13, 1960, and pro-nounced himself "thrilled" with the album.*

This was a remarkable public career for a Canadian string quartet. At that time almost no Canadian chamber music was being published, and John Beckwith noted in a 1956 survey that only *two* recordings of Canadian compositions were then available, both on the Hallmark label. Yet here was an apprentice composition by a young pianist becoming the first Canadian composition of such length and seriousness to be made available to the record-buying public, and on a major American label. It was the sort of attention that Canadian composers could only dream of in those days. When it was first performed, the quartet earned some excellent notices in

---

* Gould referred to the String Quartet as his "Opus 1," and it was so designated on the cover of the Columbia LP, though not in the published score or on the CBC recording.

Toronto and New York newspapers ("a moving and impressive work," "a work of vast maturity and clear-cut musical understanding," "a powerful, melodious work"). Yet the critics most qualified to judge, including other Toronto composers, mostly differed. The quartet was "the work of a good student," wrote the composer Graham George in the *Canadian Music Journal*. "A musician of Mr. Gould's prominence has heavier responsibilities than obscure writers, who can experiment as often as they like with no one paying any attention; and it is perhaps unfortunate that he should have allowed the publication of a work so incongruous with his stature as a performer." Other composers weighed in with similar judgements, and their opinions cannot be seen merely as sour grapes, or stereotypically Canadian undervaluing of homegrown talent, or the sniffing of modernists who felt that Gould had betrayed the avant-garde; it was sound criticism from competent judges. Perhaps if Gould had developed his compositional skills quietly, in private, rather than rushing into public with his first-born, he might have made a more auspicious debut as a composer. Still, he was more than pleased with the piece – "It's my proudest achievement!" he said in 1959 – but he also admitted that "it didn't completely come off" owing to his lack of experience with strings. As late as 1974, he advised his publishers that he "had long planned to prepare a revised edition of the quartet," though he never did.

"It would be some kind of betrayal not to live in Canada."

There is an old joke (one of many) about the Canadian character: Why don't you need to cover a lobster pot in Canada? Because if one of the lobsters tries to escape, the others will drag him down. It is an old commonplace – moribund today but not quite dead – that Canada recognizes her own talents belatedly, grudgingly, or not all, or only after they have made it big in the States. When Gould was young, it is true, foreign artists were generally thought superior to native artists as a matter of course, regardless of evidence to the contrary. "We in Canada," wrote Ernest MacMillan in 1931, "find a tendency on the part of certain sections of our public to accept anything that comes to us stamped with the magic name of New York," and Wyndham Lewis, writing during the war, noted Canadians' "distrust for anything Canadian." The Canadian artist who has a talent of international rank but chooses to stay home has always encountered surprise and suspicion: If you're really so good, why are you still *here*?

But Gould never wanted for approval in his native land. His talent was recognized early, nurtured, and admired, and he was given many opportunities to display that talent even at its most offbeat. By the end of 1954 he was recognized throughout Canada as a brilliant and highly individual musician, and had already done professional work in every available medium. Many critics, in fact, held him up as an argument against the cliché of the self-denigrating Canadian. Hugh Thomson, for instance, wrote, "A 19-year-old Toronto pianist dealt a blow last night in Massey Hall to the assumption [that] the only worthwhile soloists for symphony concerts are those with foreign names and on the international circuit." John Kraglund wrote in 1953 that Gould was evidence "that Canadian pianists can take their place among the top artists generally heard here," and a reviewer in Kingston, Ontario, the same year predicted that Gould's name would be a household word within ten years. (*Three*, as it turned out.)

Still, Canadian orchestras and broadcasters and record companies had little clout or means of dissemination in the United States or overseas, and the international music world, in those days, did not look to Canada for the Next Big Thing. It would be international concerts and a major American record label that assured Gould's worldwide reputation. But he would never make his home anywhere but Canada. "I have absolutely no intention or desire to leave Canada," he told an interviewer in 1959. "I can't see, first of all, any reason for it. Canada's been terribly good to me. And secondly, I'm much too fond of the country." Of course, remaining in Toronto was convenient for Gould, who never relished change and never chose the strange over the familiar, but he also *belonged* in Toronto, the city in which his personality and thought had been forged. "My generation of Canadians grew up believing that, if we were very good or very smart, or both, we would someday *graduate* from Canada," Robert Fulford wrote, but Gould proved that a Canadian no longer had to graduate from Canada – not in the electronic age, where an artist's choice of hometown mattered less than ever before. Gould, moreover, did not merely continue to live in Canada; he made "Canadian-ness," in many ways, the substance of his art, without compromising his international appeal. And while leaving Canada (temporarily) brought him fame and money, and with it power and freedom, staying in Canada, close to institutions like the CBC, allowed him to do the kind of work he wanted to do. That, for him, was the priority.

Opposite: Gould and the conductor Jean Martinon taking a bow after one of their performances with the Israel Philharmonic, in Tel Aviv, November-December 1958. *(Photograph by Isaac Berez.)*

PART THREE

VAUDEVILLIAN

On Tour, 1955–64

**"I was never more relaxed in my life
than in my Town Hall debut in New York."**

A Canadian performer in the mid-fifties, without the support of an American agency, was lucky to meet expenses as a concert artist, so it was hardly surprising that so many musicians fled south to earn a living. Gould was by 1955 perhaps the most celebrated and admired classical performer in Canada, and one of the luckiest: his talent, his family's money, and the expert ministrations of Walter Homburger ensured that he did not need to submit to American management or take on pupils or worry about meeting expenses. But even a Glenn Gould could not develop an international reputation without leaving the country.

Homburger made tentative plans for an American tour as early as 1953, and Gould made a brief exploratory trip to New York in May 1954, but he did not feel ready to make his American debut until January 1955. On the afternoon of January 2, accompanied by Homburger and supported by his own and his parents' money, he offered a characteristic program at the Phillips Gallery in Washington, D.C.: Gibbons's "Earl of Salisbury" Pavan and Galliard, Sweelinck's "Fitzwilliam" Fantasia, five three-part Sinfonias and the G-major partita by Bach, Webern's *Variations*, Beethoven's Op. 109

sonata, and Berg's Sonata. He even played the Webern *twice*, to stress, as he said from the stage, that there are structural similarities between it and the Beethoven. Conspicuously absent was the sort of virtuosic Romantic music by which a pianist, especially an unknown pianist in his first appearance, was normally judged, but as he said years later, "I went out of my way to pick as odd a program as I could." It got him noticed. "January 2 is early for predictions, but it is unlikely that the year 1955 will bring us a finer piano recital," wrote Paul Hume, the music critic of the *Washington Post*. "We shall be lucky if it brings others of equal beauty and significance." He concluded, "Glenn Gould is a pianist with rare gifts for the world. It must not long delay hearing and according him the honor and audience he deserves. We know of no pianist anything like him of any age."

On the evening of January 11, he repeated the same program at Town Hall, an intimate space in midtown Manhattan that was a preferred spot for debut recitals. He received little advance attention, and his name hardly stood out among those from which New York music lovers could choose that month: Benny Goodman, the Budapest String Quartet, the violinists Mischa Elman and Yehudi Menuhin, the organist Albert Schweitzer, the guitarist Andrés Segovia, and a menu of great pianists including Claudio Arrau, Gina Bachauer, Alexander Brailowsky, Clifford Curzon, Rudolf Firkušný, Myra Hess, Mieczysław Horszowski, and Solomon. The January schedule for Town Hall alone included the pianists Webster Aitken, Paul Badura-Skoda, and Friedrich Gulda. The senior music critic of the *New York Times*, Howard Taubman, attended a recital by the violinist Julian Olevsky in the more prestigious Carnegie Hall that day, leaving Gould to a second-stringer. His audience was small – some said a few dozen, Gould said 250 – and with a top ticket price of $2.88 he did not make money, for he had spent $450 to book the hall, almost a thousand more for local management and publicity. An attack of "fibrositis" stiffened his hands just before the concert, but, he said, "I found a friendly chemist and got the condition stopped just in time," and in the end, he recalled, "This was one of the few occasions when I thoroughly loved playing." He was received with great enthusiasm; there were demands for encores, and he was mobbed backstage. Thanks to the lobbying of his friend Harvey Olnick, pianists like Gary Graffman and William Kapell were in the hall. Paul Badura-Skoda, himself a Bach specialist, raved about Gould's counterpoint to a Canadian reporter, and the few reviews praised Gould's unique style and sensibility and his intellectually challenging program. John Briggs, in the *Times*, called the concert "one of the most auspicious debuts this reviewer has heard in some time." Bert Gould, who drove down for the concert, told the *Toronto Daily Star*, with his usual reserve, that his son "gave them a good concert."

The American debut was hardly a "sensation" that "stirred the concert world," as the dazzled Toronto papers put it, but Gould proved that he could achieve artistic success among sophisticated audiences without betraying his musical values. He returned home, weary but happy, to a modest schedule of recitals and concerto appearances in Ottawa, Toronto, Stratford, and Montreal. He would not appear again in the United States for more than a year.

"CBS is very patient with me!"

"All were things to which I felt most spiritually attuned, things I felt would show a versatility of repertoire but also a program that would allow the audience – hopefully populated with record executives – to hear nooks and crannies of the repertoire that for the most part had not been committed to disc." So said Gould of his unusual debut pieces, and as it turned out the audience *was* populated with record executives – with a little help from his friends. The day before the Town Hall concert, and six months after playing chamber music with Gould, the violinist Alexander Schneider was in New York chatting with David Oppenheim, director of artists and repertoire for the Masterworks division of Columbia Records, and he alerted Oppenheim to the recital. Gould, he said, "was, alas, a little crazy, but had a remarkable, hypnotic effect at the piano." Oppenheim was intrigued enough to go, and was "thrilled." Gould "set such a religious atmosphere that it was just mesmerizing," he told Otto Friedrich. The next morning, he offered Gould an exclusive recording contract – "the first time they have ever signed an artist just on the strength of his debut," Homburger told the *Toronto Daily Star*, and the first time a Canadian had signed with Columbia. A draft contract arrived in Toronto in February, Homburger negotiated through the spring, and a three-year contract was signed in May. It was a contract Gould later dismissed as "ridiculous"; he would not begin to make real money from Columbia until the late fifties.

For so unconventional and uncompromising a classical artist as Gould, Columbia was an apt choice, and he would stay with Columbia all his life. Columbia had been a major label since the infancy of recording in the late nineteenth century (its first big star was John Philip Sousa), and had acquired particular prestige after being purchased in 1938 by the "Tiffany Network," CBS, the network of Toscanini and the New York Philharmonic, of Orson Welles and Edward R. Murrow. Having played second fiddle to RCA Victor for more than forty years, Columbia dominated the record business by the end of the Second World War. In 1955 it was still run by men with priorities other than commerce. Oppenheim, for instance, was a working professional clarinetist (and husband of the actress Judy Holliday).

Columbia's guiding spirit in those days was Goddard Lieberson (1911–77), who joined the label in 1939, became Masterworks director in 1943 and president of the company in 1956. Gould called him "perhaps the most vital and inquisitive musical executive of this generation." Born in England, Lieberson was a trained composer, and had a multifarious career as record producer, broadcaster, impresario, writer, and teacher. Gould recalled that their first conversation, over lunch in 1958, was devoted to the tone row in Berg's opera *Lulu*. Lieberson was a suave, cultured man, well-travelled and well-connected, versed in many subjects besides music, fluent in several languages, noted for his charm and playful, profane wit, and he moved in glamorous social circles. But he knew how to make money. In 1948, under Lieberson, Columbia had introduced the unbreakable, "microgroove" 33⅓-r.p.m. long-playing record, to great success. Later, he cultivated popular music from which Columbia earned millions: Broadway cast albums; Mitch Miller's "Sing Along" albums; middle-of-the-road artists like Doris Day, Percy Faith, and Andy Williams; spoken-world albums; and jazz, in which field Columbia was arguably the hottest label in the early LP era. When it came to classical music, he was an idealist, and became something of a hero, for he believed that Columbia made enough money on popular music to justify taking a loss in ambitious classical projects of artistic merit. (The Masterworks department, he said, "is our artistic conscience.") Under Lieberson, Columbia recorded the complete works of Schoenberg and Webern, ran a Modern American Music series, captured Stravinsky conducting his own music, and realized the musicological significance of recording esoteric early and modern music that had little place in contemporary concert life.

Gould's earliest contract negotiations show that he was determined to control his destiny as a recording artist, and Columbia gave him *carte blanche* to record what he liked, making suggestions and occasionally played devil's advocate but not dictating repertoire. At least one executive questioned Gould when he announced that he would make his Columbia debut with the Goldberg Variations, and one can see the company's point: this was a monumental, esoteric piece that he had played only a few times in public, a piece for harpsichord, moreover, and hardly a staple of the piano repertoire or the record bins. (Only Rosalyn Tureck and Jörg Demus had recorded it on the piano, both for small labels.) But Gould insisted and Columbia immediately gave in – "and *that*," Gould recalled twenty-five years later, "is the closest thing to obstruction that I've ever encountered at CBS." His choice of debut repertoire proved canny: he was praised for his courage in tackling such a piece at the start of his recording career. And he could not have made that start at a better time. As Roland Gelatt noted in *The Fabulous Phonograph*, 1955 was an *annus mirabilis* for the record business, which almost overnight became a growth industry.

Columbia capitalized at once on their new acquisition: between June 10 and 16, 1955, just weeks after signing his contract, Gould spent four days in Columbia's 30th Street studio, a former church in midtown Manhattan, recording the variations. Though it was his first taste of the big leagues in the record business, he already showed remarkable presence of mind. Outtakes reveal that the twenty-two-year-old knew exactly what he wanted and how to get it, worked confidently with much more experienced colleagues, and was already starting to take charge of his recording sessions. Columbia quickly realized that they had not only a world-class musician but a world-class eccentric on their hands. On June 25, they issued a press release that deserves to be quoted in full:

> Columbia Masterworks' recording director and his engineering colleagues are sympathetic veterans who accept as perfectly natural all artists' studio rituals, foibles or fancies. But even these hardy souls were surprised by the arrival of young Canadian pianist Glenn Gould and his "recording equipment" for his first Columbia sessions. Mr. Gould was to spend a week recording one of his chief specialties, Bach's Goldberg Variations.
>
> It was a balmy June day, but Gould arrived in coat, beret, muffler and gloves. "Equipment" consisted of the customary music portfolio, also a batch of towels, two large bottles of spring water, five small bottles of pills (all different colors and prescriptions) and his own special piano chair.
>
> Towels, it developed, were needed in plenty because Glenn soaks his hands and arms up to the elbows in hot water for twenty minutes before sitting down at the keyboard, a procedure which quickly became a convivial group ritual; everyone sat around talking, joking, discussing music, literature and so forth while "soaking" went on.

Bottled spring water was a necessity because Glenn can't abide New York tap water. Pills were for any number of reasons – headache, relieving tension, maintaining good circulation. The air conditioning engineer worked as hard as the man at the recording studio control panel. Glenn is very sensitive to the slightest changes in temperature, so there was constant adjustment of the vast studio air conditioning system.

But the collapsible chair was the Goldberg (Rube) variation of them all. It's a bridge chair, basically, with each leg adjusted individually for height so that Glenn can lean forward, backward, or to either side. The studio skeptics thought this was wackiness of the highest order until recording got under way. Then they saw Glenn adjust the slant of his chair before doing his slightly incredible cross-hand passages in the Variations, leaning in the direction of the "cross." The chair was unanimously accepted as a splendid, logical device.

Gould at the keyboard was another phenomenon – sometimes singing along with his piano, sometimes hovering low over the keys, sometimes playing with eyes closed and head flung back. The control-room audience was entranced, and even the air conditioning engineer began to develop a fondness for Bach. Even at record playbacks Glenn was in perpetual motion, conducted rhapsodically, did a veritable ballet to the music. For sustenance he munched arrowroot biscuits, drank skimmed milk, frowned on the recording crew's Hero sandwiches.

After a week of recording, Glenn said he was satisfied with his recording stint, packed up his towels, pills, and bridge chair. He went 'round to shake hands with everyone – the recording director, the engineers, the studio man, the air conditioning engineer. Everybody agreed they would miss the cheerful "soaking" sessions, the Gould humor and excitement, the pills, the spring water.

"Well," said Glenn as he put on his coat, beret, muffler and gloves to venture out into the June air, "you know I'll be back in January!"

And so he will. The studio air conditioning engineer is getting ready for the workout.

This is the Old Testament of the Gould legend: repeated endlessly by reporters and reviewers, often accompanied by colourful photos, it set the tone for much of the press coverage he would receive, especially in North America, throughout his career. Before the record was even released word of Gould's talent and eccentricities spread, and some in the business were calling it the most hyped recording debut by the most hyped young performer in classical-music history. The album was released in January of 1956, as a monaural LP with the catalogue number ML 5060, selling for $3.98 ($5.15 in Canada). The now-famous front cover showed thirty photographs – one for each variation – of Gould at the piano and cavorting in the studio; his own liner notes graced the back cover. It was one of the most sensational classical releases ever, a popular and critical success that instantly won Gould an international reputation. It became Columbia's bestselling classical record, and one of the bestselling records in America. At one point in its first year, it was outselling a new recording by Louis Armstrong and the soundtrack of *The Pajama Game*; in 1960, in the *New Yorker*, Joseph Roddy reported that it had sold more than forty thousand copies, "which is just about as astonishing in the record business as a big run on a new edition of the Enneads of Plotinus would be in the book trade." It never went out of print, and by the time Gould died it had sold more than a hundred thousand copies. Record-industry publications named it the record of the year, of the decade, and eventually one of the greatest recordings of the century. Never had such a reputation in classical music been built on a single recording of a piece so relatively unknown.

Critics at once pronounced Gould a genius, a *Wunderkind*, one of the greatest and most promising pianists of his generation, even *the* greatest. The first reviews, almost without exception, ranged from enthusiastic to awestruck:

"This is rather unusual playing. Gould has skill and imagination, and the music appears to mean something to him. He also has a sharp, clear technique that enables him to toss off the contrapuntal intricacies of the writing with no apparent effort. Best of all, his work has intensity. . . . Obviously a young man with a future." (Harold C. Schonberg, *New York Times*, January 29, 1956)

"This 23-year-old Canadian pianist has more promise than any young North American keyboard artist to appear since the war. His Bach is sensitive and superb, and with his musicianship and technique further revelations are to be expected." (*Newsweek*, January 30, 1956)

"It is at once obvious that he is an unusually sensitive, intellectually brilliant and technically versatile pianist. He does not penetrate to the depths of Bach's soul, as the incomparable Landowska does in her recording of this miraculous work, but he brings to it freshness, ardor, honesty, and unfailing technical resourcefulness. Only a musician of remarkable talent and high purpose could have done so well. . . . Columbia is fortunate to have acquired so unusual a temperament, and we await further recordings by this brilliantly gifted young pianist with genuine eagerness." (R. S., *Musical America*, February 1, 1956)

"In this, his debut recording, he demonstrates his enormous technical and musical talents to a fare-thee-well. What is more, he has taste and temperament. Moreover, he has courage . . . the overall impression Gould leaves is so mature and capable as to be a bit baffling." (C. J. L., *American Record Guide*, February 1956)

"Everything is beautifully phrased and even the most contrapuntal sections are cleanly and clearly articulated. There is little or no pedal, and consequently no smear. . . . Taken as a whole,

this is an extraordinary performance that leaves one eager to
hear what else this very gifted payer can do." (Nathan Broder,
High Fidelity, February 1956)

"The kind of selling campaign Columbia has waged on behalf of
this artist can be exceedingly dangerous, for it is apt to irritate
sophisticated listeners to the point where they can be very hard
to please. But it so happens that Gould seems to be every bit as
remarkable a musician as the ads proclaim. His recording of the
Goldberg Variations has managed to impress almost everyone
who has heard it; the brilliance, understanding, and originality
of his playing is not to be denied." (Roland Gelatt, *High Fidelity*,
April 1956)

In those days, everyone – of Gould's generation, anyway –
played Bach in a leaner, more articulated, rhythmically tighter, and
more historically informed manner than the Romantic performers
of old. But if Gould's Bach was of a piece with contemporary trends,
it still struck even informed listeners as something new and exciting. Tureck, too, offered transparency and subtle nuance and tonal
refinement in her Bach playing, but not this sort of dynamism and
rhythmic energy, not this level of brilliant virtuosity. Gould's Bach
was so vital and vibrant that it jumped out at you, but it was
thoughtful, too – no one had ever heard such a marriage of dazzle
and erudition in Bach before. Here, moreover, was an unknown
young Canadian making a potent new case for Bach on the piano
at precisely the time when the harpsichord, after decades of lobbying, had made a comeback and become fashionable in early music.
Gould's fellow-musicians – Leonard Bernstein, Lukas Foss, Herbert
von Karajan – were astonished by the recording, and when Gould
ran into Leopold Stokowski in a Frankfurt train station in June
1957, the venerable conductor knew exactly who he was. Even the
elderly Landowska, who had almost singlehandedly rediscovered
the Goldberg Variations for modern audiences, declared herself

impressed by the album when Roland Gelatt, an acquaintance of Gould's, played her a test pressing.*

The release of the Goldberg Variations unleashed a storm of publicity in spring 1956 that made Gould the most talked-about and photographed young classical artist of the day. He was profiled in music and general-interest magazines in North America and, before long, overseas. He was one of *Glamour*'s "MEN WE'D LIKE YOU TO MEET" and one of *Vogue*'s "YOUNG MEN IN THE ARTS." A four-page photo essay in the March 12 issue of *Life*, "MUSIC WORLD'S YOUNG WONDER," introduced him to the American general public. It showed Gould in the Steinway basement, carrying his chair on a New York street, taking milk and crackers and horsing around with recording technicians, playing shoeless at the keyboard, peeling off leather gloves to reveal knitted mittens beneath, soaking his arms in the men's room, conducting thin air. Much of the early publicity presented him as a new, "cool" breed of classical musician, a corollary of cerebral bebop and cool-jazz artists like Chet Baker and Miles Davis. Reviewers were soon dubbing him "music's most successful hipster" and "the object of a sort of James Dean cult." "Ask the beats in *The Purple Onion* or *The Co-Existence Bagel* who their favorite pianist is," a journalist wrote in 1964, "and they name Glenn Gould." Some of the early publicity photos played up his youthful, doe-like, androgynous appearance, and he numbered among his fans many young women and gay men. (Women seemed to want to sleep with him and mother him in about equal measure.) Even his puritanical standoffishness proved attractive in its own way: he was desirable but not attainable. All of which made Gould, suddenly, an international celebrity, and while it was all exciting and rewarding,

---

* In 2001, Landowska's former pupil, assistant, and companion Denise Restout, director of the Landowska Center in Lakeville, Connecticut, wrote to me, "Landowska heard *Glen Gould* a couple of times and found him to be very gifted for music, but she certainly did not appreciate his excentricities [*sic*]."

it also, he later admitted, "launched me into the most difficult year I have ever faced."

One of his first acts was to take a much-needed vacation in the Bahamas, in late March, joined by Jock Carroll, who documented the trip in a colourful photo essay for the magazine *Weekend*. ("Please see that he sends out his laundry and get him to buy some decent clothes," Florence Gould said to Carroll. "If you can, try to get him out in the sun.") Back in Canada, Gould was the subject of new pride. On April 16, in a packed Massey Hall, he gave a triumphant recital that had lasted three hours before the encores ended. The next day, his picture was on the front page of the *Globe and Mail*, and the day after that the mayor of Toronto presented him, at City Hall, with an engraved wristwatch in recognition of his success.

"The easiest way to be happy at this business of making music is to treat every concert as if it were a day's work of any kind."

Gould was in demand everywhere. He had given just fourteen concerts in the 1954–55 season, thirteen in 1955–56, but barely a month after the release of the Goldberg album, Homburger was advertising that the 1956–57 season was completely booked: Gould was to give forty concerts across North America, and, for the first time, overseas – and could have given many more had he wanted to.

He made his American concerto debut in March 1956, in Detroit, as a last-minute substitute. The conductor, Paul Paray, was so overwhelmed that he refused to join his soloist in the (six) curtain calls. The orchestra's manager told a journalist, "No guest artist has received an ovation like that in my experience here – and, believe me, we get only the very best on the world circuits." The 1956–57 season included solo recitals from Watertown to Pasadena, among them a November appearance at the Metropolitan Museum in New

York, and orchestral appearances in Montreal, Dallas, Winnipeg, St. Louis, San Francisco, and Victoria. He was the first soloist under the Toronto Symphony's new conductor, Walter Susskind, and on January 26, 1957, in Carnegie Hall, he made his New York Philharmonic debut, receiving a tumultuous reception for his performance of Beethoven's Second. Said the conductor, Leonard Bernstein, "There is nobody quite like him, and I just love playing with him."

In March, Gould made his first stops in California and on his way home made his Cleveland Orchestra debut under George Szell, again in Beethoven's Second. (Ohio generally became a favourite stop on Gould's concert tours.) Szell admired Gould – it was he who famously said, to his assistant Louis Lane, "That nut's a genius" – but was not really sympathetic to his piano style, and Gould, in a 1981 interview, admitted to a "total lack of chemistry" with the conductor.* A widely circulated story grew out of their 1957 collaboration. As Gould fussed with his chair during rehearsal, Szell supposedly remarked, "Mr. Gould, perhaps if you would just shave a sixteenth of an inch off your *derrière* we could get on with this rehearsal." Gould always insisted that Szell said no such thing, and that if he had, "the Cleveland Orchestra would have been looking for another soloist that evening," but he was never able to set the record straight publicly. In 1984, the Cleveland music critic Robert Finn investigated the matter for the *Plain Dealer*, and found contradictory memories among surviving witnesses. The most reliable testimony, he decided, came from Szell's personal secretary at the time, Margaret Glove. Szell, who had a reputation for saying precisely

---

* Gould did greatly admire Szell as a musician, ranking him above Bernstein, Ormandy, Karajan, and even Toscanini, but he apparently did not admire Szell's acerbic, domineering manner. He admired the Cleveland Orchestra, which also recorded for Columbia, but the first time he considered recording with the orchestra was in 1971, the year after Szell's death. He was never sympathetic to the martinet breed of conductor. He deplored the prima donna behaviour of Toscanini, and refused to perform with the Chicago Symphony under the forbidding Fritz Reiner.

what was on his mind, *did* make some sort of exasperated comment, she recalled, and the key word *was "derrière,"* but he made the remark in the "half-joking, almost falsetto voice" he reserved for kidding around. At the time, Glove added, the orchestra was warming up and there was much laughter, and Gould, who was dealing with a stage-hand, presumably about his chair, probably did not hear the conductor's aside, and the rehearsal continued "with good humor all around." (Another first-hand account confirmed Glove's story, though recalled Szell's exact words as being "saltier.") In any event, lack of chemistry was enough to make Gould tell Homburger, the next year, that he would prefer to perform with the orchestra under a guest conductor. His subsequent concerto gigs in Cleveland were all conducted by Louis Lane.

In the 1957–58 season Gould gave more than thirty concerts, in the 1958–59 season, his busiest ever, more than fifty. He continued to perform around Canada, and added ever more American cities to his tour. Even as his international fame grew, his programs remained as uncompromising as ever; indeed, it says much about his compelling musical personality that he could attract and sustain public attention with an austere, unconventional repertoire that, in most pianists' hands, would drive away custom. He was determined to challenge rather than seduce or intoxicate his audiences, and, before modern works especially, he often made remarks from the stage. There were some who felt that his concerts threatened to become graduate seminars in music theory, and on at least one occasion, at the Vancouver International Festival, a woman in the audience rose to tell him that they had paid a lot of money to hear him so would he please shut up and play. But he could rouse audiences to fever pitch with Sweelinck and Krenek, and he was usually swamped back-stage by famous pianists and piano students alike. Occasionally his house was less than full, as when he played the Schoenberg concerto, a work he once vowed to play anytime and anywhere he was asked, but much of the time he was selling out the largest concert halls and most prestigious orchestras, sometimes causing runs on the box office and setting attendance records. When he appeared in Montreal, in August 1957, to play Brahms' F-minor piano quintet with the Montreal String Quartet, scalpers were charging the unheard-of price of $30 for some tickets, and the hall was as full as it had been the last time Horowitz was in town – this for *chamber music*.*

Gould continued to get a lot of publicity. Concert appearances were invariably preceded by colourful profiles and interviews and photographs, always documenting and usually exaggerating his eccentricities. He cheerfully answered silly questions about his pill-popping and his chair and his hands being insured by Lloyd's of London. But he also impressed journalists with his politeness and charm, his lack of pretension and self-deprecating humour, his casualness about personal appearance. After a concert, the reviews often included detailed descriptions of his onstage shenanigans, starting with the chair, the blocks, the little rug, the glass of water in the piano. (Why not a ham sandwich and a beer? asked Harold Schonberg in the *New York Times*.) He wore a tuxedo when playing with orchestras, so as not to stand out, but he was the first major performer to give recitals in a plain business suit – usually baggy and unpressed and accompanied by mismatched socks and untied shoes. The suit made him feel less nervous, he said, made him feel as though a concert were nothing more than a day at the office, but some audience members considered it insulting. He would lope gracelessly onto the stage, perhaps with his hands in his pockets, looking uncomfortable, then bow perfunctorily, sheepishly. Then came the whole spectacle of Gould playing: the sidesaddle address, the bobbing head, the crouching and pouncing and swaying and flailing, and always the conducting whenever he had a hand free. He sweated copiously. His tangled mane of hair flopped this way and that, and he sometimes wiped it back with a handkerchief. To control his stamping feet he would cross his legs – hardly a less eccentric

---

* The following day, Gould and the same quartet recorded the piece for the CBC's International Service, even though Gould would years later refer to the Brahms as "not a work that I'm all that fond of" and "a very difficult piece to bring off."

option. His mouth smiled and pursed and gaped, his lips sometimes marked the beats, and of course he sang – and hummed and clucked and buzzed.

He was no calmer during orchestral passages in concertos. He "twisted and jerked and gestured while the orchestra played," by one account; other times he would beat time with his hands, shake his dangling arms, sip his water, or just stare at the ceiling. (In the recording studio he would stand up and wander about gesticulating during orchestral passages.) His conducting distracted some players. Edward W. Said remembered seeing Paul Paray direct "murderous glances" toward Gould as he flailed away during a 1961 concert in Detroit. Keith MacMillan recalled an earlier performance, in Toronto, of Beethoven's C-minor concerto:

> On cue, Gould, a pocket score in his hand, came nonchalantly onstage with Susskind. Scarcely acknowledging the audience, he flopped down cross-legged onto his famous piano chair and buried his attention in the score (of which, of course, he knew every note). He matched Susskind's opening downbeat and thereafter conducted the concerto's famously long orchestral introduction, seemingly to himself but inescapably to the audience. As his own opening scales drew near, his head remained in the score and his legs remained crossed, until the merest fraction of a second before his first entry, when he snapped the score shut and tossed it into the air; it landed flat on the piano's downturned music rack simultaneously with the downbeat of his first entry. The timing was perfect, the legs were still crossed, and the opening scales were impeccable.

Gould used a score on occasion, in both recitals and concertos, during most of his international concert career, sometimes pasting pages from a miniature score onto large, stiff pieces of cardboard, sometimes relying on notes in his own musical shorthand, even with works, such as Beethoven's Fourth, that he had played in public since adolescence. This obviously relaxed him, and gave him something to look at besides the audience, which he tended steadfastly to ignore as much as possible.

Some critics compared Gould with the most clownish of pianists, notably Vladimir de Pachmann, though in truth there have always been high-profile grunters and flailers among classical performers – Bernstein, Casals, Gieseking, Serkin, Toscanini, and many others. The public reaction to his platform manner surprised Gould, and though he claimed it did not hurt his feelings it did make him self-conscious. "These aren't personal eccentricities," he insisted, "they're simply the occupational hazards of a highly subjective business." He occasionally provoked letters to the editor, and letters directly to himself, from outraged fans. "First of all," wrote one man in 1955, "have a hair cut. It does not increase your presentation & is in fact 'Sissie.'" Even his champions worried about the tone of the press. "He must learn not to make his musical toilette in public," said one, and in 1956 the Toronto pianist Harry Heap wrote four pages of sound advice on the subject: "Everyone is very proud of you and it hurts to find your name is greeted first with a smirk and then with a grudging admission that you are a fine artist."

Yet Gould's eccentricities never outweighed his musicianship for the vast majority of his listeners. His appearances followed a pattern: his personality would get him noticed, for good or ill, but his pianistic virtuosity and strange, compelling interpretations would seal the deal. His audiences were often startled at first – there were reports of snickering and whispering and nudging in the house – but invariably he won them over. Despite legends to the contrary, to read a large sampling of clippings from his concert days is to read almost unending praise from critics, for his playing at least. Many people eventually came to regard the Gould Show as something of a circus while still remaining loyal to him as a musician. Few people ever accused Gould of putting on a dull concert, anyway, and that is something. The American critic Robert Sabin spoke for many when he wrote that Gould "is one of the most profoundly gifted and spiritually refined pianists of his generation (in some ways unique) and therefore I am willing to accept many of his idiosyncrasies as the divine right of the supremely gifted musician. . . . This young man is a magician. If he is to be dubbed eccentric, then my reply is that we need more eccentrics!"

"It was something like being the first musician to land on Mars or Venus."

Gould's first trip overseas, in early May 1957, could not have been more sensational: a two-week tour of the Soviet Union. He was the first Canadian musician, and the first pianist from North America, to appear in post-Stalinist Russia. Yehudi Menuhin was the first foreign artist to visit Russia after the war, in 1945; French and British theatre companies visited in 1955, and a touring American opera company arrived that same year to perform *Porgy and Bess*; Isaac Stern toured in the spring of 1956. But not until 1958, with the establishment of a formal cultural-exchange program, did Western artists appear in Russia with any frequency. Gould's tour has been overshadowed in the public record by other high-profile visits, particularly Van Cliburn's triumph in Moscow in 1958, when he won the first International Tchaikovsky Competition. But Gould's impact the year before was in some ways more powerful.

Nineteen fifty-seven was a propitious time for a musician to visit Russia. Stalin had died in 1953, and the country was in the midst of a decade-long cultural thaw. In February 1956, Nikita Khrushchev had delivered his famous "secret" speech to the Twentieth Congress of the Communist Party, denouncing Stalin and the "cult of personality" that had surrounded him, and the repercussions of this unexpected event were felt throughout Soviet society, including literature and the arts. The xenophobia and isolationism of the late Stalin years began to dissipate somewhat, and Russia tentatively began reaching out to countries beyond its orbit. The thaw did not last long, but while it did last Gould was one of its biggest attractions.

In 1999, a cache of documents relating to Gould's Russian tour was discovered in the National Archives of Canada, among the archives of the federal government's former Department of External Affairs. They reveal, first, that the enterprising Walter Homburger initiated the tour. In December 1955, in a letter to Lester B. Pearson, then secretary of state for external affairs (later prime minister), Homburger noted that Russian musicians like the pianist Emil Gilels and the violinist David Oistrakh had recently appeared in the United States, and that others were due to perform in Canada in spring 1956. He proposed a reciprocal Russian tour for Gould, though External Affairs's initial response was pallid:

> I think that it is desirable for us to encourage the odd concert artist from Canada to play in the Soviet Union though we should try to ensure that nothing less than our very best go. They will not stack up against such musicians as Gilels and Oistrakh but if they can put on a respectable performance and particularly if they can play a bit of Canadian music I think their visits would have some value. I am afraid that I just do not know whether Glenn Gould can be included among the foremost Canadian musicians though of course his manager refers to him as such. If you think he is good enough I think you might suggest to Homburger that he get in touch with the Russian Embassy direct and keep us informed of his plans.

The acclaim that followed the release of Gould's Goldberg album changed all that. Canada at this time was looking to enhance its international presence through cultural exchange, and External Affairs, now enthusiastic about the propaganda value of a Gould tour, put Homburger in touch with the U.S.S.R. Society for Cultural Relations with Foreign Countries (VOKS), the Canadian and Soviet embassies, and others. By summer 1956 the Soviet government had agreed that Gould would give six concerts in Moscow and Leningrad the following May, two recitals and a concerto in each city. Negotiations turned to more practical matters: travel, visas, repertoire, and Gould's anxieties about Russian hotel rooms and food. ("I can see the Canadian Press writing from Moscow:

GOULD THROWS UP!") His fee, on top of expenses, was set at $4,000, half to be paid in rubles, which could not be taken out of Russia.

In October 1956, with signed contracts on their way from Russia, Homburger released news of the tour to the press. But it was at just this time that the Suez Crisis erupted, and in November the Soviet army forcibly put down a rebellion in Hungary. American officials denounced Russia's heavy-handedness, the American Department of State cancelled all cultural exchanges, and Gould now worried that a Russian tour might antagonize American officials enough to jeopardize his career there. Less than two years after he had opened up a lucrative market for himself in the United States, he could not afford to risk being harassed or refused entry at the border. Even earlier, Gould and Homburger had worried about the effects a tour of Russia might have on public opinion in Canada, where anti-communist paranoia and the harassment and blacklisting of "tainted" individuals was then as prevalent as (if somewhat quieter than) it was in the United States. They sought a public declaration of support from External Affairs, so in February a Canadian embassy official in Washington contacted the Department of State, and was assured that Gould's tour would not be grounds for refusing him admission to the United States in the future.*

Gould's North American season came to a close at the end of March, and he arrived in Moscow on May 5, accompanied by Homburger, fifty copies of his Goldberg album, and a book called

---

* A memorandum of conversation on the subject from the Department of State, dated February 13, 1957, is now in the National Archives in Washington. One might assume that a high-profile tour of Russia in 1957, at the height of the Cold War, would have caught the attention of law-enforcement agencies in Canada and the U.S.; after all, the Security Service of the Royal Canadian Mounted Police kept files on hundreds of thousands of Canadians at this time. I made official requests for information about Gould to the National Archives of Canada, the RCMP, the Canadian Security Intelligence Service (CSIS, the descendent of the RCMP's Security Service), and the U.S. Department of Justice, but none was found. It is possible that files on Gould did once exist but were thrown out over the years (as many files were), but for now I can only conclude that the Russian tour did not make Gould a target of investigation by either the RCMP or the FBI.

Say It in Russian. Unhappy with his accommodations in a posh hotel – he wanted a double bed, not two twins pushed together – he stayed at the Canadian embassy for the duration of his visit. On May 7 he gave his first concert, a recital of Bach, Beethoven, and Berg in the Great Hall of the Moscow Conservatory. His post-Goldberg publicity had not penetrated the Iron Curtain, and as no one had heard of him, the hall, which sat eighteen hundred, was only about a third full, and many in the audience had complimentary tickets handed out by Canadian and Soviet officials uncertain of Gould's appeal. He walked out to cordial applause, but after playing four fugues from *The Art of Fugue* and the Partita No. 6, he was greeted with a thunderous ovation and a huge basket of blue chrysanthemums. (He would swim in flowers before the tour was over.) During a typically long Russian intermission of about three-quarters of an hour, many in the audience hurried out to telephone friends about what they had just heard, and a minor riot ensued as people from all over Moscow rushed to the Great Hall; by the time the second half started, the hall was full, and many people had to be turned away. After the concert, Gould was greeted with cheers and tears and – the ultimate tribute – rhythmic clapping; he had to play a Sweelinck fantasia and ten Goldberg variations before he was allowed to stop. He was still bowing after the house lights went up, and was mobbed outside the theatre. Such genuinely emotional and excited responses were typical of Russian audiences, which tended to be musically perceptive, with real devotion and love for music, and represented a cross-section of the population, not just cognoscenti. Gould had never known audiences like this before, and was overwhelmed and moved by them – and a little frightened.

Sold-out houses, ovations, and myriad encores were the norm for his remaining concerts in Moscow: Beethoven's Fourth Piano Concerto on May 8, and a second recital (including the Goldberg Variations) on May 11, both in Tchaikovsky Hall. For the latter concert, not only were all fifteen hundred seats sold but nine hundred standees were admitted and chairs were set up on the stage. When the recital ended the applause and encores continued for half an hour, and the great pianist Sviatoslav Richter was seen to clap and cheer long after the general public had become exhausted. In those days daily newspaper coverage of musical events was rare in Russia, but for Gould newspaper and magazine reviews appeared quickly, and the critics reached for words like *poetry* and *sorcery* to convey their impressions of his pianism, his expressive power and range, and his intellectual command, which suggested wisdom beyond his years. Even his platform mannerisms were seen in a positive light. The pianist Tatyana Nikolayeva praised him as "an outstanding and original musician," but the most important review came from the pianist Heinrich Neuhaus, a distinguished professor at the Moscow Conservatory and the teacher of, among others, Richter, Gilels, and Radu Lupu. He called Gould a phenomenon, and noted "the seriousness and depth of his artistic expression. Glenn Gould is a talented, thoughtful musician, possessing a vast knowledge and understanding of past musical culture, particularly Bach. It is obvious that he studied the great German composer's works for a long time and with love, and his Bach playing captivated the audience with its polyphonic clarity, richness of dynamic nuance, timbres, colour, and rhythmic freedom, all within the framework of Bach's style."

Russian audiences had never heard anything like him. Even today, Russians who saw him in 1957 use some variant of the "visitor-from-another-planet" image to capture their feelings at the time. "I was greeted like a movie star," Gould later said, and indeed he was cheered in the streets as he walked around town, which he was permitted to do freely. He had chosen, uncharacteristically, to do a little sightseeing. "I'm a very bad tourist," he once said, but Russia "was like being on the other side of the moon," too distant and exotic to pass up. Russians at this time were often self-conscious when confronted with brash Americans, but Gould, with his Canadian deference and politeness, endeared himself to the locals, though he was always startled by the Russians' fondness for vigorous embraces.

On one of his evenings off he heard Richter in recital, and though the repertoire – Schubert's last sonata and pieces by Liszt – was hardly up his street he pronounced the performance "staggering" to a local reporter. Twenty years later he was still rhapsodizing about Richter's notoriously slow interpretation of the first movement of the Schubert, which was a revelation to him, and perhaps an influence. The two pianists remained a passionate mutual-admiration society for the rest of their lives, though they could not have been less alike in style or repertoire: they forgave each other anything.

All was not pleasant for Gould. He endured cold halls and some poor pianos and low orchestral standards: during one passage in the first movement of the Beethoven Fourth, a flutist entered several beats early but soldiered on uncorrected despite the scowls and gesticulations of the conductor. Gould was uncomfortable at the meals and receptions held in his honour by the Canadian embassy and the Soviet Ministry of Culture; he hated the speeches, the small talk, the vodka toasts, in which he declined to indulge, to general incredulity (though Richter backed him up). But he attended every event, and met some of the leading Russian musicians of the day: Richter, Nikolayeva, the cellist Mstislav Rostropovich, the violinist Leonid Kogan.

Gould's popularity was so great that he agreed to give a fourth (free) concert on the morning of May 12: a lecture-recital at the Moscow Conservatory. He gave out a generic title, "Music in the West," but his intent, encouraged by Rostropovich and others, was to introduce the music of Schoenberg and his school. Such repertoire had long been proscribed in Russia, but by 1957 there was growing (though still cautious) support in Russia for a relaxation of the bureaucratic control under which music had stagnated during the Stalin era, and for a reconsideration of the Communist Party's notorious denunciations of 1948, which had discredited Khachaturian, Shostakovich, and other "formalist" composers. The Second All-Union Congress of Soviet Composers, in Moscow, which ended just a month before Gould arrived, had offered hope that the Party's Central Committee was willing to tolerate more creative exploration and debate than it had in the past. Still, in 1957 only a few Russians played modern music, and the public was often cool toward it.

The lecture-recital took place in the Small Hall of the Conservatory before an audience of students and teachers and with the aid of one official and several unofficial translators (and in the presence of Soviet officials and young communist informants). The four hundred seats were filled and standees occupied every other available space, overflowing into the exits and down the stairs. Gould was dressed informally, without a tie, and as the concert progressed and he began to feel warm he removed his jacket and sweater, heaping them on the stage, and finished in shirt sleeves with part of his shirt-tail hanging out. "When I first announced that I was going to play the kind of music that had not been officially recognized in the U.S.S.R. since the mid-thirties, there was a rather alarming and temporarily uncontrollable murmuring from the audience," Gould wrote to the photographer Yousuf Karsh. "I'm quite sure that many of the students were uncertain whether it was better for them to remain or walk out. I managed to keep things under control by frowning ferociously." Several elderly professors did walk out, Gould said, presumably in protest. He played Berg's Sonata, Webern's *Variations*, and two movements from Krenek's Third Sonata, interspersed with some rudimentary comments about the music of the Schoenberg school, with musical examples. "It was the most exciting musical occasion in which I have taken part," he told Karsh. "There were occasional suggestions that they would prefer Bach or Beethoven, but in general the students were wonderfully attentive and receptive." To placate them, he played a generous number of selections from *The Art of Fugue* and the Goldberg Variations as encores. The ovations were deafening, and the route between Gould's dressing room and limousine was jammed with cheering students.

Back in Canada Gould's Russian success was widely reported, the Reuters and Tass services carried the news around the world, and Homburger cleverly arranged to supply regular reports to the *Toronto Daily Star*. Gould's role as a cultural ambassador was the subject of approving commentary in both Canada and Russia, but Gould himself was not too dazzled to remember to write to friends and family back home.

He continued on to Leningrad, where, on May 14 and 16, he repeated his Moscow recital programs. The first night, Bolshoi Hall was less than half full: everyone had heard of Gould's triumphs the week before, but, thanks to a centuries-old Moscow-Leningrad rivalry, they made a point of not being swayed by Moscow's response. But once again, the hall filled up after intermission. At the second recital, stage seats were added for the first time ever in the Maly Hall, and policemen with horses were called out to control the crowd of people who were unable to get tickets and were still milling about hopefully at intermission. Gould received a huge ovation after the Goldberg Variations and had to play encore after encore, one of which was the entire Berg Sonata. Finally, three hours after the concert had started, he raised his hands and used two of the dozen Russian words he had managed to learn: "Thank you, good night." On May 18, in Bolshoi Hall, all thirteen hundred seats were filled, and somehow another eleven hundred standees were packed into the hall, as Gould joined the Leningrad Philharmonic in thrilling performances of Bach's D-minor and Beethoven's B-flat-major concertos.* Backstage, he was handed a note imploring him to play some Bach without the orchestra – and so there was another marathon series of encores. "I think I might as well go home," remarked the conductor, who still had a Liszt symphonic poem to get through. Even after the piano was pointedly moved aside, the audience applauded; Gould gave his last bow dressed in his coat, hat, and gloves. As in Moscow, the reviews were adulatory – again he was confidently pronounced one of the greatest pianists in the world – and once more he played tourist and attended social events, including a meeting with young colleagues at the House of Composers. And he agreed to reprise his "Music in the West" lecture-recital at the local conservatory, where the hall was again packed with enthusiastic students who tossed flowers and programs when it was all

---

* Recordings survive of these two performances and were released in Russia during Gould's lifetime on the Melodiya label. He had not consented to their release, and when he heard them, near the end of his life, he was surprised: he did not know that the concert had been recorded. He described the performances as "full of beans" and almost worthy of release, despite the glaring wrong entry by the orchestra near the end of the finale of the Bach concerto.

over, though they had been often confused by the modern music and had shouted requests for Bach and Beethoven.*

Gould's intellectual approach to music and championship of modern repertoire challenged Russia's long Romantic tradition as well as the newer tradition of Socialist Realism, and in this Gould was an inspiration to many Russian musicians, especially young composers. "He discovered the [Second] Viennese composers for us," Rostropovich said. But it was in Bach, above all, that he made a lasting impact. Regarded as an ecclesiastical composer, Bach was frowned on by many musicians in the officially atheistic Soviet Union. Gould's Bach arrived with the force of a revelation. As more than one Russian musician would say, even decades later, they played and thought about Bach one way before Gould, another way after. He was "possessed by Bach," one of the critics said; his was an exhilarating, modern Bach. Indeed, most of the critics focused on Gould's Bach almost to the exclusion of everything else. The consensus was that he had revealed not only the intellect and structures of Bach, but the passion and lyricism and humanity, too. When Cliburn proposed playing a Bach toccata in Moscow in 1958, an official told him, "No. Don't forget, we have just had Canada's Gould here."

Gould left Russia the day after his second lecture-recital and never returned, but his reputation there did not abate. For years, Western musicians (especially Canadians) visiting Russia were pestered for news of Gould. According to Ekatarina ("Kitty") Gvozdeva, a teacher of Italian at the Leningrad Conservatory, his Goldberg album was treated as a sacred relic, and his recordings and videos, when they could be got, were hungrily devoured. Young Russians took up his repertoire and mimicked his style, especially in

---

* While preparing his 2002 television documentary *Glenn Gould: The Russian Journey*, Yosif Feyginberg discovered a cassette of recordings from this event in the possession of the pianist and professor Vladimir Tropp, and both men agreed to share the find with me. It is an incomplete dub including only recordings of works by Sweelinck, Webern, and Krenek. The whole lecture-recital was recorded, but over the years the original tapes were lost or stolen, and today only the empty, labelled box for the tapes survives in the conservatory's archive.

Bach, and took inspiration from his anti-authority stance. For years he received letters and gifts from Russian admirers, particularly Kitty Gvozdeva, who wrote long, purple letters to her "golden boy." "We need you and long for you and wish [for] you and wait for you as for no one else!" she wrote a year after he left. "You are something beyond human comprehension, something high above the earth – you are *eternal*. You are grand and epoch-making." Gould, for his part, retained an interest in Russia and Russian music, and became something of a pundit on the subject in interviews, lectures, articles, and radio and television programs.

After Russia, Gould continued to Berlin, where he was already known through the Goldberg album.* There, as part of an "American Week" at the end of the Philharmonic's season, he joined Herbert von Karajan in Beethoven's C-minor concerto. At the rehearsal the orchestra welcomed him with polite applause, but after a run-through of the piece Karajan and the players gave him an ovation, and the principal cellist told Homburger that Gould was a genius, the greatest pianist he had ever heard. Gould and Karajan were an unlikely match. Karajan was then known as the *Generalmusikdirektor* of Europe, and had the sort of worldly power and ambition that Gould neither sought nor admired: besides conducting the Berlin Philharmonic he was artistic director of the Salzburg Festival and director of the Vienna State Opera, maintained an association with La Scala in Milan, made recordings with the Philharmonia Orchestra in London and the Vienna Philharmonic, and made guest appearances at Bayreuth and around the world. As a conductor he was an autocrat, and he sometimes sacrificed musical interest to plushness of sound and what Gould called an "obsessive concern with legato phrasing." But for all this, Gould found him charming, "a dream to work with," and Karajan professed to be so in synch with Gould

---

* Until the 1960s, Columbia Records did not operate in Europe, so Gould's recordings were distributed and promoted there by the Philips label, which also lent support to his European concert tours.

artistically that he could not understand why people considered him eccentric.

After their triumphant first performance, on May 24, Karajan told the press, "This was a masterly performance which will be equalled by very few in our lifetime." Gould disagreed – he had struggled with a sluggish piano action – but a radio recording of the May 26 concert reveals one of his most scintillating performances, beautifully accompanied. The most distinguished German critic, Hans Heinz Stuckenschmidt, wrote in *Die Welt* that Gould's appearance was "one of those rare meetings with an absolute genius." Gould, he continued,

> has shown himself to be in the first rank of living musicians. The C-minor concerto, Op. 37, is certainly no rarity on our concert programs, but played as it was with such incomparable intensity, technical facility, and complete intellectual command, it was a sheer revelation. Never have we heard either the little fluctuations of tempo in the fast movements, or the cantilena of the *Largo*, sound like this. It was as if the music itself was speaking to us out of these dematerialized sounds, without the intercession of the human hand. . . . His technical facility borders on the fabulous; his fluency in both hands, dynamic versatility, and range of tone colours represent a degree of mastery that, in my view, has not been seen since the time of Busoni. A marvel, an experience, an incomparable delight, the success of which exceeds all the usual critical standards.

Back home, Gould repeated the "not-since-Busoni" remark to Robert Fulford, and sheepishly added that he had looked up the date of Busoni's death – 1924.*

From Berlin he took the train south through the German countryside, admiring the views and singing Wagner's *Die Meistersinger* in

---

* Gould once received a letter from Busoni's son, who wrote that of all modern performers it was Gould who most reminded him of his father.

tribute as he passed through Nuremberg. He managed to get his left thumb caught in a doorway en route, but was able to appear at the Vienna Festival, on June 7, in a recital of Bach, Webern, Beethoven, and Berg. The house was only two-thirds full – there was much to do in Vienna that night – but every pianist in town was present, including Jörg Demus, who was overheard to say, "I am not going to sit here while Bach is being mutilated." There were many encores, thunderous applause, a final bow in hat and coat, and near-universal critical acclaim: "An orgiastic pianist," wrote one critic; "A perfection of technique that borders on the impossible," wrote another. Homburger was still relaying news of his client's triumphs to the *Toronto Daily Star*, and Eric McLean, in Montreal, reported, "No Canadian has had such sensational publicity since the Dionne family hit the headlines."

On June 11, exhausted but elated, Gould returned home.

"At live concerts I feel demeaned, like a vaudevillian."

Some of Gould's friends thought they detected changes in his personality after he became an international celebrity: he was losing his endearing modesty, his eccentricities were getting out of control, he was now less fun to be around, too high-maintenance. But Gould tried hard to keep grounded. He remained loyal to his support network back home, did not seek a New York manager or publicist, though he had offers. He continued to live in his parents' house and cottage, and was still recognizably their son. He did not boast or show off or revel ostentatiously in his new wealth, and was often refreshingly skeptical and deprecating about his celebrity. (The Russians applaud *everyone* that way, he said.) He still liked to hang out at the conservatory cafeteria and maintained contacts with old friends. He did not give the impression that he had been elevated to a new social sphere – quite the contrary. Rather than hang out in New York society, he joked about New York society with his friends back home. "At times he seemed to love the spectacle of the music world – the gossip, the backbiting, the outrageously inflated egos – almost as much as he loved the music itself," Robert Fulford recalled. "He even took a harmless pleasure from contemplating the jealousy that his talent naturally aroused in his contemporaries." He still loved cottage country, which was a good place to keep from getting a swelled head.* The locals were well aware of his success but did not treat him like a celebrity. There he was just "Glenn" and had friends rather than fans.

He did not, in fact, consider success as a concert artist to be a particularly praiseworthy achievement. He was acclaimed, wealthy, famous, yet he hated the life of a concert artist and found no personal or artistic satisfaction in the concert hall. He booked very few concerts by the standards of his peers, cancelled many of those, and complained about the ones he did end up giving. By the time he was eighteen, working for the CBC had convinced him that his *real* career was in the electronic media. Concerts were a necessary evil – necessary for earning money and building up an audience that could sustain him through a recording and broadcasting career. In 1968, he looked back on concert life in a CBC television profile, and his words were blunt:

> I suppose I never really did *want* to give concerts. I thought of it as something that had to be got through. I thought of it as something that one *must* do while endeavouring to establish, I suppose, some sort of reputation which would stand you perhaps in good stead later on. And it didn't seem to me that there was anything very productive [about it], even at the time. There was a sense of power which I rather enjoyed when I was fourteen, fifteen, sixteen years old. That was kind of fun, to play before a live, rabid public, and give of the best one could, and

---

* Stephen Leacock was once amused to be introduced, at a dinner in Orillia, as "one of the foremost humorists of East Simcoe," and as late 1940 he had trouble cashing a cheque at a local bank because the teller did not recognize him, despite his decades of international fame.

toward which one had practised for many months. But that wears off very quickly; that's a very thin veneer indeed. And once you start doing *that* every couple of nights, and at distant points and distant lands, the charm and the glamour of that doesn't last very long. It certainly didn't with me. And I became not only thoroughly sick but I began to feel that it *was* indeed very unproductive, that I was at best competing with myself once I'd begun to make recordings. The most that I could hope would be that my public statement would be as good as the equivalent recording of that work, if I had in fact recorded it. And I often had, because one *cheats* in giving concerts. You don't explore very much new repertoire. You play the same old tired pieces that you've tried out on your recorded public as well as on other, public publics. And one does cheat, and one does try to get by with as little work as possible and play them pretty much the same way, I suppose. And there is an incredible lack of imagination that sets in; there's no longer a need to rely particularly on imagination. And one grows old very quickly. It's a dreadful life.

Gould had a litany of objections to concert life. For a performer with idiosyncratic ideas, unusually high technical standards, and very personal demands when it came to his instrument, there was little to be gained by travelling from town to town, playing strange pianos, working with different orchestras and conductors without adequate rehearsal time. Little wonder that he, like so many others, played "the same old tired pieces" wherever he went – it was safer that way. His repertoire may have been unusual but it was mostly fixed: he always played the *same* unusual pieces. Occasionally he broke out of his rut and offered (usually briefly) something new: a different Bach partita, a Mozart fantasia, Beethoven's Op. 10/No. 2 sonata, Schoenberg's Op. 19 pieces. For a time in the early sixties, he felt like playing Beethoven's "Eroica" Variations and "Tempest" Sonata. But for the most part he had little time or energy to work up new repertoire while he was touring, and little incentive once he had achieved success.

He insisted, moreover, that the concert hall was precisely the wrong venue for the kind of music he liked to play: structurally complex works that tended to be intimate in scale and rhetoric. There is some historical justification to his position: concertos aside, there was scarcely a piece in his repertoire that was conceived by its composer for performance in a large hall before a massed audience, not even Beethoven's sonatas or Brahms's intermezzi or the music of the Schoenberg school. Gould often gave whole recitals of music intended to be performed, at best, for a small, private gathering, and much of his Elizabethan and Baroque repertoire was conceived for an audience consisting of no one but the performer himself. Such music, Gould believed, was betrayed when it was projected into the distant recesses of a large hall. In 1958 he played the Goldberg Variations in an arena at the University of Kentucky, in Lexington, in front of seven thousand people, and it is difficult to imagine him conveying the subtleties of Bach's counterpoint in such a setting. (He liked to play early music with the piano lid shut, for greater intimacy.) The remarkable thing is that Gould *did*, often, make his musical points in concerts – he would not have had such success otherwise. A recording survives of his 1959 recital at the Salzburg Festival, and in the first half of his program (Sweelinck's "Fitzwilliam" Fantasia, Schoenberg's Suite, Mozart's K. 330 sonata) his flawless technique and refined tone, and the atmosphere of intimate communion he creates, are astonishing, especially in a public setting, and there is scarcely a whisper from his rapt audience.

Yet that same concert includes a performance of the Goldberg Variations that, for all its beauties, is plagued by the sort of seat-of-the-pants interpretive gimmickry that Gould always disdained. The piece seems often on the verge of getting away from him technically, and sheer nerves lead him to the sort of devices – octave doublings, for instance – that he never used when he was thinking clearly. In many ways, the clear-headed and carefully controlled playing style that he aimed for in the recording studio was impossible in the concert hall. Many of his concert performances were brash and brilliant and exciting at the expense of musical values that he held more

dear. What many listeners and critics admired about his concert performances Gould considered nervous, superficial, over-projected,
out of control. In an interview in 1968 he complained that he picked
up "bad interpretative habits" by playing pieces repeatedly in large
halls. Bach's Partita No. 5 in G Major, for instance, was a piece that
turned up frequently in his early concerts, on the program or as an
encore. When he came back from his 1957 European tour, he said,
"I decided to record it, and it was, I swear, the *worst* Bach recording
that I've ever made. It was also the most pianistic. It was perhaps the
one that the connoisseur of the piano would like best; it's the one that
I like least, because it's least Bach, it's least *me* (*vis-à-vis* Bach, in any
case). It's full of all sorts of dynamic hang-ups; it's full of crescendi
and diminuendi that have no part in the structure, in the skeleton of
that music, and defy one to portray the skeleton adequately." He
preferred his 1954 CBC recording, which was "unspoiled by concert
wear and tear" and was therefore more "integrated" and "less exhi-
bitionistic." One of the few pieces of surviving video of Gould
playing in front of an audience shows him in three movements from
the G-major partita, on the CBC television series *Chrysler Festival* in
1957, and it reveals precisely the exaggerations of tempo and
gesture, the adrenaline-fuelled playing, that he disdained.

As his concert career ground on, Gould also grew increasingly
frustrated at being asked to play the clown. At first he took innocent
pleasure from the controversy surrounding his eccentricities, and
realized the publicity value of it, but as time passed he became less
amused and more self-conscious. "Everywhere I go, they want to
photograph me taking pills," he told a reporter in Dallas as early as
fall 1956. In a 1959 National Film Board of Canada documentary
one can see a flash of anger in his eyes as he is asked to don scarf and
gloves at the piano for photographs during a recording session: "I've
had *quite* enough of that sort of picture," he says, firmly. In Europe
the comments about his mannerisms were often more elevated.
Stuckenschmidt, for instance, wrote that "Gould is a player who
seems always to be struggling, physically obsessed, in an eager search
for perfect tonal expression, a young man in a strange sort of trance,

an artist on the threshold between dream and reality" – a nice way to put it. In Vienna, one critic conjured up the "fantastical dream figures" of E. T. A. Hoffmann, the once-fashionable genius-madman theories about artists like Poe and Van Gogh, and even the "charlatanism" of Wilde and Liberace, in search of a context for the "artistic phenomenon" Gould represented. Another critic saw Gould "in a trance, possessed by demons good and evil," lost to the world. For still another, he "transcended the material world; one might even say that he is possessed by music, not in the sense of a Faustian inner drive, or a demonic power, or a virtuoso's intoxication with sound, but rather in the sense of a return to what is fundamental in all music." In Florence, his mannerisms were interpreted as a symptom of his extreme sensitivity, even suffering, at the keyboard. Gould himself observed that Europeans tended to consider music-making a "more private affair, [and] whatever you do to accomplish your ends is your own business, so long as the ends are accomplished." But even the Europeans were not above the sort of tut-tutting that he received in North America: "His orang-utang style may please admirers of Elvis Presley but it irritates or leastwise fatigues a classical audience," noted *Le Soir*, in Brussels, and in Salzburg it was reported that some in the audience fled a recital at intermission, muttering that Gould was mad.

His objections to the concert hall were ultimately moral: it was simply immoral to demand that someone display his wares in this way in front of a ravening public. "I detest audiences," he said. "I think they're a force of evil." He disliked even *attending* concerts (or plays), and claimed never to have been to one after 1967. He thought that the concert situation was a manifestation of competitive and violent instincts, of "rule of mob law," and compared the concert hall to "a comfortably upholstered extension of the Roman Colosseum." He told an interviewer in 1968, "There's a very curious and almost sadistic lust for blood that overcomes the concert listener. There's a waiting for it to happen, a waiting for the horn to fluff, a waiting for the strings to become ragged, a waiting for the conductor to forget to subdivide, you know. And it's dreadful! I mean, there's a kind of gladiatorial instinct that comes upon the hardened, the case-hardened concertgoer, which is why I suppose I don't like him as a breed, and I don't trust him, and I wouldn't want one as a friend." Gould disapproved of the audience-conquering aspect of the solo recital, and the individual-versus-the-mob aspect of the solo concerto. And of course he had nothing but disdain for the sort of music – big, virtuosic solo works and concertos of the nineteenth century – that, both musically and historically, was most appropriate to the concert medium. "A performance is not a contest but a love affair," he said in 1962, and, like a love affair, it was better conducted in private.

However valid Gould's arguments may have been – for *him*, anyway – he also admitted that they represented an intellectual scaffolding to rationalize what was in essence a profound personal discomfort with concerts. Frail and anxious, he found working before a live audience intensely uncomfortable. It is not a trivial argument: stage fright and adrenaline often wreaked havoc with his carefully prepared musical interpretations. Gould's view here is hardly unique. Musical and temperamental objections to concerts are as old as the concert itself: witness the views of performers from Mozart, Chopin, and Liszt, to Godowsky, Grainger, and Horowitz, to speak only of classical pianists.

But the depth of Gould's discomfort was unusual, and it explains many of his onstage antics, which seem to have been designed to immerse him so deeply in the music that he could shut out the audience entirely. More than one reviewer noted that Gould rarely if ever looked toward the audience while playing, or even while waiting through an orchestral passage, and that when he did glance in the direction of the hall he seemed alarmed to find people sitting out there. He allowed no one backstage before a concert – it was in his contract – and was so uptight about performing in public that he wanted his audiences to be as anonymous as possible. He asked his family and friends not to attend his concerts; the closer the friend, the less comfortable he was knowing he was in the audience (a lucky few were allowed to listen backstage). He insisted that Verna

Sandercock, Walter Homburger's secretary from 1958 to 1961, actually *leave town* (at his expense) before several of his concerts. On one occasion she headed to Vancouver, and sent him a telegram: "I VERNA SANDERCOCK OF THE CITY OF TORONTO HEREBY SWEAR THAT IN FUTURE I SHALL NOT BE A MEMBER OF A VISUAL OR LISTENING AUDIENCE OF ANY GLEN [*sic*] GOULD PERFORMANCE WITHOUT HIS SPECIFIC SANCTION." She signed it, "YOUR AFFECTIONATE HEX." On another occasion hers was the only empty seat at a Stratford Festival concert, and Gould even forbade her to listen to that concert on the radio. For Gould, the audience got in the way of the music. Discussing encores with some fellow-students at the conservatory once, he declared, "You owe nothing to your public"; the performer's debts, rather, were to the composer, to the music, to *himself*. And in a 1980 interview he said, "I can honestly say that I do not recall ever feeling better about the quality of a performance because of the presence of an audience." So why give concerts?

The actual live performing was bad enough, but the trappings of concert life were worse. For a homebody uncomfortable in strange environments he could not fully control, concert life was torture. He hated sleeping in a different bed every night, in hotel rooms with the wrong food and heating that was never right, meeting new people at every stop, having to conform to a conventional daily schedule. "I don't enjoy the business of being a concert performer," he said in 1955, at which point he had left Canada only once. "There are children of nature in the piano-playing world whom I envy because they treat it as a day-to-day business." He hated the endless round of airports, train stations, hotels, and restaurants, the unfamiliar orchestras and conductors, the press interviews (which he sought to limit), and especially the receptions and parties with their small talk, alcohol, and forced conviviality. (The violinist Fritz Kreisler once said, "My fee is a thousand dollars for the concert – three thousand if it includes a party.") He gave offence to the formidable Rosalie Leventritt, an influential grande dame of the New York arts scene, by fleeing early from the party she threw for him after his Town Hall debut. He claimed illness, but in truth he was uncomfortable in social situations with people he did not know. Mrs. Leventritt never forgave him.

Mainly Gould travelled alone, with no entourage, and was lonely most of the time. He described his attitude on tour as one of "lethargic malaise," and usually begged local managers to spare him "extra-curricular" activities. He was little interested in sightseeing (he once spent a week in the Colorado Rockies and managed to miss the mountains), nervous about upcoming performances, and always fretful about his health, so he invariably spent most of his time in his hotel room, taking his meals there and passing the time by reading, studying scores, writing and composing, keeping up with correspondence, and assuaging his loneliness by making long-distance phone calls home at ruinous cost. He preferred the anonymity of hotels, and turned down offers to stay in private homes. Sometimes he would cross paths with friends from home or fellow-performers, and his pleasure in their company was palpable, though he could rarely be pried out of his hotel room. Morry Kernerman and Victor Feldbrill saw him in Brussels in 1958, and remember his disappointment when they wanted to get out of his hotel to do some sightseeing; Kernerman later managed, with much effort, to drag him along on a shopping trip. Overeager fans, too, became a problem. "I take a powder right after a concert," he said in 1964, "because I have this kook contingent who follow me from place to place, and some of them are really teetering on the balance." To evade fans he would sign hotel registers as Orlando Gibbons or Johannes Ockeghem.

On tour he was frequently exhausted – "I'm exhausted before I leave!" he told a friend, in 1958 – and frequently depressed. Not surprisingly, his health suffered. During his concert years the legend of Gould the hypochondriac grew, but he was besieged by illnesses that, psychosomatic or not, were very real. He was forever reporting colds and flus and sinus pains, which he said were exacerbated by flying and by cold halls and cold hotel rooms, which were especially common in Europe. For him, 27°C (80°F) was "just right" as a room temperature, and friends recall seeing him in hotel rooms literally surrounded by rented electric space heaters. Once, he claimed, he rushed out of a concert hall and "caught such a cold in my face that I couldn't chew on the left side of my mouth for months." His complaints could be even more baroque: in one letter he refers to a time, in 1956, when he "came home from Texas and was deaf." He was known to stop performing in the middle of a piece in order to track down a perceived draft. Always there were aches in his back, shoulders, arms, and hands; "inflammation of the hand muscles" was a typical complaint. He wore gloves religiously, sometimes in layers, used a special foam-rubber pillow in hotels, carried an electric kettle with him for quick bouts of hand-soaking, and he visited chiropractors and therapists in various cities. He took along a supply of pills wherever he went: pills to stop perspiration or increase circulation, uppers and downers, headache pills and sleeping pills, antihistamines and vitamins. These often caused him problems at border crossings; on at least one occasion he was strip-searched. "But this pill complex of mine has been grossly exaggerated," he told Jock Carroll. "Why, one reporter wrote that I travelled with a suitcase full of pills. Actually, they barely fill a briefcase."

Like Horowitz, Michelangeli, and other fragile and neurotic performers, Gould was notorious for cancelling concerts, sometimes on short notice. Audience-loving performers like Arthur Rubinstein would fulfill engagements unless they were near death, and Van Cliburn was always heartbroken when he had to cancel, though at his busiest he played more than a hundred concerts a year. But Gould, whose schedule was comparatively light to begin with, *looked* for excuses to cancel. The smallest sniffle was enough, except under unusual circumstances, and he was known to ask doctor friends like Peter Ostwald for notes excusing him from an engagement. He routinely cancelled 20 to 30 per cent of his concerts, sometimes weeks' or months' worth in a block. He was an honourable person, and usually rebooked cancelled concerts, but these, too, were often cancelled, and more than once he left bad feelings. The cancellations cost him a small fortune in fees, and he often had to pay hundreds of dollars to a local manager in reimbursement for travel and promotional expenses and hall rental; the amount payed out in reimbursement often cancelled out much of his fee if he did rebook a concert. Considering that he viewed concerts as a means of making money in order to be able to retire from public performance, the financial hit he took must be considered sadly ironic.

"Well, who the hell said it was supposed to be fun anyway?"

Gould spent the 1957–58 season touring North America, and much of early summer 1958 recording in New York and playing at the Vancouver International Festival. In early August, with no significant break, he began a punishing four-month tour of Europe. He played Bach's D-minor concerto in a triumphant debut at the Salzburg Festival, with the Concertgebouw Orchestra conducted by Dmitri Mitropoulos, and the same concerto at the World Fair in Brussels in a special Dominion Day concert for which the Canadian government had sent over Boyd Neel's Hart House Orchestra. In late September, he played the concerto again under Herbert von Karajan. Of this last appearance, Bruno Monsaingeon related a story told to him by the flutist Aurèle Nicholet, then a member of the Berlin Philharmonic: At the first rehearsal, Gould had played only the first few notes of the piano part when Karajan, stunned, stopped conducting, took a seat in the auditorium, and simply listened to the rest of the first movement.

Gould continued to Stockholm, where he recorded a performance with orchestra for Sveriges Radio (his only audience being four heaters) and three solo sessions in a studio; he also gave one orchestral concert in public. On October 9, he gave a very successful concert in Wiesbaden, under Wolfgang Sawallisch, despite what he called a "*nicht so gut*" orchestra, then he rented a car and drove through the castle country along the Rhine to Cologne, where he stayed in a hotel overlooking the great cathedral.

Musically, he was at the top of his game, yet he had been ill since arriving in Europe. Already on August 13, newspapers reported that he caught what he called "a ferocious influenza" in Salzburg (he later remembered it as "a touch of tracheitis," for which he received an antibiotic and a thyroid stimulant); he blamed the cold of the local hotels and the generally damp climate in Europe, and cancelled a recital in Salzburg. On October 3, in a letter to Homburger, he complained of "another flu à la Salzburg (current temperature 101°)," and by the time he reached Cologne his illness had progressed to the point that he cancelled a broadcast recital with Westdeutscher Rundfunk. He flew to Hamburg, still feverish (his temperature 38.9°C or 102°F) and in pain despite the ministrations of a chiropractor. He cancelled all of his plans for later October – orchestral concerts, recitals, and broadcasts, in Cologne, Hamburg, Berlin, and Vienna, as well as recordings with Robert Craft conducting the Vienna Symphony Orchestra – and holed up in Hamburg, at the Hotel Vier Jahreszeiten. He would remain there for a month, and despite his medical problems he would later remember that month as the best – because most solitary – of his life, a period in which he led "the most idyllic and isolated existence." He could not resist comparing himself with the tubercular Hans Castorp in his Alpine sanitorium in Thomas Mann's *The Magic Mountain*, and at least one newspaper reported rumours that he actually *had* TB.

On October 18, Gould wrote to Homburger with details of his illness. X-rays had revealed "a chronic bronchitis in the right lung," for which a doctor had prescribed "milk and honey, cold cloths on the right side – all that sort of thing," without effect. His temperature was regularly creeping over 100°F, especially in the evening. He noted blood in his urine on at least one occasion, and he was shedding weight, ten to fifteen pounds after Salzburg, twenty more after Stockholm, putting him "back to the poundage of my delicate years – 150." A few days later, he reported a new after-effect of his illness: nephritis, an infection of the kidney. As he wrote to Homburger on October 24, the diagnosing doctor insisted that he stay in bed for ten days on a no-protein diet, even though his appetite was returning. The idea was "to give the kidneys a rest as much as possible. X ray showed there was nothing wrong with them whatever

organically but that they had someway been affected by this virus."
Family and friends commiserated and offered advice. Grandmother
Gould suggested mustard plasters; the harpsichordist Silvia Kind
recommended massage; Deborah Ishlon, a publicist at Columbia
Records, recommended "yogi exercises"; David Oppenheim merely
expressed pride that Gould could claim "such an unusual illness." By
the last week of October, bedrest and the no-protein diet had
improved his health, and he began to play the piano again.

He resumed his tour on November 15 with a recital in Florence.
As usual, his playing and his intellectually challenging program
(Sweelinck, Schoenberg, Mozart, Bach) were considered exceptional, but for the first time in his career he experienced hissing from
his audience, after Schoenberg's Suite. In Gould's tall-tale version of
the event, he milked the combat between hissers and cheerers by
taking six curtain calls, "and, thereafter, the exhausted audience sat
back in a liverish somnolence to attend the 'Goldberg' Variations."
He played the same program in Turin, then appeared with the
Accademia nazionale di Santa Cecilia in Rome. He had originally
programmed Bach's D-minor concerto, but the orchestra had felt
that that piece was "not very important pianistically" and asked
whether he might program, say, Schumann, Chopin, Liszt, or
Mendelssohn instead. Gould replied, from his roost in Hamburg, in
the formal tone he tended to use when annoyed: "While I should
like to do everything possible to accom[m]odate the Accademia, I
regret that it will not be practical for me to program any of the
concert[o]s which they suggested. My repertoire is built almost
exclusively around preromantic music and I think that to program a
work which I find unsuitable would be a great mistake both, for me
and for the Rome public." They compromised on the Beethoven
Second, in which, a local critic wrote, Gould played with "the touch
of an angel, a touch made of air and sky, limpid, childlike, silvery."

Gould fell ill again in Rome – a cold – and became depressed. He
cancelled several orchestral appearances in Brussels and Liège, but
a more alarming prospect still loomed: a two-and-a-half-week tour
of Israel, where he was to play as part of the celebrations honouring

the tenth anniversary of the country's founding. Israel was still a fledgling country, and there was still a frontier quality about its musical life. Gould had heard stories about bad pianos, cold halls, uncongenial food, and other discomforts, but with his new illness he felt, as he wrote to Homburger, that he had "a very good excuse and even a convincing one to get out of Israel." But Homburger was firm: the Israeli tour was too extensive and high-profile to be cancelled at the last minute. And so, beginning on November 29, Gould gave eleven concerts there in eighteen days: nine scheduled appearances with the Israel Philharmonic conducted by Jean Martinon, in Tel Aviv, Jerusalem, and Haifa (he played concertos by Bach, Beethoven, and Mozart), as well as two solo recitals in Tel Aviv added at the last minute by popular demand.

Gould had been right to worry about conditions in Israel. In Jerusalem, he had to wear a coat and scarf on stage, and surround himself with space heaters, in order to play in a cold, unfinished hall. But his tour was a triumph: he played eight times in Tel Aviv, and, he recalled, three thousand people attended each concert. As in Russia, the public was mad about music and Gould was immediately proclaimed a genius, one of the world's greatest pianists. His reviews suggest he was received as something more than a mere performer. "Such playing moves the listener to the depth of his soul by its almost religious expression," wrote a critic in *Haaretz*. "We have never heard anything like it at our concerts. Gould touches the piano and there you are captivated by those fantastic hands and you listen to his playing and you feel that it comes from another planet. Every tone is poetic, every sound a revelation." After one of Gould's recitals, A. A. Boskowicz wrote, also in *Haaretz*:

> Deep experience and competence like this cannot be acquired or even explained rationally. Only theological vocabulary can express this unique spiritual manifestation from a higher sphere. This is indeed religious music; those are religious sounds. . . . Gould's playing comes nearest to the conception of prayer. This is not virtuosity; but with its esoteric spirituality – it is beyond

virtuosity. Nostalgic yearnings for a higher world breeze over to us from this music, which cannot be translated into the language of words, and no praise, however high, could do it justice.

Gould was overwhelmed by the response, and enjoyed his visit. The Philharmonic's guest house lacked central heating, so he stayed in a hotel at Herzliya-by-the-Sea, an American colony about fifteen miles outside Tel Aviv. There, he had a room with a view of the Mediterranean, which he found inspiring. He rented a car for mad drives through the countryside, including a visit to the Arab quarter of Jaffa, where he had a minor collision with what he claimed was "a blind Arab truck driver." He made headlines after picking up an Indian man in his car and making an impromptu visit to the hitch-hiker's communal settlement within a mile of the Jordanian border. There he took tea, and when he requested some milk the man rolled up his sleeves and headed for the barn to get it. Gould "was in a very happy mental condition" in Israel, "and felt myself very much attuned to stone huts, donkey carts, shepherds and flocks of goats. I think I might even go back as a tourist!" In fact, he made plans for a return visit in 1961, but never did go back. The Israeli tour had been "one of the most exciting experiences of my life," he said, but he also admitted that he "was about done in at the end of it." After his concert on December 17, he did not rebook any of his cancelled European concerts, as he had half-heartedly promised to do. Instead, he went home.

In all, the 1958 European tour had made him "terribly depressed," and he had barely a week's respite after returning home. The day after Christmas he began what would be the busiest winter-spring season of his career – almost thirty concerts in less than four months, all over North America. And just two weeks after *that*, he had to return to Europe, first for a recital in Berlin, on May 16, 1959. ("My season begins next week and so I'm getting depressed as usual," he wrote to a friend.)

He spent much of May and June in London, where he was

scheduled to give a cycle of the five Beethoven concertos as part of conductor Josef Krips's annual series of Beethoven concerts with the London Symphony. Gould and Krips had worked together the year before, in Buffalo, and were mutual admirers: Krips, Gould once wrote, was "the most underrated conductor of our time." According to the pianist Gina Bachauer, every major pianist in England made a pilgrimage to Gould's concerts, including elders like Dame Myra Hess, and Gould received a considerable amount of advance press. Naturally, the critics and the public had a lot to say about his platform manner. In England, proper deportment in concert mattered a great deal; there was no talk in the London papers about "the threshold between dream and reality," only stern admonitions to shape up. One of the senior critics, Neville Cardus of the *Manchester Guardian*, was particularly annoyed by Gould's theatrics, and wrote a condescending review that dealt with little else; several other critics steadfastly refused to be dazzled. England would always be one place where he received mixed reviews and much criticism; in fact, his recordings were conspicuously slow to be released there. Yet even in London the public response was overwhelming, and the reviews of his *playing* were mostly enthusiastic. Some felt that his interpretations strayed too far from the composers' scores, and many felt he lacked the heroism, the sheer power, even violence, appropriate to Beethoven, but by the same token he was admired for revealing the "poetic" and "inward" Beethoven through an exceptionally refined technique. This had been his intention, in fact: as he later wrote, he and Krips endeavoured to offer interpretations that "gave short shrift to the competitive absurdities of the [concerto] form." In the end, the press mostly struck the same balance it did everywhere else. As one headline put it, "ECCENTRIC OR NOT HE'S A GREAT PIANIST."

Gould spent a great deal of time in London with the journalist Gladys Shenner, who had written the first major profile of him in *Maclean's*, in 1956, and with whom he had developed a warm (platonic) friendship. He was in high spirits in London, and they saw each other every day, leading Krips and others to wonder if they were engaged or married. He saw other friends, too, like Van Cliburn, whom he dubbed "the Texas troubadour." (Cliburn had great affection for him.) But once again, he fell ill, and in fact played only four of the five Beethoven concertos: pleading illness, he bowed out of the "Emperor" and was replaced by Louis Kentner.* It was "my inevitable European flu," he wrote home, "the ache-all-over feeling we all hear about in the Alka-Seltzer ads"; a doctor diagnosed a virus, and his temperature rose almost to 39° (102°). By this time, audiences and orchestras and reporters, to say nothing of Gould's family and friends, were becoming accustomed to his illnesses and cancellations. Even Homburger was beginning to take his constant complaints about his health with good humour, but to Gould they were becoming less and less amusing. He turned down Yehudi Menuhin's offer to appear at the Bath Festival (no central heating in the hotel), turned down an offer to appear at the Stratford Festival that summer, and left London to recuperate at Lake Simcoe.

Gould had one pleasant diversion: a pair of half-hour shows for the National Film Board of Canada, which was already renowned for its documentaries. *Glenn Gould: Off the Record* and *Glenn Gould: On the Record* were produced and directed by Roman Kroitor and Wolf Koenig for their cultural series *Candid Eye*. Filmed during the summer of 1959, at the Gould cottage and in New York, the documentaries made a considerable impact when they were released in 1960, and not only in terms of Gould's reputation. They were remarkably sophisticated films for their day. Kroitor and Koenig

---

* That was his second bout of what he called "Emperoritis" in as many months. Were these perhaps convenient cancellations? After all, he never liked the piece much. In a letter to Peter Yazbeck shortly after playing the concerto in Victoria in December 1955, he wrote that he felt, "on closer inspection, less and less happy with the work itself. Neither the 2nd nor 3rd [movements] are well-devised (in my opinion). The 3rd movt. is a particularly pedantic and uninspired creation. . . . P.S. Please do not show the above critique of Beethoven to anyone who doesn't already know me. They might get the idea that I'm stark raving mad. And they might be right!!"

had been influenced by certain innovative unscripted British documentaries of the mid-fifties, and by the candid photography of Henri Cartier-Bresson. In their own films they sought to capture a behind-the-scenes spontaneity without sacrificing the subtleties permitted by post-production. The British producer Humphrey Burton recalled that the Gould documentaries influenced him and his colleagues at the BBC when they were broadcast in Britain in 1960, and that everyone was mightily impressed by Gould himself, too. The first film, *Off the Record*, offers a portrait of Gould at the cottage, walking with Banquo, chatting with friends, hanging out at the Shang, playing Bach and Webern and even a little Schubert on the piano. *On the Record* shows Gould recording Bach's Italian Concerto and kibitzing (sometimes riotously) with producer Howard Scott and Columbia technicians, and trying out pianos at Steinway and Sons. Feeling somewhat upstaged by the control-room staff, he took to calling the second film "The Howard Scott Story," but the films are revealing of Gould in his concert days.

"This movie-making has done more for my morale and indeed enthusiasm for life in general than anything else within memory," Gould wrote to Gladys. He had enjoyed his summer and dreaded going back on tour the way he had once dreaded going back to school. He even had bad dreams when a concert tour loomed. In late summer 1959, he returned again to Europe, and, as though on cue, caught a bad cold. He was due to be in residence at the Salzburg Festival from August 5 to 12, but cancelled both of his scheduled concerts. He recovered in time to record two radio recitals for the BBC in London – one on August 17 (Bach, Haydn, Hindemith) for broadcast the next day, the other on August 21 (Sweelinck, Bach, Krenek, Berg) for broadcast on April 18, 1960.* Four days later, he gave a rescheduled recital at the Salzburg Festival, and a week after that he appeared at the Lucerne Festival with the Philharmonia

---

* The BBC apparently did not keep the original tapes, and the National Sound Archive of the British Library did not record the broadcasts off the air. Unless these recitals were recorded by a private collector, we must assume they are lost.

Orchestra. He played Bach's D-minor concerto, his piano sur-rounded by the strings, as was his preference in Baroque concertos; Herbert von Karajan obligingly conducted from the lip of the stage. Gould still had a high fever and had wanted to cancel, though by all accounts, and despite perspiration running into his eyes, he gave a brilliant performance; even he remembered the performance fondly. He received ovations and rapturous reviews. One critic wrote, "In a trance, this quiet ecstatic transports us to a magical sphere of sound, creates tones seemingly drawn from the spirit realm rather than the strings of a concert grand." Another asked, "Did it really take a young Canadian to show us how to play Bach?"

Gould cancelled a scheduled appearance with orchestra in Salzburg, returned home, and never left North America again. He would field offers from around the world for years and occasionally made plans for overseas visits, but he always changed his mind. He had begun his overseas career in good faith, with enthusiasm. In 1957, he wrote home from Vienna to say that he was having a wonderful time in Europe. That same year, he told a correspondent he hoped someday to give concerts in India, and he once told Bruno Monsaingeon that he had entertained plans to tour China and Japan, countries that fascinated him. But the good intentions did not last long. As he was embarking on his 1958 European tour, he said to Homburger, "This tour in Europe is crazy and I won't do it again. After all, I can make that money just doing two or three concerts here." After the travails of 1958 and 1959, he no longer had the stomach to travel overseas. Even Hawaii held no attraction: he can-celled an appearance in Honolulu scheduled for December 1960.

He also cancelled an extended tour of Australia. As early as age twenty Gould had come to the attention of the Australian Broad-casting Corporation (ABC) through the conductor Bernard Heinze, but they did not really become interested until the release of the Goldberg Variations, at which point they began a lengthy corre-spondence with Homburger. Gould had his usual concerns about playing in so exotic a place – airplanes, the weather, income-tax regulations, the food, the state of local concert halls and hotel rooms, the quality of local orchestras, pianos, critics. Moreover, the ABC liked to arrange busy, country-wide tours, while Gould resisted playing more than three times per week, and they liked their visiting artists to give speeches, attend receptions, and give their time generously to the press, not hide in their hotel rooms. By the end of 1958, after protracted negotiations, Homburger and the ABC had settled on detailed plans for a tour running from October 26 to December 10, 1960, and featuring a total of nineteen recitals and concerto appearances, in Sydney, Brisbane, Melbourne, and Adelaide. Gould agreed to the arrangements, but a month after returning home from Lucerne he sent Homburger a letter from Uptergrove:

> I have been studying the schedule for the Australian tour with increasing concern and anxiety. While it certainly conforms admirably with the conditions which were mutually agreed upon for the tour I wonder whether, in view of my recent unfortunate experience in Europe, my health will be able to endure the strain of such an intense and protracted series of engagements. I am particularly worried that during my visit in Australia a sickness may befall me, as it did last winter in Europe, which might make it impossible for me to continue the tour which would be of great embarrassment to the ABC.

He left open the possibility of coming to Australia in the near future for "a shorter and less arduous series of engagements, which could possibly be part of a holiday in the Far East," but he was just being polite: the Australian tour was off. The ABC was not happy, though its representative in New York expressed relief at the cancellation: "Since it has become common knowledge in New York that Mr. Gould was scheduled to tour Australia in 1960, more than one person in the music world here has spoken in warning terms of Gould's unreliability due only to his constant anxiety for his health."

"I guess I am just too delicate for this world."

On December 8, 1959, Gould visited the Concert and Artist Department of Steinway and Sons, in their office at Steinway Hall, on West 57th Street in Manhattan. There he chatted with the department's manager, Frederick Steinway, and his assistant Winston Fitzgerald. After a while, the three were joined by William Hupfer, the department's legendary chief concert technician. A Steinway employee since 1917, Hupfer's admirers had included Paderewski and Rachmaninov. What transpired next was summarized in "The Glenn Gould Case," an internal Steinway and Sons document apparently prepared in the spring of 1961:

> Hupfer entered the office (Gould's back being to the door) and, in greeting Gould, Hupfer placed a hand on his shoulder. All three Steinway employees are quite emphatic in stating that this was not a "slap on the back" and that no pressure was applied by Hupfer to Gould's back or shoulder. However, Gould cringed away from the physical contact and protested to Hupfer on account of the contact. Hupfer apologized. There was no evidence whatsoever of an accident or injury, as those words are commonly understood; although Gould sulked somewhat, he remained in the office and continued his conversation with Fitzgerald for at least half an hour.

Later that same day, Gould attended a screening of the two NFB films at Canada House and "appeared to be in an excellent mood," saying nothing about Hupfer, and on December 10 he gave a recital in Syracuse.

At the same time, however, he began claiming that Hupfer, who was a large man, had injured his left shoulder. As he wrote in a letter on January 27, "The initial injury was to the left shoulder and when x-rayed the shoulder blade was shown to have been pushed down about one-half an inch. That problem has basically been cleared up now but has caused a secondary reaction much more troubling. The [ulnar] nerve which controls the fourth and fifth fingers of my left hand has been compressed and inflamed or whatever with the result that any movement involving a division of the left hand, as in a sudden leap to the left side of the keyboard, is, if not actually impossible, accomplished only by a considerable effort of will." He complained of constricted muscles, pain, intense fatigue after brief bouts of playing, and loss of co-ordination in his left arm, hand, and fingers (especially the fourth and fifth).

He consulted five doctors with different physio-therapeutic approaches within the first two months, and claimed that all concurred that a nerve had been compressed by cervical vertebrae, though doctors in Toronto and Baltimore who examined Gould and shared their findings with Peter Ostwald denied that he had suffered any real injury. He had orthopaedic and chiropractic treatments every day, sometimes twice a day, in Toronto as well as New York. (His medical files in the National Library of Canada include records for 117 treatments between January 8 and October 22, 1960.) He cancelled three months' worth of concerts, including a European tour planned for February 1960, though to spare Steinway embarrassment he told the press that he had "a dislocated shoulder resulting from a fall." Winston Fitzgerald visited him in Toronto in February and noticed no physical impairment, and the company, long aware that Gould was "a hypochondriac to the Nth power," did not take his complaints very seriously, even when, annoyed at Fitzgerald's skepticism, Gould dragged his X-rays into Steinway Hall. By February his correspondence begins to suggest a growing desperation, but by March he was reporting some good progress with cortisone, though it made him nauseated. On March 2 he tried out the shoulder in a concert with the Baltimore Symphony, and he continued to make orchestral appearances into April, though he cancelled solo recitals, which he considered too strenuous.

After an apparently brilliant performance of the "Emperor" Concerto in Montreal, on April 19, Gould cancelled the rest of his engagements for spring 1960 and decamped for Philadelphia, where, on the recommendation of the conductor Eugene Ormandy, he sought treatment from a well-known orthopaedic surgeon, Irwin Stein. For six weeks, from late April to the end of May, he was holed up at the Drake Hotel. He spent an entire month immobilized in an upper-body cast, in order to bring the shoulder up toward the neck and reduce the stretch of the nerves in the shoulder, then more time with his left arm in a sling; for a period afterward, he wore a cervical collar while practising. Back home, his assessments of his weeks in Philadelphia were contradictory, but mostly negative, though he made many return visits to Dr. Stein. "To be perfectly truthful I find greater enjoyment in composing than I do in concert work," he had told the *Globe and Mail*. "So if I do not play again I won't be terribly distressed." This was brave, yet privately Gould was desperate at the thought that he might be permanently disabled, and he was anxious and depressed in Philadelphia, so much so that he never performed there again. As he later wrote to the Philadelphia Orchestra, he developed "a totally foolish and illogical phobia" about playing in that city. Yet, despite the continuing left-shoulder problems, which would flare up on occasion for years, Gould fulfilled a heavy recording and performing schedule beginning in June 1960.

As early as January 1960, he had considered taking legal action against Steinway and Sons, and his resolve to do so may have stiffened when a disability claim with his own insurance company was rejected because he was still giving concerts. On December 6, by which time he was back on a full schedule, he filed a civil suit in the United States District Court for the Southern District of New York, against both the company and Hupfer, claiming damages totalling three hundred thousand dollars. His suit claimed that "Hupfer approached plaintiff from behind and wilfully or recklessly or negligently brought both his forearms down with considerable force on plaintiff's left shoulder and neck, driving plaintiff's left elbow against the arm of the chair in which he was sitting," resulting in "injury to the nerve roots in his neck and spinal discs in the neck region." The press treated the story as another act in the ongoing Gould comedy, and blew up Hupfer's greeting into "effusive slaps," a "pally overture," a "thump" on the back. The suit dragged on for almost a year, with Steinway disputing not only with Gould but with its own insurers. In March 1961, after a face-to-face meeting between Gould and Steinway representatives resolved nothing, he was temporarily banned from Steinway Hall, and his status as a Steinway artist was reconsidered.

All of which must be understood in light of Gould's always fractious relations with the company. He had been dealing with the New York office since early 1955, though he had considered himself a Steinway artist even when he was dealing only with Steinway representatives in the Eaton's department store in Toronto. From the start, despite his youth, he was confidently suggesting ways in which the company's product could be improved, though Steinway's technicians, whose instruments satisfied more than 90 per cent of the world's concert artists, naturally felt that they already had some small insight into their job. Gould even wanted the company to undertake scientific studies on different piano actions in order to better understand his needs. The problem was that he was not a conventional pianist, and could never be placated with a conventional piano even if it was the world's best. Steinway's pianos are designed first and foremost for the Romantic music that is at the core of the piano repertoire. Qualities for which the Steinway has always been renowned include its projecting power, its potent, "growling" bass, a sustaining pedal that produces an unusually complex wash of sonority, and above all a sustained, animated, singing tone. Rossini once reportedly referred to the Steinway's sound as "a nightingale cooing in a thunderstorm," and Paderewski once said that anyone could make a Steinway sing.

These, needless to say, were not qualities Gould sought when he played Gibbons or Webern; he was not interested in filling large halls with massive sounds, did not like to pound away in the bass, used the sustaining pedal sparingly when at all, almost never to create a tonal haze, and was no fan of the piano's "smug, silken, legato-spinning resource" (though his tone did sing, in its own way). He sought, instead, a hair-trigger action, and perfect control of articulation and tonal nuance, especially at the quieter end of the dynamic spectrum.

He wanted no aftertouch and immediate damping; in other words, he wanted the depression of the key to stop once that hammer had been thrown, and he wanted a note to stop sounding completely the instant he let his finger off the key. And given his finger-oriented technique, he wanted a light, tight action that required minimal effort to push the key down into its bed, even if it meant sacrificing some degree of dynamic power. In short, he cared more about how the instrument felt under his hands than how it sounded. In fact, he once told an interviewer, "I don't happen to like the piano as an instrument. I prefer the harpsichord." And his preferred piano tone, he said, was "a little like an emasculated harpsichord."

Gould campaigned tirelessly to find suitable pianos, either at Steinway Hall or on tour, and he borrowed, rented, and purchased various instruments over the years. As early as December 1957, Alexander (Sascha) Greiner, who had been head of the Concert and Artist Department at Steinway since 1934, and had a reputation as personable, unflappable man with a gift for mollifying star egos, lamented in a memo that "Glenn Gould has been and is extremely difficult to satisfy with our instruments." The problem was that the new Steinways could never meet Gould's standards without substantial modification. Something was always wrong: the tone was too plush or too insistent; the action was too heavy or too sluggish; the white or black keys were too long or too wide, or even too smooth (rough keys suited his fondness for a touch that he once compared to stroking a dog). He also used the soft pedal a lot, pervasively in music composed before about 1800, even when playing *forte*. In the mid-fifties he became convinced he needed wider-than-usual spaces between the white keys, so he could wiggle them in imitation of vibrato on a string instrument, a notion that is mechanically absurd though psychologically revealing. Sometimes he would suggest putting the action of one piano into the body of another, even pianos of two different makes.

The Steinways that Gould did accept were invariably older models from between the wars, a period many consider the company's glory days. He often shipped pianos from city to city in North America, at his own expense, in order to keep congenial instruments at his side, and he sometimes felt that Steinway was slow to accommodate his schedule, and overcharged him. In January 1955 he discovered one instrument, designated CD 174, that he considered almost ideal; it was built in 1928. He used it to record the Goldberg Variations, and had it shipped around eastern North America for concerts, despite racking up freight bills to the tune of almost four thousand dollars. But in March 1957 CD 174 was dropped and damaged in transit, and had to be completely rebuilt – which, to Gould, meant ruined. "Maybe there are no more pianos," he lamented while seeking a replacement. (He used no less than *three* pianos in his 1958 recording of Beethoven's C-major concerto.) He deplored Steinway's policy of withdrawing old pianos from circulation, for at times not a single new piano in the factory satisfied him. "This is of no use and benefit to Steinway & Sons whatever," Greiner wrote in a 1958 memo. "We are not in the business of promoting and selling Steinway pianos which were made 50 or 100 years ago but our business is to promote the present product." The instruments Gould found suitable were often not only older than usual but smaller than usual, and sometimes instruments that, in the company's view, were all but worthless, among them an old German piano that had been nicknamed "The Crock." As Greiner put it, "what he likes is anything but a Steinway piano."

If shiny new Steinways could not meet these demands it is no surprise, for the piano Gould always had in mind as an ideal was a baby grand made by the Boston-based firm of Chickering (once a great rival of Steinway) in 1895. This extraordinary instrument, he said, "is quite unlike almost any other in the world, an extremely solicitous piano with a tactile immediacy almost like a harpsichord's. It gives me a sensation of being so close to the strings and so much in control of everything." With its crisp, feather-light action, tightly focused bass sonority, and unusually dry, refined tone in the upper registers, the Chickering was useless as a concert instrument in Liszt or Rachmaninov, but for that very reason suited Gould's fingers and temperament and repertoire perfectly.* It gave him, he said, "the illusion of complete premeditated control and rapport." The Chickering is often referred to as Gould's "childhood piano," though in fact he came to know it only in his early twenties, when it was being rented by a friend of his. He practised on it in preparation for his New York debut, and liked it so much that he eventually took over the rental and installed the instrument at the cottage; he purchased it outright in November 1957 for $555. When he fled to the cottage at the end of a concert tour, he was not just seeking sanctuary by the lake, he was restoring his treasured image of what a piano should be. It was always the Chickering to which he pointed when explaining his needs to Steinway's staff, even though some in the piano business who knew the instrument cordially dismissed it as junk.

Gould did admire the Steinway brand, and the company was pleased to have an artist of Gould's calibre on its roster, but his idiosyncratic demands meant almost continuous conflict. Gould's frustrations over pianos led to bad feelings, including one letter from December 1956, revealing a rare flash of anger, referring to "the incredible negligence on the part of your firm, of which I have been victim since our first dealings 18 months ago. Surely no artist of the undersigned stature has ever received such lack of consideration, has so conspicuously failed to reap those advantages of personal consideration which, through popular legend, have become a trademark of Steinway and Sons." Occasionally, with Steinway's consent, Gould would use a piano of another make on tour when there was some problem with the local Steinway product or service, and sometimes he would threaten to switch his allegiance permanently. In fall 1958, he became furious with the Steinway representatives in Hamburg, accusing them (for unexplained reasons) of "thievery" and "unprecedent[ed] exploitation of their name and my dependence on it" so much so that he made a quick, "top-secret" side-trip to Berlin to

---

* Gould can be heard playing the Chickering only in the NFB's *Glenn Gould: Off the Record* and in some of his own private recordings.

explore "a possible defection of allegiance" to Bechstein. (He also visited East Berlin while he was there.)

Admittedly, arrogance has long been a trait for which Steinway and Sons has been criticized. The company has a reputation for being high-handed about confronting pianists over what is "proper" when it comes to tuning, regulating, and voicing their pianos, and for being unwilling to admit to imperfections. But even the most gracious company might have met its match in Gould, whose demands Steinway often considered absurd, even "childish," and certainly not showing their instruments in the best light. Gould also had a history of personal clashes with William Hupfer. His lawsuit claimed that, in the past, Hupfer had been prone to "unduly strong handshakes and other demonstrative physical acts" toward Gould, of which he had complained. In this context, it is tempting to assume that Gould psychosomatically magnified the effect of Hupfer's touch on the shoulders. For what, really, could Hupfer possibly have done to Gould, short of jumping on him, that could have put him out of commission and in medical therapy for months? Of course Gould was fragile, and a childhood back injury had left him predisposed to musculoskeletal aches (more on that later); still, a pianist who requires a year's therapy to recover from even a hearty pat on the shoulder is a pianist who, by rights, should be too frail to put fingers to keys. (To some friends he claimed that Hupfer had violently shaken him.) There was surely more involved here: built-up resentment toward the company and especially Hupfer, and perhaps anger over what Gould felt to be Hupfer's condescending or over-familiar greeting. And once Gould had convinced himself that Hupfer had "hurt" him, the situation could easily have been inflated in his own mind as he stewed over the insult, and especially when he perceived Steinway insinuating that his injury was not real. As we will see, Gould was hypochondriacal enough that even a trivial or non-existent injury could be worsened through his own anxiety about it. He always had some complaint about his musculoskeletal system; Hupfer may not have caused or even exacerbated a problem so much as *reminded* Gould of a problem, and his mind did the rest.

The timing of the incident is surely significant. The cancellation of the Australian tour had been embarrassing, and Gould was probably, at least subconsciously, looking for an excuse to back out of his planned 1960 European tour. He reported good days and bad days with his left shoulder, but the timing of those days was often suspiciously convenient. Gould cited the shoulder injury when cancelling his European tour – "the jinx which Europe has for me must still be there" – and he pointed to flare-ups of the shoulder injury when making several cancellations during the busy 1960–61 season, during which period he generally travelled with a physiotherapist in tow. He continued to cite the injury long afterwards when he wanted to bow out of a distant engagement, though despite the excuse some cancellations with orchestras in San Francisco and Seattle caused considerable acrimony. He would use the shoulder as a reason not to shake hands, attend receptions, or, frankly, to do anything else he didn't want to do.

Yet, magically, his shoulder permitted him to make a high-profile American television debut on January 31, 1960, in the CBS series *Ford Presents* as part of a program entitled "The Creative Performer," whose other guests included Igor Stravinsky and the soprano Eileen Farrell (he gave a magnificent performance of the first movement of Bach's D-minor concerto with Leonard Bernstein and the New York Philharmonic). He was also pleased, as always, to play at festivals in Vancouver and Stratford in the summer of 1960, and did so without complaint or evidence of trouble; in fact, four members of the Steinway family travelled to Stratford to hear him play. He had to cut short some studio work early in July, after making a "superb" recording of Beethoven's "Tempest" Sonata, but in September he recorded a whole album of intermezzi by Brahms, which he described as "perhaps the best piano playing I have done." He did not pass up the opportunity, in early December, to give the first public performances in Canada of Schoenberg's Piano Concerto with the Toronto Symphony, performances that led John Beckwith, in a thoughtful *Daily Star* review, to call him "the eighth wonder of the music world." In February 1961, he was well enough to give, in three concerts, a complete Beethoven cycle with the St. Louis Symphony, which included all five piano concertos (no "Emperoritis" this time) as well as the Triple Concerto for piano, violin, cello, and orchestra – his only performance of this piece.

What is not in doubt, however, is that Gould honestly *thought* he had been seriously injured: he was hypochondriacal, and could be paranoid, but he was never devious or dishonourable; not even Steinway and Sons claimed that. In the end, the lawsuit was resolved by personal arrangement between Gould and Henry Z. Steinway, then the company's president. The two were brought together in a New York hotel room in August 1961 by Schuyler Chapin, who had replaced David Oppenheim as Columbia's Masterworks director in 1959. Gould was really interested only in recovering his medical and legal expenses, which he calculated as $6,522.35 and $2,850 respectively. He did not even claim all of his physiotherapy costs: he deducted a thousand dollars to cover situations in which he had had a physiotherapist on standby and did not need him. And, over his own lawyer's objections, he made no claim for lost concert income, even though it amounted to more than twenty thousand dollars, and made no punitive claims for "pain and suffering" or "emotional distress." To their mutual relief, they made a final settlement of $9,372.35, paid to Gould on November 9, 1961, and the suit was withdrawn. To this day, what Henry Z. Steinway remembers of the whole incident is not Gould's neurotic fretting but his honesty and graciousness when it came to the settlement: he wanted only reimbursement for legitimate expenses of what he considered a real injury. Recalling the lawsuit more than thirty years after the fact, Steinway wrote, "In my opinion this settlement is entirely due to Glenn's lack of any trace of a vindictive nature, and perhaps some feeling for Steinway & Sons at least trying to satisfy his piano needs."

A September 1961 memo to all Steinway Hall personnel restored Gould's good standing with the company: "He is to be received with all the graciousness and courtesies due to any Steinway Artist," Frederick Steinway wrote. "It is absolutely paramount that there will be no handshaking or physical contact with this artist in any way whatsoever – no matter what the circumstances. The reasons for this are self evident."

"I know that no one believes me, but this will definitely be my final tour."

Gould's resentment of concert life increased through the early 1960s. He accepted fewer and fewer bookings, but still cancelled many concerts: "I don't go to concerts," he quipped, "sometimes not even to my own!" Not counting the Stratford Festival, he made only eighteen stops on his 1961–62 tour (including Chicago, where he finally played after *three* cancellations); only nine stops in 1962–63; and only three in 1963–64. Still, the pressure and drudgery of touring continued to wear him down; concert life seemed to make him pricklier and more depressed with each passing year. While he hated travelling in general, flying caused him particular concern, and not only because he was neurotic: he had experienced one or two traumatic close calls in planes, and was acutely aware of those famous musicians who had already died in plane crashes: William Kapell, Guido Cantelli, Ginette Neveu, Jacques Thibaud, Glenn Miller, Ritchie Valens, Buddy Holly. One day, in 1962, he simply said to himself, "What are you *doing*?" and never flew again. Not that he enjoyed spending hours on trains, either: travelling by rail to San Francisco, he said, "is almost as bad as crossing the Atlantic." And more than ever before, he was resenting the publicity surrounding his eccentricities; even his admirers were beginning to tire of his act.

Just five months after the Steinway Incident was resolved came the Brahms Incident, which set tongues wagging in the press once more. On April 5, 6, and 8, 1962, he was to play Brahms's monumental D-minor concerto with the New York Philharmonic under Leonard Bernstein. He had been playing the concerto in public since the

1959–60 season, though as the New York performances loomed he took to calling Bernstein to alert him that he had a highly unusual interpretation to offer. Once more he wanted to give short shrift to the competitive absurdities of concerto form by taking an determinedly "unspectacular" approach to this spectacular piece. He wanted to minimize the dramatic contrasts of piano and orchestra and of "masculine" and "feminine" themes, to play down the elevated, often tragic rhetoric of the music and the barnstorming virtuosity of the solo part. Instead, he wanted to read into the music "the analytical standpoints of our own day" – of Schoenberg. He wanted to emphasize continuity over contrast; he wanted to underscore organic connections between themes and motifs within movements, and to forge a long-range continuity between movements. (He saw the piece as "a giant fresco.") More than that, he wanted a performance based on an ethic of contemplation rather than competition – an introspective rather than merely exciting performance. To achieve these ends, he chose unusually slow tempos in all three movements, and sought to maintain those tempos consistently throughout a movement, in contrast to most performances, which underscore changes of mood and theme with fluctuating tempos. He also levelled some of Brahms's dynamic markings, and dug into the contrapuntal fabric of the music at every opportunity. The three chosen tempos, moreover, were to have a proportional relationship – one of the first important examples of Gould's use of tempo relationships to bind a whole multi-movement work together.

Bernstein had more conventional ideas about the piece, and said so, but he was willing to play it Gould's way, *pour le sport*, and instructed the orchestra accordingly. The first performance, on April 5, was a Thursday-night "Preview Concert," on which occasions Bernstein was in the habit of speaking to his audience from the podium. He had intended to talk about Nielsen's Fifth Symphony, the other work on the program, but, with Gould's consent, he instead introduced the audience to Gould's Brahms interpretation. He spoke for four minutes, with good humour, noting that he and Gould disagreed about the Brahms but that he wanted to play it Gould's way, "because Mr. Gould is so valid and serious an artist that I must take seriously anything he conceives in good faith," and because the interpretation offered all sorts of new insights into the music. He added, to general laughter, "I have only once before, in my life, had to submit to a soloist's wholly new and incompatible concept, and that was the last time I accompanied Mr. Gould." In the end, the sheer sense of adventure in Gould's interpretation convinced him that it was a worthy undertaking. Gould then walked onstage, smiling, and touched fingertips with Bernstein, then sat at the piano before his pasted-up miniature score. The audience cheered, then settled down expectantly. (That expectation is palpable in the recording of the performance made on April 6, on which occasion Bernstein repeated the speech.) At the end, fifty-three minutes later, the performers received an ovation, and Bernstein later wrote, "I never loved him more."

Everyone got the point and took it in the right spirits – except the critics. In the days that followed, Gould and Bernstein were almost universally condemned in the press – Gould for a "funereal" interpretation that arrogantly disregarded venerable traditions, Bernstein for the "betrayal" of a colleague. His remarks were widely misinterpreted and usually misquoted, and sensational accounts of the "duel" between conductor and soloist were widely reprinted, even overseas. Most damaging was Harold Schonberg's review, "Inner Voices of Glenn Gould," in the *Times*. The piece was couched in the form of a letter, in dialect, from one pianist to another: "Such goings-on at the New York Philharmonic concert yesterday after-noon! I tell you, Ossip, like you never saw . . ." Bernstein, in Schonberg's interpretation, had washed his hands of Gould's per-formance, and committed a breach of decorum by speaking out against it. He had strong words for the interpretation itself: "The Gould boy played the Brahms D minor Concerto slower than the way we used to practice it. (And between you, me and the corner lamppost, Ossip, maybe the reason he plays it so slow is maybe his technique is not so good.)" He criticized the performance for lacking power ("Once in a while maybe a forte came through"), faulted Gould for fussing inordinately with buried inner voices, and, finally, accused him of lacking professionalism. Gould's champions, and many fellow-critics, found the tone of Schonberg's review distasteful and insulting to Gould both musically and personally,* though in fact most concurred with his judgement of Bernstein's speech, and agreed that Gould's aberrant performance had been heavy and brooding, lacking grandeur, power, and vitality. The musicologist Paul Henry Lang, in the *Herald Tribune*, denounced Gould as "at present suffering from music hallucinations that make him unfit for public appearances," and Irving Kolodin, in *Saturday Review*, wrote that "Gould didn't show the breadth of pianistic style or the technical resource to play this work impressively at any tempi, even his own."

Neither Gould nor Bernstein could ever set the record straight. "We're still good friends," Gould told a reporter in Cincinnati later that year. "Bernstein showed me his notes of what he was going to say before I played. I said, 'Sure.' So he made the speech." Two years later, he told an interviewer that "we were in agreement about his speech. . . . I don't know why so many grim people got into the act." He never strayed from this line in public. Privately he came to believe that the speech had perhaps been a tactical mistake, but he insisted that it had been a mutual decision. Moreover, he told more than one friend he was charmed by the speech – it *was* charming –

---

* Gould and Schonberg had met only once, through the publicity department of Columbia Records, for what Schonberg described as a very awkward lunch that deteriorated when Gould scoffed derisively at Schonberg's interest in obscure Romantic piano fare. Gould had never been fond of Schonberg's critical style or musical tastes. After the Brahms review, he took to parodying Schonberg as "Homer Sibelius," music critic of "the *New York Square*," and he liked to circulate the old canard that Schonberg's career as a music critic was preceded by a tenure on the sports desk. In a letter to Diana Menuhin in 1966, he wrote that "anything Homer Sibelius can know about on Monday, I can know about on Sunday!"

and took the whole thing in a sporting spirit.* He wrote a program essay explaining his interpretation called "N'aimez-vous pas Brahms?" when he played the concerto, at faster tempos, in Baltimore in October 1962. Regrettably, because of the brouhaha, Schuyler Chapin cancelled a planned Columbia recording of the concerto, with the consent of Gould and Bernstein – a decision Chapin came to regret. The controversy over the Brahms concerto proved to be Gould's most unpleasant professional experience, and was a key factor in his decision to give up playing concerts for good.

"We want to try some far-out things."

Gould found more congenial and creatively fulfilling concert situations at summer festivals back home. In July 1958, he participated in the ambitious inaugural season of the Vancouver International Festival, organized by his friend Nicholas Goldschmidt. He gave three concerts: a recital, a concerto, and a mixed all-Bach program, the latter announcing a new interest in thematically unified programs that would come to dominate his festival concerts as well as his broadcasts. He returned in summer 1960 to give a recital and a two-concerto evening, in addition to which he managed to draw an audience of twelve hundred to an all-Schoenberg lecture-recital that included *The Book of the Hanging Gardens*, with the Swedish mezzo-soprano Kerstin Meyer.

---

* The two never performed together again. Gould cancelled an appearance with the New York Philharmonic in 1963, due to illness, and was replaced at the last minute by the sixteen-year-old André Watts, whose career was launched by that concert. But Gould's concert career was effectively over by this time, anyway, and this is no evidence of a permanent falling-out with Bernstein, as some have claimed. Two months after the Brahms performances, Gould was talking to Columbia about recording Strauss's *Burleske* with Bernstein, to be coupled perhaps with the *Bourgeois gentilhomme* Suite or the *Tanzsuite* after Couperin, in celebration of the Strauss centenary in 1964 (the project did not materialize). Eventually the two stopped seeing each other, but that reflects only a general thinning of Gould's circle of contacts after his retirement from concert life.

His last summer season in Vancouver, in 1961, included his two strangest evenings at the festival. On August 7, he presented "A Piano Lesson with Glenn Gould," in which he chatted and played for an hour before almost three thousand children. His talk dealt with the interpretation of a Beethoven sonata – Op. 31/No. 3, which he was performing for the first time in public – and he could not resist the urge to ham, putting on broad accents and funny hats to play French, German, and English colleagues offering their own views of the sonata. His message, that a performer should be true to *himself* before even the score or the composer, was a serious one, of great importance to him, but did six-year-olds understand it, or care? Most of the children found it funny, though the adults felt that Gould should not be encouraged along these lines. The show was broadcast on CBC television, and David Oppenheim offered to let Gould repeat the lesson for the American television series *Omnibus*, though he never did. In his last appearance at the festival, on August 9, he served as soloist, conductor, and lecturer in an all-Bach concert that included two concertos and a cantata. For this evening Gould unveiled his latest plaything: the "harpsi-piano," a small grand piano specially adapted for him by Steinway and Sons in New York. T-shaped metal pins were inserted into the piano's hammers, causing the instrument to produce a metallic twang intended to imitate the sound of the harpsichord while retaining the dynamic capabilities of the piano; Gould once described it as "a neurotic piano that *thinks* it's a harpsichord." He used this curiosity in several concerts and broadcasts in the early sixties, and for one terrifying moment considered recording all of Bach's *Well-Tempered Clavier* on a similar instrument that Columbia Records kept on hand for Rosemary Clooney, but Columbia balked and he came to his senses. For most people, the "harpsi-piano" was a great talking point, and an annoyance.

Gould's overseas touring schedule kept him from returning to the Stratford Festival until 1960. There, as in Vancouver, he said, he could "dare to try new things" (in the 1963 season, he told a reporter, he played only one work that was not new to his repertoire).

In the years since 1956 the festival had become increasingly open to experiment, and its music season had expanded to offer symphonic and choral works, early music, opera and operetta, as well as jazz and folk music. There was now a real sense of community at the festival. The turning point had come in 1959, when Louis Applebaum organized the first annual Orchestra Workshop, a group of two dozen professional instrumentalists from around North America who attended master classes and formed a core of resident musicians for the whole season. Moreover, Stratford now had a proper theatre, seating nearly 2,300, into which the music events were moved in 1960, and concerts were now permitted on Sundays.

Gould returned with a splash in 1960, playing in two chamber-music concerts with two distinguished American colleagues, the violinist Oscar Shumsky and the cellist Leonard Rose.* All three were designated "Artists-in-Residence" for the season, and in addition to performing they coached in the Orchestra Workshop; Gould was particularly enthusiastic about the sessions devoted to the performance of modern music. In his first concert, he joined Shumsky and Rose in an all-Bach program that included the D-minor clavier concerto and the Brandenburg Concerto No. 5, with Gould doing triple duty as soloist, continuo player, and conductor, all at the "harpsi-piano." Later he participated in a program of chamber music by Beethoven, of which recordings survive of the Cello Sonata in A Major, Op. 69, and the "Ghost" Trio, Op. 70/No. 1. Thanks in large part to Gould's star power, the concerts sold out. The Beethoven concert sold out weeks in advance, in fact, and more than a thousand people seeking tickets had to be turned away; Gould's friend Jim Curtis remembers standing in line for two and a half hours to get a ticket that permitted a view only of Gould's legs. "The son-of-a-gun sure sells tickets," one of Gould's associates said, and that

---

* A 1959 letter from Applebaum to Walter Homburger reveals that Gould had suggested playing a concert in 1960 "in duet with Van Cliburn," but it did not materialize. Later, he gave Cliburn a standing invitation to give a concert at Stratford – "the zanier the better."

would remain true throughout his tenure at Stratford; when he did not perform, the theatre was often only half full. The public response to the concerts was wildly enthusiastic, though there were a few dissenting voices – people who hated the "harpsi-piano," who found his vocalizing and other mannerisms intrusive, who thought his interpretations odd. The concerts in which Gould participated were always dominated by his personality, and every summer there were critics who noted that he tended to overwhelm his partners in chamber music.

Applebaum retired from administrative duties after the 1960 season, and Gould, Shumsky, and Rose agreed to return to the Festival in 1961 with a new joint title, "Directors of Music," which they would hold through 1964. (His fee for 1961 was $7,000.) It is difficult to imagine Gould as an administrator, helping to deal with quotidian matters like scheduling, women's committees, and the press, but he did just that, and his willingness says much about his commitment to Stratford. He helped raise funds to restore one of the Festival's theatres, weighed in on such matters as whether "God Save the Queen" should be played, and sought out new repertoire and guest artists, soliciting some of the leading composers of the day: Britten, Shostakovich, Lukas Foss, Karl Amadeus Hartmann, Hans Werner Henze. Ezra Schabas found Gould "rude and close to dictatorial" as an administrator, however, especially when he confronted some difference of opinion. Schabas actually quit his position as music manager after the 1961 season because of Gould, and there was always some tension in Gould's relationship with Shumsky and Rose.

Gould continued to perform – three concerts in 1961, with Shumsky and Rose, each devoted to a single composer: chamber music by Brahms; concertos by Bach, on the "harpsi-piano," as well as Cantata 51, with Lois Marshall; and an eclectic program of works by Richard Strauss, including the Violin Sonata in E-flat Major, Op. 18, as well as a set of songs and the ravishing closing scene from Strauss's last opera, *Capriccio*, with soprano Ellen Faull. (*Capriccio* had "possessed" him, he said, since he saw a production of it in Berlin in 1957.) Gould opened both halves of the Strauss concert with lengthy remarks from the stage, which, to judge from the reviews, were relaxingly informal but often impenetrable (one reviewer found them "coy and forced"). He ranged widely, from Strauss's skill in musical characterization, to his "subtle contemporizing" of eighteenth-century idioms, to the overall motivic unity in some of his operas, and he briefly sang Elektra to Faull's Chrysothemis to make a certain point because, he joked, "the budget could not afford another singer."

This concert was one of the first shots in Gould's career-long campaign for the music of Strauss, which he championed in concerts, recordings, television and radio programs, and published writings and interviews for the rest of his life. In those days, the heyday of serialism, Strauss's reputation was much in decline, especially among young musicians, and it was provocative to declare, as Gould did at Stratford, that Strauss was "the greatest man of music of this century." But he always hated the "snob culture" of the avant-garde, the competitive jockeying for position, and rejected the notions of "progress" and "fashion" in art so common among the "'ism'-devotees" of his day. (For another Stratford concert, in 1963, he organized a program that polemically juxtaposed music by Schoenberg and Strauss.) The calendar was a tyrant, he liked to say, and should be ignored: music was good, or great, or bad, without regard for whether it is fashionable, and he (correctly) predicted that Strauss's musical reputation would rise again when the fashions of the post-war years no longer pertained. At the time, he was a lone voice. John Beckwith spoke for many young colleagues when he wrote, in 1962, "Seeing Glenn Gould through his current Richard Strauss phase is for the Canadian public a little like seeing a difficult child through mumps."

As Gould's concert career declined, his enthusiasm for Stratford increased, as did his talent for arousing controversy. In 1962, he played, lectured, and wrote program notes for a series of thematically unified concerts, the first of which was devoted to Bach. Before the last number, instrumental arrangements of pieces from *The Art of Fugue*, he gave a speech in which he criticized the custom of automatic applause at concerts, which he derided as immoral and insincere – "an easily induced mob reaction" – and considered particularly inappropriate after such esoteric fare. He requested that the audience refrain from responding, and, to emphasize his point, had the lights dimmed to black during the final phrases of the last fugue. He had a point: applause after *The Art of Fugue* is like a cheery curtain call after a late play by Beckett. But the audience was startled by the request, and, though most complied with it, the result was not the reverent silence Gould had wanted, but tittering, nervous coughs, and embarrassed shuffling. As early as age sixteen, he had wanted to found his own concert society in which all audience responses be forbidden – shades of the Society for Private Musical Performances that Schoenberg ran just after the First World War. "Some artists seem to place too much reliance on the sweaty mass response of the moment," he told a *Globe and Mail* interviewer a few months later. "Applause tells me nothing. Like any other artist, I can always pull off a few musical tricks at the end of a performance and the decibel count will automatically go up ten points." (In a 1962 article, "Let's Ban Applause!" he unveiled the "Gould Plan for the Abolition of Applause and Demonstrations of All Kinds.") He received sixty letters about the Bach concert, half of which were supportive, and only one of which was abusive, but many people were becoming fed up with his antics. The composer Udo Kasemets wrote in the *Toronto Daily Star* that he had once "believed that some day the pampered wonder-boy would grow up and concentrate on straight and honest music-making. Time has proved me wrong. Glenn Gould has changed indeed, but the change has been for worse."

Gould wrote program notes for "The Schoenberg Heritage," a concert of music by Schoenberg, Webern, and Foss given in 1962, and performed in two more concerts devoted to favourite composers: "Hindemith – The Early Years," in which he joined Lois Marshall in a triumphant performance of the 1923 version of *Das Marienleben*; and an all-Mendelssohn concert, which included the Piano Trio in D Minor, and in which he knocked his ever-present glass of water onto the keyboard, to general hilarity. His sympathy for this often-sentimental early-Romantic fare came as a pleasant surprise to many people, though Kasemets noted that "Mendelssohn occupies a very special place in Anglo-Saxon hearts" and criticized the all-Mendelssohn program as akin to "reviving the spirit of artistic colonialism that still has a frightening grip on our country and population" – which goes to show how insecure Canada's independent identity remained in some quarters even a few years before the country's Centennial.

Gould once praised the Festival Theatre's three-sided stage because its intimacy "brings out the ham in me," but there was too much ham for most tastes in his last concert of the 1962 season. "Panorama of Music of the 20's" would prove to be the strangest public appearance of his life. He did not play at all in the first half; instead, he served as master of ceremonies and comedian. He strode onto the stage dressed, according to one review, "in baggy beige plus-fours, knee-high olive-green socks, and a black cloth cap. He straddled a chair, cupped his head in his hands, and said: 'You didn't expect music, did you? . . . My name is Plummer.'" That got a laugh – Christopher Plummer was playing Cyrano at Stratford that summer – but then Gould launched into a long lecture on music in the twenties, contrasting the "significant" trends (the Schoenberg school) with the neo-Classical music that he considered sterile and trivial, particularly that of Stravinsky. He left the performing to others, "partly because I'm lazy and partly because I'm proud." Many beyond the front rows could not hear him, and grew frustrated, while those who *could* hear were put off by his tart comments and pompous manner. Everyone quickly grew tired of his shenanigans. During the performance of Stravinsky's *Rag-time* he sprawled across the closed piano lid, produced a bottle from his pocket, and took a sip, remarking, "Purely medicinal!" Before the first half was over, people began to walk out – one by one at first, then en masse. Those who remained, by one account, expressed their displeasure through "impatient rhythmic applause." The walk-outs rattled Gould, but his apology to the weary crowd fell on deaf ears. Joyce Goodman, in the *Montreal Star*, recorded this uncomfortable exchange:

Suddenly a masculine voiced boomed from the balcony, "We still can't hear you." (A feminine voice had lodged the same complaint during the first half of the program.)

Mr. Gould apologized and said, "I'm tired."

"So are we," answered the voice.

Even after Gould retired through a trap door in the stage, audience members continued to leave, and the performers grew increasingly flustered. At the end of William Walton's *Façade*, he reappeared through the trap door dressed in a huge raccoon coat that had belonged to his grandfather, and bearing a sign that announced intermission. On the lawns outside the theatre, the audience – what remained of it – was abuzz over the antics, and many did not return. But for the second half Gould changed into formal attire and played Schoenberg's Suite and Berg's concert aria *Der Wein*, with the soprano Ilona Kombrink, and these performances, introduced only with brief, impromptu remarks, were received with great enthusiasm. The press reacted without mercy – Gould's behaviour was "infantile," "unethical," "insultingly unfair" – and Gould's fellow-directors were reportedly miffed. "I agree that the 'Music of the 20's' episode was a complete disaster," he later told the *Globe and Mail*. "It all looked marvellous on paper" – it did? – "but it simply didn't come off." Six years later, on CBC radio, he referred to that "crazy afternoon" as the first-ever "happening" in Southern Ontario. "And, although I couldn't really encourage experiment along quite such kooky lines, I hope that some sense of [the] excitement that sponsored experiments of that kind will not ever be lost at Stratford."

Gould performed only twice at the 1963 festival, first in another all-Bach concert that included the Clavier Concerto No. 6 in F Major (which he never recorded) and Cantata 170; once more he conducted from the keyboard, though he finally traded in his "harpsi-piano" for a real harpsichord. Three weeks later he participated in an uncharacteristic program covering about a hundred years of Romantic and modern songs and chamber music by Russian composers: Glinka, Musorgsky, Prokofiev. He was scheduled also to accompany the soprano Phyllis Curtin in a performance of songs by Dowland, Schoenberg, Mozart, and Strauss, but came down with the flu and was replaced. For the first time, he left Stratford without committing to any future concerts at the festival.

"I enjoy recording more than any other phase of making music."

The decline of Gould's concert schedule was due in part to his growing insistence on exploring his potential in other fields – as a recording artist, broadcaster, writer, composer – and as the number of his concerts plummeted his work in these fields achieved new sophistication. As long as he was a busy concert artist he was a rather conventional recording artist, sticking close to his concert repertoire and concert interpretations. He had not the time nor energy to develop new repertoire for recordings, and Columbia Records was not averse to albums forged out of the music with which he had had success in concerts. The albums released during his first eight years as a Columbia artist, with only minor exceptions, document the same Glenn Gould that concert audiences came to know:

- Bach, Goldberg Variations (recorded in 1955/released in 1956).
- Beethoven, Piano Sonatas Nos. 30 in E Major, Op. 109; 31 in A-flat Major, Op. 110; 32 in C Minor, Op. 111 (1956/1956).
- Bach, Clavier Concerto No. 1 in D Minor; Beethoven, Piano Concerto No. 2 in B-flat Major, Op. 19, with Leonard Bernstein, Columbia Symphony (1957/1957).
- Bach, Partitas Nos. 5 in G Major and 6 in E Minor; Fugues Nos. 14 in F-sharp Minor and 9 in E Major from Book Two of *The Well-Tempered Clavier* (1956–57/1957).
- Haydn, Sonata No. 59 in E-flat Major; Mozart, Sonata No. 10 in C Major, K. 330; Mozart, Fantasia and Fugue in C Major, K. 394 (1958/1958).

- Bach, Clavier Concerto No. 5 in F Minor; Beethoven, Piano Concerto No. 1 in C Major, Op. 15, with Vladimir Golschmann, Columbia Symphony (1958/1958).
- Berg, Sonata, Op. 1; Schoenberg, Three Piano Pieces, Op. 11; Krenek, Sonata No. 3, Op. 92/No. 4 (1958/1959).
- Beethoven, Piano Concerto No. 3 in C Minor, Op. 37, with Leonard Bernstein, Columbia Symphony (1959/1960).
- Bach, Partitas Nos. 1 in B-flat Major and 2 in C Minor; Italian Concerto (1959/1960).
- Gould, String Quartet, Op. 1, with the Symphonia Quartet (1960/1960).
- Brahms, Ten Intermezzi (1959–60/1961).
- Beethoven, Piano Concerto No. 4 in G Major, Op. 58, with Leonard Bernstein, New York Philharmonic (1961/1961).
- Bach, *The Art of Fugue*, Volume 1: Contrapunctus 1–9, on the organ (1962/1962).
- Mozart, Piano Concerto No. 24 in C Minor, K. 491, with Walter Susskind, CBC Symphony; Schoenberg, Piano Concerto, Op. 42, with Robert Craft, CBC Symphony (1961/1962).
- Strauss, *Enoch Arden*, with Claude Rains, speaker (1961/1962).
- Bach, Partitas Nos. 3 and 4; Toccata in E Minor (1962–63/1963).

Eight of these albums featured Gould's own liner notes, which he was particularly fond of writing in his early years. Whether discussing the repertoire at hand, championing or denigrating some cause, tackling some historical or stylistic issue, or explaining the premises behind his own interpretation, the Gould liner note was inevitably stimulating and usually provocative, if often unappealingly baroque in style. All of his albums sold unusually well, if not at the level of the Goldberg Variations – and some of them, like his first concerto album, became bona fide hits.

But for all their commercial success, and artistic brilliance and originality, these recordings did not long satisfy Gould; by the end of his life, he found "many of my earlier recordings" – including the greatest of them – "very irritating to listen to." He was disenchanted with the "performance-oriented" nature of the recordings, the way in which he had transplanted his concert interpretations wholesale into the recording studio without making allowances for the medium itself; in other words, these were not recordings by a real *recording artist*, offering interpretations prepared especially for the recording medium and crafted to the highest technological standards. Gould was more interested in the process of mechanics of recording than were most classical artists, even as a young man, and moved easily in that realm. But his concert schedule simply did not permit close involvement with post-production or development of a real aesthetic of recording. Early recording sessions had to be fitted into his concert schedule. By his later standards, these recordings were made very quickly, whole albums in just two or three or four days. Some of his early recordings even include uncorrected errors of the sort he would never have let by in later years, evidence of the hopeless task of trying to make corrections by international telegram.* Once he recalled regenerating a segment of tape in a Mozart rondo because he had a train to catch.

Nevertheless, these first albums did show off the full range of his pianistic talent in his twenties. His dynamic Bach style was the real revelation for most of his early listeners, of course, yet his other albums from this period include some performances that he never surpassed. Consider his rococo delicacy in Mozart's K. 330 and his hard-as-nails potency in the K. 394 fugue, his vital, witty Haydn, his passionately argued program of Berg, Schoenberg, and Krenek, which made a compelling case for the Second Viennese School – the Krenek, in particular, would remain one of Gould's richest and most beautiful recordings. His unabashedly Romantic reading of Schoenberg's concerto, with a superb accompaniment by Robert

---

* Two examples, from Bach: a flubbed bass entrance (bar 25) in the Fugue in C Minor from Book One of *The Well-Tempered Clavier*; and a dropped note (melody, bar 178) in the finale of the Italian Concerto – one of his most brilliant recordings.

Craft (whom he greatly admired), is both poetic and dramatically charged, and his surprisingly powerful reading of Mozart's K. 491 concerto,* despite some controversial embellishments to the score, impressed the conservative critic B. H. Haggin so much that he called it "one of the greatest performances I have ever heard."

Gould's recording of the first part of *The Art of Fugue* marked his public return to the organ after almost fifteen years. The recording was (mostly) made on a new, Baroquish Casavant organ at All Saints' Church (Kingsway), in Toronto, though at least one fugue was recorded later, in a chapel in New York. Gould loved the Casavant's "gloriously eccentric registration." His organ style – fast, loud, highly articulate, monotonal, closely miked – was an implicit challenge to the lush Romantic organ and the reverberant acoustics of most organ recordings, but the album had many admirers as well as detractors. Gould enjoyed the experience enough to talk of making other organ albums, even one a year, of works like sonatas by Mendelssohn and Krenek, and Schoenberg's *Variations on a Recitative*. In the end, though, he did not even record Volume 2 of *The Art of Fugue*, despite plans as early as mid-1962. For one thing, he said that playing the organ had exacerbated his "never too dormant shoulder trouble," and in 1966 the Casavant he so loved was destroyed in a fire.

His patience with concert life waning in the early sixties, Gould began to explore new repertoire in the recording studio. As his first

---

* In his liner notes Gould refers to K. 491 as "not a very successful concerto," and in 1974 he told an interviewer that it was "the only Mozart concerto that I've recorded because it's the only one that I sort of halfway like." In 1959 he had spoken of wanting to do an album of Mozart concertos with a chamber orchestra and without a conductor, as Serkin and Bernstein and others had done – a "relaxed and informal" approach – and at one point, to John Roberts, he hinted that he might even record *all* of Mozart's concertos. He had studied the "Coronation," K. 537, and other of the concertos under Guerrero. During his concert days he and Homburger announced on several occasions that he was willing to program the G-major and A-major concertos, K. 453 and 488, respectively. In 1970 he talked about performing the C-major concerto, K. 503, on television. But in the end, he never performed or recorded any Mozart concerto but K. 491.

ten albums had been devoted to Bach and to Classical and modern music, many fans were surprised when he produced two albums of late-Romantic music in a new though still highly individual style. His album of ten intermezzi by Brahms, one of the glories of his discography, offered a survey of a repertoire he loved but had only sampled in concerts. Gould had mixed feelings about Brahms's piano music. He deplored the "mechanistic" virtuosity of the great variations sets, but admired the "remarkable gentleness and restraint" in the late, shorter pieces. In his Brahms album, he favoured the most intimate of the intermezzi, and played them, he told an interviewer, "as though I were really playing for myself, but left the door open." The album offered "the sexiest interpretation of Brahms intermezzi you have ever heard," he added. "I have captured, I think, an atmosphere of improvisation which I don't believe has ever been represented in a Brahms recording before." The album recalls the free, flexible style of earlier generations of pianists to a surprising degree. Gould described his style not just as "sexy" but as "aristocratic," a style in which "the Teutonic element is left in abeyance." Perhaps he meant "old-fashioned," for like the Romantic pianists of yore he plays here impulsively, with great rhythmic power and freedom (and often slow tempos), pushes and pulls the music, dynamically as well as rhythmically, to expressive effect, with great attention to tone colour, and arpeggiates chords pervasively in the process of digging into Brahms's counterpoint; moreover, he creates an atmosphere of nostalgia and melancholy, of very personal and intimate communion. The album was widely praised but had detractors who scoffed at Gould's unabashed and bygone Romanticism: John Beckwith, in the *Toronto Daily Star*, dismissed it as "sloppily reminiscent of suppermusic," and another critic remarked, skeptically, "Perhaps Gould believes this is the way Brahms may have played these pieces." But Gould was right. The pianist Moriz Rosenthal, a pupil of Liszt, once recalled that Brahms always arpeggiated chords when playing his music, and Brahms himself wrote of his B-minor intermezzo, Op. 119/No. 1, not only that it must be played slowly (it is marked *Adagio*) but that "every measure and every note must sound like a *ritardando*" – a request for the most exaggerated, aching sort of Romantic expression.

Even more unexpected was Gould's recording, with the actor Claude Rains, of Strauss's early drawing-room piece *Enoch Arden*, a melodrama for speaker and piano, consisting of Tennyson's poem with musical accompaniment. Gould himself wrote that it contains "Strauss's most uncomfortably sentimental music," but he played it with great feeling and with real understanding of its late-Romantic idiom.

These albums should not really have surprised anyone familiar with Gould's concert performances and other recordings, for the Romantic was never far from the surface, even in his high-modernist Bach (the sarabandes, for instance). Many critics noted his tendency toward effusive expression and Romantic performance practices in, for instance, the slow movements of Beethoven's concertos and late sonatas. In such works – Op. 109 and the G-major concerto come to mind – Gould's flexibility of texture and rhythm, his impulsiveness, and what one critic called his "swooning sensuality" were, by the standards of his day, throwbacks to another era, melodrama that was unfashionable in the mid-twentieth century.

Indeed, his highly anticipated follow-up to the Goldberg Variations, an album of Beethoven's three last sonatas, was widely regarded as a disappointment. Harold Schonberg, in the *New York Times*, condemned the performances as "immature" and "inexplicable," and he was not alone. Many listeners were disturbed by Gould's often unconventional tempos – in the variation finale of Op. 109, or in the first movement of Op. 111, with its admittedly thrilling, damn-the-torpedoes forward momentum* – and there were all sorts of quirky, melodramatic turns of phrases and departures from the score. (In his concerts, Op. 109 was often conspicuous in its failure to please.) Many were further enraged by Gould's irreverent liner notes, in which he suggested that these cherished pieces perhaps "do

---

* Of this first movement Gould once said to John Beckwith, "It's such a bad piece; I want to get on to the finale."

not yield the apocalyptic disclosures that have been so graphically ascribed to them." The critic Abram Chasins, in his book *Speaking of Pianists* . . ., was moved to sarcasm. "There was a time," he wrote, "when we were deluded into believing that these sonatas were full of profound and inspiring ideas. I blush to remember how hood-winked we were in our youth, especially by a wily old fox named Schnabel, and we are no end grateful to Mr. Gould for awakening us to Schnabel's sharp practices."

Yet even this album received more than a little gushing praise from reputable quarters, and indeed the reviews of Gould in his first decade as a recording artist closely matched those of Gould the concert artist; here, too, it is mere legend that his evident eccentric-ities seriously undermined his appeal. The majority of his listeners willingly followed him as he sought new interpretive paths through familiar repertoire, and few felt that his idiosyncracies outweighed his merits. The late-Beethoven and Brahms and Strauss albums all received many flattering reviews, and his organ recording, which has a reputation of having been trashed in its day, received many posi-tive, high-profile reviews from critics who found his playing style buoyant, stimulating, brilliant, transparent, and a refreshing change from Romantic clichés. As he did in concert, he was able to win over listeners who disagreed with some or many or even all of his inter-pretive choices if they considered his approach worth listening to. Most of his audience was persuaded by his conviction about his own positions, and they enjoyed performances in which they could never be sure what lay around the next corner. He was noted for "individ-uality" more often than for "eccentricity," and in his early days, at least, his eccentricities were most often interpreted as evidence of serious commitment, not mere whim.

"I, myself, have been Bernsteining in all directions."

"From the moment I began broadcasting," Gould said in 1980, "that medium seemed like another world." But through the 1950s his broadcasting, like his recording, was mostly an adjunct to his concert life. His first decade's worth of broadcasts, on both radio and television, was limited mostly to straight studio performances or live-concert broadcasts, and while some were devoted to single composers or repertoires, he was not yet crafting the sort of sophisticated theme concerts he enjoyed organizing at summer festivals. He appeared in a variety of music series on both the English and French networks of CBC radio and television, and was a popular subject for interviews and profiles. The first important broadcast portrait was *At Home with Glenn Gould*, an hour-long, wide-ranging, unscripted (though edited) conversation with Vincent Tovell, which first aired in December 1959. His television broadcasts, of course, went out live to air until the early sixties; however, by the mid-fifties the CBC was pre-taping some of its radio-music programs, though it would be some years more before they made provisions for corrective tape-editing.

His early broadcasting repertoire hewed closely to the solo works and concertos of his concert repertoire, but there were some noteworthy departures: sonatas by Scarlatti, fugues from *The Well-Tempered Clavier*, a wider range of solo works by Beethoven, Schoenberg's *The Book of the Hanging Gardens* (with Roma Butler), and chamber music by Beethoven, Schubert, and Brahms. To some extent he was trapped within the confines of his concert reputation – as a Bach player, above all – and he increasingly resented it. When he was to appear on CBC television's *Chrysler Festival*, in 1957, he decided, as he later told an interviewer, "that it would be very great fun if I could make my reappearance as a Chopin player," his usual fare seeming too severe for a popular variety show aimed at the widest TV audience. He devised a little speech, too: "Ladies and gentlemen, there have been nasty rumours going around that because I do not play Chopin I *cannot* play Chopin, and tonight, once and for all, I intend to *prove* that I cannot play Chopin." His plan was to play an "old warhorse," the Waltz in A Minor, Op. 34/No. 2, "in the schmaltziest fashion I could devise," to which end he dug out Horowitz's classic 1945 recording and "copied all the rubatos." The producer was on board, but in the end the sponsor's agent objected: they wanted something more associated with Gould. And so he dropped Chopin and played . . . Bach.

"I do some of my happiest playing on TV," he said, and CBC television, which became a truly nationwide network in the summer of 1958, did much to establish his Canadian reputation. In the early sixties he began to do more ambitious projects for television, moving beyond the filmed-concert format to develop theme programs – perhaps inspired by his Stratford Festival experiments – that included staged spoken commentary.* In those days, there were producers interested in making serious, innovative classical-musical programs, and there was money to support them – enough, in fact, to make the prime minister complain of "hog-wild spending" by the CBC. Also in the early sixties, television made the transition from live broadcasting to pre-taping. At first, pre-taped programs still had to be shot in large segments – a whole movement of a sonata, for instance – and fine tape-editing was not an option. Still, for Gould this development was crucial: it permitted him to put together programs that would be too complicated to risk undertaking live. Before he was thirty years old, he would be acknowledged as a pioneer among broadcasting musicians.

He made a breakthrough with his first talk-and-play special, *The Subject Is Beethoven*, taped in 1960 and broadcast on February 6,

---

* One particularly promising theme program, alas, never got made. In the late fifties a CBC producer had the bright idea of bringing Gould together with Toronto's other world-class pianist, Oscar Peterson. Both men jumped at the idea, and plans were formulated for a ninety-minute show involving classical music and jazz, with each pianist performing solo, in a small ensemble, and with full orchestra, and swapping ideas in conversation. A taping date of April 26, 1960, was set, but because of persistent scheduling problems with both Gould and Peterson, the show never materialized. Every few years – as late as May 1982 – the CBC approached Gould with new plans for a televised Gould-Peterson summit, either a talk-and-play show or a joint interview, but while he remained interested he never committed. Peterson told Timothy Maloney that Gould did not show up at an appointed meeting for the original 1960 show, and offered no explanation; Peterson was miffed, and was less disposed to working with Gould after that. Curiously, though the two pianists lived in the same city, and admired each other, they never met.

1961. He spoke briefly about Beethoven – he worked hard on his script – gave an exciting performance of the "Eroica" Variations, and joined Leonard Rose in the Op. 69 cello sonata. The producer, Franz Kraemer, had heard them play the sonata at Stratford and insisted that they commit their interpretation to tape. Good thing: it may be the finest chamber-music collaboration in which Gould ever participated. Rose recalled, more than twenty years later, that his music stand proved to be a problem for the cameramen at the rehearsal. He had the sonata memorized, but, he told Kraemer, "Glenn is using the music." Gould jumped in at once: "Leonard, do you want to play it from memory? I'll play it with you from memory tomorrow." And he did. The show attracted a great deal of attention. Some critics thought Gould's commentary verbose and pompous, but the show also earned some glowing reviews, and it prompted many enthusiastic letters to the CBC and to Toronto newspapers; it was so popular that it was repeated later in the season, and was seen by more than a million people.

Impressed by the success of *The Subject Is Beethoven*, the CBC offered Gould a contract to create four more hour-long television specials. He was given *carte blanche* as to subject, repertoire, script, and collaborators, and the network invested generously: the last of the four shows cost about thirty thousand dollars. Gould created two Sunday-afternoon specials in early 1962: *Music in the U.S.S.R.*, and *Glenn Gould on Bach*. In the first show, he lectured from the keyboard on Russian music of the nineteenth and twentieth centuries, gave his first preserved performance of Prokofiev's Seventh Sonata, and, with the Symphonia Quartet, offered sensitive readings of several movements from Shostakovich's Piano Quintet, his only performance of music by that composer. In the second show, another Stratford-inspired program, he opened by playing the "St. Anne" Prelude and Fugue on an organ, and spoke at length about Bach's style and place in music history. Moving to the "harpsi-piano," he played Contrapunctus 4 from *The Art of Fugue*, then conducted (from the keyboard) a string orchestra in a moving if stylistically eccentric performance of Cantata 54, *Widerstehe doch der Sünde*, with the

American counter-tenor Russell Oberlin, and the Brandenburg Concerto No. 5, with Oscar Shumsky on the solo-violin part. His third program, *Richard Strauss: A Personal View*, broadcast in October 1962, was a sort of replay of his all-Strauss Stratford concert of the previous year, and once again his performances, including the first movement of the Violin Sonata (with Shumsky), songs with Lois Marshall, and music from the *Bourgeois gentilhomme* Suite, illustrated a polemical defence of Strauss's style. "I've always been addicted to his music the way some people are addicted to chocolate sundaes," he said. "I find it absolutely irresistible."

The final program of his contract, *The Anatomy of Fugue*, broadcast in March 1963, was his most ambitious. In one hour, he tried to cram in a comprehensive primer and history of the fugue, including music by de Lassus, Marenzio, Bach, Mozart, Beethoven, and Hindemith. He performed along with a handful of colleagues and talked at length at the keyboard, his musical examples including a brief stab at a fugue based on "Do Re Mi" from *The Sound of Music*, and a contrapuntal marriage of "The Star-Spangled Banner" and "God Save the Queen." The program was a tour de force for Gould even without its finale: the premiere of his own composition, *So You Want to Write a Fugue?** – a clever five-minute fugue, itself a capsule primer and history of the genre, scored for vocal quartet and string quartet and set to a comic text of Gould's own devising. (Typical line: "But never be clever for the sake of being clever, for a canon in inversion is a dangerous diversion . . .")

These specials had no precedents in Canada, and very few

---

* Gould's first sketches for *So You Want to Write a Fugue?* date from 1958. That year, in the *Globe Magazine*, it was noted, "This summer he worked feverishly on a 90-minute program for the CBC called History of the Fugue from the Sixteenth Century to the Present Day. The program is being recorded slowly, [and] will probably be broadcast some time next year. . . . The windup piece on the program is something tantalizingly called 'So you want to write a fugue?' Gould grins about it, [and] says it will probably sound a little jazzy." Why his work on the program was interrupted is a mystery.

anywhere else. Of course Gould knew Leonard Bernstein's ambitious, acclaimed, high-profile educational programs for the CBS cultural series *Omnibus*, the first of which aired in the fall of 1954, and his broadcasts of the New York Philharmonic's *Young People's Concerts*, also on CBS, beginning in 1958. For *Omnibus* especially, Bernstein covered a wide range of topics – Beethoven's Fifth Symphony, jazz, conducting, American musical comedies, modern music, Bach – and he, too, had a didactic bent that led him to supplement his performances with generous commentary. (Tom Wolfe once dubbed him a "village explainer.") But Bernstein tried hard to appeal to the broadest audience, including children, while Gould, though he consulted a little with Bernstein on some of his television projects, acknowledged that his programs might not appeal to the masses.

Gould's subjects, for one thing, tended to be more highfalutin than Bernstein's, inherently difficult for the average TV viewer. And unlike the extroverted Bernstein, Gould did not, in those days, have a knack for talking clearly and plainly about classical music for non-professional viewers. He could not tailor his prose to suit his audience, and aside from the odd flippant or slangy remark, his texts were often too technical and long-winded, written in that peculiar, knotty Gouldese that is often difficult to assimilate at spoken tempo – especially as Gould's spoken tempo tended to be rather brisk – with its endless subordinate clauses, digressions, asides, and odd turns of phrase. Two of the local headlines after *The Anatomy of Fugue* read: "Glenn Gould: Talk, Talk, Talk" and "Anatomy of English Might Aid Glenn Gould." Even Eric Till, who produced the show, claimed he didn't understand much of what Gould was saying. Bernstein talked just as much as Gould, but so accessibly that no one minded. Moreover, Gould lacked Bernstein's ease and charm on camera; he was more nervous, and often seemed not to know quite what to do with his arms and legs. His insecurity showed in his tendency to veer toward the pompous in his commentary – thrusting out his chest and strutting professorially with his hands in his jacket pockets. Some of his theatrics – in the Russian show, wandering about a large space and pouring tea out of a samovar – seemed contrived, and he failed to sound natural and spontaneous while reading from a teleprompter.

Still, Gould was making innovative and provocative television, and his ambitions extended far beyond the often inane classical-music programming of his day. He derided the sort of program in which, say, the Marlboro Festival crowd "all sit around telling each other how much they love music." (Think *Live from Lincoln Center* on PBS.) He was fascinated by the medium of television, and he *believed* in it, as he believed in radio and recording, mostly because, in his view, it vitiated the need for concerts. As he told a reporter in 1962, "When Aunt Minnie can turn on her four-screen television and watch the Berlin Philharmonic we will have reached total inwardness on the part of the audience." He dreamed of being a TV director himself, and artistically, at least, he exercised authority over even his first specials. Eric Till told a reporter, "The producers, like myself, who were assigned to the show, were there simply as a service to Gould. We had no creative part in the show."

His literary limitations notwithstanding, Gould *wanted* to talk, to proselytize, to explore issues, not simply perform. There was not a great deal of room for talk in *The Subject Is Beethoven*, but in *The Anatomy of Fugue* the music is there to illustrate the commentary, not the reverse. Gould wanted, in fact, to make programs in which he did not perform at all. In radio that breakthrough came early, in June 1961, when he was commissioned to create a program about Schoenberg. His two-hour documentary *Arnold Schoenberg: The Man Who Changed Music*, a sophisticated mélange of interviews and recorded music, was broadcast on August 8, 1962, and enjoyed considerable success. It was Gould's apprenticeship in a genre in which, after he had left concert life behind, he would do some of his most creatively stimulating work.

"I really would like the last half of my life to myself."

On Thanksgiving weekend, 1959, Gould gave two concerts with the Cleveland Orchestra, performing Schoenberg's Piano Concerto and Bach's Brandenburg Concerto No. 5, neither one a staple of the concert repertoire then or now. He wrote a three-thousand-word program note about the Schoenberg, and while he was in town delivered, without notes, a forty-five-minute lecture on Schoenberg for the orchestra's women's committee, on the same program as the American premiere of his String Quartet. Everyone was duly impressed by the range of his talents, and he was clearly in his element, but he had little opportunity for such stimulating events in his regular concert season. It was predictable that his excitement over creative experiments in radio and television in the early sixties would make him increasingly less patient with concert life, in which he could find no artistic fulfillment. "I want some time for thinking," he would say when explaining his desire to retire from concerts. By the time of *The Subject Is Beethoven* and *Arnold Schoenberg: The Man Who Changed Music*, to say nothing of his increasingly wide-ranging work for Columbia Records, it was clear that the kind of media work he wanted to do was too ambitious to be fitted into the cracks of a concert schedule.

Gould was announcing as early as 1962 that he would quit for good, probably around 1964, and his reduced bookings and increased cancellations should have tipped people off; in fact, he had been announcing his desire to quit since he had first become a professional performer, before he had even left Canada. Few people really believed him, and most were surprised, even stunned, and certainly disappointed when he finally did so. On the evening of Friday, April 10, 1964, Gould gave a recital at the Wilshire Ebell Theater in Los Angeles, a rescheduled concert he had earlier cancelled. He played four fugues from *The Art of Fugue*, Bach's Partita No. 4 in D Major, Beethoven's Op. 109, and Hindemith's Third Sonata, and was still impressing critics with his repertoire, technique, poetic sensibility, and musical insight. The near-capacity audience was as enthusiastic as ever, and both the public and critics forgave his eccentricities on the basis of his playing.

He had one more concert booked: Mozart's C-minor concerto in Minneapolis, on April 17. But he cancelled, and never gave a concert again.

Opposite: Gould in a CBC radio studio in the late 1960s, around the time of his first "contrapuntal radio documentaries," *The Idea of North* and *The Latecomers*. *(Photograph by Herb Nott. CBC Still Photo Collection.)*

PART FOUR

RENAISSANCE MAN

A Higher Calling, 1964–75

**"I have been announcing my retirement every year
since I was 15. This time I might just pull it off."**

Some time in the early sixties Gould seems to have decided to give
up his concert career at the end of the 1963–64 season. Verna Post
(née Sandercock) recalls that he was taking no bookings beyond
1964 when she left Walter Homburger's office in 1961. But there
would be no farewell tour, and he did not announce that his recital
in Los Angeles in 1964 would be his last concert. At first, in fact, he
implied he would still give concerts from time to time. Walter
Homburger – presumably on Gould's authority – advertised "very
limited availability" for the 1964–65 season, and tentatively booked
a few concerts as late as 1966. Gould referred to 1965 as a mere "sabbatical" year, and talked of perhaps giving concerts again after a
break of, say, five years, but he was just letting his fans down easy:
he probably knew in Los Angeles that his concert career was over.

He did not retire because he wanted for opportunities or appreciation. He ranked among the handful of most admired and most
discussed classical pianists in the world; few if any classical musicians
have made so powerful and widespread an impact while so stingily
rationing their public appearances. He gave fewer than two hundred
concerts in his life – that was two years' touring for Van Cliburn or

1

(1) Glenn at seven-and-a-half months of age, with the Shipman children – today, Ruth Morawetz and Dr. William Shipman – who lived next door at 34 Southwood Drive. This photograph appeared on a Christmas card that the Goulds sent out in 1933. *(Ruth Morawetz.)*

(2) Glenn as a toddler, and the signature he wrote on the back of this photograph. Originally he spelled his surname "Gold"; at some later date, a *u* was crudely inserted, by him or by someone else, to make "Gould." *(Uxbridge-Scott Township Museum and Archives.)*

2

(**3**) The Gould family home at 32 Southwood Drive. *(Photograph by Alex Schultz.)*

(**4**) Glenn with his maternal grand-mother, Mary Catherine Greig (née Flett). "As soon as he was old enough to be held on his grandmother's knee at the piano," Gould's father recalled, "he would never pound the keyboard as most children will, with the whole hand, striking a number of keys at a time; instead he would always insist on pressing down a single key and holding it down until the resulting sound had completely died away. The fading vibration entirely fascinated him." *(Estate of Glenn Gould.)*

(**5**) Glenn at age two, with his mother, Florence Emma Gould (née Greig). *(Estate of Glenn Gould.)*

6

7

(6) Gould's great-grandfather, the Reverend Isaac Gold. *(Uxbridge-Scott Township Museum and Archives.)*

(7) Russell Herbert (Bert) and Thomas George Gould, Glenn's father and grandfather. *(Uxbridge-Scott Township Museum and Archives.)*

(8) Glenn as a young teenager, with his English setter, Sir Nickolson of Garelocheed (Nicky), at the Gould family's cottage on Lake Simcoe. *(Estate of Glenn Gould.)*

8

9

(9) The prodigy at age ten, 1942. *(Photograph by Charles Du Bois.)*

(10) Chilean-born Alberto Guerrero, Gould's only piano teacher besides his mother. *(Photograph by Margaret Privitello.)*

10

11

(11) Glenn at fourteen, at the organ of the concert hall of the Toronto Conservatory of Music. This photograph appeared in the December 1947 issue of the service-club publication *Lion News: A Magazine of News and Views of Canadian Lions*, to accompany an article entitled "Music and Canada's Children." *(Photograph by Page Toles.)*

(12) One piano, four paws: Glenn and Nicky in duet. This photograph accompanied a profile of the sixteen-year-old pianist and composer that ran in the *Evening Telegram* on February 5, 1949, and was picked up by other Ontario newspapers.

12

The twenty-two-year-old Gould at the piano **(13)** and soaking his arms **(14)**, in Columbia Records' 30th Street studio in New York, during the recording sessions for his first Columbia album, of Bach's Goldberg Variations, June 1955. *(Photographs by Dan Weiner. Sony Classical.)*

(15) Gould around 1956, composing at the cottage, which remained a sanctuary for him at least into the late 1960s. *(Photograph by Fednews.)*

(**16**) Gould at Massey Hall, with the Toronto Symphony conducted by Sir Ernest MacMillan, probably rehearsing Bach's D-minor concerto for their concert in Hamilton, Ontario, on March 21, 1956. Barely two months earlier, Gould's album of the Goldberg Variations had made him suddenly an international star.

(**17**) Gould during his appearance in the CBC television series *Chrysler Festival*, February 20, 1957, before a live audience at Loew's Uptown Theatre in Toronto. *(CBC Still Photo Collection.)*

18

19

Gould in recital **(18)**, meeting the pianist Sviatoslav Richter backstage in Moscow **(19)**, and giving a lecture-recital at the Leningrad Conservatory **(20)**, during his triumphant May 1957 tour of Russia. *(Photographs 18 and 19 by E. I. Ivano.)*

20

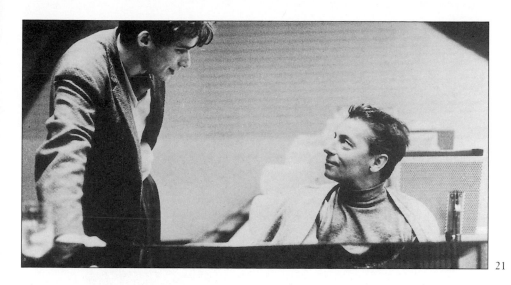

21

(21) Gould and the conductor of the Berlin Philharmonic, Herbert von Karajan, at a rehearsal in the concert hall of the Hochschüle für Musik in West Berlin, late May 1957. *(Photograph by Erich Lessing. akg-images, London.)*

(22) Gould greeting Van Cliburn backstage after one of his Beethoven-concerto performances in London, May-June 1959. This photograph ran in the June 5, 1959, issue of the *Toronto Daily Star*, with a caption noting that both pianists had a reputation for not shaking hands.

(23) Gould rehearsing Bach's Brandenburg Concerto No. 5 with members of the Detroit Symphony, conducted by Paul Paray, for a concert on October 13, 1960. *(Photograph by Lare Wardrop.)*

22

23

24

(24) Gould trying out pianos at Steinway and Sons, in New York, 1958. Behind him, at right, is Frederick (Fritz) Steinway, then manager of the company's Concert and Artist Department. *(Photograph by Don Hunstein. Sony Classical.)*

(25) Gould in the upper-body cast he wore for a month in Philadelphia, April-May 1960, as treatment for the injury he claimed to have suffered a few months earlier at the hands of a Steinway and Sons employee. *(Photograph by Adrian Siegel.)*

25

(26) Gould and a string quartet rehearsing for his July 9, 1956, concert at the Stratford Festival – a tour de force that included piano works, Schoenberg's *Ode to Napoleon*, and the first public performance of his own String Quartet. *(Photograph by Herb Nott. Stratford Festival.)*

(27) Gould in Stratford with (left to right) the composer Louis Applebaum, the cellist Leonard Rose, and the violinist Oscar Shumsky. When this photo was taken, in the summer of 1960, Applebaum was director of music at the Stratford Festival and the others were artists-in-residence; the following summer, Gould, Rose, and Shumsky became joint directors of music. *(Photograph by Peter Smith. Stratford Festival.)*

28

Gould with some high-profile collaborators: **(28)** Leonard Bernstein (left) and Igor Stravinsky, during the taping of *The Creative Performer*, a CBS television special that aired on January 31, 1960; **(29)** Leopold Stokowski, during the recording of Beethoven's "Emperor" Concerto, with the American Symphony, in Columbia Records' 30th Street studio in New York, March 1966; and **(30)** Yehudi Menuhin, in October 1965, rehearsing for *Duo*, a CBC television special that aired the following May. *(Photograph 29 by Don Hunstein; Sony Classical. Photograph 30 by Barry Wilson; CBC Still Photo Collection.)*

29

30

31

32

(31) Gould in his penthouse at 110 St. Clair Ave. West, in midtown Toronto, 1963. *(Photograph by Walter Curtin.)*

(32) Gould's chair, at one of the direst points in its evolution, probably in the later 1960s. *(Photograph by Robert C. Ragsdale. CBC Still Photo Collection.)*

(33) Gould recording in Columbia Records' 30th Street studio in New York, March 1963. *(Photograph by Don Hunstein. Sony Classical.)*

33

34

35

(34) Gould with Lorne Tulk in the green room of Eaton Auditorium, 1971, listening to a playback of recordings he made for a broadcast recital for the European Broadcasting Union. *(Photograph by Walter Curtin.)*

(35) Gould exercising one of his most appealing attributes: his infectious, cackling laugh. *(Photograph by Don Hunstein. Sony Classical.)*

(36) Gould driving one of his big American cars through Toronto, April 1974. *(Photograph by Don Hunstein. Sony Classical.)*

36

37

38

Gould in costume as three of his fictitious alter-egos – **(37)** "the dean of British conductors," Sir Nigel Twitt-Thornwaite; **(38)** "the brilliant German reductionist" Karlheinz Klopweisser; and **(39)** "the brilliantly articulate American actor" Myron Chianti – taping three television commercials advertising the radio series *CBC Tuesday Night*, 1974. *(Photographs by Robert C. Ragsdale. CBC Still Photo Collection.)*

39

40

(40) The studio Gould maintained, at the Inn on the Park hotel, in the suburb of Don Mills, from September 1976 until his death. *(Photograph by Lorne Tulk.)*

(41) Gould recording and videotaping his new interpretation of the Goldberg Variations, April-May 1981. *(Photograph by Don Hunstein. Sony Classical.)*

41

Sviatoslav Richter – and fewer than *forty* overseas. He was widely regarded as a genius, and in some respects he had an influence on younger musicians comparable to that of Vladimir Horowitz (in a very different way) a generation before. Knowledgeable sources declared him the greatest pianist since Busoni, since Backhaus, since Gieseking. One of the New York critics wrote that Gould "even at his worst is a musician so far in advance of most of his contemporaries that there is no legitimate basis for comparison"; B. H. Haggin wrote that he "stands out above all other pianists young and old," and credited him in the early sixties with "possibly the most remarkable and exciting musical intelligence operating in musical performance today."

Other pianists, even elder statesmen like Arthur Rubinstein, revered Gould. Cliburn, among others, wanted to play for him and get his advice. Richter, after hearing him play the Goldberg Variations in Moscow in 1957, decided then and there never to admit that piece into his repertoire. Gina Bachauer ranked him as one of the four best musicians in the world, and José Iturbi said in 1966 that among the younger pianists of the day "Glenn Gould is the outstanding one." His fans included Menuhin, Rostropovich, and countless other instrumentalists, as well as singers: Maureen Forrester wrote that she was "in awe of his mind" and felt inadequate in his presence. Every orchestra wanted him, and most conductors. "He created a style which led the way to the future," said Karajan. "He gives me a whole new interest in music," said Bernstein, who "worshipped the way he played." Josef Krips called him "one of the greatest musicians of our time, if not the greatest of all," and Erich Leinsdorf called him "perhaps one of the all-time greatest (and in my view perhaps also the kindest and gentlest) artists." The venerable Bruno Walter thought him a genius – even though he didn't like the way he played. Stokowski offered to record with him in 1966, though he had rarely consented to record a concerto since, a generation before, he had recorded Rachmaninov concertos with the composer at the piano.

Gould counted major contemporary composers like Samuel Barber, David Diamond, and Lukas Foss among his fans. "You play like a composer," Aaron Copland told him in 1957, adding, "I haven't heard a legato like that since Paris in 1849," referring to the year Chopin died. Later Copland told John Roberts, "When listening to his Bach, it is as though Bach himself is actually performing." Gertrude Schoenberg said that Gould's interpretation of her husband's piano concerto was unrivalled. Stravinsky, too, was a fan – the same Stravinsky, who, in his *Poetics of Music*, raged against the interpreter who puts his own musical vision before that of the composer. Stravinsky professed astonishment at Gould's musicianship when they both appeared in a CBS television special in 1960, and after hearing him play the Op. 110 sonata in Los Angeles a year later Stravinsky sent him a handwritten note saying that he had never understood Beethoven's late sonatas until that night.* Stravinsky made many visits to Toronto between 1962 and 1967, to conduct concerts and make recordings and broadcasts, and he badly wanted to record his *Capriccio* for piano and orchestra with Gould. Roberts brought the two together over lunch, but Gould, no Stravinsky fan even in the composer's presence, deftly changed the subject whenever the *Capriccio* came up, then bowed out before dessert; later he refused even to glance at the score. Curiously, Stravinsky also told Roberts that Gould was one of the handsomest men he had ever seen.

And, of course, there were his legions of admirers among the general public (and not only among the classical-music aficionados), his already burgeoning cult following, his high-profile admirers in every field, from Oscar Peterson and many other jazz musicians to Rolling Stones guitarist Brian Jones, from Roland Barthes to Samuel Beckett. No one, in short, had less cause, practically speaking, to retire from concert life than Glenn Gould did in 1964. Until his death he continued to get offers for concerts from all over the world, but already in 1968, after "four of the very best years of my life," he was certain that "it would be a terribly retrogressive step to retreat

---

* Stravinsky's note is lost, but Gould's two-line reply, dated May 9, 1961, survives in the Stravinsky Archive at the Paul Sacher Foundation, in Basel, Switzerland.

back into the embrace of the concert." He could not be enticed back, even by offers of up to a million dollars for a single recital.

"I never have been able to resist forums, soap-boxes, or Hyde Park corners."

For a time he continued to lead a public life. He returned to the Stratford Festival in summer 1964 for his final season as a director of music, but he did not perform, and the festival felt keenly the loss of its brightest musical star. He had a brief career as a public lecturer in the mid-sixties. In April 1963, he delivered one of the inaugural Corbett Music Lectures, a high-profile series at the University of Cincinnati, and a happy by-product of the lecture was *Arnold Schoenberg: A Perspective*, a short monograph published in 1964 by the University of Cincinnati Press.* In July 1963, on short notice, he gave the inaugural MacMillan Lectures at the University of Toronto, at the request of Sir Ernest himself, who had to withdraw for medical reasons. He responded with three wide-ranging and provocative papers: "Forgery and Imitation in the Creative Process"; a repeat of the Schoenberg lecture; and "Music in the Soviet Union," based on his 1962 CBC television special.

In 1964 he gave just two concerts but seven lectures, the most important of which were a pair entitled "The History of the Piano Sonata," delivered at Hunter College, in New York, and repeated at the Isabella Stewart Gardner Museum, in Boston. On June 1, he accepted an honorary Doctor of Laws degree from the University of Toronto, and, though he had been expected to perform, gave a convocation address entitled "An Argument for Music in the Electronic Age." On October 9 he returned to Cincinnati to present "Music in the Soviet Union" as a Corbett Lecture, and on November 11, in his

---

* In a letter from late 1965, he claimed that this monograph was "really just a preparatory sketch for a longer work which I have been commissioned to write next year." But he never wrote that book.

last public lecture, he addressed the graduating class of the Royal Conservatory of Music, urging them to resist conventional systems of thought and instead to seek new ideas by relying on their own imaginations – presumably not a message the faculty wished to hear.

Gould had no trouble attracting large audiences to his lectures, and he cut an attractive and personable figure on stage. (A noticeably large number of young women attended his MacMillan Lectures.) His lectures were usually though not always well received. He was nervous and insecure in public situations, and seemed oblivious to his audiences' expectations. At Hunter College, he spoke in dense, often technical prose in a rapid speaking voice, and, as the critic Eric Salzman wrote, "Somehow one had the uneasy feeling that maybe five people in the audience were interested, alert and able to follow." His appearance had been advertised as a "lecture-recital" but he stubbornly insisted on discoursing. "It was obvious that some listeners would have preferred to hear Mr. Gould make music and not talk," wrote Raymond Ericson in the *New York Times*. "After he had played just a few measures early in the evening, he was greeted with prolonged applause. To this he merely shook his head, indicating that he was intent on giving his lecture." He spoke without a break for almost two hours, offering barely ten minutes of musical examples at the piano. His audience grew restless, and some people walked out; the audience for the second lecture was noticeably smaller, though this time he indulged them by playing the whole Berg Sonata at the end.

Some knowledgeable critics found the Hunter College lectures challenging, stimulating, even brilliant. Now with a growing reputation as a thinker and writer, he was increasingly in demand to lecture, serve as a visiting professor, attend symposiums, teach seminars and master classes. To the end of his life he would receive offers from august institutions like Stanford, Berkeley, Dartmouth, Indiana, Juilliard, Oberlin, the New England Conservatory, and the Metropolitan Museum. Harvard pursued him for years, at one point offering to appoint him Horatio Appleton Lamb Visiting Lecturer, a position previously held by Enesco, Holst, Bartók, Copland, and

Boulez. But he said he was put off by the "most awesome responsibility" of teaching – he was one of very few professional performers never to have had a single pupil – and the mixed success of his lectures did not encourage him to continue communicating his ideas in public.

With his last lecture, his life as a public figure effectively came to an end. He turned down invitations to festivals and conferences, refused to attend gala events for the prime minister or the Queen. He won many record-industry awards in North America and overseas, and major honours like the Canadian Confederation Medal (1967), the Canada Council's Molson Prize (1968), the Diplôme d'honneur from the Canadian Conference of the Arts (1976), and the Canadian Music Council Medal (1981), and after 1964 he was offered a handful of honorary degrees, but he accepted awards only if he did not have to pick them up at a public ceremony.* He was simply no longer interested in appearing before the public except through the intercession of the electronic media.

"Isolation is the one sure way to human happiness."

Quitting the concert circuit for the recording studio led Gould to reassess his personal life, which he had come to view as cluttered. Throughout the early sixties and especially after 1964, many people who had known him in his twenties stopped seeing or hearing from him, and he was no longer a part of the local music scene. In his late twenties, home was still his parents' house, where he was comfortable and doted on. Though he spent a lot of time at the cottage, his needs and the hours he kept were taking a toll on his parents (his mother was approaching seventy). Friends finally convinced him that he ought to find his own place. He moved out in 1959, at first

---

* Gould refused many offers over the years to have his name brought forward for the country's highest honour, the Order of Canada. He was put off by the competitive implications of the "stratification" – the various levels – of the Order.

into two suites (one for his piano) at the Windsor Arms, a dowdy hotel whose atmosphere of faded Edwardian splendour suited him perfectly, and where a sympathetic switchboard operator shielded his privacy. Then, in December of that year, having heard that Van Cliburn had just bought a house, he got a whimsical "longing for grandeur" and leased a mansion called Donchery, about fifteen miles outside Toronto. He described it in a letter to a friend:

> The estate, let me tell you, had 26 rooms, if one counts the 7 bathrooms, the breakfast room, the scullery, the dog kennel, and every other partition which could conceivably be construed as a room. It also had on the property, which by the way was beautifully wooded with a river running through it, a swimming pool and tennis court. The swimming pool was surrounded by a four-car garage and boys and girls dressing rooms (no bacchanalian revelries for us!). The house was situated some 60 steps above the river (known as the Don) and the view from down below looking up and especially at night with flood lights was like looking at Salzburg castle from your own strawberry patch. Oh yes, there was one of those too on the other side of the Don.

Gould was embarrassed when word of this indulgence was leaked to the press; still, with John Roberts's help he gamely went about furnishing the mansion. But when the movers arrived, he realized that the whole thing was mad. "The brooms and the pyrex dishes arrived and I was filled with all the horror of the domestic idyll I had been courting," he wrote. "Suddenly 'Donchery' represented a snare." He jumped into his Buick and fled to Toronto, returned everything he had bought, and in mid-January, at considerable expense, got out of his lease.

He spent the first half of 1960 at the Algiers Apartments, on Avenue Road, but the heating was not to his liking; later that year he found more congenial digs at Park Lane Apartments, at 110 St. Clair Avenue West. Park Lane is a striking, glamorous, U-shaped brown-brick edifice built in 1938 in the style known as Depression

Modern, an architectural equivalent of Art Deco. Gould leased No. 902, a penthouse with six large rooms and a terrace whose garden was overgrown with weeds unless a friend volunteered to tend it. Park Lane was a quiet building in a quiet neighbourhood. The tenants were mostly retired people, and the management guarded their privacy. For Gould it was perfect, and he lived there for the rest of his life.

He had offices of sorts around town, too. He was a ubiquitous, beloved figure at the CBC, so much a fixture that Roberts, who became supervisor of music for the English Service in 1965, fixed him up with a makeshift office by putting partitions around a desk in an unused corner of the music department. ("We were Glenn's family," the CBC technician Lorne Tulk said.) Gould continued to do business through Homburger's office, and in the mid-sixties, when he became more directly involved with his recordings and broadcasts, he rented a studio at Film House, at 22 Front Street West. It says much about his new priorities that his rent at Film House was higher than at Park Lane.

Everyone warned Gould that he would take a financial hit if he retired from concert life. In classical music, money was to be made in concerts, not recordings, and Gould knew it: in 1956, by his own calculation, he earned $13,750 for about twenty concerts, but only $1,485 in royalties from his bestselling recording of the Goldberg Variations. His concert fees ranked near the top for pianists of his day. The year after the explosion of international fame in 1956 his price, which had been $500 to $750 for one recital, rose to more than $1,000, then to $2,000 a year later, which is not much less than Cliburn was earning after winning the Tchaikovsky Competition in 1958 and becoming the biggest name in the business. By the end of his concert career Gould was charging $3,500 or more. (His fees were lower for concerto appearances and for concerts overseas.) In a document from 1956, he gave his average annual income for the past six years as $20,000 (about $140,000 today), and his income grew until it topped $100,000 (well over $600,000 today) at least once in his later concert years. In a letter to an insurance company, his lawyers put his average gross income between 1956 and 1966 at $50,000 per year (close to $300,000 today). In the mid-sixties one could still buy a five-bedroom house in Toronto for $15,000, and a secretary made about $100 a week.

Gould did take a big pay cut. In fact, he retired just as concert fees in the classical-music business were beginning to explode, making artists of his stature very rich men. Had he still been on the concert circuit at age fifty, he might have been making, like Horowitz, tens of thousands of dollars per concert. His record sales did not plummet after he stopped giving concerts, as predicted, but it was years before his royalty income began to rival his concert income: financial records among his papers reveal royalties of about $23,000 in 1966, $32,000 in 1970, $47,000 in 1973, and $102,000 in 1981. He earned a fee of $2,500 in 1959 for the NFB documentaries, and $2,000 for his two lectures in Boston in 1964. His writing brought in very little and his published compositions brought in a pittance: a hundred dollars in 1962, a little over *two* dollars in 1974, nothing in 1975. Away from the concert hall, Gould earned a decent wage by the standards of the average gainfully employed person, but little by the standards of star performers.

He had saved income from his concerts, however, was responsible with money, and lived modestly.* In 1960 he incorporated a private company to represent his artistic ventures: Glenn Gould Limited, which had initial capital of forty thousand dollars (about a quarter of a million today). He was not naive about money. He was closely involved with the negotiation of his contracts, checked his royalty statements line by line, kept his own accounts. From the mid-fifties, as soon as he had real money of his own, he was investing wisely, and became proficient at playing the stock market, from which much of his income would derive. He understood the markets, and enjoyed researching stocks and keeping track of details

---

* In an insurance document from 1962, Gould calculated the total value of his possessions – pianos, furniture, paintings, recording and medical equipment – at $19,800, somewhat more than a hundred thousand dollars today.

about capital gain and tax-shelter provisions and negative options and ratios of debt to total portfolio value. He had a large circle of contacts with whom he traded stock tips, including Homburger, colleagues at Columbia Records, colleagues like Yehudi Menuhin, and a well-placed head waiter at the Royal York Hotel. Brokers were impressed by his acumen. During the recession years of the early eighties, his broker told him that he was his only client making a profit.

His executor, Stephen Posen, put Gould's net worth at the time of his death at about three-quarters of a million dollars – not much for a musician of his standing. When Horowitz died in 1989 his estate was valued at between six and eight million American dollars, and when Karajan died the same year his estate was conservatively estimated at about three hundred million. But Gould was not interested in money as a source of status or luxury and was willing to maximize his income only in ways compatible with his lifestyle and artistic goals. What he wanted from money was freedom, independence, privacy, and the resources to do the work he wanted to do, and by that standard he was plenty rich.

"My idea of happiness is two hundred and fifty days a year in a recording studio."

Abandoning the concert hall was a radical act, but it was the right move for Gould, and the proof is in his output. He made an astonishing number and range of recordings in the first decade after 1964 – in 1973 alone, he released six new albums – even as his musical and technological standards rose. The following is a list of the albums from that first decade. It does not include re-releases, compilations, Columbia Record Club releases, and the like, all of which contributed to Gould's consistently high visibility in the record market.

- Bach, *The Well-Tempered Clavier*, Book One, in three volumes (recorded in 1962–65/released in 1963, 1964, and 1965).

- Bach, Two- and Three-Part Inventions (1964/1964).*
- Beethoven, Piano Sonatas, Op. 10/Nos. 1–3 (1964/1965).
- Schoenberg, Piano Pieces, Opp. 11, 19, 23, and 33, and Suite, Op. 25; Songs, Opp. 1 (with Donald Gramm, bass-baritone) and 2 (with Ellen Faull, soprano); and *The Book of the Hanging Gardens*, with Helen Vanni, soprano, (1958, 1964–65/1966).
- Beethoven, Piano Concerto No. 5 ("Emperor"), with Leopold Stokowski, American Symphony (1966/1966).
- Beethoven, Piano Sonatas, Opp. 13 (*Pathétique*) and 14/Nos. 1 and 2 (1966/1967).
- Bach, Clavier Concertos, Vol. 1: Nos. 3, 5, and 7, with Vladimir Golschmann, Columbia Symphony (1958, 1966/1967).
- Schoenberg, *Ode to Napoleon*, with John Horton, narrator, and the Juilliard Quartet; Fantasy for Violin and Piano, with Israel Baker (1964–65/1967).
- *Canadian Music in the 20th Century*: Morawetz, *Fantasy in D*; Anhalt, *Fantasia*; Hétu, *Variations pour piano* (1966–67/1967).
- Beethoven-Liszt, Symphony No. 5 (1967–68/1968).
- Mozart, Piano Sonatas, Vol. 1: Nos. 1–5, K. 279 through 283 (1967/1968).†
- Bach, *The Well-Tempered Clavier*, Book Two, in three volumes (1966–67, 1969, 1971/1968, 1970, and 1971).
- Prokofiev, Sonata No. 7; Scriabin, Sonata No. 3 (1967–68/1969).
- Mozart, Piano Sonatas, Vol. 2: Nos. 6, 7, and 9, K. 284, 309, and 311 (1968/1969).
- Bach, Clavier Concertos, Vol. 2: Nos. 2 and 4, with Vladimir Golschmann, Columbia Symphony (1969/1969).

---

* The Inventions finally released were all recorded in two sessions in March 1964, most of them on the first take. Gould noted in 1966 that he had previously attempted integral recordings of the Inventions in 1955 and 1963, "and on both occasions had rejected the results out of hand."

† This was the first Gould album to be released in stereo format only. His albums were released in mono sound only up to summer 1958, then in both formats until 1967.

- Schumann, Piano Quartet in E-flat Major, with the Juilliard Quartet (1968/1969).
- Beethoven, Piano Sonatas, Opp. 13 (*Pathétique*), 27/No. 2 ("Moonlight"), and 57 ("Appassionata") (1966–67/1970).
- Beethoven, Variations, WoO 80 and Opp. 34 and 35 ("Eroica") (1960, 1966–67/1970).
- *A Consort of Musicke Bye William Byrde and Orlando Gibbons* (1967–68, 1971/1971).
- Mozart, Piano Sonatas, Vol. 3: Nos. 8, 10, 12, and 13, K. 310, 330, 332, and 333 (1965–66, 1969–70/1972).
- Schoenberg, Songs, Opp. 3, 6, 12, 14, and 48, and Op. posth., with Donald Gramm, Helen Vanni, and Cornelis Opthof, baritone (1964–65, 1968, 1970–71/1972).
- Handel, Suites, Nos. 1–4, on the harpsichord (1972/1972).
- Grieg, Piano Sonata in E Minor; Bizet, *Premier Nocturne* and *Variations chromatiques* (1971–72/1973).
- Bach, French Suites, Nos. 1–4 (1972–73/1973).
- Mozart, Piano Sonatas, Vol. 4: Nos. 11 and 15, K. 331 and 545; K. 533, with Rondo, K. 494; Fantasia in D Minor, K. 397 (1965, 1967, 1970, 1972–73/1973).
- Beethoven, Piano Sonatas, Op. 31/Nos. 1, 2 ("Tempest"), and 3 (1960, 1967, 1971/1973).
- Hindemith, Piano Sonatas, Nos. 1–3 (1966–67, 1972–73/1973).*
- Wagner-Gould, Prelude to *Die Meistersinger*; "Dawn" and "Siegfried's Rhine Journey" from *Götterdämmerung*; *Siegfried Idyll* (1973/1973).
- Bach, French Suites, Nos. 5 and 6; French Overture in B Minor (1971, 1973/1974).
- Bach, Sonatas for Viola da Gamba and Harpsichord, Nos. 1–3, with Leonard Rose (1973–74/1974).
- Beethoven, Bagatelles, Opp. 33 and 126 (1974/1975).

---

* This was the first Gould album to bear the new label designation "CBS Masterworks" rather than "Columbia Masterworks."

- Mozart, Piano Sonatas, Vol. 5: Nos. 14, 16, and 17, K. 457, 570, and 576; Fantasia in C Minor, K. 475 (1966, 1970, 1973–74/1975).

Gould's new life liberated him, and he began exploring new repertoire with relish. One never knew what he might do next. Suddenly the great Bach pianist and self-professed modernist was playing Handel on a harpsichord, playing chamber music by Schumann, playing orchestral music in transcription, revealing himself to be a closet Wagnerite, and putting himself in direct competition with classic Horowitz recordings of sonatas by Prokofiev and Scriabin. He was championing music by contemporary countrymen, in a special album honouring Canada's Centennial. He was returning to Romantic repertoire, after having largely ignored it for a decade, in an album of rare works by Grieg and Bizet. And he was now free to explore in depth music he had only sampled in concerts (Byrd and Gibbons, Hindemith), and to survey whole repertoires that interested him (the keyboard music of Bach and Schoenberg, the sonatas of Mozart and Beethoven). Columbia, as the producer Paul Myers recalled, "was happy to release any record he wanted to make."

He was eager to promote his albums, too, now that he was no longer generating publicity on the concert circuit, sometimes through essays and promotional recordings made especially for Columbia. The unlikeliest such project was *Glenn Gould über Bach*, a seventeen-minute recording he made in 1971 for CBS in Germany, to promote his just-completed cycle of *The Well-Tempered Clavier*. Against a seamless "musical tapestry" of excerpts from fugal works by Bach, he read his own text translated into German, a language he did not speak, with excruciating results. In April 1968, Columbia released an album entitled *Glenn Gould: Concert Dropout*, an hour-long, carefully planned and edited conversation between Gould and John McClure, director of the Masterworks division. (It was packaged as a bonus album with the Beethoven-Liszt Fifth Symphony.) He referred to the interview as a "position paper" on his new life, and it touched on many classic Gouldian themes: recordings versus concerts; radio and television broadcasting; his preferences among pianos; his working methods in the recording studio; his approach to interpretation; the contemporary avant-garde; the Canadian North; and his views on musicians ranging from Bach and Beethoven to Strauss and Schoenberg to Petula Clark and the Beatles.

Gould's ambition as a recording artist at this time was astonishing. In addition to all those he completed, he began at least a dozen major recording projects that he never finished, including Strauss songs with a soprano he adored: Elisabeth Schwarzkopf. A session in New York, in January 1966, was squeezed into Schwarzkopf's schedule while she was busy preparing *Don Giovanni* at the Metropolitan Opera – Take 1 counted as their rehearsal. Despite their mutual admiration, they had artistic differences. "Schwarzkopf thought she would have a very distinguished accompanist," the producer, Paul Myers, recalls. "Glenn thought he was going to have a very distinguished *collaborator*, and that's a slightly different thing." The *Ophelia-Lieder* "went like a dream," according to Myers, and three other songs were recorded without incident. Gould was proud of his ability to transpose several of the songs, including the difficult "Heimliche Aufforderung," at sight, to accommodate Schwarzkopf's voice. But when they came to the popular "Morgen!," an early song Gould never liked, "Glenn went into his full experimental mode," playing fast and loose with Strauss's score – something Strauss himself, incidentally, did when accompanying his songs. Schwarzkopf, by her own account, was disturbed by Gould's improvisational approach to the piano part – "he was fantasizing about Strauss, which is not what you should do" – and by his insistence on staying at the piano and playing rather than discussing the songs between takes. (Perhaps he was somewhat cowed by her presence, as he was, later that year, when he ran into another soprano he adored, Barbra Streisand, at Columbia Records.) The session ended, and that evening Schwarzkopf's husband, Walter Legge, called Myers to announce that she could not work "with a man like that." The album was cancelled.

Gould began but abandoned other major recording projects in the late sixties and early seventies: sonatas by Scarlatti and C. P. E. Bach, the former album aborted after one session because he got bored ("a little Scarlatti goes a long way"); Beethoven's experimental sonatas of Opp. 78, 79, 81a ("Les Adieux"), 90, and 101, all of which he loved, as well as the mighty "Hammerklavier" Sonata (he recorded only Op. 78, and taped the "Hammerklavier" for CBC radio in November 1970); all of Scriabin's sonatas; and all of Beethoven's symphonies in Liszt's transcriptions. He talked of recording all of Bach's double concertos (presumably through overdubbing), all of Handel's suites, all of Haydn's dozens of sonatas, music by Carl Nielsen, "a 2, 3, or even 4 record set which would detail a history of the variation form," chamber music by nineteenth-century Russians like Glinka and Borodin – but there was never enough time. In 1971 he surprised everyone by deciding to record Grieg's popular piano concerto, a piece he had claimed to hate.* (A downturn in the stock market had once prompted him to quip, "Another bad week like that and I'll have to record Grieg and Tchaikovsky to recoup.") He made firm plans to record the concerto that fall, with the Cleveland Orchestra, but cancelled, citing illness.

Away from concert life, Gould was no longer plagued by the vagaries of unfamiliar pianos. He had found his ideal instrument in 1960: CD 318. ("CD" denotes a Model D Steinway grand piano held in the Concert Division for use by Steinway artists.) CD 318 was built in New York in 1945 and shipped that fall for consignment to Eaton's in Toronto, the local Steinway dealer; it was this very piano,

---

* John Roberts was in Gould's apartment when a package arrived containing a score of the concerto, which Gould claimed never to have studied. He needed to tell Columbia once and for all whether he would record it, and so decided to sight-read it on the spot. A few years later Roberts wrote about what followed: "He sails through the first movement, including the cadenza, without a wrong note or the faintest blemish. The last movement is sight-read at breakneck speed, again flawlessly. It sounds like Horowitz, only better. At the conclusion Gould says, 'Somehow, I feel this is not for me,' and shuts the score." Later, obviously, he changed his mind, at least temporarily.

Gould noted, that "assisted in many of the memorable moments in my career as child prodigy." From 1960, CD 318 was routinely shipped back and forth between Toronto and New York, despite the hassles at customs, for Gould's use in concerts and recordings; it was the instrument on which he made almost all of his Columbia recordings over the next twenty years.*

Gould adored the lean, bright, "translucent" sound of CD 318, and its quick, tight action. Near the end of his concert career the piano, though still owned by Steinway, was given over to his exclusive use and he was permitted to make mechanical adjustments that ran contrary to factory specifications in order to refine its native attributes and create a "harpsichordistic" piano particularly suited to the music of Bach. "I wanted a much lighter action than is the Steinway norm," he said, "with the hammers somewhat closer to the strings, so that one gets a more immediate bite"; he also wanted little or no aftertouch, immediate and total damping, and a shallow key dip. ("Key dip" is the distance a key travels from rest to a fully depressed position.) He wanted maximum responsiveness with minimum effort, and in the process of trying to get it from CD 318 he became one of Steinway's most demanding clients.

As long as he was recording in New York, his principal tuner and technician was Franz Mohr, who joined Steinway in 1962, became

---

* He had two practice pianos in his apartment: his old Chickering baby grand, and a Steinway Model B grand built in 1932. According to a comment published in 1979, he received the Steinway on loan in January 1960, and he claimed that "I last had it tuned in January 1963, and through all types of meteorological vicissitudes, it has stayed perfectly in tune." Nonsense, says his Toronto piano tuner, Verne Edquist: the instrument was half a tone flat. The National Library of Canada in Ottawa maintains CD 318. The two Yamaha grand pianos he bought in his last years are now housed at Roy Thomson Hall, in Toronto, and at The King's University College, in Edmonton. The two pianos he kept in his apartment, the Steinway grand and the Chickering baby grand, are, respectively, in Rideau Hall (the Governor General's residence in Ottawa) and in the lobby outside Glenn Gould Studio. All have been serviced and restored to varying degrees over the years, and none can reliably be said to retain the precise, very idiosyncratic standards of touch and tone that Gould cherished.

William Hupfer's assistant in 1965, and became chief concert technician when Hupfer retired in 1970. Hupfer had stopped working for Gould after the lawsuit, and when Mohr took over he was told, "Franz, please don't go near him. Don't touch him. Just tune!" At first, the hair-trigger action Gould demanded produced a disturbing side effect: in the middle register, at moderate and slow tempos, a hammer would sometimes glancingly strike a string a second time before returning to rest, creating a tonal anomaly Gould dubbed a "hiccup." In the first album on the newly adjusted CD 318, the Two- and Three-Part Inventions, the hiccup is obvious from the first bar of the first invention, though in a disclaimer on the album cover Gould professed to "now find this charming idiosyncrasy entirely worthy of the remarkable instrument which produced it." (Few listeners agreed.) After a few more years of tinkering, the "hiccup" had mostly disappeared.

Columbia had more to deal with – the squeaks of Gould's knackered chair, the stamping of his feet, his tendency to begin discussing a take before the reverberations of the last notes had faded away. And there was his constant singing, all the more difficult to avoid or muffle given his penchant for close-up miking. Once, in 1956, it was jokingly suggested that he wear a gas mask while recording, and as a gag he actually picked one up at a war-surplus store and emerged wearing it at his next session. A *Life* photographer happened to be in the studio at the time, and, as Gould recalled, "there had been so much nonsense about the various things I do that we decided that the great American public would really take this thing seriously. And we had one heck of a time to get those pictures suppressed – it was dreadful!" His mannerisms were not put on – he can be heard singing away even in private recordings – and he knew they were a problem. But of his singing he said, "I can't do without it. I would if I could. It's a terrible distraction. I don't like it. . . . I can only say I play very much less well if I don't indulge in a few vocal elaborations." Considering the precision and polish of his piano playing and his fastidiousness as a recording artist – he would ask for retakes to correct flaws his producers could not detect – it is revealing that he would accept so many intrusive sounds into his recordings. But as long as the piano *felt* right he didn't care if it hiccuped, and as long as the performance and recording were perfect his squeaking and stamping and singing did not count, any more than a crinkling candy wrapper counts at a concert.

Then there were his interpretations. In the studio Gould felt free to undertake creative experiments with the music he played, and his interpretations could be, depending on one's point of view, either personal or self-indulgent, refreshing or perverse. In most everything he played, particularly in popular, canonical works with entrenched traditions of interpretation, he could be counted on to forge some idiosyncratic image of the music through extreme tempos, upside-down textures and dynamics, curious turns of phrase, weird ornamentation, his trademark *détaché* articulation, or even a little rewriting of the composer's pitches and rhythms. He was predictably unpredictable; he took nothing for granted. When he did play a piece in a more or less conventional way, one sensed that it was only because he happened to agree with the convention, after having considered other options.

Every Gould recording features at least a few eccentric details – a quirky arpeggio, a hammered-out bassline, a surprising refusal of the sustaining pedal, or some other calling card that marks it as unmistakably *his*. But there are also movements and whole works in which he radically reconceived an entire musical structure, in effect creating a new piece. In the first movement of Mozart's popular A-major sonata, K. 331, he treats a conventional theme-and-variations cycle as a cumulative structure: the tempo increases with each variation, and as a consequence the theme (marked *Andante grazioso*) is set out in slow motion, while the penultimate variation (marked *Adagio*) is played quickly. In the "Appassionata" Sonata, whose "egoistic pomposity" and "combative," "belligerent" rhetoric he deplored, he resorted to parody, dissecting phrases and textures, in a plodding tempo, in order to sabotage the very qualities that gave the piece its nickname. Yet, in the fast movements of Beethoven's three C-minor sonatas, and the finale of the "Moonlight," all of which might also be labelled *appassionata*, Gould gives wild, unrestrained readings at breakneck tempos. For him, apparently, exaggeration at either end of the spectrum was fair game, and the only enemy was compromise. His ability to realize such aberrant interpretations with conviction points to digital and mental facility of a very high order, as well as a feeling for "how far to go too far."

Gould usually knew what traditions he was upsetting: after Take 1 of that movement from K. 331, according to the producer, Andrew Kazdin, he exclaimed, "There! That'll bug the critics!" Once, on television, he played some of Mozart's K. 333 sonata, beautifully and in an absolutely conventional manner, in order to show off how different *his* interpretation was – stocky, upright, articulated, contrapuntally alive. (His way, he said, "adds vitamins to the music.") Sometimes, though, he confessed to having no idea how a piece was usually performed, and he obviously did not care: his goal was to play everything as though no traditions existed. He offered intentionally prejudiced interpretations, passing the work through the prism of his own aesthetic sensibility to see what the process might yield. He denied that an ideal, comprehensive, permanently valid interpretation was ever possible or even desirable, and he had no problem leaving aside some aspects or possibilities in a work in order to illuminate others.

Like Marshall McLuhan, Gould was sending out "probes" for the purpose of upsetting conventional ideas. (The more entrenched the idea, the more outrageous the probe: he tended to be most creative – most outrageous – in the works whose performance traditions were most entrenched, such as Mozart's and Beethoven's sonatas.) McLuhan said that he preferred questions to answers, that he wanted his words not necessarily to be believed but to make people think. "I'm making explorations. I don't know where they're going to take me," he said in his 1969 *Playboy* interview. His books, he added, "constitute the *process* rather than the completed product of discovery; my purpose is to employ facts as tentative probes, as means of insight." Gould, likewise, through his performances, was putting forth theses, exploring new terrain, seeking new paths through scores. And, like McLuhan, he used exaggeration, irony, jest, surprise, bombast – anything that might throw new light on a familiar work. (He did that as a writer, too.) For McLuhan, moreover, a "probe" also served to make the medium itself visible, and in many of Gould's interpretations there was a self-conscious foregrounding of the interpretative process, like a Brechtian "alienation effect."

Gould could have made many more recordings than he did, but as a recording artist he considered his task to be something more than "playing a piece." For him a performance was a discourse with the work, an opportunity to analyze it and to say something about its form, its genre, its composer. Once he had stopped recording his concert repertoire, Gould would record not necessarily the music he liked best, but the music about which he felt he had something to say – some point to make or case to plead. His Mozart cycle is a good example. He admired the early sonatas but disdained the later ones because of their perceived hedonism and theatricality; he considered Haydn's sonatas better-constructed and more individual works. But he spent a decade committing Mozart sonatas to tape because he wanted to address what he considered long-standing misconceptions about Mozart, about the sonatas, and about the "lavender-and-lace," "Victorian" approach to performing Mozart on the piano, which, in his view, still prevailed. And so he conspicuously downplayed the lyrical and *galant* aspects of Mozart's style in his dynamic, cleanly articulated, light-hearted (frequently hilarious) and "deliciously straightforward" readings of the sonatas, sometimes taking amazingly fast tempos and turning Mozart's textures and dynamic markings upside-down and inside-out, yet putting over his "Baroque-ish" conceptions with spectacular clarity and conviction. The Mozart project, he said, was "a joyous task," not because the pieces ranked high in his pantheon but because he had so successfully said what he wanted to say about Mozart.

He was clearly not one of those performers who give much thought to the composer's intentions. As his beautiful but idiosyncratic album of Canadian music revealed, he was not the least reluctant to tinker with works by living composers. He was still a teenager when he defended his impertinent reading of Oskar Morawetz's *Fantasy* to the composer himself. When Morawetz raised an eyebrow at Gould's too-fast tempos and discretion with the sustaining pedal, and at his highly contrapuntal reading of what were supposed to be conventional tune-plus-accompaniment textures, Gould replied that Morawetz did not really understand his own music, and he refused to change his interpretation. This was not mere arrogance: it was a belief that a performer was a creative force not bound by the limits of the composer's wishes. He did not bother to consult Jacques Hétu before recording his *Variations pour piano* in 1967. Hétu found out about the recording through a letter from Columbia a few weeks before it was released, and, though impressed by Gould's analytical grasp of the piece in the liner notes, he was shocked by the performance (he couldn't sleep for three days, he said); years later, however, he came to feel that Gould's interpretation of the *Variations*, despite its fundamental departures from the score, had its own integrity and offered a viable alternative to the composer's vision of the piece.

Gould was, as Hétu put it, "an authentic creator," a "recomposer": he viewed the act of interpretation as something more than the execution of a series of instructions. In this he took Bach's music as a model. Bach's scores, for the most part, consist of pitches and rhythms only; they are mostly devoid of instructions as to tempo, dynamics, phrasing, expression. There is a kind of abstraction to Bach's music that makes it frequently amenable to widely diverging interpretations, a quality Gould eagerly exploited. He left five recorded performances of the E-major fugue from Book Two of *The Well-Tempered Clavier* with the following metronome speeds for the half note: 65 (CBC radio, 1954); 38 (Columbia, 1957); 100 (Columbia, 1969); 100 (CBC television, 1970); and 35 (film, 1980). More radical was that Gould treated *all* scores as though they had been written by Bach, as sets of notes the realization of which was for the performer alone to decide, and it did not matter how specifically the composer had tried to notate his intentions.

To say that he was a *creative* performer is to say that, for all his high-modernist ideas, he was a *Romantic* performer – more so, indeed, than any other of his generation. The musicians and conductors he admired in his youth, even where he did not seek to emulate their styles, were invariably "ecstatic" Romantics for whom a score was a vehicle through which to express their own personalities and visions of music. Those Gould performances that outraged so many listeners in the mid-twentieth century will seem less shocking to the listener with a long memory or good collection of historical recordings, the listener familiar with Busoni and de Pachmann, Paderewski and Friedman, and others (not just pianists) from the early days of the recording era. His contrapuntal readings of Mozart's sonatas will not alarm the listener familiar with the Mozart recordings of Gieseking, Horowitz, Landowska, Novaës, Schnabel. His souped-up Variation 5 from Mozart's K. 331 has a precedent in Rachmaninov's 1919 Edison recording. His very leisurely stroll through the first movement of Beethoven's *Pastoral Symphony* has precedents in orchestral performances led by Furtwängler and especially by Pfitzner, and some of his extreme tempos in Beethoven's sonatas came straight out of Schnabel's recordings. In Bach, his very slow tempos had precedents in the recordings of Tureck, his very fast tempos in those of Gieseking, whose 1950 recordings of the six partitas all fit on a single CD (Gould managed only five). Sometimes, admittedly, Gould outdistanced even his Romantic predecessors. His two recordings of Wagner's *Siegfried Idyll*, in which he sought to underscore the "languor" he thought implicit in the music, come close to the twenty-five-minute mark, longer by several minutes than even his closest competitors in this perverse race, like Knappertsbusch. But then, Wagner himself wrote that "the pure Adagio cannot be taken slow enough."

Still, after 1964 more and more listeners and critics, including the sympathetic ones, came to despair of Gould. To this day many consider the Gould of the concert hall and the early Columbia albums to have been a great pianist later betrayed by his eccentricities. Some consider his approach to music in his later years neurotic, unhealthy; some assume that he was just pulling people's legs; some accuse him of capricious perversity, of following any bizarre notion that popped into his head. They are not always wrong – Gould was a naughty boy as well as a serious, probing artist. There was an attention-seeking, look-at-me aspect to some of his interpretations in addition to his sense of fun and play. Before recording the slow movement of Bach's G-minor concerto he said to his producer, Andrew Kazdin, "I'm going to play all sorts of inner voices and syncopations – very Wanda Landowska with a touch of Modern Jazz Quartet – so don't be surprised at what you hear." Turning on the tapes, Kazdin replied, "I've never been yet."

With Gould there was no such thing as consensus – no opinion was self-evident, no response universal. He was dismissed as a gadfly, but also placed within the long, proud tradition of Canadian explorers.* A reviewer of the first volume of *The Well-Tempered Clavier* pronounced himself "occasionally irritated, often enthralled, usually impressed, and constantly fascinated" – and that about sums up the Gould literature. For every critic who scoffed at, say, his Byrd-Gibbons album there was another who found it a revelation. (Gould thought it "the best damn record we've ever made," rivalled only by the Prokofiev-Scriabin album.) For every critic who deplored his unidiomatic harpsichord style in the Handel album, another pronounced himself dazzled by the colour and animation of his playing. In two high-profile reviews of the Beethoven-Liszt Fifth Symphony, one critic praised a "magnificent" display of "virtuoso brilliance and temperament" that "forces us (literally) to listen to this familiar music with fresh ears," while another lamented "the waste of one of this generation's most impressive native talents" in this "absurd release." Of the Wagner album, Joseph Horowitz wrote that "Gould's tactile

---

* Northrop Frye noted that the idea of the frontier – "the unknown, the unrealized, the humanly undigested" – is built into the Canadian character: "The sense of probing into the distance, of fixing the eyes on the skyline, is something that the Canadian sensibility has inherited from the *voyageurs*." Indeed, he wrote, "There would be nothing distinctive in Canadian culture at all if there were not some feeling for the immense searching distance, with the lines of communication extended to the absolute limit, which is a primary geographical fact about Canada and has no real counterpart elsewhere."

engagement with the music fosters a wealth of living, breathing nuance. His trademark chiseled articulation does not preclude another, less advertised Gould trademark: all the lines, even the improbably long ones, sing." His piano recording of the *Siegfried Idyll* – intimate, lyrical, tonally resplendent, immaculately paced – may be his greatest performance, yet Vladimir Horowitz, after hearing it, told Harold Schonberg, "He played like a stupid ass."

Sometimes divided opinion came from the same critic: Harris Goldsmith, who called the recording of Mozart's K. 533 "loathsome," admitted that he had been swept away, in the early sonatas, by the "heady brilliance and ravishing detail" as well as the sheer confidence of Gould's playing. Some considered his Beethoven among the finest of the age. Gould admitted that his reading of the "Appassionata" was "the most perverse in history," adding, "I don't think there was a critic anywhere who had a good word to say about it," yet Allen Hughes, in the *New York Times*, nominated it as "the most extraordinary, and, in a way, refreshing, item of Beethoveniana to be issued in this 200th anniversary year of the composer's birth." Even those who disagreed with his interpretations often welcomed them as respite from tradition and cliché.

We always read about the critics who accused Gould of ignorance, insensitivity, impiousness, even insanity when it came to Mozart. "It is very difficult to see what Gould is out to prove," wrote one of them, "unless the rumor that he actually hates this music is true." Another compared Gould in Mozart to "a tremendously precocious but very nasty little boy trying to put one over on his piano teacher." (Fair enough.) But the Gould legend exaggerates the degree to which the idiosyncrasies of his later recordings outraged listeners and critics. Gould exaggerated it himself – it reinforced his status as a proud iconoclast. It is actually surprising how many of his quirkiest albums – the organ recording of the *Art of Fugue* and the harpsichord recording of Handel suites, the sonatas of Mozart and Beethoven – earned glowing reviews precisely *because* of their freshness. Of his traversal of Horowitz's terrain in Prokofiev and Scriabin, the Russian musicologist Alexei Kashperov, a Scriabin

authority, praised Gould's "genius" and said he had never heard
Prokofiev's Seventh Sonata so well played, "not even when Prokofiev
himself played it."

Gould's recordings always compelled attention, and often
received a great deal of space in magazines and newspapers. Each
new production that emerged from the snows of Toronto became an
event in the classical-music world, to be taken seriously, chewed
over, debated. Columbia Records rode the controversies about
Gould's recordings all the way to the bank. Of the first volume of
Mozart sonatas, a Columbia publicity memo noted, under the
heading "CONTROVERSY": "These are far from conventional interpretations – some movements are taken at breakneck speed – others
lingered over with great care – what emerges are interpretations of
exceptional virtuosity which will cause comment and excitement.
Result: S A L E S."

"I don't see any point in utilizing the technology as a delivery system and ignoring its much more important philosophical implications."

"Canada's principal contribution to North American thought consists of a highly original, comprehensive, and eloquent discourse on
technology," Arthur Kroker wrote, in *Technology and the Canadian
Mind*. "The Canadian mind may be one of the main sites in modern
times for working-out the meaning of technological experience.
Indeed, a general fascination with the question of technology extends
like a brilliant arc across the Canadian cultural imagination, from
cinema and music to literature and philosophy." Technology, above
all *communications* technology, he concluded, was at the heart of the
Canadian identity.

Gould was every inch a Canadian in this respect. He was one of
the first truly modern classical performers, for whom recording and
broadcasting were not mere adjuncts to the concert hall. When it
came to technology and media, he was interested in mechanical

minutiae as well as philosophical implications, and not only in music and recording: he knew his McLuhan intimately, read books like *Technic and Civilization* by the American social critic Lewis Mumford, studied the reflections on technology by the theologians Jean Le Moyne and Pierre Teilhard de Chardin.* He belongs within the "Toronto tradition" that included the media theorists Harold Innis and McLuhan and other writers including Northrop Frye and George Grant. In his own field he earned an international reputation as a philosopher of recording: his 1964 convocation address was the first shot in a twenty-year multimedia campaign of stimulating and controversial reflections on technology. His magnum opus was "The Prospects of Recording," published in the April 1966 issue of *High Fidelity* and based on a radio documentary he made for the CBC the year before. It is a manifesto on the ramifications of a musical life devoted to the electronic media.

Prophets of technology were scarce in the staid world of classical music, though hardly unknown among Canadians who came of age just after the Second World War.† In Canada, the history of communications and the psychological, social, political, and cultural effects of the mass media were hot topics in intellectual circles,

---

* Gould knew McLuhan and Le Moyne personally. In the later sixties McLuhan lived not far from him, and (as Eric McLuhan recalled) Gould was an occasional visitor to McLuhan's study. The two corresponded and spoke often on the phone, and Gould interviewed McLuhan twice for CBC radio projects. Gould thought him "a dear and wonderful man," despite his penchant for monologue and reluctance to give straight answers to questions, in which respects he out-Goulded Gould. McLuhan admired Gould's media work, and wrote, in *Counterblast* (1969), "Bless Glenn Gould for throwing the concert audience into the junkyard." Le Moyne met Gould in 1968, in which year both received the Canada Council's Molson Prize, and Gould interviewed him for a 1969 radio program about the Moog synthesizer.

† Robert E. Babe, in *Canadian Communication Thought: Ten Foundational Writers*, made the fascinating observation that virtually all of the writers he studied – Innis, McLuhan, Frye, Grant, and others – were greatly influenced by their mothers, read voraciously as children, had intense religious training as children and retained profound religious sensibilities as adults, did not have a prototypically "masculine" view of the world, were "outsiders" by disposition, and were concerned with the moral implications of technology. Sound familiar?

subjects of scientific research as well as philosophical speculation, and Gould absorbed the theorizing no less enthusiastically than he took to the machines themselves. He was comfortable with technology because he had grown up with it. It was not through concert-going that he really learned about music, but through radio and records. No wonder he extolled the virtues of quiet, sheltered, domestic listening that encouraged "a state of contemplation": that was how he had really come to know music in his formative years.

He knew McLuhan's work well before McLuhan was discovered in the United States and became a pop-culture sensation in the mid-sixties. Gould was skeptical about his trendiness, his "hot" and "cool" terminology, and so on: "I personally find his books a somewhat infuriating combination of analytic brilliance and sheer nuttiness," he wrote in 1966. (Look who's talking.) But he recognized that McLuhan was "an intriguing and important figure" who had "put his finger on some of the central issues of our time." The influence of McLuhan's ideas on media is unmistakable in Gould's writings – in, for instance, his concern with the effects of media on human psychology and behaviour, the issue encapsulated in McLuhan's catchphrase "The medium is the message." And he was not immune to McLuhan's vocabulary: witness his fondness for terms like "linear" and "tactile."

McLuhan wrote that "it is only too typical that the 'content' of any medium blinds us to the character of the medium," but Gould was not blinded. He recognized that recording was not intended to produce "a picture postcard of a concert," but was an entirely separate art form, "with its own laws and its own liberties, its quite unique problems and its quite extraordinary possibilities" – and its own ethics. (For him, the live concert recording was thus the worst of both worlds.) He insisted that recording was exactly analogous to filmmaking, and considered the standards and ethics of the concert hall no more relevant to recording than those of the theatre were to film. Assembling a performance outside of real time through splicing and other techniques was not dishonest; it was merely how a recording (like a film) was made. He coined terms like "creative cheating" and "creative lying" to emphasize the creative aspect of the process. In recording, as in film, "the musical end justifies the editorial means" – or, more cheekily, "the tape does lie and nearly always gets away with it." These were banal truths in the field of contemporary pop music, which embraced an aesthetic of recording that ignored the limitations of live performance; Gould's radicalism was to advocate the same creative engagement with the new technologies in his own more reactionary *métier*.

He was a new kind of classical performer – the musical equivalent of a film actor. Indeed, he was sometimes compared with the revolutionary Method actors of his day, like Marlon Brando and James Dean, when he first appeared on the international scene. Just as the development of the microphone and electronic amplification in the 1920s had encouraged a more intimate style in popular singers like Bing Crosby and later Frank Sinatra, it offered a perfect forum for a classical artist like Gould, whose repertoire and style were scaled to "the acoustic of the living room." Like a film actor, he was aware of the magnifying effect of the electronic media, which do not reward the outsized theatrical gesture. The "extreme definition," the "clarity, immediacy, and indeed almost tactile proximity" afforded by the drier recorded sound enhanced the analytical transparency of a performance and the sense of intimate communion with the listener. In other words, recording enhanced the style Gould was already trying to get with his fingers.

He was amazed at those colleagues who resisted the implications of recording. Rubinstein, for instance, herded people into the studio so that he could have an audience to play to, while Richter recorded in public because he needed the stimulus of an audience to play his best. Gould did not care how many people were in the studio as long as they were working on the recording, but he never permitted visitors: with even one extra person present, a recording session became a concert. (He was mortified whenever someone happened to overhear him practising in private.) Yet, he was no less concerned about communicating with his listeners than Rubinstein or Richter or anyone else. As he insisted in 1978, "there is no greater community

of spirit than that between the artist and the listener at home, com-
muning with the music." When Stokowski quit his post with the
Philadelphia Orchestra and turned his sights on recording and on
Hollywood, he announced, "I go to a higher calling," and Gould
shared that view: communicating with people individually (though
in great numbers) through the media was artistically and ethically
superior to doing so in the concert hall.

Gould deplored the impermanence of concerts. He once wrote,
"I never have been able to understand how theatre people can bear to
abandon their dramatic offspring once reared." In concert performances he saw only an endless series of imperfect, transient experiences
of a work, which became stale and distorted through over-exposure.
(His own interpretations did not improve through repetition in concerts.) But in a recording he saw a permanent document in which he
could leave a fixed, definitive statement of an interpretation, and
he accepted the responsibility of that position. He recorded a piece
as though he would never encounter it again, which was often the
case. He focused all of the mental and physical and technological
resources at his disposal on making that one experience of the work
as close as possible to ideal. "The new intensity of the interpreter's
role now encourages him to attempt a contact with the work which
is very much like that of the composer's own relation," he wrote in
1965. "It permits him to encounter a particular piece of music and
to analyze and dissect it in the most thorough way, and to make it
a vital part of his life for a relatively short period; and then to pass
on to some other challenge and to the satisfaction of some other
curiosity." (He compared himself to soap-opera actors who learn
and forget lines on a daily basis.) This attitude explains the still
astonishing polish and intensity of Gould's recordings, especially
after 1964; to paraphrase Shaw, they make us do with our ears what
we do with our eyes when we stare.

For Gould the permanence of recording meant he could con-
tinually expand his repertoire, well beyond the limits imposed by
concert life; and it meant that on those rare occasions when he
recorded something for the second time after the passage of years –

suites and fugues by Bach, the Goldberg Variations, Haydn's Sonata No. 59, Mozart's K. 330, Berg's Sonata – he had an opportunity to offer a completely new take on the music: the fact of the first recording absolved him from the need to put forward the same interpretation. The permanence of recording was in fact a crucial part of his creative approach to interpretation. Thomas Edison invented his tin-foil cylinder phonograph in 1877, and commercial recording began, with vertical-cut wax cylinders, in 1890; the catalogue of available recordings was already huge when Gould began adding to it. He realized that a recording artist was adding to a pile that grew larger by the year, and so needed to find unique and personal interpretations to justify doing so. He outlined his approach in the *Concert Dropout* interview:

> I think that if there's any excuse at all for making a recording it's to do it differently, to approach the work from a totally recreative point of view, that one is going to perform this particular work as it has never been heard before. And if one can't quite do that, I would say abandon it, forget about it, move on to something else where you *can* feel a little differently about it. . . . I wouldn't want to take the nice, easy, mean line in a [recorded] performance if only because there are nice, easy, mean-line performances available all throughout the *Schwann* catalogue and I would incline to buy those myself if that's what I wanted. I don't think there's much excuse for another Beethoven Fifth Concerto unless one has a totally different approach. Now, if that approach is based *only* on eccentricity, only on the idea that you want to shake people up and get dreadful reviews because of that shaking-up that you're trying to instate, then forget it. Obviously that's not a sufficient excuse to do anything. There has to be some quite convincing reason behind all that eccentricity. But if you *can* somehow manage to forge those two things, to actually make it convincingly Beethovenian eccentricity that really does catch everyone unawares, then by all means do it. That's the excuse of making records, I'm sure.

For Gould, the studio was a creative laboratory that offered a perfect marriage of freedom and control. The *Concert Dropout* interview, once more:

> This sounds a very strange thing to say, but I have in many cases come to studio without the least notion of how I was going to approach the work that we were to play that day. I've come in perhaps with five or six (as it then seemed to me) equally valid ideas, and if we were lucky, and if time permitted, and if the producer had the patience, we would try all five or six of those possible interpretations. And perhaps none of them worked, in which case we'd come back in a couple of weeks and try a seventh. If two or three did work, we [would] then repair to an editing cubicle within a week or so and listen to them – and really the week, at least, is necessary for some kind of perspective. . . . We know precisely what we want to do with that recording by the time we come to treat it as a finished product. We *don't* treat it as a finished product in the studio; we don't even think of it as that. I very often learn on company time, of course; fortunately CBS is very patient with me!

Like a filmmaker, Gould felt free to take chances "on the set," to bring an "improvisatory open-mindedness" to his performing and examine the work from various angles, because the post-production process left him time to reflect – and he sometimes let years elapse between recording and editing. One of his favourite examples was the A-minor fugue from Book One of *The Well-Tempered Clavier*, which he recorded in 1965. As it turned out, there were two usable takes at the same tempo, one "pompous, rather turgid, rather Teutonic," the other lighter, more "skittish"; neither worked all the way through, yet by splicing back and forth between them he created a more varied and structurally transparent interpretation, one he had not conceived in advance of the recording.

"Most of the ideas that have occurred to me as a performer have related in some measure to the microphone," Gould said in 1966, and in fact his early years with Columbia coincided with a period of experimentation and of great improvement in recording standards throughout the record business. Some of the albums from his concert days reflected an awareness of the impact the recording process itself could have on an interpretation. In his 1961 album of Brahms intermezzi, for instance, the "very discreet, recessed" sound matched the intimacy of the music itself, and in his 1962 album of *The Art of Fugue* he made "no attempt to glamorize the sound, to imprison it within a halo of resonance"; he used close-up miking to get an organ sound appropriate for domestic listening, not one that mimicked a recital in a church. But "the first records that really reflect a total concentration, a total respect for the medium," he said, came a couple of years after the end of his concert life, precisely when he began to exert authority over his own editing. Eventually, as Andrew Kazdin wrote, Gould came to understand tape splicing as well as a professional editor.

Many people assumed, on the basis of his vocal advocacy of technology, that Gould was a sort of mad scientist who assembled recordings literally note by note. That is nonsense – and if he *had* done so he would have bragged about it. His use of recording technology was mostly conservative, with takes and inserts recorded and edited in conventional ways. His producers have testified that he spliced less often than some classical artists, and because he rarely hit wrong notes and always had a solid architectural grasp of the music he was playing, needed splicing less than most performers. Some of his recordings, in fact, contain no splices at all. But he had no scruples about the practice: "I see nothing wrong in making a performance out of two hundred splices, as long as the desirable result is there." Regardless of the number he used, Gould was extraordinarily fussy about the quality of the splicing, pushing the comparatively rudimentary recording technology of the 1960s to its limits.*

---

* Andrew Kazdin noticed that Gould accepted minor flaws like small, unwanted shifts of tempo if they originated in his performance, but not if they were the result of imperfect splicing.

A page from Gould's score of Hindemith's song cycle *Das Marienleben* (original 1923 version), which he recorded with the soprano Roxolana Roslak, 1976-77. Like most of his scores, this one is largely devoid of interpretive markings – phrasing, fingering, and so on – but is black with editing notes. He would write such notes into a score while listening to his various takes of the piece, and after jotting down his final editing decisions he would convey them, often by telephone, to his producer – in this case Andrew Kazdin – who would splice the master tape accordingly, in New York. *(Estate of Glenn Gould.)*

Gould allowed recording techniques to influence his interpretations in other ways, some of them conventional – altering the balance of piano and orchestra, using electronic reverberation, regenerating a piece of tape in order to create an exact match between repeated passages. In the *Meistersinger* and *Götterdämmerung* excerpts in his Wagner album he tried a more radical option: overdubbing himself in order to give three- and four-hand performances. (True to form, he bragged about doing so in the liner notes.) He was enthusiastic about the possibilities of quadraphonic technology in the late sixties and early seventies, and envisioned recording fugues one line at a time for quadraphonic playback; he did no more than make a rudimentary, though promising, experiment with the technology during some leftover studio time in 1969, and anyway the fad for quad soon faded.

Influenced by film, Gould came to think more "dimensionally" about recorded sound after 1964, to the point of questioning the assumption that a recording must, like a concert, present an unvarying audio image. In 1970, he recorded Scriabin's Fifth Sonata using a process he called "acoustic orchestration" (and sometimes "acoustic choreography"), which required four pairs of microphones arranged throughout the hall: two inside the piano almost on top of the strings; two at Gould's usual perspective about five feet from the piano; two about eight or nine feet from the piano; and two pointed at the back of the hall to pick up ambient reverberation. The intent was to record the performance on eight-track tape in all four audio perspectives at once, then, in the mixing, to shift between or variously combine those perspectives so that the sound of the piano changes – gradually or suddenly, subtly or blatantly, rarely or frequently – in ways that underscore the different moods, structural features, and even details of the music. Gould compared the process to a filmmaker's use of close-ups, medium and long shots, hard cuts, dissolves, pans, zooms, and other camera techniques. He talked of using acoustic orchestration, perhaps in quadraphonic sound, in the later sonatas of Scriabin, though he abandoned his Scriabin cycle before mixing the Fifth

Sonata.* The only recording he released with this technique was his 1977 album of pieces by Sibelius. He later admitted that the understated music of Sibelius did not really *need* such sonic enhancement, but this evocative album did make a compelling case for the potential of his approach. Many listeners and critics were unconvinced: "the weirdest (ab)use of multi-miking techniques ever ventured by anyone for any misbegotten reason"; "the disruptive changes of focus can only be condemned"; and so on.

Gould, wearing his McLuhan hat, liked to point out how "electronic media have drastically altered the effect of music upon our society," how recording had made available whole repertoires of classical music (particularly early music) that in his day had limited relevance to the concert hall, how electronics had influenced twentieth-century composers. But for him, recording, like everything else, was ultimately about ethics. His powerful artistic ego notwithstanding, he approved of the "democratic" and "anonymous" nature of recording, which is a collaborative process undertaken in private settings, out of the public eye and away from the constraints of real time, and unburdened by "personality" in the way that a concert performance is. As he wrote near the end of his life, "I think that the finest compliment one can pay to a recording is to acknowledge that it was made in such a way as to erase all signs, all traces, of its making and its maker."

Gould noted that recording was changing the relationship of composer, performer, and listener, roles that had been increasingly separated since the later eighteenth century but were becoming, he said, "rather hopelessly and joyfully muddled" by the 1960s. It was a notion that McLuhan, Cage, and many others were talking about at the time; indeed, his advocacy of open borders between the roles

---

* Except for some comments about the opening bars, in his 1974 *Rolling Stone* interview – the recording was to have commenced with a striking rapid "zoom" from a "long shot" to a "close-up" – Gould left no mixing instructions for the Fifth Sonata. When Andrew Kazdin edited it for a posthumous CD in 1986, he declined to attempt a speculative acoustic orchestration of his own, and so the recording is available to the public only in a conventional, unvarying audio perspective.

of composer, performer, and listener is but one respect in which he was a sort of postmodernist *avant la lettre*. His creative approach to interpretation, for instance – that free, subjective, self-conscious engagement with musical texts without regard for inherited traditions or the composer's intentions – calls to mind contemporary literary ideas like Umberto Eco's "open work," Roland Barthes's *nouvelle critique*, and the whole phenomenon of reader-response criticism, even, in some ways, deconstruction. (There is no contradiction between labelling that freedom both Romantic and postmodern; in fact, according to one school of thought postmodernism is nothing but a kind of late-late Romanticism, anyway.) His atemporal, ahistorical view of musical works, his advocacy of a mixing of styles (as in his String Quartet or his "Baroque-ish" Mozart performances), his defiance of avant-garde factions and opposition to the notion of "progress" in the arts – all resonated with intellectual trends of his day, in various fields, to such a degree that we might call Gould the first postmodern performer of the Western classical canon.

He extended his postmodern belief in creative freedom to its logical limit, advocating the direct participation of the listener in the creative process, through the intercession of technology. He believed that the modern listener had the same right to tinker with the recording artist's work as the performer had to tinker with the composer's. "Dial twiddling is in its limited way an interpretative act," he noted, and the hi-fi listener was by nature a creative force: even to adjust volume, tone, and balance on a crude home stereo of the 1960s was to impose oneself creatively onto the work. "I'm all for the kit concept," he said in 1968. "I'd love to issue a series of variant performances and let the listener choose what they themselves most like. Let them assemble their own performance. Give them all the component parts, all the component splices, rendered at different tempi with different dynamic inflections, and let them put something together that they really enjoy – make them participant to that degree."

Such ideas sounded crazy to most people in the sixties, though not those on the cutting edge in Gould's field; the trail-blazing

English record producer John Culshaw credited him with "the break-through in this line of thought."* But even without the "kits" he envisioned, recording, Gould said, "compels the performer to relinquish some control in favor of the listener, a state of affairs, by the way, which I happen to find both encouraging and charming, not to mention aesthetically appropriate and morally right." It is a pity that Gould did not live to explore the digital technologies of the late twentieth and twenty-first centuries, technologies, like the Internet, that democratize and decentralize the institutions of culture to a degree he never imagined, creating precisely the sort of society that McLuhan described as "all centre without margins." He would have admired the ethical implications of such technologies – and would have had fun playing with them.

Gould was an optimist, a Utopian, a transcendentalist when it came to technology, unlike some theorists of the media, including his countryman George Grant, and even more so than McLuhan, who was not necessarily a champion of the media he sought to understand. Gould believed that technology had an infinite capacity for emancipating people and bettering human society; his personal experience of technology had always been positive, and, characteristically, he believed that everyone else's should be, too. He apparently gave very little attention to the potential dark side of technology, for instance its dehumanizing effects – something McLuhan wrote about. Just like his parents, but in a more sophisticated, more modern way, he wanted to "do good" and foster an intimate relationship with his community through his music, and he could do this

---

* Forty years later, digital technology has made Gould's prophecies eminently feasible. There have been CDs, including classical CDs, in which the disposition of the contents is left open – for instance, a recording of Beethoven's Violin Concerto offering fifteen alternate cadenzas for the first movement – and the typical DVD resembles in many ways a Gouldian "kit." In the movie business, to the horror of the studios, the "director's cut" now has competition from the "viewer's cut": computer aficionados have lately been circulating their own edited versions of certain movies online. The "fan edit" has also become popular among some pop-music fans, though classical-music types, typically, have been slower to catch on to such things.

better from a distance, through technology, than he could in person. "Art on its loftiest mission," he once wrote, "is scarcely human at all."

"I saw myself as a sort of musical Renaissance Man, capable of doing many things."

Gould was not a piano machine, the kind of performer whose life is the practice room and whose thinking is bound up with his instrument. "Anyone who is really interested in music should combine as many fields as possible," he told a reporter when he was sixteen. "A Canadian writer, composer, and broadcaster who happens to play the piano in his spare time" – that was how he once described himself. It was never quite true, though he did spend an increasing amount of time away from the piano after 1964, even as he was becoming more prolific as a recording artist. He saw his mission as far broader than that of a performer: he wanted to make statements, about music and culture and life, and to this end the piano was just one of many means.

Had he not been a musician, he said, he would like to have been a writer, and after 1964 he worked more and more with his pen. (And it *was* a pen: this prophet of the electronic media hated typing, preferring to draft writings by hand and then dictate to a secretary.) He produced a flurry of magazine and newspaper articles, liner notes, reviews, lectures, scripted interviews (including *self*-interviews),* and texts for radio, television, and films, as well as private letters that sometimes amounted to dissertations. He recycled a lot – reprinting articles as often as three or four times in different forms, reusing radio pieces as articles (and vice versa), stealing the odd phrase or sentence or paragraph from himself – but the quantity of his output

---

* After retiring from concert life Gould rarely gave conventional interviews. Usually he either wrote out both questions and answers, sometimes on the basis of a preliminary impromptu conversation, or granted an unscripted interview on the condition that he could edit it for publication.

was still impressive: well over fifteen hundred pages of written and spoken material by Gould have been published to date. Not even counting public lectures and his vast output for the CBC, he published some forty pieces in the decade beginning in 1964, liner notes as well as pieces in periodicals like *Saturday Night*, *Saturday Review*, Toronto's *Globe and Mail* and *Star*, the *New York Times*, and particularly *High Fidelity/Musical America*.

In his concert days he wrote mostly about composers and works, but from the early sixties he cast his net wider; just about the only subject he *refused* to write about was "the trials and tribulations of piano playing." Those forty pieces cover an impressive range of subject matter: composers including Bach, Beethoven, Bizet, Byrd, Gibbons, Grieg, Hindemith, Ives, Korngold, Krenek, Mahler, Prokofiev, Schoenberg, Scriabin, and Strauss; Yehudi Menuhin and Petula Clark; rare Romantic repertoire and Canadian music of the twentieth century; the performance of early music on the piano; the nature and history of fugue; the role of the imagination in interpretation; the art of piano transcription; conductors; recording; the Moog synthesizer; his innovative approach to radio documentary; music on television; musical competitions; the National Youth Orchestra; the ethical underpinnings of his aesthetic positions; musical ephemera that struck his fancy (the British musical psychic Rosemary Brown, the fictitious P. D. Q. Bach); and his baby steps as a Leacockian humorist.

In the fifties, on the basis of little more than a handful of record-jacket notes, he already enjoyed a reputation as learned and provocative thinker. Over the years he was besieged with offers to write a regular column, by magazines like *Piano Quarterly* and *Contemporary Keyboard*, even *Opera News*, and he was asked to contribute to books and to the *Encyclopaedia Britannica*.* As early as 1959, Knopf offered to publish a book under his name, and over the years he was solicited (sometimes repeatedly) by more than a dozen major houses in North

---

* He also received several offers to supervise new editions of Bach's keyboard works, but he turned them down.

America, Europe, and Japan to publish either a collection of essays or an original book. Gould actually announced forthcoming books several times in the early sixties, but he never went beyond preliminary discussions with publishers.

His reliable outrageousness may have attracted publishers as much as his actual writing. He was passionate about communicating his ideas, and from the start his writings were never without brilliant insights and provocative theses, but as a writer, at least until middle age, he was at best uneven, at worst awful. He was terribly insecure as a writer, as revealed by his reluctance (and, when he was famous enough, refusal) to allow his writings to be edited, and by his admission that he was far more sensitive to criticism of his writing than of anything else. He was not really a writer at all, in fact – he was a raconteur. As a conversationalist he was animated, engaging, provocative, witty to the point of riotous, and usually dominating through the electricity of his ideas and his sheer volubility.* In October 1963, *Holiday* magazine commissioned Leonard Cohen to interview him and write about his impressions of various cities. The two met in the Hotel Bonaventure in Ottawa, but Cohen, according to his biographer Ira B. Nadel, "became so enthralled by Gould's conversation that he forgot to pursue the line of questioning he had prepared." He never did write the story.

Some of his conversational dazzle found its way into his writing. Mendelssohn, he wrote, "has in certain circles been regarded as the goody-two-shoes of music," while Hindemith, near the end of his career, "drew consistency around him like a Linus blanket." He described the third movement of Ives's Fourth Symphony as "a fugue of the sort that Taneyev might have written had he chanced to recompose Brahms's *Academic Festival Overture*," and when introducing a clip from Terry Riley's minimalist work *In C* on the radio, he quipped, "And you thought Carl Orff had found an easy way to

---

* To judge from the testimony of his friends, I doubt that Gould was drawing on personal experience when he wrote that "unembarrassed silence" was "the true mark of friendship."

make a living?" But he was not a *craftsman* when it came to writing, a Flaubert fretting and sweating over the rhythm of his sentences. Often he was merely a stenographer for thoughts that came off the top of his head, and his volubility tended to come across as pompous, not charming, on the page. To study his drafts is revealing: a remarkable number of his writings ended up in print in almost exactly the form in which they first escaped from his pen, minimally revised, sometimes with glaring weaknesses left untouched in draft after draft. He did not mind putting in long hours as a writer, but he did not naturally possess the craft for making polished prose out of the products of this teeming brain.

Gould's surviving high-school essays already reveal a fondness for pretentious verbiage, over-ripe metaphor, embarrassing alliteration, excruciating word play, and forced, heavy-handed attempts at humour. His teachers had to contend with the likes of this: "Far down, through the concrete channel, a myriad of flustered flotsam floundered against a flurry of the wind-squall. . . . The rain struck against my streaming window pane and the torrent glanced gleefully groundward to plague the plodding plutocrat and proletarian alike." He was in Grade 13, eighteen years old, when he wrote that; later that same year, he would presume to lecture on Schoenberg to his conservatory colleagues. In later life he never fully outgrew the literary sins of his youth. One might forgive a writer for using the redundancy "vacant emptiness," for concocting the adverb "idée-fixedly," for observing that late-Romantic tonality was "choking on the catarrhal drippings of its own sentimentality" if his basic usage was at least sound, but Gould's often was not; he did not even spell particularly well, and his punctuation, though he fussed over it, was lousy.

He seemed to equate long, tortuous sentences with seriousness and sophistication, and he was prone to false formality – playing professor. He could not resist using two words where one would do: multi-movement works were works "employing a multiple movement mechanism," a passage that stays in the same key was a passage that "limits the confines of modulative area within its structure." In his early prose especially there is often a drone of pseudo-academic babble that some readers (and Gould) mistook for erudition. Here is a typical paragraph from his liner notes for his first Columbia album, in which he is saying only that the ornate melody of the opening Aria is not the fund from which later motifs in the Goldberg Variations are drawn:

> One might justifiably expect that in view of the constancy of the harmonic foundation the principal pursuit of the variations would be the illumination of the motivic facets within the melodic complex of the aria theme. However, such is not the case, for the thematic substance, a docile but richly embellished soprano line, possesses an intrinsic homogeneity which bequeaths nothing to posterity and which, so far as motivic representation is concerned, is totally forgotten during the thirty variations. In short, it is a singularly self-sufficient little air which seems to shun the patriarchal demeanor, to exhibit a bland unconcern about its issue, to remain totally uninquisitive as to its raison d'etre.

When writing about recording, say, or writing autobiographically, Gould's tone was more natural and genial, his texture lighter, even if overwriting remained always a temptation, but when writing analytically about music he seemed unable to avoid tangled prose. The result could be the likes of this (take a deep breath):

> *Metamorphosen*, for example, which one need not praise by noting that its composer was then eighty, is a work in which the harmonic consequences of triads that divide between them the twelve-tone capacity of the chromatic scale – the same triad relationship that Schoenberg developed as the basis of the tone row in his, coincidentally, contemporaneous work *Ode to Napoleon Bonaparte* – are mined here not for the significance of their mutually complementary interval relationships (upon which Schoenberg develops his structure) but rather for the comparison of those relationships to the casual but never perfunctory

sequences of purely diatonic cadence that they resemble and by which they are, at most pivotal moments in the work, quietly supplanted.

That 115-word sentence may well reveal a fantastic insight into the harmonic idioms of both Strauss and Schoenberg, but who can tell?

He was tempted by pseudo-academic prose because he sought legitimacy as an intellectual, but temperamentally he was not a scholar – he was an enthusiast. He retained some of the excitability of adolescence all his life, and he could not take up some new idea or cause without quickly fancying himself an authority on it. To make a case for a pet love or against a pet hate was a major motivation of his writing. The pet loves fared better. On the subjects he was passionate about – Strauss and Schoenberg, recording and radio – he was informed, original, provocative. But when he let fly at his *bêtes noires*, he often revealed a surprising ignorance of basic sources and a willingness to accept trite and spurious ideas. His musical rationales for disliking late Mozart and middle-period Beethoven – and Schubert and Schumann and Chopin – were feeble, as were his efforts to divide up musical forms into sheep and goats (fugues good, nocturnes bad, sonatas so-so). He disliked fantasias because they were fantastical; he disliked jazz, in effect, because they just made it up as they went along. He once poked fun at a Grade 2 teacher who used round-singing as a metaphor for "the heroic achievements which were possible" – this was during the war – "if we would *all pull together*," yet he was himself prone to simplistic moral and sociological thinking about musical forms: "autocratic" sonata forms, "competitive" concerto forms, and so on. Such thinking was backed up by a conveniently spotty and outdated command of music history, and a fondness for vaulting generalizations, which made Gould prone to undergraduate platitudes like this: "The age in which Bach lived was very proud to define itself as an age of reason." (That would have been news to Bach.) He was blissfully unaware that some of the ideas he considered original and exciting were in fact discredited clichés.

None of which matters. Gould was a pianist, not a writer; an interpreter, not a musicologist; a creator, not a scholar. He thought like a composer. He was not interested in forming an objective image of music and music history, but in buttressing the image that best supported and validated his creative ideas and goals. His learning was filtered through – bounded by – his needs as an artist. And if that meant bending or ignoring aspects of music history or style, he was up to it. Whether he knew that it was questionable to assess Bach or Mozart or Liszt by the standards of Schoenberg is irrelevant: to do so was essential to his own creative project. What matters is what he *did* with those assessments. Just as a great opera can come from a shoddy libretto, a great performance can be founded on shoddy musicology. Writing and playing require different kinds of thinking, and what makes a performance compelling, integrated, logical has little to do with musicology, even if musicologists claim otherwise. Gould's Mozart performances unfold with a conviction that his written and spoken comments on Mozart never attain – even if those comments remain indispensable to understanding the recordings.

So Gould *was* an intellectual, but he did his most important intellectual work at the piano, not at his desk. What is touching is that he never quite accepted this himself; despite uneven success with his pen he never stopped yearning for the particular kind of intellectual respectability that comes through writing, even if he didn't need it. "He said ridiculous things which made me mad," Rudolf Serkin recalled, after hearing Gould talk on the radio. "But then at the end he played, and everything was all right."

"It's Op. 2 that counts!"

There would be no Op. 2. After completing his String Quartet in 1955, Gould would never again finish a serious, substantial composition. When he was just eighteen his press kit noted that "Mr. Gould hopes to be able to divide his time always equally between composition and the piano." Later, when he talked about leaving concert life behind and having "the last half of my life to myself," it was always in order to devote himself in large part to composition, which he saw as his true calling. He knew he would have to give concerts or make records in order to earn money; he was aware that "composers must eat" – even if they required only one meal a day. "An ideal arrangement," he said at Stratford in 1956, "would be if I were able to play my limit of twenty-five concerts a year all in two or three months and have the rest of my time for composing." On his concert tours he could find little leisure or energy for composition, even during down times. He admitted to John Roberts that he spent much of his free time on tour simply staring out hotel-room windows, and between tours there were recording sessions, broadcasts, and other commitments to keep him busy.

He still managed to compose in those years, sometimes on odd bits of hotel and airline stationery. In February 1959, in a letter to David Diamond, he reported, "I am struggling with the sonata for clarinet and piano, which I am desperately trying to prevent [from] becoming a quintet. My piano writing always has a habit of getting over-rich and assuming a sort of organ pedal for the left hand."* He described the music as Straussian, "arch-romantic," like that of the String Quartet. Some surviving sketches dated as early as July 14, 1957, appear to be for this piece. It begins strikingly, in purest C major, with a twenty-seven-bar outpouring of unaccompanied melody for the clarinet. (Gould was probably influenced by the opening of Strauss's oboe concerto.) Neither the clarinet nor the piano writing is idiomatic except in terms of range: the sketch reads like an exercise in pure three-part counterpoint, like one of Bach's sonatas, and Gould gives little thought to the clarinetist's need to breathe. Over the summer of 1957 he wrote only six pages (less than seventy bars) of the sonata, and by December just a page more. But it is clear that

---

* A month before, he had told a reporter that the sonata was finished, yet in a 1962 interview he said he had "a work sitting around that began as a wood-wind quintet, then altered itself and became a clarinet sonata. It has taken three different forms in the past four years. It is 95 per cent completed."

he intended to develop his themes in imitative counterpoint, including fugue, and through the sort of Schoenbergian "developing variation" he had essayed in the String Quartet. More pages of the clarinet sonata survive – as many as three dozen – from a year or two later,* but his efforts to develop his material tended to degenerate into verbose sprawl.

As his concert schedule dwindled in the early sixties, he spent more time composing, and planned some ambitious works. Between about 1959 and 1964, he worked on what he described as "a John Donne portrait," a song cycle for mezzo-soprano and piano based on Donne's Holy Sonnets. At least two dozen pages of sketches survive for settings of at least four of the nineteen sonnets: No. 1 ("Thou has made me, And shall thy worke decay?"), No. 6 ("This is my playes last scene"), the famous No. 10 ("Death be not proud"), and No. 14 ("Batter my heart, three person'd God"). The last seems particularly to have interested him. Again, the harmonic idiom was late-Romantic – tonal but highly chromatic, though in spots almost purely diatonic, too – and Gould's fondness for angular, expressionistic melody hints at the influence of Schoenberg's songs.

He conceived another ambitious vocal work in fall 1961 when he read a series of letters written by German soldiers in January 1943, shortly before their surrender after the bloody, failed siege of Stalingrad. (First published in the Autumn 1961 issue of *The Hudson Review*, the letters appeared as a book, *Last Letters from Stalingrad*, in 1962.) He was particularly moved by the seventh letter, which begins: "You are the wife of a German officer; so you will take what I have to tell you, upright and unflinching, as upright as you stood on the station platform the day I left for the East."† The officer

---

* None of his sketches is labelled "clarinet sonata," but there are internal clues to their identity – mainly the abbreviation "cl" in various spots. (The accompaniment is unmistakably for piano.)

† He was apparently also struck by the first letter, one line of which – "Monica, what is our life compared to the many million years of the starry sky!" – he set to music in several sketches.

expresses his love for his wife, notes the "hopeless situation" of the German army ("misery, hunger, cold, renunciation, doubt, despair and horrible death"), acknowledges "my share of personal guilt in all this," and implores her to be strong, not bitter. The letter ends, "Don't forget me too quickly." The text, Gould said, is "an extraordinarily moving thing, in which he instructs his wife in how she must conduct herself in the catastrophe of their world. He exhibits the remarkable schizophrenia of the German military character, coupling sentimental nostalgia with arrogant autocracy."

Gould soon began sketching *A Letter from Stalingrad*, which he described as a "concert aria" for soprano, ten or fifteen minutes long, with piano but eventually to be orchestrated. He said he was writing it for Lois Marshall, though she said after his death that she knew nothing about it. He worked on the piece for several years, most intensively around the time of his last concerts, and at least about fifty pages of sketches survive. (His compositional shorthand can be difficult to decipher, and he was no neater a penman as a composer than as a writer.) "It's a very personal piece for me," he told the CBC *Times* in spring 1964. The music consisted of "loose variations" on a theme from one of the pieces he loved most: Strauss's *Metamorphosen*, which, appropriately, was completed in Germany during the last weeks of the Second World War. The theme in question was the brooding, harmonically unstable utterance Strauss gives to the cellos and double basses in the opening bars, though Gould's sketches also allude to other motifs from *Metamorphosen*. The sketches, which include several vocal themes as well as an instrumental introduction and interludes, reveal a lyrical, richly contrapuntal late-Romantic style, some strategic use of tonal ambiguity and atonality for expressive and dramatic purposes, at least one outbreak of fugue, and a few hints of agitated "war" music. (One sketch includes an angular, wide-spaced "Fate motive.") The music is impassioned, at times expressionistic, in its rhetoric, suggesting early Schoenberg and Berg.

Gould's ambition extended even to opera. When he was twelve he sketched the libretto for an opera dealing with nothing less than

A sketch, from the early 1960s, for the beginning of Gould's unfinished soprano cantata *A Letter from Stalingrad*. The opening bars are for an instrumental introduction; the vocal line begins at the end of stave 1 and continues on stave 9 ("You are the wife of a German officer"). The chord progression noted in musical shorthand on staves 4–7 is from the opening bars of Strauss's *Metamorphosen*, here transposed to F minor – the main key of Gould's String Quartet and probably also of the cantata. *(Estate of Glenn Gould.)*

the destruction of the human race in a nuclear holocaust and its replacement by a "species of morally enlightened frogs, fish, and associated reptiles" – he dubbed it, in perhaps his most gruesome pun, "an aquatic *Toad und Verklärung*." There was to have been one human role, he said, for a boy soprano – "and I'll give you one guess as to who was to get it." He said he also wrote some music for a chorus of frogs, but it does not survive. Early in 1956 he told reporters he was planning an opera for CBC television based on Kafka's story "The Metamorphosis," with a libretto, "just finished," by "a friend in Montreal." The opera was to run an hour and a half, to have a cast of seven with a chamber orchestra, and to feature "modern techniques." He claimed to be working on it, but no identifiable music is extant.

In the early sixties, when his championship of Strauss was at it most intense, he had an idea for an opera inspired by the composer. About forty pages of work on a libretto and music survive, revealing at least two main stages of work. The first drafts of the libretto – the literary merit of which is poor – date from around 1960–62, and suggest a one-act work, set in the present day, revolving around a sixtyish composer addressed (like Strauss) as "Doctor." In the opening scene, two musicians of modernist sympathies challenge his latest opera, the hero of which has abandoned "the world of action" and "retreated into the half world of dreams." They dismiss the work as bloated, pompous, saccharine, over-orchestrated, full of arcane devices like overture and fugue and sonata – as, in short, a Romantic relic "that does not belong in spirit to the times." The scene ends with the composer's passionate defence of artistic individualism: "One cannot close ranks without suffocating." Other early drafts survive for a different opening scene, in which the composer's daughters, concerned with advancing his career, urge him to ingratiate himself with influential people: "Think of it father – your opera given by Karajan – your sonata played by Cliburn – your symphony given by Bernstein." But the composer chides them, insisting that the satisfaction of the work itself counts more than public acclaim. Later, Gould conceived of a *two*-act opera focused on a serenely detached composer who "lives a strong interior life," and in yet another (possibly still later) draft, the opera is explicitly about Strauss, set in his villa in the Bavarian Alps in 1940, the year he began his last opera, *Capriccio*. Only a few lines of this draft survive, and a title: *Dr. Strauss Writes an Opera*.

Near the end of his concert career Gould returned to this project, at first in a present-day setting with characters of noble rank and a chorus of orchestral musicians. In his final take on the subject, around 1964, he settled on a structure of one long act, a setting in the eighteenth century, characters including a count and countess and other nobles, an allegorical plot with a poetic libretto, and a score featuring a good deal of eighteenth-century pastiche (recitatives, arias, choruses, fugues) – all of which is lifted straight out of *Capriccio*. The count and countess patronize many artists, one of whom, an elderly composer, is condemned for writing unfashionable music: "Old man you're failing/Old man you're dying/Old man your world will simply fade away/You claim your art's refined/Become yourself resigned/At this our court you've long outlived your day." Gould finally sketched some music, at least fifteen pages' worth, most of it for an argumentative vocal fugue that recalls the laughing-and-squabbling Octet in *Capriccio*. It was a fascinating idea, to take a work like *Capriccio*, a self-reflexive opera about opera, and add a new layer of meaning to it – an opera about an opera about opera. Gould called it a "quasi-autobiographical opera," his aim being to explore in a creative new way cherished ideas about progress and fashion in music, about artistic integrity versus worldly success – ideas that for him had always revolved around Strauss.

But neither this nor any other of his major compositional projects advanced beyond rough sketches,* and his surviving sketches reveal an enormous disparity between plans and reality. In moments

---

* It may be that some compositions were more complete in his head than on paper. John Roberts recalls hearing him play music from *A Letter for Stalingrad* for as long as thirty or forty minutes – perhaps he was improvising on ideas he had only roughly sketched, or had worked out more music in his head than on paper.

of honesty he admitted that "I specialize in unfinished works" and that his composing was "much more talk than action," yet he never stopped boasting publicly of major works that were just around the corner – vocal music, chamber music, works for piano and orchestra. In late 1962 he told a reporter, "Right now, I'm working on a symphony I think I like."* He would claim that such works were underway or nearly finished when his sketches reveal nothing or only rudimentary work – at such times, his longing to be treated as a composer is poignantly evident.

As early as age sixteen he told a local paper, "I would like to do more composing but at present haven't the time," and when high school was behind him it was concert life that provided an excuse. His compositional ambition grew stronger as his disenchantment with concert life intensified, but at the point at which he actually stopped giving concerts his composing effectively ceased.[†] After spring 1964, faced with the prospect of a life devoted in large part to composition, he balked. He was insecure as a composer, and hypersensitive to criticism, and aware that his preferred compositional style – Strauss by way of Schoenberg – was growing increasingly unfashionable. But the main problem was simpler: as a composer, his reach vastly exceeded his grasp.

He had the temperament to be a composer, and he had talent. The String Quartet revealed a command of motivic manipulation and late-Romantic harmony, and *So You Want to Write a Fugue?* – despite its jokey premise – revealed a command of formal counterpoint. But he had no training as a composer, and was too proud to solicit advice from others, especially after he had become internationally

---

* The closest thing to a symphony I have discovered is a curious "Sonata" in E-flat major from around 1964, scored for flute, oboe, bassoon, two horns, two trumpets, and strings. Gould did nothing more than rudimentary sketching for first and second themes, in a harmonic idiom so resolutely diatonic that the prepubescent Mozart would have found it conservative.

† The break is strikingly obvious in his surviving sketches – unless one assumes that boxfuls of compositional manuscripts from after 1964 once existed but have since vanished, which, since Gould was a packrat, is unlikely.

famous and had had several pieces published. Some of his compositional ideas had promise, but they tended to elude him just where
training and craft became most necessary. Often he got caught up in
spinning out ideas, and the music got away from him, lost in a sprawl
he could not control. Many sketches reveal the same turgidness, too-
dense counterpoint, and busy but prosaic rhythmic profile that
plagued his String Quartet. But his greatest stumbling block, as he
told an interviewer in 1959, was that he had "absolutely no home
base idiomatically" – just the fatal flaw he saw in Stravinsky's eclecti-
cism. "As a composer, I'm a maker of grafts," he admitted in 1967,
"which I suppose is a fancy way of describing an attitude to composition which some would call eclectic and others, less well disposed,
derivative." As a composer he never found a distinctive voice – precisely what he *did* have, so spectacularly, as a pianist.

Sadly, the only music he actually completed in the last half of his
life was humorous occasional pieces that – like *So You Want to Write
a Fugue?* – relied on his gift for pastiche. In spring 1964, for instance,
he composed a little madrigal for four solo voices and piano, in
honour of Goddard Lieberson's twenty-fifth anniversary with
Columbia Records, and taped a hilarious performance of the piece
rather than attend a testimonial dinner in New York. He wrote the
text himself, and filled it with in-jokes about Columbia's commitment to esoteric music ("We're all uncommercial here, our sales get
worse from year to year") and references to Columbia artists like
Szell and Serkin, Stravinsky and Craft. The four movements –
chorales framing a recitative and fugue – include some witty parody
of the Elizabethan madrigal; a Baroque-style fugue that begins,
"Lennie Bernstein wants to do Boulez, Nono, Stockhausen, Nono,
Lennie, no, you can't, why must you be so damn avant, damn avant,
damn avant?"; and a brief eruption of atonality at the text, "For art
gone mad this company's gone broke."

But his failure as a serious composer must have hurt: it was the
most significant failure of his career, since it meant abandoning
his most cherished ambition. It has been suggested that Gould's
compositional efforts reflected a longing for immortality, and he was

indeed frustrated as a concert performer because "you don't create anything that lasts." But his real longing was to be a truly *creative* artist, and he did in fact succeed in being one, in his own way. When he gave up trying to be a composer in the conventional sense, he did not lose his creativity; he simply channelled it into other pursuits. The less original music he composed, the more he exercised his creativity in his performances of other people's music. Permanently preserving deeply personal interpretations through the medium of recording – here was at least some of the creativity and immortality that Gould had craved since childhood.

Not all, however. The decline of his compositional efforts also coincided precisely with the start of a new career in which he would realize his creative ambition with astonishing originality, albeit in a venerable medium: radio.

"I'm devoted to radio. It's home for me."

It was radio that Gould described, in 1968, as "my favourite medium." He was an *aural* person. His senses of sight and taste and smell were poorly developed, but what he took in through his ears, be it music or speech or noise, affected him deeply, and what he put out for the ears of others, as a pianist or telephone companion or disembodied voice on the radio, was unusually compelling. It was the nature of radio, as well as its content, that moved him. "It's always occurred to me," he said, "that when those first people sat glued or wired to their crystal sets, what they really were recognizing was the phenomenon of another human voice. It wasn't a fact of news reportage, it wasn't vital weather information, it was the phenomenon of that human voice, the sheer mystery and challenge of another human voice being five blocks away and being heard. It didn't matter whether what was being said was being said accurately or inaccurately, or was senseless or serious – none of that counted. What really counted was that there was a voice, there was a way of communicating something – no matter what – one person to another, and not being in the same room, in the same acoustical area."

Radio was the perfect medium for an introverted loner who wanted both physical distance from and intimate communication with his public. Already as a child he considered radio drama "somehow more pure, more abstract" than live theatre, to which his "puritan temperament" objected. Gerald Nachman, in *Raised on Radio*, wrote that radio is "an entirely interior experience, closer to reading than anything else, a quiet, contemplative thing," and Northrop Frye called it "the blind man's medium." To listen to the radio is to eavesdrop on something private, to *overhear* something – precisely the effect Gould seemed to want in his recordings. The intimacy of radio gives it great power over its listener. McLuhan noted "the power of radio to involve people in depth" (for good or ill). "I live right inside radio when I listen," he said. This nature of radio was most obvious when the medium was new and still a thing of mystery and wonder; what Gould eventually came to seek was a radio style which recaptured that original sense.

"Gould and his contemporaries were the first radio generation – and the last," wrote Robert Fulford. "I'm speaking of those born shortly before or shortly after 1930. . . . We were the first to grow up with radio all around us, and pretty well the last to grow up without television." Like many Canadians, Gould believed in and supported public radio, and public radio returned the favour. The CBC supported him generously through the fifties, sixties, and early seventies, even as its attention was turning increasingly to television. He was a genuine fan of the CBC, and kept up with its internal politics and with developments in the radio industry generally. Margaret Pacsu once ran a contest on her radio show inviting listeners to call in if they could identify the music she was playing, some obscure early songs by Schoenberg. Only one person in Canada called in, and of course it was Gould, though he declined the prize: it was one of his own records.

When Gould stopped giving concerts, creative and progressive people still held positions of authority at the CBC, budgets for cultural programming were relatively generous, and demand for

Canadian content was high. He was given *carte blanche* to make whatever programs interested him, within the limits of the network's resources. In the later sixties he was contracted to give four recitals and make two documentaries per year for the radio network, though it was difficult to keep him on schedule. His recitals now tended to be integrated, thematic programs, featuring works related in some way (nationality, composer, genre, key) and including his own commentary, which often took the form of a scripted conversation with a CBC announcer. He tried to make these conversations sound spontaneous, but when a staff announcer would, say, refer to Beethoven's G-major piano concerto as "a rather stingy piece motivically," it was obvious who was really doing the talking.* Gould often performed major works on the radio and nowhere else: Beethoven's "Hammerklavier" Sonata and *Pastoral Symphony*, for instance, and the Sonata No. 2 by the Norwegian composer Fartein Valen, which he considered a masterpiece. He explored repertoire he would never have recorded.† In 1970 he surprised everyone by programming Chopin's B-minor sonata, which he had decided was a better piece than he had realized once he actually picked up a score. Encouraged, he said, by the "aesthetic cross-breeding" typical of the permissive artistic environment of the 1960s,** he offered a rhythmically straightforward, "symphonized," resolutely "Teutonic" reading, resisting "the temptation to succumb to the enticing roulades in which this music abounds" and imposing instead a Mendelssohn-ish

---

* Gould wrote to a correspondent in the late sixties that he had wanted to release albums, too, that included spoken commentary, but Columbia Records had rejected the idea.

† Also, his technical standards were a little lower in one-time broadcasts. There were poor splices in some of his radio performances that he would never have countenanced in one of his albums.

** The program in which the sonata was broadcast included a ten-minute capsule-history of recent musical trends, which, according to Lorne Tulk, was extracted from a much longer documentary on music in the sixties that Gould made for the CBC and edited into various forms, but that ultimately never aired. To my knowledge, the full-length version does not survive.

rectitude. It was, he said, "a great experiment," and of course the performance did no justice to Chopin, as he admitted. When Columbia asked him to record the sonata, he refused.

After 1964 he ventured more and more beyond the conventional radio recital. The twenty-four-week series *The Art of Glenn Gould*, which ran in 1966–67, was another of his post-concert "position papers," a comprehensive survey of his recordings and musical predilections. Public interest in the series was so great that it was reorganized for a second run in 1969, and this time Gould's commentary ventured farther afield, into topics ranging from Bach's fugues and suites to the Moog synthesizer, from Mozart and Schnabel to "the psychology of the virtuoso," and interviewed a wide range of guests: István Anhalt, Walter Carlos, John Diefenbaker, Jean Le Moyne, Norman McLaren. He made more and more programs in which he did not perform: *Anti Alea* (1968), in which he wove commentary, music, and interviews into a documentary on contemporary "chance" music, which disturbed him; an interview-documentary for the series *The Scene* (1972), in which he used sports as a metaphor for competition in all facets of life. He even dreamed, from childhood, of reading the news on the air some day, and came very close to doing so one evening. He happened to be hanging around the CBC when a newsreader failed to show up. Gould was actually sitting in front of the microphone, ready to pinch-hit, when the announcer arrived at the last minute.

Gould was not getting rich at the CBC. In 1962, he earned $1,500 for producing his two-hour Schoenberg documentary, and in the late sixties he earned a total of $10,000 for a season of four hour-long recitals. In 1974 he earned $2,000 for producing a ten-week series about Schoenberg – which is to say that, reckoning in today's dollars, he earned almost three times as much money giving a single concert in 1964 as he did producing ten hours of radio a decade later. In at least one case, in 1961, his CBC fee was so small that he regarded it as hilarious (was it the $11.35 payment he noted on that year's income tax?), and he wrote an elaborate letter of mock-gratitude to John Roberts: "I cannot tell you, sir, how much this assignment and its colossal attendant fee means to myself, my good wife, my ill-clad children and my dog . . ." Even factoring in residuals and the like, one high-profile comeback concert at the end of his life might have netted him more money than thirty years' work for the CBC. But it was never about the money: he loved radio, and the CBC, and willingly took a pay cut in order to do work he wanted to do.

He loved television, too, and in that medium as well his work became increasingly ambitious after 1964. As on radio, he branched out from his recorded repertoire, particularly in chamber music, and offered provocative new interpretations of works he *had* recorded – Mozart's K. 333 sonata, Beethoven's Op. 34 variations, Berg's Sonata. The first high-profile telecast of his post-concert years aired in May 1966. *Duo* was a one-hour special that featured Gould talking and performing with the violinist Yehudi Menuhin, whom he greatly admired as both musician and man (in a 1966 profile he compared Menuhin to Albert Schweitzer). In *Duo* they performed Bach's C-minor sonata and Schoenberg's *Phantasy*, and gave a glowing account of Beethoven's Op. 96 sonata. Between works, they discussed the *Phantasy* (Menuhin, no fan of twelve-tone music, had learned it especially for the occasion) and the interpretation of Op. 96 – discussed *impromptu*, it should be stressed, for Menuhin balked at reading the scripted dialogue Gould had presumed to write for the occasion.* Gould's first colour telecast was in 1967, when he performed Bach's G-minor concerto and Strauss's *Burleske* with the Toronto Symphony – another Centennial project.

By the later sixties Gould was looking to television as another way to disseminate "position papers." The first of these was *Conversations with Glenn Gould*, a series of four programs, co-produced by

---

* After *Duo* Gould badly wanted to make records with Menuhin, who was under contract to EMI, and was bitterly disappointed when he and Menuhin could not convince either EMI or Columbia to make the necessary contractual concessions. The two taped another conversation, on the subject of recording, in June 1978, for Menuhin's television series *The Music of Man*. Menuhin again declined to read from Gould's carefully prepared script, and in the finished program the encounter seems strained.

the CBC and BBC, that Gould made with Humphrey Burton in 1966. The programs were unscripted, though talking points were selected in advance after many hours' discussion between the two, and Gould had his quips and musical examples at the ready. (As Burton put it, "The spontaneity was rehearsed – a paradox Glenn enjoyed.") There was a behind-the-scenes feel to the conversations, which took place in an undressed studio with the back wall and miscellaneous equipment exposed – Gould wanted to expose the trappings of the medium, rather than mimic a proscenium setting or fireside chat. The programs focused, respectively, on Bach, Beethoven, Schoenberg, and Strauss, but the first two were more wide-ranging, dealing with Gould's views on recording and his creative approach to interpretation. The series fascinated and outraged viewers when it aired in September 1966; the first program in particular created a lively storm in England. The *Times* ran an editorial ("WHY GO TO CONCERTS?"), and *New Statesman*, in an admiring review, noted Gould's "colonially brash theories." The half-hour profile *Variations on Glenn Gould* (1968), in the CBC series *Telescope*, offered a television counterpart to the *Concert Dropout* interview: a carefully packaged portrait of the artist. Interviews alternating with documentary material show Gould in the recording studio, making innovative radio programs, traipsing through the wilds near Wawa, Ontario, all the time setting out some the premises of his new life – his disdain for concerts and love of recording, the importance of imagination and the restorative powers of solitude.

Gould's devotion to the CBC was never more obvious than in 1970. That fall the Italian pianist Arturo Benedetti Michelangeli, no less reclusive and eccentric than Gould, was in Toronto making a Beethoven-bicentennial television program for the CBC, but at the last minute he backed out of a scheduled performance of the "Emperor" Concerto with the Toronto Symphony. Gould happened to place a call to the show's producer just when the conflict with Michelangeli was coming to a head, and when apprised of the problem he offered, to the astonishment of everyone, to fill in if needed. The evening before the scheduled taping, Gould was given the nod. He duly showed up at the CBC the following morning, played the concerto almost flawlessly, from memory, and received a standing ovation in the studio. He later taped Beethoven's Op. 34 variations and one of the Op. 126 bagatelles to complete a one-hour program, which was broadcast December 2. The program was widely distributed and received considerable acclaim, but the performance of the "Emperor," though it testifies to Gould's mental and technical gifts, has been over-rated. Working on just a few hours' notice, he could do nothing more than offer a carbon-copy of the interpretation he recorded with Stokowski four years earlier, albeit now fitted into Karel Ančerl's more conventional, much faster tempos – and it was a poor fit. Seat-of-the-pants performing went against everything Gould believed in by 1970; he did this only as a favour to the CBC.

He also appeared on American television in the sixties and seventies – on the NBC News series *Comment*, for instance, in 1971. He was even solicited by the talk shows (Johnny Carson, Dick Cavett), though he always turned down requests for impromptu interviews. ("I'd like to do a talk show, but only if I were host.") In April 1968, he appeared on *PBL*, a Sunday-night magazine program produced by National Educational Television (NET), the American public broadcaster, in a short program provocatively entitled *How Mozart Became a Bad Composer*. He took issue with the "facility for improvisation" that, he claimed, led Mozart to an over-reliance on conventional formulas in his compositions, most obviously in the "jaded, world-weary" works of his later years. In the C-minor piano concerto, K. 491, a work whose ingenious and original structure, expressive power, and proto-Romantic rhetoric are universally admired, Gould heard only "an appalling collection of clichés" of no greater potency than "inter-office memos." The program outraged viewers in both the United States and Canada, including formerly sympathetic fans and critics.

Gould wanted to forge a new kind of television that ignored the standards of the concert hall. His first great experiment in this vein was a "somewhat McLuhanesque TV essay" called *The Well-Tempered Listener* (1969), an hour-long CBC-NET co-production that featured conversation segments with Curtis W. Davis, NET's director of cultural programs, intercut with musical examples, and concluded with performances of four preludes and fugues from *The Well-Tempered Clavier* (two on piano, two on harpsichord). Gould described the program as "a montage of sights and sounds which I hope adds up to an overall impression of Bach's music," and the supervising editor, John McGreevy, recalled that it was "murderously difficult to put it together," because technologically Gould was "pressing the envelope all the time." In one sequence, Gould used a split screen to give a three-hand, overdubbed performance of a three-part Bach fugue; in another, he intercut between performances of the same fugue on piano, harpsichord, and organ, in order to demonstrate Bach's idealism; in another, he intercut between performances of *different* fugues, on different instruments, in order to demonstrate, curiously, the "Muzak-like" aspect of fugal evolution. *The Well-Tempered Listener* also featured *Spheres*, a seven-and-a-half-minute film by the NFB animators Norman McLaren and René Jodoin that illuminated contrapuntal procedures by providing an abstract visual accompaniment to Gould recordings of Bach.

In the end, Gould never achieved a really satisfying breakthrough when it came to presenting music on television – "I think that most of us have got an awful lot of experimenting to do before anything of *that* kind can be claimed as yet." He knew that such a program should be something more than a staged, filmed concert, and knew that "audio and video should serve one another rather than simply come packaged together." And he envisioned an era in which the regrettable "disposability" of television would give way to home video, allowing him to create music programs that had the status of permanent works. But he never became a theorist or artist in television the way he did in radio (and recording). For one thing, he did not enjoy the same degree of creative control and independence in television: the technology was too complicated and unwieldy and expensive, the required crew too large. The CBC could not afford the time or money required for Gould to really experiment, to *play* with television. But he never lost his faith in television as an art form or as a medium for bringing music and ideas to large audiences.

"The north has fascinated me since childhood."

Gould saw radio, like recording, as an art form with vast untapped potential for original creative expression, and he had not long retired from public life before he set about exploring it. He had a forum at hand: *Ideas*, a nightly CBC radio show on contemporary thought created in 1965. His first contribution, in November 1966, was *The Psychology of Improvisation*, a half-hour amalgam of talk and music in which he again took on "chance" in music, from Baroque continuo and the Classical cadenza to aleatory music and the jazz riff. More significant was *The Search for "Pet" Clark*, on December 11, 1967,* in which he used the British pop singer Petula Clark, whom he had discovered on the radio on long drives through Northern Ontario, "as a launching pad for some observations which I felt compelled to make about pop music trends in the 60's." It was his first hands-on experience with an "artistic" brand of radio involving precise and subtle use of montage to unite text and music. Clark herself heard the program, and was surprised and flattered by Gould's interest, though miffed at his observation that her voice was "fiercely loyal to its one great octave," and at his remark that she was "my age if she's a day" – she was two months younger.

In the program that really launched his career as a radio artist Gould tackled a subject close to his heart: the Canadian North. "In my school days, I used to pore over whichever maps of that region I could get my hands on," he wrote. "The idea of the country intrigued me, but my notion of what it looked liked was pretty much restricted to the romanticized, art-nouveau-tinged, Group-of-Seven

---

* The program was based on an article Gould had published that fall in *High Fidelity*. The magazine had insisted on "Petula Clark" in the title, but Gould's preference was "'Pet' Clark," which he duly restored in the radio version.

paintings which in my day adorned virtually every second school-room, and which probably served as a pictorial introduction to the north for a great many people of my generation. A bit later on, I began to examine aerial photographs and to look through geological surveys and came to realize that the north was possessed of qualities more elusive than even a magician like A. Y. Jackson could define with oils." He had no first-hand experience of the Arctic; his "North" was the rugged shore of Lake Superior, country "that is absolutely haunting in its emptiness and bleakness and starkly magnificent beauty." He was nourished by the isolation of such country; his thinking, he said, was clearer, sharper in the North. He was particularly inspired by the quality of Northern light – Southern light depressed him. For him the North was more than a place: it was a way of life, a way of thinking, and he associated his personal and aesthetic values with a Nordic temperament. There is a photograph of Gould sitting on the beach in the Bahamas, in cap, sunglasses, coat, long pants, and shoes, studying a Bach score – that says it all.

In any country there is an intimate relationship between geography and psychology, geography and culture. Some 40 per cent of Canada lies north of the sixtieth parallel, and though relatively few Canadians ever experience it directly the North exerts a profound influence on the Canadian sensibility. It is incarnated everywhere in Canadian art and letters – including music, and not only in programmatic music inspired by the Canadian landscape or works that draw on indigenous folk music. A. Y. Jackson believed in a national art created by artists "with their feet in the soil," and Gould, though he rarely put his feet in anything but carpeting, was one of those artists. Some listeners have detected a "northerliness" in his playing. David Dubal wrote that "Gould's Bach is sparse, abstract, yet mysterious. It is never pretty, certainly not sensuous. It is a northern Bach, piercing the listener like the cold." And George Steiner heard in Gould's Bach "a luminosity, sharp and dry and as strangely intoxicating as a Canadian winter morning." In Gould's playing – clearly articulated, contrapuntally transparent, closely miked – there is an unusual sense of space and dimension and chiaroscuro. One is always aware of the pregnant silence between and behind the notes, which are set in high definition as though imposed onto a vast backdrop of empty space, like scattered stands of trees dotting a Northern landscape. What Northrop Frye called "the melancholy of a thinly-settled country under a bleak northern sky" – one *hears* that in Gould's playing, most obviously in his spare later recordings of Bach.

With concert life behind him, the North became an increasingly potent force in his thought, and he longed to see it in person. And so, in June 1965, he travelled by train the thousand miles north from Winnipeg to Churchill, Manitoba, on the southwestern shore of Hudson Bay. Churchill was not really the North – it was above the tree line but still hundreds of miles south of the Arctic Circle – though it was the farthest north one could travel by train. The trip inspired him. On the train, known fondly as the "Muskeg Express," he encountered a crew of raconteurs including Wally Maclean, a retired surveyor who worked for the Canadian National Railway in Dauphin, Manitoba. Maclean was a well-read, garrulous conversationalist and something of a cracker-barrel philosopher, fond of quoting Shakespeare and Thoreau, William James and Kafka. Gould was captivated by him. They met in the dining car and embarked on a free-wheeling eight-hour conversation on topics including the metaphorical and literary significance of surveying.

Gould returned home elated, and hoping to make many more trips north. He planned to spend a month in Alaska and the Yukon in late spring 1966, and expressed a more ambitious desire to "spend a winter in the dark" in the Arctic. He never did take another trip to or near the North (did fear get the best of him?), but Churchill had sufficed: back home, he began to read books and compile data about the North, and to consider the artistic implications of his experience. As early as August 1965 he reported that the CBC had just asked him to write "a mockumentary for radio – a sort of Arctic 'Under Milkwood,'" and a year later he was planning a debut as a playwright, with *The Festival at Tuk*, which "deals with the purported founding of a sort of Arctic Bayreuth" in Tuktoyaktuk, N.W.T., and

in which prominent figures in the Canadian arts would play themselves. (He was still talking about producing this play, on stage or on
the radio, as late as 1970, but it was never finished.)

Early in 1967, Janet Somerville, the producer of *Ideas*, gave him
the means to focus his thoughts about the North: a commission to
make a documentary about the Arctic as a special Centennial
project. Gould spent most of that year thinking about the program
and rounding up interview subjects. He did not want to make a conventional documentary in which he dispensed fact and opinion, but
a more impressionistic "mood-piece" in which he brought together
the different views of people whose lives had been touched by first-
hand experience of the North. After considering a larger cast he
settled on five subjects. "We wanted an enthusiast, a cynic, a government budget-watcher, as well as someone who could represent
that limitless expectation and limitless capacity for disillusionment
which inevitably affects the questing spirit of those who go north
seeking their future," he later wrote. "We felt, however, that we also
needed someone whose experience of the north effectively encompassed all of these positions, who was at once a pragmatic idealist, a
disillusioned enthusiast."

It was obvious whose voice encompassed all four positions:
Wally Maclean, whose discourses on the North had got Gould's cre-
ative juices flowing in the first place. Maclean became the program's
narrator, the axis upon which it turned, and it was Maclean whom
Gould interviewed first, in Winnipeg, on Thanksgiving weekend.
Later, in Toronto and Ottawa, he recorded his other characters.
The enthusiast was J. R. (James) Lotz, a biologist, geographer, and
anthropologist and a professor at St. Paul University, in Ottawa; his
perspective was idealistic, visionary, Utopian. The cynic was Francis
G. (Frank) Vallee, a professor of sociology at Carleton University, in
Ottawa, formerly employed by the federal government in the central
Arctic; he found the reality of the North ugly, and was skeptical
about the romantic illusions of others. The government budget-
watcher was R. A. J. (Robert) Phillips, a federal official and member
of the Privy Council; he was pragmatic about the North, and

believed that the government could play a role in making people's lives there better. All three men were prolific authors and editors of published writings about the North. Finally, the voice of disillusioned expectation belonged to Marianne Schroeder, a nurse who had worked in a mission in Coral Harbour, Southampton Island, in the northwest corner of Hudson Bay; her initially awestruck and sentimental reaction to the North, captured in the first speech of the program, disappeared when she experienced the rough reality of it.

Even in late fall 1967, with all five interviews in the can, Gould was unsure what form his documentary would take. At one point, he envisioned a series of five programs, one for each character, and in a memo dated as late as November 15, Somerville wrote that Gould was producing "two one-hour dream documentaries." Eventually he gathered up transcripts of his interviews, sequestered himself for a few weeks in a motel room in Wawa, and returned with a script. He worked frantically through December to have the program finished by the end of the Centennial year, and was still at it the day before the broadcast.

He was developing some innovative radio techniques, and working to standards so exacting that they pushed the available technology to its limits; the project required hundreds of hours of studio time for a program that ran just under an hour. The technical supervisor was Lorne Tulk, with whom Gould had first worked on *The Search for "Pet" Clark*. Tulk had been with the CBC since 1959 but was still in his twenties at the time. He would become one of Gould's most trusted colleagues in his later years, and a close friend. He recalls working up to sixteen hours a day, more than a hundred hours a week, to complete the program on time; often he and Gould would emerge from the studio at three or four in the morning, and would take an early breakfast at Tulk's house. The work was exhausting, but Gould seemed indefatigable, driven by his enthusiasm for the project; moreover, the CBC's support was unwavering, and Tulk was devoted to Gould and to his new brand of radio. (Gould's contracted fee for the program was $1,500 – a pittance given the work involved. He once told Tulk that his radio documentaries cost him three to five times more than he was paid for them.) Gould called his "dream documentary" *The Idea of North*. Its airing on December 28, 1967, had been widely promoted and received a great deal of attention across Canada.*

In *The Idea of North* Gould revisited his 1965 train trip as allegory, and drew on a contemporary source for inspiration: Katherine Anne Porter's novel *Ship of Fools*, published in 1962 and adapted as a film, directed by Stanley Kramer, in 1965. (The novel was still among Gould's effects when he died, and Tulk remembers seeing the film in his company.) Set in 1931, the novel chronicles a voyage from Mexico to Germany by a shipload of diverse passengers, but, as Porter makes explicit, the story is an allegory: the ship is a world, the passengers a society, a cross-section of nationalities, classes, occupations, personality types, moralities, prejudices. In *The Idea of North*, that shipload became a trainful of passengers representing a cross-section of perspectives on the North. Gould admitted to being influenced by the episodic and indeed contrapuntal structure of *Ship of Fools*, too, in which characters interact with each other in ever-changing combinations and, in the process, cause broad themes to emerge. The novel is set out in three unequal parts, comparatively short sequences ("Embarkation" and "The Harbors") surrounding a long central sea voyage ("High Sea"). In *The Idea of North*, likewise, a short prologue and epilogue frame the central train trip. The idea

---

* A television adaptation of *The Idea of North*, a co-production of the CBC and NET, produced and directed by Judith Pearlman, had its premiere on August 5, 1970. The program, for which the radio version, with some editing, serves as the soundtrack, includes images of the locations that originally inspired Gould, for which purpose Pearlman and her crew took the "Muskeg Express" to Churchill in November 1969. Two actors appear – one plays Wally Maclean, the other a new, non-speaking character, a young man taking his first train trip north – and the other four characters appear as themselves. Gould appears briefly, on a boxcar in Toronto's railway yards, to deliver his introduction. He supported the production in a variety of ways and loved the results, and Pearlman credited him as "associate producer" out of gratitude. But he was not really involved with the shooting or post-production, even though, in speaking to the press, he sometimes abetted the misconception that the program was a joint effort or even his own show.

of Wally Maclean as narrator, a character who is first among equals, apparently came from the film version of *Ship of Fools*, in which the dwarf Glocken addresses the camera at the beginning and end. *The Idea of North* is not merely *Train of Fools*, however; Gould was not, like Porter, attempting social commentary and satire on a universal scale, but he *was* chronicling his own allegorical journey. Porter reminds us that such allegory was already "very old and durable and dearly familiar" when her own model, the German poet Sebastian Brant's *Das Narrenschiff* (The Ship of Fools), was published in 1494, and that *The Idea of North* thus belongs within a tradition that is as old as literature.

Once the three-minute prologue is past,* Gould's dramatic conceit is that his five characters are all riding the "Muskeg Express" to Churchill and discussing the North en route. The journey, during which the sound of the train is ever present, comprises five acts dealing with different aspects of the Northern experience: the effects of isolation; the development of the North; disillusionment with the North; the effects of white settlement on the indigenous people; and the possible future of the North.† The nine-minute epilogue belongs to Wally Maclean alone: a rambling monologue in which he sets out his "poetic vision" of the North and summarizes the program's themes against a musical backdrop of the finale of Sibelius's Fifth Symphony – the only music in the program. (Gould used Karajan's 1965 recording with the Berlin Philharmonic, which he considered "the ideal realization of Sibelius as a passionate but antisensual composer.") The program ends on an optimistic note:

---

* Between the prologue and the start of the train trip, Gould interpolated his own two-minute introduction. It was his only misstep in *The Idea of North*. The autobiographical comments, the introduction of the characters, and the tone of Gould's overwritten prose – "that incredible tapestry of tundra and taiga," and so on – are jarring in this context.

† One whole, partly edited sequence – it dealt with "the media in relation to northern experience, in relation to sensory deprivation" – was ultimately cut because the program was running long. To my knowledge no tape or transcript of this sequence survives.

Maclean rejects both naive and cynical views of the North, but retains a belief in the importance of the region as an archetypal experience and an alternative to the spiritual emptiness of modern urban society.

The Idea of North offers little hard data about the history, geography, population, sociology, politics, or economy of the North; about the burgeoning interest in the North after the Second World War, especially after the creation of the federal Department of Northern Affairs and Natural Resources in 1953; about the aboriginal-land-claims issues being thrashed out in the late sixties. In fact, Gould intentionally edited most topical references out of his interviews, in order to treat his themes metaphorically, universally. But he never pretended to offer indigenous perspectives of the North and Northerners; Inuit society, for instance, is examined solely from the standpoint of the white man. *The Idea of North* is really about visiting Southerners who "come to measure their own work and life against that rather staggering creative possibility" of the North, and are spiritually transformed by the experience. "It was a program about the Canadian North, ostensibly," Gould said a year later; "what it was *really* about, as a friend of mine very kindly said, was the dark night of the human soul. It was a very dour essay into the effects of isolation upon mankind."

Gould knew what he wanted when he set up his interviews. His five subjects, he said, "were all people who'd experienced isolation in some very special way," and in his interviews his questions mainly focused on the effects of solitude – a subject much on his mind at the time. He was then in the midst of a frontier experience of his own, having dropped out of public life in order to cultivate the physical and intellectual isolation he considered necessary for creativity. The dialectic of opinion in *The Idea of North* thus reflected ideas about solitude that were bouncing around his own mind in the later sixties. Pointedly, Gould did not use his characters' names outside his spoken introduction. For his purposes they were not people so much as disembodied voices representing points of view, and by abstracting them, by taking names and personalities (and hard data and topical references) out of the equation, he was underscoring the metaphorical and autobiographical import of the program. And so in this respect the train trip in *The Idea of North* stands in for the *inward* journey Gould had been taking since 1964. "It's very much me," he said of the program. "In terms of what it says, it's about as close to an autobiographical statement as I am probably going to make at this stage of my life."

"It was, in fact, a documentary which thought of itself as a play."

"Contrapuntal radio" was Gould's term for the art form he invented in *The Idea of North*. The operative principle was really montage, in the cinematic sense – creating new forms, effects, and emotional connotations through strategic editing. (He owned two books by Sergei Eisenstein, the Russian director who was one of the pioneers of cinematic montage.) But the sequences that caused the most comment and controversy, that had listeners cursing their radios over what they took to be cross-talk, were those in which two or more voices speak at once, in counterpoint. In fact, the prologue, which introduces the program's themes and techniques, is a piece of pure three-part counterpoint, painstakingly edited to enhance transparency and thematic significance. Gould dubbed it a "trio sonata" – in early drafts it was a quartet – though it more closely resembles a fugue: three voices representing contrasting views of the North (Schroeder, Vallee, Phillips) enter one after the other and eventually all talk at once before drifting off into silence. But the contrapuntal climax of the program is in Act 4, what he called his "Eskimo scene": he creates two simultaneous conversations (Vallee-Schroeder, Phillips-Lotz) in the dining car, and places the listener in the position of a waiter trying to take them both in.

"It's perfectly true that in that dining-car scene not every word is going to be audible," he wrote, "but then by no means every syllable in the final fugue from Verdi's *Falstaff* is, either, when it comes to that. Yet few opera composers have been deterred from utilizing trios, quartets, or quintets by the knowledge that only a portion of the words they set to music will be accessible to the listener – most composers being concerned primarily about the totality of the structure, the play of consonance and dissonance between the voices – and, quite apart from the fact that I do believe most of us are capable of a much more substantial information intake than we give ourselves credit for, I would like to think that these scenes can be listened to in very much the same way that you'd attend the *Falstaff* fugue." He was seeking a kind of radio in which the listener was "caught up," forced to solve a puzzle with his ears, as one does when lost in the rich textures of music by Bach or Strauss.* In *The Idea of North* this was a matter of form serving content: as he said in 1971, in "Radio as Music," a published conversation with John Jessop, then a student preparing a thesis on his radio documentaries, he wanted "to create a structure in which one could feel free to have different approaches and responses to the same problems emerge simultaneously." The vocal counterpoint underscored the dialectical nature of the subject matter.

This counterpoint was certainly innovative, and impressive technically, especially given that Gould and Tulk were working with monaural sound, analogue recording, razor blades, and splicing tape. But no less original in *The Idea of North* was Gould's synthesis of three principles: documentary, drama, and music. For all its abstraction and artiness it *is* a documentary about the North, but the documentary material is dramatically charged, conveyed through confrontations of characters with different perspectives, blended evocatively with other sounds. (The confrontations were created with the razor blade: the five subjects did not know each other and were interviewed

---

* Even in his more conventional radio programs Gould tended to eschew foreground-background distinctions where someone speaks against a musical backdrop: voice and music tend to be equally loud, forcing the ear to listen contrapuntally. He deplored the venerable tradition of turning down the music track in the background as soon as someone begins to speak.

separately.) Gould clearly saw himself within the Canadian traditions of documentary production and radio drama. There were radio
plays in Canada as soon as there was radio, but after the formation,
in 1938, of the CBC's Drama Department – effectively the country's
first national professional theatre – radio drama developed into a
potent and influential genre, and the young Gould was hooked on
it. He was particularly impressed by *Stage*, a popular Sunday-night
series of innovative radio plays, founded in 1944 under the guidance of the young national supervisor of the Drama Department,
Andrew Allan, whom the broadcaster Knowlton Nash called "the
sun king of the golden age of radio." For people of Gould's generation, *Stage* was a school. "On the *Stage* series many of us heard our
first Shakespeare, our first Sophocles, our first Ibsen," Robert
Fulford recalled, "and also heard for the first time that Canadian
writers were producing entertaining and socially engaging work."

In *Stage* Gould had an early model for a style of radio that
combined principles of documentary and drama in the service of
ambitions that were moral and social as well as artistic. The *Stage*
dramatists, who emerged out of the Depression and Second World
War, were socially committed and tackled taboo subjects like religion, politics, war, class, and sex in addition to those less controversial, including the Canadian North. "A lot of that kind of ostensibly
theatrical radio was also, in a very real sense, documentary making
of a rather high order," Gould said in "Radio as Music." "At any rate,
the distinctions between drama and documentary were quite often,
it seemed to me, happily and successfully set aside." The young
Gould was also impressed by the idiomatically "radio-istic" nature
of the *Stage* dramas, and by their technical skill. He noted the innovations of *Stage* dramatists like Gerald Noxon, who came to radio
from film and imported cinematic concepts of montage in order to
draw listeners into the subject; he heard, for instance, some "very
sophisticated microphone placement," which inspired his own later
efforts to convey "space and proximity" in radio.

But "contrapuntal radio" was something more to Gould. *The
Idea of North*, he insisted, was a piece of music. (Janet Somerville

called it "a *Finlandia* for Canada.") Always fascinated by the appropriation of musical principles by artists in other fields (Thomas Mann, for instance), Gould came at radio from this perspective. His thinking about editing voices and sound effects was musical – it was all about rhythm, texture, tone, dynamics, pacing, and the strategic, integral use of silence. He would describe structures and effects in his radio programs in musical terms – sonata and rondo, canon and fugue, *crescendo* and *decrescendo* – and he referred to his scripts as "scores." In the studio he would "conduct" playbacks in an effort to get the rhythm of a sequence right – R. A. J. Phillips recalled that Gould "conducted" even during their original interview – and in the process of editing raw interviews into more polished vocal "music" he was often splicing word by word, syllable by syllable. He called the ever-present sound of the train the program's "basso continuo," and fussed over the tone and rhythm of that backdrop in the editing; shifts in the "basso continuo" articulate structure and evoke different settings (compartment, lounge car, coach car, dining car). In his "score," Gould could not resist labelling the sound effect that separates Act 5 from the epilogue a "train cadenza." He even took to referring to his radio documentaries by opus numbers, *The Idea of North* being "Op. 1."

All of which was radical as documentary but *au courant* as music. The principle of collage was central to art of many kinds in the sixties, particularly where electronics were involved, but of even more relevance was the view, shared by many composers of the day, that the spoken word could be the stuff of music. The Canadian composer István Anhalt noted that "speech compositions," by composers ranging from Schoenberg and Milhaud to Berio, Kagel, Ligeti, Lutosławski, Stockhausen, and eventually many others, amounted to "one of the significant developments in the recent history of Western music,"* and McLuhan, in a 1965 interview with Gould, remarked that "the spoken word is music, pure music, at any time. It is a form

---

* Gould was impressed by one of Anhalt's own works in this vein, *Cento* (1967), and interviewed Anhalt about the piece on CBC radio, in 1969.

of singing." Not just speech but all sounds increasingly became the stuff of music after the Second World War, in, for instance, *musique concrète* and some of the aleatory works of Cage, but not only among composers: Samuel Beckett conceived his later stage, radio, and television plays musically, and the score for Hitchcock's film *The Birds* consists of a kind of music forged out of electronically processed bird sounds. Gould, admittedly, took little pleasure in the electronic and concrete and aleatory music of his day, yet he explicitly placed "contrapuntal radio" within this context.

Even where identifiable musical techniques were not involved, the "contrapuntal" documentary is connotative as well as didactic, in a way that deserves to be described as musical. The forms and techniques are always at one with the content: when, for instance, Marianne Schroeder complains about women being relegated to the background in Inuit society, her voice trails off into silence, overtaken by the masculine voice of James Lotz. Gould felt that the listener would eventually become so familiar with the point of view of each character that he could treat their voices as instruments, relying on their established connotations. By the second half of *The Idea of North*, he said, "they had become such archetypes that we no longer *needed* the precise word to identify them and their position, we needed only the sound of their voice and the texture of its mixing with other voices to do this." This is a powerfully evocative kind of radio, precisely the kind of "music" that Stockhausen was referring to when he wrote that "electronic music has liberated the inner world": a wholly interior, private thing, best experienced at home, alone, preferably with the eyes closed, and with the imagination free to ponder its patterns and implications. In a sense, Gould sought to recapture that intense engagement with disembodied sounds experienced by the first generation of radio listeners.

"To some extent or other, all of the subjects that I've chosen have had to do with isolation – even the musical ones."

The Idea of North surprised, challenged, and confused many listeners, but it was still widely praised as ambitious, innovative, poetic, and technically polished – as, indeed, all of Gould's major radio documentaries would be. He was proud of the program, and eager to work again with this new kind of radio. In the spring of 1968, the CBC commissioned him to create a program in order to promote its new FM stereo service, and he at once set about creating a companion-piece to *The Idea of North* focused on a new Canadian subject: Newfoundland. In August and September 1968, he spent a month in Newfoundland collecting interviews, a trip he later called "one of the most exhilarating experiences of my life." This time he assembled a larger cast, of thirteen, some of them colourful, bardic raconteurs, though the whole cast appears only twice, in a prologue and epilogue, "as a kind of Greek chorus." (Seven of the characters, in fact, appear *only* in these outer sections.) The script gestated for a year; the program was not edited until fall 1969, and required well over three hundred hours of studio time (it also runs just under an hour). On the air date, November 12, a new stereo facility in Ottawa was inaugurated, one of only three in Canada at the time, but the program was too complicated for the monaural sound of AM radio.*

Gould called this documentary *The Latecomers*. Newfoundland had become a Canadian province only in 1949, and twenty years later it was still struggling with issues relating to its identity within Confederation. The program, Gould later wrote, "was obviously to be about the province as island; about the sea, which keeps the mainland and the mainlanders at ferry-crossing's length; about the problems of maintaining a minimally technologized style of life in a maximally technologized age." But it was also about "separateness"

---

* In order to bring the documentary to a national audience, CBC Learning Systems released it as an LP in 1971. *The Idea of North* was also released the same year.

– being at once a part of Canada and isolated from the mainstream of Canadian life – and about "the cost of nonconformity." Solitude and isolation, again, this time seen from a cultural perspective, with Newfoundland as the metaphor. The documentary hook was a contemporary *cause célèbre* in Newfoundland: the abandonment of outport villages. According to Lorne Tulk, Gould had been outraged when he read in the newspaper that the province's premier, Joey Smallwood, had proposed a bill suggesting that people from the outports be transplanted to larger centres for economic reasons. But he did not channel his outrage into social commentary. As in *The Idea of North*, he kept his politics private, eschewed topical references, and created a more universalized "mood-piece." His dramatic conceit was that all thirteen characters came from the same village, St. Joseph's, which at the time was pulling up stakes and becoming a ghost town (only some of his subjects were actually from St. Joseph's). This time the "basso continuo" is the sound of ocean waves beating against the rocky shoreline; Gould manipulated those waves to convey the impression that the listener approaches the island at the beginning of the program and pulls away from it at the end.

He relished the chance to work in stereo. Even with the monaural sound of *The Idea of North* he had played with filters in an effort to create the illusion of depth, but now he could create more "sculptural," multi-dimensional textures. To documentary, drama, and music he was effectively bringing a fourth influence: film. He could now reinforce didactic and dramatic points by putting his characters in motion, moving sound sources around within the stereo spectrum, a process he discussed by analogy with film techniques – pans, zooms, dissolves, and so on. He used space to imply relationships among his characters. In one scene, for instance, he positioned an elderly minister within the spectrum in such a way that he seems to speak from a spot higher than the other characters, as though from a pulpit. In another scene, he created an apparently intimate relationship between a man and woman who in fact did not

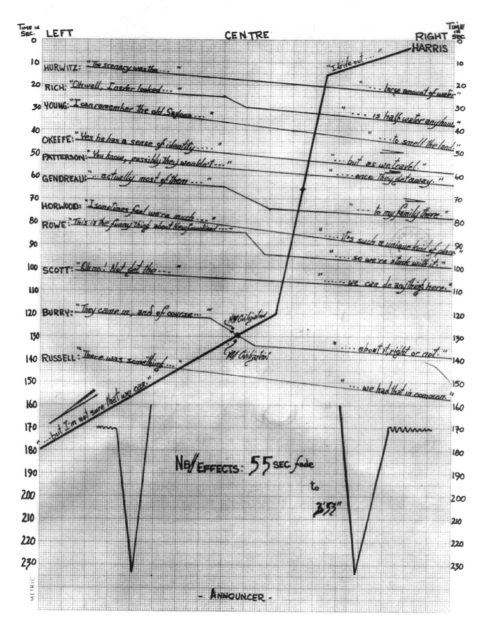

Graph, in Lorne Tulk's hand, of the epilogue of Gould's "contrapuntal radio documentary" *The Latecomers* (1969), showing the movement of the narrator (Dr. Leslie Harris) across the stereo spectrum, from right to left, his encounters with other characters along the way, and his eventual merging with the "basso continuo," the waves that pound against the shores of Newfoundland. *(Estate of Glenn Gould.)*

know each other; they speak on different sides of the spectrum, separated by the sea. In the four-minute epilogue, as the character who acts as narrator talks about driving across the country, his voice, previously confined to the right speaker, begins to move slowly across the spectrum, and as the epilogue unfolds he encounters, en route, all of the other characters, who are moving in the opposite direction. The narrator's optimism about Newfoundland conflicts with the views of the other characters, a situation for which Gould created an audio metaphor: the narrator literally "moves past" the other characters. At the very end, the narrator appears to walk right off the island and merge with the sea, and Tulk recalls that in the process of getting this effect he and Gould had the studio strewn with yard-long tape loops threaded around the backs of chairs, music stands, and anything else that would hold them up at the right height – Gould held one aloft with pencils in his hand.

In 1969, at John Roberts's suggestion, Gould began preparing a radio documentary on Leopold Stokowski. He considered the commission something of a relaxation from the enormous complexities of *The Latecomer*, but the subject did genuinely attract him. He was a passionate Stokowski fan of long standing, admiring his subjective, "ecstatic" interpretations, his championship of new music, his "search for moral correlatives of his aesthetic undertakings," his openness to experimentation, and above all his commitment to recording and other electronic media. Stokowski was the Glenn Gould of the early twentieth century, proselytizing on behalf of recording and broadcasting and film, and working with engineers to improve recording technology and recording methods. In December 1969, three years after recording the "Emperor" Concerto with Stokowski, an experience he had relished, Gould interviewed the conductor in his New York apartment. (The interview was filmed by a crew from NET, which was preparing its own documentary on Stokowski.) Completed in August 1970, *Stokowski: A Portrait for Radio* was broadcast on February 2, 1971. (The NET program aired on CBC television the following night.) In a sense, the Stokowski documentary, and Gould's later documentaries on musicians (Casals, Schoenberg, Strauss), continued his interest in the theme of solitude and isolation, for all were men who stood somewhat outside the musical mainstream of their day.

Once again Gould eschewed facts-and-figures documentary in favour of a "mood-piece." His intent was not to create a capsule-biography, but, as he wrote to Stokowski, to reveal "the aesthetic ideas which have been prevalent throughout your career." After Gould's five-minute introduction the only voice is that of Stokowski, who was loquacious enough to sustain the hour-long show. Gould aimed, he wrote, for "an effect at once relaxed and concentrated." This time his "basso continuo" was "a continuous and, I hope, seamless musical texture consisting of fragments drawn from works which you have recorded through the years. None of the works are, of course, heard in their entirety and they all are treated, in cinematic terms, to an extended dissolve so that a consistent harmonic climate prevails throughout the musical background." Technically, the program was less complicated than his previous documentaries, but he still used montage with great precision and subtlety; the voice and music tracks complement and counterpoint each other in various ways, and distinct spaces are carved out within the stereo spectrum. In one astonishing sequence, over which Gould laboured long, Stokowski is talking about folk music against a backdrop of the first movement of Shostakovich's Eleventh Symphony, so Gould weaves strands of folk music from several countries into the backdrop. The obvious thing to do – except that the folk excerpts fit *perfectly* in counterpoint with Shostakovich's harmonies. Gould, in other words, made a clean musical match out of discrete sources of recorded music, giving remarkable evidence of his acute ear and technical finesse.

Despite heavy recording commitments, he was eager to keep making radio art. In spring 1971 he began to prepare a documentary in which he would examine the "moral tenor" of the sixties through the words of Christopher Booker, the author of *The Neophiliacs: A Study of the Revolution in English Life in the Fifties and Sixties* (1969). Again he planned to use the techniques of "contrapuntal radio"; an interview with Booker would form the "basso continuo." And again the subject at hand would be treated not journalistically but metaphorically: phenomena like the Angry Young Men and Swinging London afforded him an opportunity to raise one of his pet themes, the dangers of notions like "progress" and "fashion." As he thought about this program he came to feel that he needed a "strong counter-motif," and he found one as far away as possible from Swinging London, in the adamantly conservative Mennonites of southern Manitoba, whose traditional way of life was threatened by modern trends and technologies. That same spring, he was mulling over a suggestion that he create a documentary about the Canadian West, and his first impulse was to tackle the subject from the perspective of the Mennonite, Hutterite, and Doukhobor communities. But he soon put aside the sixties,* and the Canadian West, and fixed his gaze on the Mennonites, with whose lifestyle and ideas he clearly empathized.

In July 1971 he spent two weeks in Winnipeg, interviewing local Mennonites. (A newspaper reported that he stayed in four different hotels – the air conditioning bothered him in one of them, the carpeting in another.) He edited the vocal tracks, mostly in his own studio, in early 1972, and in November he recorded two services, one each in English and German, at the Waterloo-Kitchener United Mennonite Church, in Waterloo. The program had originally been intended to air in 1973, but he only resumed work on it late that year: according to his letters, he was delayed by a CBC engineers' strike, then by a dispute the gist of which was "whether or not the technicians union has jurisdiction over products produced in my own studio." In 1974 he was distracted by radio projects celebrating the Schoenberg centenary, and so the Mennonite documentary, now entitled *The Quiet in the Land* (Mennonites have long used that phrase

---

* Aspects of the Booker project lingered in his mind. In September 1971 he proposed to Helen Whitney, of NBC News, a television program that would "look at the Thoreauvian way of life as evidenced in present-day America," a "south-of-the-border adaptation of *my* theme . . . the relationship of isolation and solitude to one's productive capacity." The program, which was never made, might have looked at "the revolt against certain aspects of materialism" in the youth culture of the sixties.

with pride to describe themselves), was not completed until summer 1975; even so, it was not broadcast, owing to "bureaucratic entanglements," until March 25, 1977, when it aired as an *Ideas* special.

With *The Quiet in the Land* Gould had a genuine Solitude Trilogy: he used the Mennonite community to represent all people who attempt to live outside the mainstream of society. Solitude and isolation, once again, this time seen from a religious perspective, and this time with particularly strong autobiographical resonances: the Mennonite motto, "In the world not of the world," might have been engraved over Gould's penthouse door. He had hoped to extend the stereophonic techniques of *The Latecomers* still further by producing *The Quiet in the Land* in quadraphonic sound. He corresponded with a CBC radio-drama producer who was planning some experimental quadraphonic specials in which he wanted to participate, but in the end quadraphonic radio came to nothing. Still, the program was more complicated even than *The Latecomers*: it made his previous documentaries, he said, seem like Gregorian chant by comparison. There was a cast of nine and an especially complex backdrop of sound effects and musical excerpts. (The Mennonite service is the "basso continuo.") At the beginning of the program, while several speakers discuss the motives behind Mennonite isolation, Gould evokes the warring forces of spirituality and materialism with counterpoint of two musical excerpts: a cello suite by Bach, and Janis Joplin singing "Mercedes-Benz." Throughout the program, Gould's technique is of a new order of elegance and refinement, and his use of montage is not just impressive but often deeply moving.

While work on *The Quiet in the Land* was held up, Gould produced another portrait of a contemporary musician – a rather surprising choice: the cellist Pablo Casals. Gould's approach to performance, especially in Bach, had little in common with that of Casals, though he did acknowledge Casals's great musicianship, including his "incredibly underrated" conducting. He also admired Casals's sacred choral composition *El Pessebre*, and it was a Casals recording of Bach he used to represent the spiritual in *The Quiet in the Land*. He was impressed, too, by Casals's breadth of culture and vision, and his enlightened moral and political views. (For such a rigid and puritanical artist Gould had an interesting soft spot for more open and generous colleagues.) Casals was still active, and in August 1972 Gould travelled to Vermont for a week to interview him at the Marlboro Festival (he was taken aback by the vigour of the old man's handshake); he also interviewed some of Casals's pupils and colleagues. Casals's voice was too aged and too heavily accented to sustain an entire program, so for narration Gould chose the marvellously orotund voice of Albert Kahn, author of the Casals biography *Joys and Sorrows*. The program was completed but had not aired when Casals died, in October 1973, at age ninety-six; nonetheless, *Casals: A Portrait for Radio* was broadcast unaltered (it runs about seventy-six minutes) on January 15 the following year.

"Contrapuntal radio" obviously demanded a new kind of radio audience, closer to the audience for contemporary music than for news and entertainment. Gould's documentaries are too complex to be absorbed at first hearing, but he clearly thought of them as *works* that would outlive their original function as radio specials and survive as recordings, to be enjoyed and studied like pieces of music. And they do repay close scrutiny, though they have been widely underrated even among his admirers. Except for his best performances, they are the most original and polished creative work he ever did, and deeply personal statements on themes of great importance to him. They are recognized as such among those people in North America and Europe who take radio seriously as an art form. Richard Kostelanetz, for instance, considers him perhaps the greatest radio artist in North America, and his own radio works have been influenced by Gould. In Germany, where, as Kostelanetz notes, "radio is culture," Gould's radio has been admired and influential. Klaus Schöning, for instance, founder of the Studio for Acoustical Art of Westdeutscher Rundfunk, credits *The Idea of North* as an important early specimen of the kind of experimental radio drama he calls the "*neue Hörspiel*" or "*ars acustica.*"

Gould, in any event, was convinced of the artistic validity of "contrapuntal radio," and had no doubts about his own mastery of the genre, none of the insecurities that plagued his writing and composing. "In the last few years, I've spent roughly half my time working on radio and television programs that have nothing at all to do with music," he said in 1970, and of course there were many people, including fans and friends, who wished he would make more recordings instead of frittering away his time making incomprehensible radio programs. But Gould did not think his creative energies were being misplaced. His enthusiasm and energy seemed bottomless when it came to radio, and he was so committed to the medium that, as his correspondence reveals, his recording commitments for CBS sometimes became, in his mind, if not quite necessary evils then at least runners-up to his radio work for the CBC. Gould would expound at great length, with evident glee, upon his artistic intentions and techniques in interviews about his radio work – such was his delight with the process and his pride in his own skill and imagination.

His enthusiasm is easy to understand: creating successful works in a new genre of radio art took much of the sting out of his failure as a composer. He never doubted that when he was making "contrapuntal radio" he was really making music. As he said in *The Well-Tempered Listener*, "It has occurred to me in the last five years that it's entirely unrealistic to see that particular kind of work – that particular ordering of phrase and regulation of cadence which one is able to do, taking, let us say, the subject of an interview like this one to a studio 'after the fact' and chopping it up and splicing here and there and pulling on this phrase and accentuating that one and throwing some reverb in there and adding a compressor here and a filter there – that it's unrealistic to think of that as anything but composition."

Opposite: Gould at Caledon, Ontario, January 1970. Another photograph from the same session graced his 1970 album of three sonatas by Beethoven, and Gould came to think of it as his favourite picture of himself. *(Photograph by Don Hunstein. Sony Classical.)*

PART FIVE

A PORTRAIT OF
THE ARTIST

"I don't think I'm at all eccentric."

That is a hallmark of a true eccentric – not thinking you're at all eccentric, even when your every thought, word, and deed seems to set you apart from the rest of the world. From the start of his career Gould was pinned with the label "eccentric," and he was usually good-natured about it, realizing its publicity value, though he became petulant if too much attention was paid to his personality at the expense of his music. It was true; he *was* a queer duck. His eccentricity was real, even predictable given his extraordinary talent. (As Sir Francis Bacon said, "There is no excellent beauty that hath not some strangeness in the proportion.") But Glenn Gould was perhaps no more eccentric than, say, Vladimir de Pachmann, Percy Grainger, Ervin Nyiregyházi, or Vladimir Horowitz, to name just a few pianists who lived in his century. In some respects he was standard-issue as eccentric artists go, and in some respects he was downright normal. This has not stopped writers from offering dark interpretations of his personality and lifestyle. *Newsweek* once called him "a musical Howard Hughes" – he was interested in Hughes, by the way – and the image of Gould as a misanthropic, paranoid hermit, perhaps autistic or mentally ill, is remarkably widespread. Many writers likely judge him by their own standards or by those of some putatively normal person – i.e., If I lived like Gould, I'd be miserable. But Joseph Roddy was right when he wrote, near the end of Gould's life, that "it would be a mistake to categorize Gould as a lonely Phantom of the Concert Hall. His world is rich, if hidden."

The clichés about Gould have always leaned heavily on the voluminous and colourful publicity generated while he was on the international concert circuit, yet these were precisely the years when the lifestyle he was forced to lead was most at war with his temperament. Many of the Gould legends are exaggerations or misinterpretations of mundane facts, though admittedly he sometimes abetted the legend-making by selectively overstating or suppressing aspects of his real personality for public consumption. Consider his refusal to shake hands – even leaving aside the whole idea that a professional pianist who is unusually fussy about his hands may not necessarily be a lunatic. It is true that he usually refused a proffered hand, and posted notices about his reluctance to shake hands outside his dressing room, but he had experience on his side: early in his career he had found that his hand was likely to be crushed by at least one fan in five; the worst, he said, were short men and college boys. Once even a *doctor* had "squeezed my hand like a vice – darn near broke it." But he worried only where he was confronted with unfamiliar hands; privately, he often shook hands, sometimes on his own initiative, with people he trusted to be gentle. Kerstin Meyer remembered shaking his hand: "It was like . . . a lump of jelly."

The friends and colleagues who knew Gould best, who saw him at close quarters, privately, in relaxed and congenial settings like the CBC, Eaton Auditorium, or his own apartment and studio, saw a less caricatured, more balanced personality. It is clear from speaking to them that many of his legendary eccentricities represented default positions to which he cautiously deferred in situations he could not fully control or with people he did not know well. He readily modulated or abandoned these behaviours in the right circumstances, which makes one wonder if they should really be called eccentricities at all. Often his behaviour, though unconventional, was logical, where it served to maintain the specific conditions and environments and schedule he needed to function contentedly and productively. Through the last twenty years of his life, he increased his direct control over every aspect of his life and work by narrowing his sphere of operations, demanding that the world come to him: he stopped travelling overseas, then stopped flying altogether, then quit the concert circuit, then moved his recording operations from New York to Toronto, then took over his editing work in his own studio. The lifestyle he cultivated was all about eliminating contingencies and distractions, maximizing opportunities, relating to the outside world on his own carefully controlled terms. To the outside world he became more eccentric with age, but he was really living precisely the way he wanted and needed to live, which is why he didn't think he was at all eccentric – and why, perhaps, he was right. The truth about Glenn Gould is at once more surprising and more banal than the legend: for all the personal demons with which he wrestled, he was, in the end, a mostly fulfilled and liberated person. If he was eccentric his was the brand of eccentricity John Stuart Mill described as coming from "strength of character" as well as "genius, mental vigour and moral courage."

Gould had no hobbies: his life was his work. "I don't think that my life style is like most other people's and I'm rather glad for that," he told an interviewer in 1980. "[T]he two things, life style and work, have become one. Now if that's eccentricity, then I'm eccentric." He did not ply a typical middle-class trade but was still a workaholic in the Scotch-Presbyterian tradition. Geoffrey Payzant was correct when he wrote that "his private life is in fact austere and unremarkable,"* and a private diary Gould kept for three months in 1980 reveals that his life was just as dull as it seemed: writing and editing, some practising, various errands, a modest amount of human contact for professional and personal reasons. This apostle of the electronic age was a classic Old Torontonian, a confirmed homebody whose idea of a good time was to stay in alone, or meet

---

* I leave it to my readers to decide whether Payzant was also correct when he added, "A book on his life and times would be brief and boring."

with at best one or two friends. As an artist he had a reputation as a radical, yet in many ways his temperament was that of a banker, not a bohemian. His monastic lifestyle, like his fondness for the recording studio, was tied up with his ethics. Pascal famously wrote, "The sole cause of man's unhappiness is that he does not know how to stay quietly in his room," but Gould did know, and the result, for him, was a relatively happy life, and a *good* one.

He was not tempted to lead a splashy celebrity life, and considered fame to be mostly inconvenient. He was frightened when mobbed by fans in public, and took pains to avoid such situations. He did not use his wealth for the sake of status or personal display or creature comfort. He employed secretaries and housekeepers and technicians as needed, and had a personal assistant in his last decade, but had no entourage, and lived as modestly and self-sufficiently as possible. He read and answered his mail personally, did many of his own mundane daily chores, dealt with the minutiae of his business affairs.

Always fragile and fussy, Gould was unusually vulnerable to the ordinary vicissitudes of life. Not surprisingly, he was drawn to the comfort of the familiar and found change traumatic. He spent his whole life in his hometown. He lived with his parents for almost thirty years, then lived in the same apartment on St. Clair Avenue for more than twenty. He worked for the same broadcaster for more than thirty years, for the same record label for more than twenty-five. He had the same accountant, the same stockbrokers, the same doctors and chiropractors for years, and his posthumous affairs are still directed by the law firm he was with in the mid-1950s. He remained loyal where possible to old friends and colleagues, and had only two managers in thirty-five years. He had his one favourite piano, his one favourite chair. In his 1980 diary he left an account of a working trip to New York in which he reported endless problems finding a hotel room that suited him – problems with room service that shut down at night, with bad mattresses and air conditioning, with traffic noise and new-paint smells. It was a short trip, but it was an ordeal, because he found it almost impossible to compromise. As he confided to the diary, "I'm not cut out for traveling, strange mattresses, or meeting a hectic itinerary."

Before that same trip he fretted about all the people he would have to "meet with and/or entertain," for he found socializing onerous. He lived alone and guarded his privacy jealously, giving out his unlisted address and telephone number only to a trusted few. He was a classic introvert, drained rather than energized by prolonged contact with others, especially crowds, and he discovered early that isolating himself from society was essential to his happiness and security, and to his art. "Solitude nourishes creativity," he wrote, and "colleagual fraternity tends to dissipate it." Physical isolation helped protect the intellectual isolation he cultivated. "I need spinal resilience when I'm confronted with opinions not my own," he said. "I separate myself from conflicting and contrasting notions. Monastic seclusion works for me." Gould's ego was as fragile as it was strong; his isolation made him appear at once like an insecure provincial and like one of those heroic loners among Canada's legendary explorers.

"I'm a very private person," he said, and it was true, but when he declared on various occasions that he was Canada's "most experienced hermit," that "my fantasy is to develop to the fullest extent a kind of Howard Hughesian secrecy," that "I just don't like seeing people," he was feeding his own legend. He was not immune to loneliness; he accepted it as a necessary cost of the kind of work he wanted to do. And he was never alone for long; he sought out company frequently, not only for professional purposes though always on his own terms. He needed human contact, and, privately, did not pretend otherwise. Often he made the CBC his first stop of the day, not necessarily because he had work to do there but just to hang around, collect his mail, see what was going on, catch up on gossip. (He enjoyed gossip, as long as it was not malicious.) Legends notwithstanding, his apartment and studios were not off limits the way Howard Hughes's hotel suite was, as long as the people and the conditions were "safe." Many friends and even a fair number of acquaintances, as well as secretaries and others who worked for him, visited him on his home turf, as did musical collaborators with whom he had to practise.

"Technology," Max Frisch wrote, "is the knack of so arranging the world that we don't have to experience it," and for Gould that was technology's blessing, not its curse. When he was not seeing people in person he was plugged in by telephone, and on this instrument, too, he was a virtuoso. To befriend him was to become part of a wide international circle of friends and acquaintances to whom he devoted much time on the telephone and with whom he would often chat more openly than he did in person. (His letters are frequently friendly, funny, and informative, sometimes revealing, but rarely intimate.) He called when it suited him, and if *you* called *him* you got an answering machine or service, even when he was in. He would place calls to help himself wake up in the afternoon, but also called very late at night, and some of his friends have reported falling asleep while he chatted happily away. Even his long-distance calls could be hours long, and he seemed unaware of the concept of the time zone. He was known to read whole essays and books, to sing whole pieces of music over the phone, and several of his musical collaborators have recalled that he even liked to rehearse over the phone, singing through his piano part. He became adept at exploiting the CBC's free tie-line, which linked the Toronto, Ottawa, and Montreal stations, and as soon as the technology was available he had a phone in his car. His phone bills routinely ran to four figures; from January through September of 1982, his last year, his phone bill ran to nearly thirteen thousand dollars. That he owned stock in Bell Canada is nicely appropriate.

Gould poked fun at his obsession with the telephone in a mock personal ad that he scribbled down toward the end of 1977 but presumably never published:

Wanted: Friendly, companionably reclusive, socially unacceptable, alcoholically abstemious, tirelessly talkative, zealously unjealous, spiritually intense, minimally turquoise, maximally ecstatic, loon seeks moth or moths with similar qualities for purposes of telephonic seduction, Tristanesque trip-taking and permanent flame-fluttering. No photos required, financial status immaterial, all ages and non-competitive vocations considered. Applicants should furnish cassette of sample conversation, notarized certification of marital disinclination, references re low-decibel vocal consistency, itineraries and sample receipts from previous, successfully completed out-of-town (moth) flights. All submissions treated confidentially, no paws [?] need apply. Auditions for (all) promising candidates will be conducted to, and on, Avalon Peninsula, Nfld.

Gould spent most of his time holed up in his apartment or studio, in an artificial environment that was hardly healthy but offered him the cocoon he needed. "I don't approve of people who watch television," he told an interviewer in 1959, "but I am one of them." He called himself a "vidiot," and watched a lot of TV for relaxation. (He was a big fan of *The Mary Tyler Moore Show*, and his video-tapes of various episodes are soberly catalogued among his papers in the National Library of Canada.) He listened to recordings and CBC radio, at least six or seven hours a day, by his own estimate. Often he would have, say, a TV and two different radio stations (news and music) playing in different rooms of his apartment, and he would keep them on while working or talking, reading or practising. (He read several newspapers a day and a handful of books a week.) He used heavy drapes to keep the sun out. His sleeping schedule was not set in stone – he occasionally *had* to deal with the outside world during working hours – but he generally went to bed at five or six in the morning, around dawn, sometimes catching the headlines on *The Today Show* just before turning in. He started his day in the early afternoon, and for a Torontonian in the winter months that meant seeing no more than an hour or two of the sun, assuming one stepped outside at all. Sometimes he would not emerge until dusk, "with the bats and the raccoons"; when he went out earlier, he wore dark glasses. The apartment and studio were heated to at least 80°F, and his windows were permanently sealed against fresh air. He had an aversion to "pushed air," whether it was heating or air conditioning; he preferred radiators and electric heaters. He would walk into a restaurant and raise an arm to test for drafts; if there was one and it could not be quelled, he ate elsewhere – yet he apparently had no problem being outside in the dead of winter. He would change hotel rooms or even taxicabs several times if the air was not right, and he would do no TV interviews in air-conditioned studios.

He cared nothing for status or beauty when it came to his surroundings, which were Spartan and utilitarian. His living quarters sufficed as long as they met his needs in terms of size, heat, light, and quiet. He had mostly ordinary furnishings, some of which came with his apartment, and these were shabby by the end of his life. He decorated or designed only to the extent of ensuring that nothing imposed itself on his eye: he wanted no bright colours or sensuous trappings. His brain was orderly, but his apartment, studio, and car were a mess, as was his desk at the CBC and any other space into which he moved more than briefly. He described one of his hotel rooms in his concert days as "the workroom of the Marquis de Sade." Friends could find no surface on which to sit down in his apartment, and his own housekeeping consisted of little more than straightening up the less stable piles, though he claimed to know where everything was. He hired housekeepers who fought vainly against the clutter – some of them, middle-aged immigrant women who did not know who he was, thought him odd and even frightening – and he sent his laundry out. In domestic matters he could be forgetful and disorganized; to lend him a book or record was to say goodbye to it forever. And he was no host. Friends might spend the better part of a day with him without being offered so much as a glass of water. He occasionally stocked some favourite beverage for a particular person, but his larder was usually bare. The lunch he served Harvey Rempel consisted of arrowroot biscuits and instant coffee made with hot water from the kitchen tap.

He was often oblivious to niceties like holidays. He thought nothing of asking, say, a recording technician to work on Thanksgiving or Christmas, and this has sometimes been interpreted as an assertion of personal power. More likely, he simply neglected to notice the comings and goings of holidays, or assumed that everyone was as oblivious to them as he was. When he received the inevitable reply – "Er, Glenn, tomorrow is *Thanksgiving*" – he would merely apologize and reschedule. He forgot birthdays. Walter Homburger had to send flowers to Florence Gould on her birthday and sign her son's name to them. Sometimes he forgot to make a Christmas-card list until after Christmas, and some friends recall cards arriving in February. (Was the insecure Gould first waiting to see who sent cards to *him*?) Some of his friends, though, did receive thoughtful gifts from time to time.

Gould gave little thought to his personal appearance. He was nattily attired only as long as his mother was dressing him; as a child, in photos taken in school or in public or at the piano, he is usually wearing a tie with a sweater or jacket. As an adult he insisted on drab, dark colours. His clothing might be expensive and of high quality, but it was usually baggy, mismatched, or old-fashioned, and he would heap it on the floor. It often looked slept-in, shabby, and soiled. Shirts and socks might be full of holes, pants split up the seat, shoes held intact by a rubber band.* His socks were often mismatched, his shoes untied. Always cold, he dressed in many layers. Reporters occasionally compared him to a Gypsy, a *clochard*, a hobo; it did not help that he was sometimes unshaven and liked to carry his belongings around in a garbage bag. In Florida, in 1957, he was picked up by police in a park on suspicion of being a vagabond, and he was sometimes refused entry to hotels until his identity was made clear.

Calvin Trillin observed that concert pianists "are as a group undoubtedly the most devout searchers-out of quality restaurants."

---

* Most of Gould's clothing was donated to charity after his death, though some representative samples were kept, and are now stored at the Canadian Museum of Civilization in Gatineau, Quebec. In 1996, the Bata Shoe Museum, in Toronto, announced the acquisition of a pair of shoes and a pair of galoshes belonging to Gould.

Not Glenn Gould, whose life was ascetic and abstemious, and who seems to have felt that there was something sinful about bodily needs like eating. He did not smoke and drank nothing stronger than coffee. He told friends that when he once drank a little alcohol at a party at Leonard Bernstein's, he felt ill, and found his thinking, co-ordination, and piano technique affected; that sufficed to make him a teetotaller for life. His insistence on drinking only spring water (especially Poland Water) had nothing to do with refinement of taste: he was afraid of germs in tap water. He confessed to being "almost totally indifferent to food," and considered eating and drinking to be duties rather than joys. He did not even like candy as a child, and once expressed amazement that other people could tell different foods apart. Raised on the drab English fare typical of Old Toronto, he stuck to it, and doused his meals with ketchup as though to kill what taste they had. He did not cook and relied on restaurants and room service. By his own admission he could barely open a can, and he once started a fire at the cottage when he tried to use the stove. On his drives he sometimes stopped at all-night truck stops to drink coffee, eat, and chat. He was a frequent customer at Fran's, a local chain of friendly diners open twenty-four hours a day; there was one down the street from his apartment, where he would eat in a back booth in the wee hours of the morning.

"Gould eats only once a day and confesses that if he eats more often he feels guilty," an interviewer wrote in 1964. That one meal, eaten sometime in the early-morning hours, would be supplemented only by arrowroot biscuits and Ritz crackers, as well as tea, coffee, milk, juice, or bouillon. "On the day of a recording he wouldn't eat at all," his producer Andrew Kazdin recalled. "He claimed fasting sharpened the mind." In his later years he professed to have become a vegetarian out of respect for animals (the idea of abattoirs horrified him), yet several of the private notepads from his last years have lists of foods that seem to represent meals he actually ate, and they include roast beef, veal, chicken, and Dover sole, in meals that usually included soup, salad, potato, vegetables, and sometimes melba toast and ice cream. A typical meal at Fran's consisted of scrambled eggs, salad, toast, juice, sherbet, and decaf, and an employee at the Inn on the Park hotel recalled that Gould's after-midnight meal, in his last years, was often nothing more than scrambled eggs and orange juice, though he sometimes visited the hotel's Vintage Room restaurant for a steak. His pallid diet may have had more to do with native squeamishness about food than with animal rights. The pianist Anton Kuerti, who met him from time to time on the concert circuit, saw Gould flee in horror from a restaurant in Salzburg after the waiter brought the local delicacy Kuerti had ordered: *Hirn mit Ei*, calf's brains with scrambled eggs. Gary Graffman witnessed a similar disgust at escargots.

Gould's pianistic lifestyle, too, was Spartan. He went days, even weeks, without playing, and claimed that the "best playing I do is when I haven't touched the instrument for a month." He was not a slave to the piano, though he became insecure if he was away from it *too* long. He practised less than most virtuosos during his concert years, and after 1964 needed an even smaller amount of time at the piano; he could not understand why most of his colleagues practised so much. In his last interview, in 1982, he said that he did not know Brahms's Ballades, Op. 10, at all before he prepared to record them that year. His two months' preparation consisted of studying the score for six weeks, then practising in the two weeks before the recording, usually no more than an hour a day. For him, getting the interpretation right, a mostly mental process, was more a concern than actually rendering the music on the piano. "Do you realize that this sounds quite unbelievable?" his interviewer, David Dubal, asked. Yet Gould's private notepads suggest that it was true. From the mid-seventies, he was practising, when at all, as little as half an hour a day, usually about one hour, never more than two. He devoted the same or more time to reading, studying scores, writing, dictating, editing, even to his mail.

Though by the 1970s he was no longer using the Lake Simcoe cottage, Gould tried to get out of the city for an extended period at least once or twice a year, most often in the late summer, albeit for *working* holidays, for he was not the type to play volleyball on the beach. The 1962 holiday in the Bahamas was a fluke: his destinations of choice were almost always north, and included Manitoulin Island, in Georgian Bay, as well as Sault Ste. Marie, Wawa, Marathon, Thunder Bay, and other towns along the rugged, lonely north shore of Lake Superior, where he admired the "Group of Seven woebegoneness" of the countryside. "As you know, I have a special fondness for your town," he wrote to a high-school principal in Terrace Bay in 1965, "since I find it an ideal place in which to catch up on some writing and score studying and most of all, thinking. Indeed, I sometimes wonder whether those of you, who have the opportunity to live in what can only seem to an urban southerner as blessed isolation, do in fact appreciate the wonderful advantages that that isolation offers." He spent some time in Quebec and the Maritimes, too, and in the last few years of his life, he took to visiting certain remote islands off Georgia and the Carolinas, which he had discovered on tour in 1959. Yet he could be lonely when vacationing by himself, for all his talk about the glories of solitude. Jessie Greig recalled that he invariably returned from his American holidays earlier than anticipated.

He usually drove himself when he left town: he was one of those North Americans who are in love with their cars. For someone who liked to be in the world but not of the world the automobile was a perfect metaphor, a travelling apartment from which he could see the world at arm's length. Beginning with the brand-new Plymouth Plaza he bought in 1956, for a little over two thousand dollars, his preferred cars were big and American, and he bought or leased a whole succession of different makes and models; in his last years he had a Chevrolet Monte Carlo that he named Lance, and a Lincoln Town Car named Longfellow. On cars he willingly lavished a good deal of money and attention, though his driving, by all accounts, could be appalling: All of his friends tell stories about their terror at occupying what one of them dubbed the "suicide seat" in his car. He learned to drive on his father's knee at the cottage, and hinted at his future driving career by steering the family car into Lake Simcoe. (He drove boats no more safely.) For someone so anxious about so many things, Gould apparently felt invulnerable in a car, but then in most situations he felt comfortable and safe as long as *he* was in control. Not even a long record of accidents and traffic violations could rid him of the idea that all was well when he was behind the wheel. Yet he could not keep his mind on the road, particularly when someone else was in the car. He would talk volubly as he drove, and had the disturbing habit of turning to a passenger while addressing him. Even alone, he would become wrapped up in music on the radio, singing and conducting, and sometimes kept a score open by his side. He often drove with his legs crossed, with his left foot working the pedals, sometimes with one finger on the wheel, at high speeds regardless of the visibility or the road conditions, always with the windows and vents closed and the heater turned up. The only good thing about his driving was that he did not tailgate: he was afraid of inhaling fumes from other vehicles.

He was involved in many fender-benders and other minor accidents, even in his own parking lot, though miraculously never a major crash. He would spin out of control on slippery roads, plough into snow banks, run into guard posts on the highway, and drive up onto the sidewalk, endangering trees and parked cars. Jessie Greig recalled an occasion when he hit a truck in a snowstorm and ended up in the river. John Roberts remembers the passenger door flying open on one occasion as Gould's car spun out of control on black ice, and only Gould's quick, strong hand keeping him from falling out.

Gould's driving put him constantly in trouble with the authorities. Speeding, running stop signs and red lights, making U-turns downtown during rush hour, veering between lanes, driving the wrong way up a one-way street – he repeatedly made every sort of violation. He was forever paying fines, receiving demerit points on his licence, and getting warning letters from Ontario's Driver Control Branch. He had to appear in court from time to time, or report to the Branch for an interview or re-examination; at least once, in 1963, he had his licence temporarily suspended, a fate that loomed on other occasions. In the summer of 1979, the police investigated him for "leaving the scene of an accident." On one occasion he got into trouble while a reporter was in the car, and in fact his driving was fodder for the newspapers from at least the summer of 1958, when the headline "Gould Freed in 4th Crash" appeared in a local paper after he skidded forty feet into a truck. He was hauled into court in Beaverton, Ontario, but the judge, who said he was a music fan, merely praised the honesty of his testimony, dismissed the careless-driving charge, and sent him to a safe-driving clinic. "He was a very nice man," Gould said. "I didn't have to say a thing. We obviously understood each other." (It was not the last time he would benefit from sympathetic judges, attorneys, or policemen.) "He just couldn't seem to comprehend that he drove like an idiot teenager," one of his passengers recalled, but Gould was incorrigible. "I suppose it can be said that I'm an absent-minded driver," he once said. "It's true that I've driven through a number of red lights on occasion, but on the other hand, I've stopped at a lot of green ones but never gotten credit for it."

"I think one really has to live one's life with a spiritual direction in mind."

Going up a mountain track, I fell to thinking.

Approach everything rationally, and you become harsh. Pole along in the stream of emotions, and you will be swept away by the current. Give free rein to your desires, and you become uncomfortably confined. It is not a very agreeable place to live, this world of ours.

Those are the opening sentences of Natsume Soseki's 1906 novel *The Three-Cornered World*. A fan Gould met on a train in 1967 introduced him to the novel, which he came to consider one of the greatest of the twentieth century. The book tells of a painter and poet who, tired of the mundane world, goes on a spiritual journey in which he attempts "to rise above emotions, and to view things dispassionately," though the "sublime detachment from the world" he desires proves difficult to achieve, and he must struggle to come to terms with challenging sensory experiences. As Gould wrote in 1981, *The Three-Cornered World* "is, among other things, about meditation versus action, detachment versus duty, about western versus eastern value systems, about the perceived perils of 'modernism'" – all issues he himself struggled with. The opening sentences of the novel could stand as a motto for Gould, encapsulating as they do an essential dilemma of his life: how to balance reason and emotion. He was certainly not comfortable poling along in the stream of emotions. "There is a Sicilian strain in the people of Toronto, ready at any moment to shatter their exterior of blancmange-like calm," Robertson Davies wrote, and while no one could mistake Gould for a Sicilian ("I'm not a southerner; there's not a drop of Latin in me"), he was a man of great passion who was never happier than when he was controlling his emotions beneath an exterior of blancmange-like calm. "I rather approve of restraint," he told a reporter in 1962, with perfect restraint. He might have cited Pascal again: "When the passions become masters, they are vices."

Intense, overt emotions, his own or someone else's, disturbed and embarrassed him, and he avoided situations in which they might arise. In extraordinary cases, with close friends, he could be frank, and he would not flee a room if a friend was in tears; on the contrary, he could be solicitous and consoling. But wherever possible he preferred to keep things light. The prospect of losing control of his emotions filled him with anxiety, and when an unavoidable emotional confrontation with another person loomed, he needed more than spinal resilience to deal with it; he needed Valium. Even small confrontations disturbed him. Otto Joachim, remembering some musical disagreements that arose when Gould performed with the Montreal String Quartet, said, "Whenever Glenn defended his opinion, he closed his eyes and began to stutter." On other occasions when, say, a professional situation slipping away from his control – Yehudi Menuhin's refusal to stick to the script, for instance – he got a nervous tic around his right eye, clearly visible in some of his television programs. The soprano Joan Maxwell once telephoned Gould and, disguising her voice, pretended to be a small-town piano student and fan. She strung him along until she realized he was genuinely upset at the thought that his personal security had been breached. She apologized profusely but he felt angry and betrayed, though he often played precisely this sort of gag on others. Andrew Kazdin saw him develop elaborate strategies for avoiding unwanted meetings or phone calls. Gould tried to control social situations in advance. If someone was to visit his apartment or studio, he would often carefully prepare the visit, cueing up recordings and videotapes, preparing his comments – in effect, planning a program. He sometimes prepared for face-to-face conversations or telephone calls with written notes, followed by a tranquilizer. Yet once a meeting was underway he could be open to spontaneity, depending on how things went. He needed the rituals of preparation to calm him and give him confidence, but the anxiety, while real, was not necessarily overwhelming.

Gould saw moral issues everywhere, and saw them in black and white – another legacy of his puritan heritage. Musically and personally he tended to view options in terms of opposing extremes. Curiously, though, he apparently had no fixed views on politics or religion. In his youth he was already fascinated by Canadian and American politics, and in later years he eagerly followed the Watergate scandal, the Quebec referendum, and so on; his surviving videotapes show that he was a news junkie whose television was often tuned to political events. Sheltered and privileged all his life, he had no first-hand experience of poverty or intolerance, and his native reticence did not dispose him to public activism even on behalf of issues he held dear, like pacifism and animal rights. Though some of his favourite musicians – Strauss, Furtwängler, Karajan, Schwarzkopf – had been tainted by association with the Nazi regime, Gould never made this a bar to appreciating them; he seems never to have discussed the issue, except, once, to describe Strauss as "apolitical" and "naïve" in the 1930s. In his personal conduct he was deeply conservative, a "square," and he poked (gentle) fun at Beats, hippies, and the like, but politically he was neither a reactionary nor a leftist. He never advocated a system that trampled on individual rights; when he told one of his radio technicians, Donald Logan, that life would be much better in a benevolent dictatorship in which he was the dictator, it was with a twinkle in his eye. He claimed to hold vaguely socialist views that are not necessarily contradicted by his individualism and fondness for the stock market, and he would berate the capitalist system even as he admitted his dependence on it. He seems to have picked up some of the liberal social conscience typical of the United Church and, earlier, Methodism. His family, through their church, had worked on behalf of social causes. As he noted in his eulogy, his mother, near the end of her life, was devoted to a group of underprivileged mothers in a large downtown church "where, weekly, she tried, through music and inspiration, to make their lives a little more meaningful." He believed in social justice and racial equality and in caring for the poor, and approved of policies that supported "the Peace, Order, and good Government of Canada," to cite the famous phrase of the country's original constitution.

When it came to contemporary politics, Gould's views had more to do with personalities than with policy. He disapproved of flamboyant politicians. He was put off by the glamour, the "Camelot" mystique, around John F. Kennedy, preferring the awkward, insecure Nixon (though he once claimed to be "in love with Jacqueline Kennedy"), and he deplored the cult of personality around Pierre Elliott Trudeau during the "Trudeaumania" of the late sixties. When, near the end of Gould's life, Trudeau notoriously made an obscene gesture to some protesters outside his train in British Columbia, Gould was disgusted. The Beach, Robert Fulford recalled, invariably elected some Tory "nonentity," and Gould seems to have inherited a fondness for dour, conservative politicians whom he admired as ethical men. He was a fan of Robert Stanfield, the sober head of the Progressive Conservative Party and leader of the Opposition during the early Trudeau years, and he admired the young Joe Clark, who succeeded Stanfield in 1976. Gould offered to write a profile of Clark for the *Canadian Magazine* that year, for which purpose he contacted Clark's press officer about an interview, collected clippings, and jotted down notes, but in the end he never did make a foray into political commentary.

Just as he had no party-political affiliations, Gould had no denominational or even well-defined religious beliefs, though he was fascinated by religion and indeed by all sorts of otherworldly phenomena. He believed in ESP and telepathy, took omens and "coincidences" seriously, was frightened by ghosts and the occult. A mind-reading game once so disturbed him he abruptly quit playing. He believed in the significance of dreams, too, and eagerly discussed his dreams with many friends and occasionally interviewers.* He was deeply superstitious. He would cancel a concert or airplane flight if he believed it would turn out to be "unlucky," and he panicked when friends ignored his dire warnings about their own flights. He would sometimes rewrite a cheque over and over because he considered the signature to be somehow "unlucky," though his friends never figured out what his criteria were. (This is one reason he hated to give out autographs.) Among his notepads is a page from 1978 on which he obsessively practised his signature – always with one *n* in "Glenn" – and in other notepads he used up five or six pages just to write a one-sentence note to his assistant or make a list of "accounts due," restarting over and over, sometimes writing no more than part of the first word on a page, because something about the note was not quite right. This is not necessarily surprising in someone who prided himself on his reason: to a rational man the irrational is bound to

---

* Among the dreams he discussed with others were some whose meaning was ambiguous (being without form and looking down on the earth from above), some that caused him anxiety (standing in at the last minute for an indisposed baritone in an operatic duet with Maria Callas only to make a terrible musical error; grabbing on to something just as he is about to plummet over Niagara Falls; looking out his bedroom window at the cottage and seeing only an expanse of barren rock), and some that put him in a heroic light (guiding a damaged airplane to a safe landing). "I'm very much the anti-hero in real life," he once said, "but I compensate like mad in my dreams."

hold a morbid fascination. Phenomena he could not explain were phenomena he could not control, so perhaps his fascination with them was in part an effort to control them by figuring them out.

Though he had no definite theology, Gould had religious tendencies. Different people remember his religious persuasion differently, and his own comments were contradictory. To Donald Logan he described himself as "agnostic going on atheist," but others recall that he definitely believed in God, if not necessarily a fixed or conventional notion of God. To the interviewer Elyse Mach, in 1980, he set out some of his beliefs with surprising frankness:

> I can only say that I was brought up as a Presbyterian; I stopped being a church-goer at the age of about eighteen, but I have had all my life a tremendously strong sense that, indeed, there is a hereafter, and the transformation of the spirit is a phenomenon with which one must reckon, and in the light of which, indeed, one must attempt to live one's life. As a consequence, I find all here-and-now philosophies repellent. On the other hand, I don't have any objective images to build around my notion of a hereafter, and I recognize that it's a great temptation to formulate a comforting theory of eternal life, so as to reconcile one's self to the inevitability of death. But I'd like to think that's not what I'm doing; I'd like to think that I'm not employing it as a deliberate self-reassuring process. For me, it intuitively seems right; I've never had to work at convincing myself about the likelihood of a life hereafter. It is simply something that appears to me infinitely more plausible than its opposite, which would be oblivion.

But he believed that the afterlife had to be *earned*, through an honourable life and good works.

Gould read a great deal of theology – books by Jacques Maritain, Jean le Moyne, Pierre Teilhard de Chardin, Paul Tillich, and many others – and some of the philosophers whose work he read (Kierkegaard, Nietzsche, Schopenhauer) dealt with religious matters. Jessie Greig remembered having many discussions about religion with Gould in his later years, and said that he "was full of humility" when it came to matters of faith. He knew the Bible well, and was particularly fond of the New Testament, especially Revelation. His appreciation of the Bible seems to have been more ethical and even aesthetic than doctrinal, but he took comfort from certain Biblical texts. One favourite was "Lord, grant us the peace the earth cannot give," another was "Let your light shine before men that they might see your good works." He was familiar with many hymns and other traditional religious music, and was genuinely moved by the spirituality he perceived in composers like Gibbons, Bach, Mendelssohn, and Bruckner. He once said, "I believe in God – Bach's God." For all his apparent structuralism, he believed that art and artists should ultimately seek transcendent experiences. "Art is not created by rational animals," he wrote, rather surprisingly, in 1964, "and in the long run is better for not being so created." He said he disliked the label "intellectual" because he was "primarily interested in art that communicates spiritually" and was only interested in music that met his ethical and spiritual standards.

To work out one's own answers to religious questions without relying on inherited dogma is characteristic of mysticism, and various strains of mystical thought had made significant inroads even in staid Ontario in the generations before Gould was born: Christian Science, theosophy, Neoplatonism, Rosicrucianism, anthroposophy, and perhaps most significantly the transcendentalism associated with R. M. Bucke's *Cosmic Consciousness* of 1901. Mystical ideas were still in the air when Gould was young – they had motivated many Canadian artists, for instance – and even the United Church had some ministers who held liberal views on matters like mysticism. An Uxbridge woman who worked for the Goulds as a nanny recalls (admittedly vaguely) that Florence Gould had some mystical-sounding religious ideas that were unusual for her milieu. For instance, she apparently believed that her son was the reincarnation of one of the great composers – a Russian, possibly Tchaikovsky – and told him so.

It is not absurd to posit a strain of mysticism in Gould's thinking, for Gouldian idealism and individualism and rejection of dogmas are all typical of mystical faiths. Gould's God was not the fire-breathing law-giver of the Old Testament, but something more akin to the transcendentalist or pantheist or Spinozist God, a timeless spiritual ideal, and like many mystics he worshipped, in some ways, the centrality and restorative power of nature. His notion of "ecstasy" – of art transporting the perceiver so that he stands outside himself and outside time, caught up in an ideal realm – recalls mystical notions about transcending individuality and communion with the eternal, joining the "great soul of mankind." His favourite "Lord, grant us the peace the earth cannot give" is practically a definition of the theosophical concept of Nirvana. Northrop Frye considered the painters of the Group of Seven – still influential in Canada in Gould's youth – to be theosophical given their "commitment to painting as a way of life, or, perhaps better, as a sacramental activity expressing a faith, and so analogous to the practising of a religion." For all its Wordsworthian Romanticism, this sounds like Gould, too, for whom everything from choice of repertoire to rendering of trills was a statement of a larger world view with ethical implications. Even his views on technology were ultimately spiritual. Like Jean Le Moyne, he believed in "the charity of the machine," the idea that technology is benevolent, as when, for instance, recording removes music from the "gladiatorial" realm of the concert hall. And like Pierre Teilhard de Chardin, whom he read prolifically, he considered the growing integration of technology with human life to be a positive force in the ethical and spiritual evolution of mankind. Teilhard's Utopian notion of a "noösphere" – of a sort of envelope of thought surrounding the globe, born of the "unified consciousness" and knowledge of all mankind – was supported by his observation of the growing worldwide network of machines and technology; such ideas, Marshall McLuhan's and Gould's among them, have new resonance in the age of digital technology and the Internet.

Gould viewed art as ultimately an instrument of salvation, and he must have appreciated reading, in *The Three-Cornered World*, of Soseki's belief that artists "can obtain salvation, and be delivered from earthly desires and passions," and so "enter at will a world of undefiled purity." Western mysticism in fact overlaps in many ways with Eastern religion and philosophy. (Emerson, for instance, was a fan of Asian literature.) Gould sometimes poked fun at the fashion for Eastern thought in the sixties and seventies and its musical manifestations in, for instance, the work of John Cage, but while hardly a dharma bum he was not immune to this particular trend: he read authors like Kahlil Gibran and Alan Watts, and books about Japan and China. In Eastern cultures he admired a lifestyle, an ethic, and an aesthetic devoted to order, restraint, contemplation, tranquility, and the pursuit of repose,* the latter a concept of great importance in Soseki's novel. "The purpose of art," Gould wrote in 1962, "is not the release of a momentary ejection of adrenaline but is, rather, the gradual, lifelong construction of a state of wonder and serenity." The Japanese writer Kobo Abé, whose novel *The Woman in the Dunes* Gould greatly admired,[†] told a CBC radio interviewer that Gould would have made a good Zen Buddhist monk, and his friends recall that he took an interest in Zen Buddhism in his later years. His views on ethical and spiritual matters often had an Eastern and anti-Western flavour – for instance, his distrust of the egotism, worldliness, and competitive instincts implicit in capitalism. Of course, Western mystics and Eastern philosophers also praised intuition rather than reason as the key to understanding, questioned the validity of logic and analysis, and tended to prefer the simple to the complex, all of which was anathema to Gould. "An artist," Soseki wrote, "is a person who lives in the triangle which remains after the angle which we may call common sense has been removed from this four-cornered world." Much as he wanted to be a perfect spiritual creature, Gould knew he could not fully succeed. He could not quite do without that fourth corner.

---

* One of his few material indulgences was an oil painting by the Chinese artist Zao Wou-Ki, which he valued, in 1962, at $4,200.

[†] He considered Hiroshi Teshigahara's 1964 film version of the novel "quite possibly the greatest film ever made," saw it dozens of times, and claimed to have studied it frame by frame.

"You know what an uncurable romantic I am anyway."

Gould had great anxiety about his body, and in his later years rationed his physical contact with others to a manageable degree. He shied away from contact with unfamiliar people, and usually even with friends: it is not only Steinway and Sons employees who say, "You never touched Glenn." A lot of it was concern for his physical health, not merely fear of intimacy. He was not as averse to physical contact as most people assume, and was known to embrace or physically comfort people he knew well. Once again, it depended on the person and the situation; the no-touching rule was another default position that he willingly surrendered in the right circumstances. He almost certainly desired more physical contact than his anxiety permitted him to enjoy.

Gould guarded no aspect of his life more jealously than his sexuality, about which there has been much mystery and speculation. All but his closest friends risked immediate and permanent banishment if they inquired into his love life, and for the most part his friends have kept his secrets. He never married, was never linked publicly with a woman, seemed indifferent to the attentions of female fans, and in interviews refused to answer prurient questions about his private life (his definition of "prurient" was strict). He deplored "the repetitive, tasteless, and ultimately unproductive inquiries into Boulez's sexual proclivities" in Joan Peyser's biography of that composer, which he reviewed in 1976, and he admired Liberace for successfully suing an English journalist who had implied that he was homosexual – clearly, Gould believed that a public figure had the right to keep his private life private.

Not surprisingly, many people assumed, and still assume, that he harboured some secret vice he was keen to hide, presumably homosexuality. Rumours that he was gay were fed by the androgyny of his appearance – so striking in many early photographs – and by his superficial sexlessness, which could be interpreted either way; it probably did not help that on concert tours he sometimes travelled with a male massage therapist. He was not uncomfortable or disapproving around homosexual friends, and had a significant following among gay men who considered him "one of us." In Kevin Kopelson's odd little book *Beethoven's Kiss: Pianism, Perversion, and the Mastery of Desire*, published in 1996, Gould's homosexuality is a *donnée* not requiring proof, and he is discussed, alongside Horowitz, Cliburn, Pogorelich, and others, as a closeted gay pianist – as, indeed, "a touchstone of queer pianism."

His piano style fed such assumptions, to judge from the reviews. In concertos by Beethoven and Brahms, for instance, he was praised for introspection and poetry but criticized for lacking power and "virility," and over the years some of his detractors used words like "frail," "lightfingered," "swooning," "effeminate," and "mincing" to describe performances low in bravura, with which he was never comfortable. ("Mincing" is one of the very words that sent Liberace to court.) George Szell criticized Gould to his face for using the soft pedal pervasively in a Beethoven concerto, because "It makes a very *feminine* sound." Gould said years later, "I had the feeling that he intended a sexual connotation to this whole matter, but I pretended I didn't notice." Robert Sabin, reviewing the 1960 album that included Gould's gorgeous recording of Bach's B-flat-major partita, compared him favourably with the "over-trained young keyboard athletes" of his day, admiring his "exquisite tactile sense," his "gentleness," "grace," and "charm." Gould, he wrote, "is a poet, a seeker of beauty in hidden places," and he concluded that "sensitivity" was the keynote of his playing. Meant as high praise, this sort of thing was also fodder for those who considered Gould's playing insufficiently masculine, and some of his critics drew on notions of decadence, exoticism, and femininity that have long been used as code for homosexuality.

Admittedly, Glenn Gould was no one's idea of a powerful argument for heterosexuality, or any other sexuality: he did not ooze sex. And his private sexual thoughts were doubtless no less ambiguous than the average nominally heterosexual man's. But no evidence suggests that he was privately homosexual or had or desired homosexual experiences. Not even his gay friends claim that: one of them recalls that when they were students he made a pass at Gould, who "practically fell out of the window." Gould was not oblivious to the rumours, and was upset when they were aired publicly, though he could be good-humoured on the subject in private. Ben Sonnenberg asked him what he said when people asked if he was gay, and he replied, "I always quote Horowitz, that there are three kinds of pianists: homosexual pianists, Jewish pianists, and bad pianists. And I add, pianists who play better than Horowitz."*

Ravel, an apparently asexual composer widely assumed to have been homosexual, once said, "The only love affair I ever had was with my music," and Gould liked to make similar claims: "Music is *my* ecstasy," he told Nicholas Kilburn. This was his party line with the press. A 1959 interview in the *Toronto Daily Star* included this priceless exchange:

> Dennis Braithwaite: Are you engaged, or do you have a steady girl friend?
> Glenn Gould: I am not engaged.
> Dennis Braithwaite: Getting back to your music . . .

Gould reportedly had dates with women when he was a teenager and young man, though they were, by all accounts, friendly, chaste meetings with much talk of books and music.

Andrew Kazdin believed that Gould lacked experience with women. "In many ways, Gould displayed a kind of arrested development," he wrote, "certainly in his emotional behavior. From a social standpoint, it seemed clear to me that Glenn viewed women with a kind of prepubescent naïveté." As Kazdin recalled, Gould once decided that *Stereo Review* was giving him bad reviews because the magazine's classical-music editor was jealous that Gould had been friendly with, and perhaps attracted to, his wife, who had

---

* To this day there are rumours that he had homosexual encounters as a young man, and while I do not dismiss them as necessarily absurd on their face, I know of no evidence to support them.

worked for Columbia Masterworks. "The whole episode," Kazdin wrote, "appeared to me like something one could unearth from a teenager's diary." Gould's naïveté showed in his puritanical streak, too: he strongly disapproved of Kazdin's wife's reading *Cosmopolitan*, and professed to be "absolutely shocked" that there was such a thing as pornography. We can imagine his embarrassment when Leonard Bernstein, at a party after their first performance together, told him, "You played so beautifully in the cadenza that I almost came in my pants." Yet despite his prudishness he was fascinated by tales of the sexual exploits of friends, and Paul Myers recalls that Gould liked to go to risqué movies and would watch sex scenes with boyish wonder.

Gould couldn't help but attract women, who responded to his physical beauty (as a young man, at least), his talent and intelligence, his charm and wit, his celebrity. He told friends of uncomfortable occasions on his concert tours when he had to fend off unwelcome advances from women, including the wife of a diplomat in Russia. "No wonder the pianist Glenn Gould needs the Chevrolet he is driving in Tel-Aviv," wrote a journalist in Israel in 1958. "Gould, a bachelor of 25, is simply 'chased' by the beautiful ladies of Tel-Aviv, and apparently he has no other way of escaping them than by dashing away in his car. From a reliable source it was disclosed that Gould cares nothing for all those pretty admirers, and he spends almost every free minute playing the piano."

His standoffishness seemed only to make him more desirable. He was more frightened than flattered by groupies, though he often had to deal with them. A note from Walter Homburger among his papers reads, "Watch yourself – I think that she'll be poison. She is a piano teacher and obviously is trying to obtain publicity for herself." One young woman, from the CBC, would come to the house and, to his mother's consternation, literally sit at Gould's feet while he practised. A woman wrote to him in 1961 asking if he was married or engaged, and if she could come to Toronto to see him; "my future," she wrote, "depends entirely upon your answers." Gould felt pity for such women, though he was rattled by more persistent and perhaps dangerous fans. Ray Roberts, Gould's assistant in the 1970s, got a call from him one night because some woman was pounding on his door. "And then," recalled Roberts, "there was that crazy woman from Texas who kept writing him letters. She wrote him every day. She said she was going to come up and start shooting people on the corner of Bloor and Yonge unless he agreed to marry her." A Swedish woman claims that he wanted to marry her, and that he visited Sweden secretly, shortly before his death, to see her and receive medical treatments for his back, but evidence contradicts her story, which is as plausible as a lost Gould recording of the Tchaikovsky concerto.*

Gould seemed to get along better with women than with men, and had warm friendships with many women over the years. There was Deborah Ishlon, who was working in the publicity department at Columbia when Gould first signed with the company, and the journalist Gladys Shenner, who was close to him throughout his international concert career. There was Verna Sandercock, Walter Homburger's secretary, and Susan Kocsis, who was director of publicity at CBS Masterworks during the last years of Gould's life. He relished such relationships, though sometimes, perhaps unintentionally, they threatened to become more serious, more intimate, a prospect that apparently made him anxious even where he seemingly desired it.

Evidence points to a number of relationships with women that may or may not have been platonic and ultimately became complicated and were ended. Gould found the most intimate sort of relationship difficult to sustain, for he feared that too close an emotional bond would engulf his life and thoughts, undermining him and ultimately his art. When conflicts invariably arose with the women he got close to, he had difficulty confronting them, preferring to cut the relationship off with at best some written explanation. Among his papers is, for instance, a handwritten note to a woman, from the early sixties, that begins, "Of course, we parted friends. Why shouldn't we? However much I may have upset you it was, at worst,

---

* I called her to talk about it, but she hung up on me.

the result of a thoughtlessness sometimes characteristic of me but never the intent of deliberate malice. So you must believe that I could not but think of you kindly." Another document from the same period, presumably a draft of a letter, implies a relationship that, in his opinion, was becoming too intense or demanding:

> I gather you tried to call me yesterday, so this letter – though difficult – is necessary.
>
> You are as well aware as anyone by what intuition I am sometimes governed, upon what "unreason" my decisions are sometimes based. And this intuition in the business of human relations is a force which I serve quite without question; and when it seems to demand isolation from one person or from everyone – that too is obeyed. However illogical and unpredictable, and infuriating this may be to others, I have found in this obedience – however arbitrarily I may have used it – a source of immense strength.
>
> And I can only ask you to be charitable and forgive me, and *believe* me when I tell you that you are in no way responsible for this – except in the sense that we are all of us responsible for the world's becoming – to try to understand when I say that the one thing I will not do is to analyze – to explain my reactions – except to myself, and once again to believe me when I tell you that I hold you in as much affection as ever.

Such situations genuinely distressed him, and though his stated explanations sound contrived – "the world's becoming"? – he seems to have been at once anxious not to hurt the other party and determined to make the necessary break.

Gould had an intimate relationship, in the early and mid-1950s, with a woman somewhat older than he whose letters to him were addressed from "Faun" to "Spaniel," and Gladys Riskind remembers seeing Gould with a woman friend around this time – the same woman? – lying with his head in her lap as she stroked his hair in a manner that was more than friendly. In both cases, he assumes the role of beloved pet, as he had with his mother, and his close bond with his mother surely influenced his later relationships with women, with whom he was generally gallant and considerate. He brought out the mother in some women; he needed nurturing, praise, pats. Sometimes it is unclear what he was looking for in a particular relationship – a friend? an intellectual companion? a lover? a mother? Sometimes, it seems, neither he nor the woman in question was certain. He revered certain women from a distance, including those artists whose work particularly affected him: Elisabeth Schwarzkopf, Barbra Streisand, Petula Clark. (And Mary Tyler Moore?) He seems even to have fallen in love with the occasional *fictional* woman, including the mysterious Nami in *The Three-Cornered World*, perhaps "the woman in the dunes," and, near the end of his life, the disabled Rowena in the film version of Timothy Findley's novel *The Wars*.

As to whether Gould had a real sexual life, some of the evidence is admittedly ambiguous. The former manager of the Wawa Motor Inn, for instance, recalls that Gould did not always check in alone, but was sometimes with a woman ("some CBC woman" was his not entirely confident memory). On the other hand, they took adjoining rooms (the two at the end, farthest from the office), which merely raises the question: Was she a secretary? A colleague? A friend? A lover? Other evidence of his travels with female companions is equally ambiguous. Among his papers is a fragmentary text, to (or about) someone named Dell, that has been much discussed by his fans, for some of whom it is a smoking gun analogous to the mysterious "Immortal Beloved" letters of Beethoven. Here is the text in its entirety:

> You know, I am deeply in love with a certain beaut[iful] girl[.] I asked her to marry me but she turned me down but I still love her more than anything in the world and every min[ute] I can spend with her is pure heaven; but I don't want to be a bore and if I could only get her to tell me when I could see her, it would help. She has a standing invit[ation] to let me take her anywhere she'd like to go any time but it seems to me she never has time

for me. Please if you see her, ask her to let me know when I can see her and when I can –

There was, according to all available evidence, no one named Dell in Gould's life. The page on which the letter appears offers few clues, except as to the date. At the top of the page is a sequence of keys relating to the editing of his album of preludes, fugues, and fughettas by Bach, released in the late summer of 1980; in the middle of the page is a bordered phrase that apparently reads, "Chopin's block plump and silvery," whatever that means; the letter follows. At the head of the text Gould wrote "– love letters to Dell –" (the letter is written to a third party *about* the woman in question). Of great significance is a harmless-looking emendation near the bottom of the letter, in the clause "She has a standing invit[ation] to let me take her anywhere she'd like to go." Instead of "to let" Gould had originally written "and let"; later, with a different pen, he struck out "and" and replaced it with "to," correcting an obvious error, but at that same time he also put a question mark in the margin. This is a telling detail, for there is no reason for him to have questioned a per-fectly reasonable correction in something he himself was writing; the question mark makes sense only if he was presuming to correct something that someone *else* had written. In other words, Gould did not write the Dell letter; he *copied* it, as he often copied out quota-tions and bits of text that struck him in some way. (The use of the plural in the heading – "love letters" – suggests that the letter is one of a collection.) Mysteries still remain: Why did he copy this letter? From what source? But the text cannot simply be interpreted as a "love letter" in the usual sense of the term, and does not seem to refer to real people and situations in Gould's later life.

It is tempting to assume that Gould was asexual, an image that certainly fits his aesthetic and the persona he sought to convey, and one can read the whole Gould literature and be convinced that he died a virgin. As he liked to say, he, rather than the hero of George Santayana's novel, was "the Last Puritan." (He was a great fan of that novel.) Sex was not discussed in his family when he was growing up:

his house seems to have been one of those in which sensuality was equated with a want of virtue. But while it is easy to believe that such an environment must breed fear or guilt about sex, we should not assume that Gould lacked normal sexual feelings, was riven with guilt and shame on the subject, and was incapable of sexual intimacy given the right circumstances. (Even puritans manage to procreate.) One well-known Toronto musician, who knew Gould in the early fifties, had the privilege of walking unannounced through an unlocked door, in a house he owned, to discover Gould *in flagrante delicto* with a female friend. Gould himself told Ray Roberts that he had had "a torrid affair" in his twenties, on tour in the United States, and there were rumours of girlfriends in Montreal, in New York, in California. A woman who knew him well in the late fifties recalls that they "flirted like a couple of teenagers" and that he unequivocally sought to initiate a sexual relationship. (She declined, he was respectful and gentlemanly about it, and their friendship continued.) Reliable sources supply further plausible second-hand testimony suggesting that other of his later relationships became sexual, though one does not get the sense that there were many such affairs. In any event, let there be no more talk of Saint Glenn never sullied by the touch of Woman.

The most serious romantic relationship of Gould's life was with an American woman who was married and had children. They met not long after the release of his first Columbia recording, and presumably their relationship blossomed over time. Around 1967, she left her husband and moved, with her children, to Toronto. She stayed first with one of Gould's friends, then in a hotel, before taking her own apartment in the Deer Park neighbourhood not far from Gould, and she lived there for four years. The woman was herself an artist with a lively mind, and by all accounts Gould adored her. He spent a lot of time at her apartment,* and they spent hours

---

* "He shacked up with a broad for about a year," his accountant, Patrick J. Sullivan, told Peter Ostwald. "I know, because I saw the expenses." I, however, have seen no evidence that the two lived together for any period of time.

talking on the telephone, sometimes until they fell asleep; he was also fond of her children. The two sometimes socialized with friends like John Roberts and Paul Myers, and Gould talked about her to his friends. Kazdin saw them together in November 1967, in New York, at a private screening of one of Gould's television programs for NET (Herbert von Karajan was also present). "It was a different Glenn Gould that I saw during that day," Kazdin wrote. "Instead of the self-absorbed center of attention, I witnessed an attentive escort to [the woman]. Was she comfortable? Could he get her anything? My current mental image of them during the actual showing of the tape is of [her] sitting in a large lounge chair and Glenn perching on the arm of same, sort of draped over the back of it. Throughout this period, there was no doubt that [she] held a special place in his life." They were a couple, their relationship (according to one of the woman's friends) was "very passionate and very physical," and their life was as close to domestic as Gould's ever got. According to Otto Friedrich, who interviewed the woman, Gould wanted to marry her; it was she who refused, and, around 1971, moved back to her husband. "Gould telephoned her every night for two years, she says, until she finally persuaded him to stop. They never saw each other again."

Gould admitted to thinking a lot about marriage, and at some level yearned for domesticity. He was intently interested in other people's families, and often grew close to the wives and children (and pets) of his friends and colleagues. He was eager to hear news of the families he knew, and seemed to enjoy visiting people at home, as though he took vicarious pleasure from being in the presence of domestic harmony. He loved children all his life. Jessie Greig, who was a teacher, said, "Glenn had a deep interest in my work and about how I was trying to challenge the children. Often he proffered advice and suggestions." He was friendly with children who lived around his family's cottage, taking them along on his walks, joining in their games, sometimes inviting them and their mothers into the cottage to have a little fun with his tape recorder, and he never talked patronizingly to them. "I can still see him bounding up the stairs of our house in Toronto to tell bedtime stories to our children, stories which flowed spontaneously from his imagination," John Roberts recalled. (The only problem was stopping him and getting the children to sleep.) With the children of other friends he played table hockey and other games, or showed them how to splice tapes, and the closest he ever came to giving a piano lesson was to provide a little encouragement or advice to a young pianist within his circle.

It seems that Gould would have liked a domestic life himself but knew it was impossible, partly of course because he was an odd, difficult, high-maintenance personality, but mostly because marriage was incompatible with the solitude demanded by his art. Angela Addison remembers him sitting in her practice room at the Royal Conservatory, in the early fifties, in tears, pouring out his frustration over a relationship with a woman. The problem was not that he was incapable of or did not want a real relationship or marriage, but that he could not reconcile it with his artistic needs. It is a dilemma familiar among creative artists; Beethoven's biographer Maynard Solomon called it a "conflict between a defensive narcissism and a wild, thrusting desire to break out of a painful isolation." Brahms put it more pithily when he said, "Unfortunately I never married and am, thank God!, still single."

If Gould worried that a wife might overwhelm him and his art, it is probably because he himself was prone to obsession and jealousy in a romantic relationship. "Those who have had little opportunity of expressing or sharing sexual feelings tend to alternate between suppressing or repressing sexuality and overvaluing it to the point of idiocy," Anthony Storr wrote in *The Dynamics of Creation*. "It is those who have had little practice in handling their own sexuality who are likely to 'fall in love' in a devastating manner; and who treat the whole matter of love in an all-or-nothing fashion." That sounds remarkably like Gould. To relationships, as to work, he brought an exhausting intensity, and great anxiety. He was indeed like a teenager: many of his relationships read like infatuations, or crushes. In one of his notepads, he makes an anagram from the letters of a woman friend's name, as a teenager might carve initials on a tree. His devotion was intense but always on his own terms, his own schedule, and his romantic feelings, though powerful, could be ambiguous, not always clearly readable. Greta Kraus told Peter Ostwald of one affair in which Gould "was possessed with absolute jealousy," constantly talking about the woman in question, longing to see her, but ultimately overwhelming her. A woman with whom he had an intimate relationship when he was in his early twenties was in part relieved when she eventually lost touch with him, for his emotional needs and his demands on her time – keeping her up all night on the phone, and so on – had become too much to handle. There are similar tales involving other women later in his life, sexual relationships as well as close platonic friendships. And when a passionate relationship inevitably ended, his pain was such that he would eliminate the woman from his life with an "all-or-nothing" ruthlessness.

The relationship with the married woman may have been a watershed for Gould, proof that he was not going to achieve a lasting domestic union. He continued to have at least a few romantic relationships in the last decade of his life, including at least two that overlapped for a time in the later seventies, both of which seem to have ended (poorly) around 1980, and Susan Kocsis says she wondered, on the basis of some of Gould's comments and behaviour, if and how her relationship with him might have developed had he lived longer. But Ray Roberts observed that Gould "was much less involved with women" in his later years, and the evidence bears this out. It appears that Gould sought, in his forties, to avoid the problems that had doomed his earlier attempts at long-term relationships. This, at least, is the conclusion that comes to mind from a long handwritten text in one of his notepads from 1980, the same year as the Dell letter:

How good *is* our friendship?
In my opinion, so good that it has created an almost tensionless atmosphere.
Because; we met and dev[eloped] it when we were seemingly of one mind: one purpose; we both fell in love talking about tranquillity

of spirit *and* we re-inforced each other's determination to find
that quality and bring it into our lives.

= I talked about hierarchies of friendship i.e. that I didn't believe
in them. I said that there are moments of intensity which have
nothing to do with longev[ity], intimacy, proximity etc. We, in
my opinion, reached that plateau. very quickly and till now have
maintained ourselves there in a miraculous fashion

= We've also reached that plateau because, like all good Navajo
café customers, it hasn't made any sense to play games, to employ
strategies of any kind; we've behaved, I think, as though we really
might never see each other again and have therefore between [=
"been"] completely honest.

= Which, however, doesn't necc[essarily] mean we've made ourselves as clear to each other as we'd like to think.

Last w[ee]k, we had the first (and, I hope, last) mini-fallout from
unclearness. I took a little too much for granted; I just assumed
that my prevailing interest in a reclusive life style was understood. and I didn't realize how ready you were to interpret that
as rejection

= But I think now we reach a larger problem, and a more urgent
need for clarif[ication].

Because our rel[ationship] has, no doubt about it, escalated;
there's a psychic intensity which is really quite extraordinary – it's
also imm[ensely] prod[uctive] and comforting and re-assuring.

But it can resemble – if one wants to let it – a physical intensity;
or, if not that, one can easily convince oneself that its natural
course is in the direction of physical intensity.

And that isn't necc[essarily] so, in my opinion,

[in margin:] most people *do* try to make it so: some succeed,
most fail

and if there is a confusion of purpose between us and a cor-
res[ponding] need for clarif[ication], that's where it's going to arise.
Because nothing that's happened, or could foreseeably happen
in our relationship, is going to change or begin [?] to change the
way of life that I decided many y[ea]rs ago to lead.

= Flashback if absol[utely] necc[essary]

A B A

A¹ insuff[icient] clarity in the psychic exam. [?]

A²   "   "   resulted in jealously etc

[struck out:] Therefore, so as to ensure that we

= Theories of physical relations = psychic deterioration.

Years of prep[aration] for this way of life. Change would be destructive and produce the kind of resentment that would rather quickly cause our relationship to flounder.

Therefore: no change is contemplated.

can *you* live with that? i.e. is psychic energy per se [read "alone"?] hard for you to deal with?

I tell you this now only to avoid the kind of confusion that could add even a moment's uneasiness to what is a really remarkable relationship.

I intend that, if you are willing to continue, we will bring each other such peace as "passeth understanding"

This reads like notes for a letter or conversation, and there is no reason to take it as anything other than what it appears to be: a draft of a communication to a woman with whom Gould has shared a quickly growing emotional bond that has threatened to become sexual, resulting in a tension he felt needed to be cleared up in a characteristically detached and logical way. That most Gould fans will be surprised to find Gould in this intimate, confessional mode shows how the legends about him have obscured his very real relations with the opposite sex. The phrase "fell in love" is hardly ambiguous, and his equation of "physical relations" with "psychic deterioration" implies that he knew whereof he spoke, that he had suffered experiences he did not want to repeat. This communication does suggest that late in his life Gould had made a definite decision to lead (or *try* to lead) a more literally monastic life, though it also reveals that he was by no means seeking to live without close relations with other people.

As his friend Margaret Pacsu said, "Glenn was one of those people who take vows," which certainly seems true of his later years.

But he did not necessarily "take vows" for moral reasons, to remain pure in an impure world; more likely he meant to avoid the problems he seemed unable to avoid in sexual relationships. Given his inflexibility and self-involvement, but also his genuine desire not to hurt others, the demands of his art, and his one, failed long-term relationship, he must have been tempted, in his forties, to leave behind the whole business of romance. His friend Carl Little once asked him what advice he would give to a young artist who aspired to a professional career. Gould replied, "You must give up everything else."

"They say I'm a hypochondriac, and, of course, I am."

Gould is talking to a friend on the telephone when the friend happens to sneeze, or cough, or say that he might be coming down with a cold, and Gould, in a hypochondriacal panic, hangs up. It is the classic Gould anecdote, and a surprising number of people insist they witnessed it at first hand. One aspect of the Gould legend that has never been exaggerated is his all-consuming hypochondria. He was one of those intellectuals for whom the body was an inconvenient but necessary vehicle for carrying around the head (and hands), and he longed to keep his body, like his emotions, at a distance. At the same time, he was obsessed with it, fixated on the minutiae of its functions to the same degree that he fussed over his pianos and his editing. As he sought to control everything in his life, he sought to control his body, as though it were a machine rather than an unpredictable organism. From that day when he watched a classmate throw up in school, he feared losing control of his body. He brooded over it, studied it, tried to fix it, yet no amount of attention sufficed to convince him that it was under control. On the contrary, the more he fussed and fretted over his body the more helpless he seemed, for he appeared only to discover problems, never solutions.

Gould was not a small man. He stood just an inch shy of six feet, and in his younger days his weight fluctuated between about 150 and 180 pounds, making him lean but not emaciated. (And for the record:

light brown hair, blue eyes.) Nevertheless, to many he appeared gaunt, like someone who did not look after himself, and he never lost his constitutional fragility and extreme sensitivity. His mother worried constantly that he was making himself sick, and continued to minister to him when he was an adult. She wrote helpful notes to him: "Keep lemon in refrigator [*sic*] – you can take a dessert spoon to make a cup of hot-lemonade should you get a cold." He was a rather angelic-looking child but an awkward-looking teenager, and he never grew out of his adolescent body. All his life he had a teenager's slouch and a hunched, loping, splay-footed gait, and he was physically clumsy: John Roberts has said that Gould could not carry a cup of coffee across a room without spilling it.

To be sure, he had genuine medical problems. His whole musculoskeletal system was a constant source of concern, not only in his concert days when he was playing often and under stressful conditions. When he was ten years old he suffered a serious back injury at the cottage: he fell out of a boat as it was being hauled down a rail into the lake, and landed hard on the ground. "He was in great pain," his father said, and over the next few years he was taken to many doctors, though only his neighbourhood chiropractor, Dr. Arthur Bennett, helped. As an adult Gould gave every evidence of being a typical sufferer of chronic back pain, and Bennett had no doubt that Gould's persistent later musculoskeletal complaints stemmed from his childhood injury. Dr. Herbert J. Vear, the Toronto chiropractor who inherited Gould when Bennett retired, and treated him from 1957 to 1977, says unequivocally that Gould's "observed spinal problems were real and clinical." There was, Vear says, "early cervical disc degeneration observed on cervical x-rays" and "functional biomechanical stress to other areas, in particular the upper and mid thoracic spine." His main complaints were in his neck, shoulders, and arms, including the hands – particularly the left arm and hand – but Vear also recalls that "he had mild thoracic pain and discomfort which often affected the lumbar spine as well." His anxiety about physical contact was particularly acute when someone touched or leaned on his shoulders. He frequently complained of swelling, stiffness, and pain in his joints, and apparently feared that he was genetically predisposed to arthritis. Some of his musculoskeletal complaints were strange. He told Peter Ostwald, for instance, that "the bones of my back easily get out of alignment with my ribs," and in his last years he recorded some bizarre symptoms in his notepads – for instance, in 1978, unusual arm pains and pressures after "sub[stantial] juice or tea intake," and "extreme neck tension" triggered by long conversation or laughter.

Vear places most of the blame for Gould's musculoskeletal problems on his chronically poor, unstable posture, made worse by the hunching keyboard posture he acquired under Alberto Guerrero, though Gould was forever seeking more "scientific" diagnoses, or at least terminology, to explain his problems. For instance, from at least the mid-fifties he claimed that stiffness in his fingers was caused by "fibrositis," which is allied to rheumatism, and thought the condition dated from early 1950 when he fell through the ice on Lake Simcoe and was badly chilled. After his bout with nephritis – the kidney infection – in 1958, he frequently returned to that diagnosis, to the end of his life, to explain back pains that seemed to emanate from the area of the kidneys. In the late seventies he frequently referred to "sub-clinical polio," a mild, transient form of polio infection that can cause various forms of discomfort and malaise as well as stiff and aching muscles (he said he first experienced it in 1958). Even after 1964, when he was playing the piano less and less, he complained of persistent muscle, nerve, and joint pain throughout his upper body. His notepads from the last decade of his life include references to severe tension and pain throughout the upper body, which sometimes made straightening up difficult and interfered with his sleep. A note in one of his private papers alludes to a "1966 fall and subsequent brace-experience" (back brace, presumably), and his chronic problems were certainly inflamed on other occasions. It was almost impossible to find a mattress that suited him, and when considering a new car he would take it out for a "seat trial" rather than a road test, always searching, usually in vain, for a car in which he could sit comfortably on a long journey.

Chiropractors, physiotherapists, masseurs, and radiologists were a regular part of Gould's life. He depended on therapy during his concert years, especially after the Steinway injury. Cornelius Dees, a Dutch masseur, treated Gould for many years in his apartment, where he had his own massage table, and joined him on some of his concert tours. From Dr. Vear he received conventional chiropractic manipulations and some "trigger point therapy" of the sort pioneered by Dr. Janet Travell. (Dr. Bennett had advised Vear that Gould needed "patience and understanding, as well as treatments which were not painful.") After the Steinway injury Gould continued to see Dr. Irwin Stein, in Philadelphia, off and on for treatments and injections; the last visit was in December 1981, when he received X-rays of the hands, lumbar spine and pelvis, and cervical spine. He tried mechanical aids. Around the time of the Steinway injury he acquired his own Siemens diathermy unit, which used a high-frequency electric current to produce heat, as well as a locally manufactured ultrasound unit that emitted high-frequency sound waves to stop pain and tension (they cost about five hundred dollars each); Dr. Vear sometimes used such machines to treat him, too. In the mid-seventies he began to consult Dr. Dale McCarthy, an orthopaedist, who found no explanation for Gould's continuing musculoskeletal complaints beyond poor posture at and away from the piano. He prescribed non-steroidal anti-inflammatory drugs like Indocid, Naprosyn, and phenylbutazone, usually given to arthritics; Gould was also prescribed analgesics like Fiorinal, which has sedative properties and is generally prescribed for headaches. In short, he tried everything to ease his pains – everything, that is, but sitting up straight and getting a little exercise.

Gould's sleeping habits were never good, and it did not help that he sometimes had to reconcile normal working hours with his preference for an upside-down schedule; one may assume that he often suffered from sleep deprivation, particularly during his concert years. From early adulthood he took sleeping pills of various kinds for his chronic insomnia, including Placidyl and Dalmane as well as the barbiturates Nembutal and Luminal. He was a long-standing user of Valium, which he took sometimes to sleep as well as to relieve stress and anxiety. In the mid-sixties Dr. Stein at least once prescribed Stelazine, an anti-psychotic medication sometimes used to treat anxiety, and in 1976 John A. Percival, Gould's regular G.P. from February 1971 until the end of his life, prescribed the sedative Librax after he complained of stomach cramps that were presumably anxiety-related. For most of 1978 he tracked his sleep in detail. He averaged around six-and-a-half to seven hours per night, sometimes more, sometimes less, which for most people would be less than refreshing but not quite alarming, though his sleep was generally interrupted and inconsistent; a block of six or seven hours' uninterrupted sleep was rare enough to warrant special note, as was sound sleep without medication. He was sometimes sleepy during the waking hours, to judge from the amount of napping he recorded – snatches of sleep here and there, fully dressed, in a chair or on a chesterfield, even in the bathtub. He almost always slept with the TV on; "television," he once said, "is one of the greatest sedatives in the world."

From at least as early as 1976 until the end of his life, Gould was tested and received treatment for elevated levels of uric acid in the blood, which may account for some of the swelling and pain he felt in his joints, as he noted in some of his private papers. He worried about kidney stones, and was reluctant to believe negative tests for them. He was prescribed anti-inflammatory medications of the sort used to treat gout and prevent uric acid and kidney stones, like allopurinol.

Of Gould's genuine medical problems the most significant was high blood pressure. Dr. Percival first diagnosed him as borderline hypertensive in March 1976, and though Percival was not unduly concerned Gould took the diagnosis very seriously. He had a particular fear of hypertension, which ran in his family: Bert Gould and Jessie Greig both suffered from it, and his mother had died of a stroke less than a year earlier. He at once began to consult other doctors, including Alexander G. Logan, a kidney specialist. Logan found no internal problems, but put Gould on a low and later

moderate dose of the anti-hypertensive Aldomet, and shortly afterward on a low dose of the beta-blocker Inderal, which is used to treat
anxiety, tension, panic attacks, phobias, some types of pain, and other
symptoms, as well as high blood pressure. He received other such
drugs over the years – clonidine, HydroDiuril – and it is not unusual
for hypertension patients to use several drugs in combination.

Gould purchased several different kits to measure blood
pressure, and in his notepads duly recorded his readings (and sometimes pulse rate) at intervals throughout the day, sometimes hourly
or even more often, especially after meals, trips to the bathroom,
doses of medication, or even just an animated conversation. His
blood-pressure readings reveal low and moderate levels of hypertension at different times, but also many normal readings. Generally
only the diastolic reading (the number to the right of the slash) was
high; the systolic reading was usually normal. The drugs apparently
worked, keeping his blood pressure mostly within acceptable param-
eters in the later 1970s, though friends have testified that it could
rise alarmingly when he did not take his medication, as once happened after a mix-up at the pharmacy. Still, Gould fretted about his
blood pressure, and it is even possible his own anxiety on the
subject, coupled with his tight control on his emotions, could have
exacerbated the problem. The highest reading among his papers is
a very high 180/118, which he recorded in his diary, in 1980, after
getting angry over a family matter – that says much about the source
of the problem.

So musculoskeletal pains, insomnia, uric acid levels, and hypertension were all real problems for which Gould received appropriate medical treatment. But his health concerns did not end there,
not in his own mind at least: his *fear* of getting sick never abated.
In fact, his hypochondria only worsened with age, and he never
stopped imagining that his body was perennially under siege and
claiming medical problems for which the evidence was questionable.
He always insisted, for instance, that he had poor blood circulation,
an idea planted in his head by his first family doctor, Colin A. McRae,
and one he could never shake: "Circulation pills," he remarked to a

reporter in 1955; "if I don't take them, well, I don't circulate." He seemed to feel cold, or at least to act cold, much of the time.* Some of Gould's friends have said he was cold to the touch, yet Morris Herman, his G.P. in the fifties and early sixties, denied that he had a real circulatory problem, and found that his skin was warm and moist – that he was in fact sweating beneath all those layers of clothes. In 1956, Gould told Jock Carroll that he was suffering from "a spastic stomach, diarrhea, and tightening of the throat. I've got three doctors treating me for it now." Peter Ostwald thought Gould might have had a psychosomatic disorder, and Gould was always sensitive where the gut was concerned. "What did you eat that disagreed with you, Glenn?" a friend once asked. "Food?"

From childhood Gould dreaded germs, and his mother's concerns about the Canadian National Exhibition apparently resurfaced in his mind after he signed a lucrative contract to play at the Hollywood Bowl in August 1957. According to Peter Yazbeck, Gould had not realized that the Bowl was an *outdoor* amphitheatre, and when Yazbeck told him he panicked and cancelled the concert. He feared germs in tap water, in groups of people, in hospitals – even when greatly concerned about a sick friend he could not bring himself to visit a hospital and would instead keep in contact by phone. He had cans of Lysol disinfectant spray around his apartment and packed disinfectants whenever he travelled. He avoided the company of anyone who seemed the slightest bit ill; he would not even enter a room or car or elevator a sick person had recently occupied. June Faulkner, a theatre-company manager who worked on the television program *Glenn Gould's Toronto* in 1978, recalled seeing him roll around on the floor with her hacking, wheezing dog. "But I gave a tiny sneeze and he was out the front door like a shot and bolted into his car, which had a telephone. He sat there in front of my house and we conducted our business by telephone." When Ray

---

* In some of his notepads from the late seventies, he reported symptoms like "chills," "on occ[asion], absolutely uncontrollable shivering," and "freezing sensations – shivers – top of nose," which he associated with rises in his blood pressure.

Roberts came down with a bad cold just before they were to travel to New York, in 1980, Gould insisted they take separate cars, and so Lance and Longfellow made the trip in convoy.

Gould knew he was a hypochondriac, and often seemed to treat the matter lightly with friends, doctors, and the press. And he knew it was part of a very profitable public persona. In 1958, a reporter saw him stop in the middle of a recording session, groan, and announce, "I think I have appendicitis." It turned out to be a minor cramp – he had been sitting too long – and he joined everyone else in laughing about it. "I am sure you look forward to the interesting symptoms that I shall dig up for you in the future," he once wrote to Dr. Herman. The French filmmaker Bruno Monsaingeon recalled that, during their first filming session in 1974, Gould "very, very gently" bumped his head on a microphone, collapsed in a chair, and cried out, "My God, a concussion!" He listed the symptoms that were bound to follow over the next few hours, then finally admitted, "Well, I know, I know, once I let my imagination go, I'm lost." On June 12, 1980, he noted in his diary "some odd spots . . . on my abdomen – right of the navel, and in the area where the hiatus hernia is often knotted up – and, indeed, has been so for the last couple of days." At the end of that entry there is a P.S.: "Have taken bath; spots have disappeared." They were marks from a pen. Some dialogue from the film *Hannah and Her Sisters* comes irresistibly to mind:

> Julie Kavner: Two months ago you thought you had a malignant melanoma.
> Woody Allen: Naturally – the sudden appearance of a black spot on my back!
> Julie Kavner: It was on your *shirt*.

We ought not to laugh, though: the anxiety required to fuel this level of hypochondria cannot have made life easy for Gould.

He required a stable of doctors to meet his needs. He saw a doctor at least every few weeks in the latter part of his life; it was simply a part of his routine, like a weekly squash game. He probably chose his family doctor for his convenience: Dr. Percival's office was at 262 St. Clair Avenue West, not far from Gould's apartment building. He saw dozens of doctors, often several at the same time, and he could be crafty in dealing with them, sometimes receiving prescriptions for the same medication from different ones (he would not necessarily tell one doctor that he was seeing others). His doctors were rarely as impressed with his symptoms as he was, and his doctor-shopping was often motivated by his dissatisfaction at not getting the answers he wanted to hear. He demanded many tests, which his doctors often felt compelled to conduct if only to set his mind at ease (there was little chance of that, alas). He frequently had X-rays, internal as well as skeletal; the radiologist Dr. A. A. Epstein recalled that "Glenn worried constantly about his chest and having pneumonia all the time," and worried about having cancer. From his later years there are many records of hospital appointments for assessments of various musculoskeletal, gastrointestinal, and neurological complaints, and for all sorts of tests: liver and spleen and kidney function, blood chemistry, glucose tolerance, potassium levels, cholesterol, uric acid. He would also request urine tests, rectal and prostate exams, and barium enemas. These are intimate procedures for someone normally shy about his body, but he was so anxious about his health and had so much experience with doctors that he apparently overcame his natural reticence in a medical (read: safely rationalized?) setting. In any event, all his tests usually showed that nothing medical was wrong. This merely caused him more anxiety, because it meant only that the real problem had yet to be found, and so it was on to the next round of theories, doctors, and tests. Gould could not interpret the lack of evidence as the absence of a problem – a good definition of a hypochondriac.

He was convinced that he was the master of anything he put his mind to, and just as he told his record producers and lawyers and accountants and stockbrokers how to do their jobs, he presumed to instruct his doctors, who knew that he had very little insight into the body – just enough to be dangerous to himself – and that his long-winded medical explanations were mostly rubbish. Dr. Vear recalls that Gould would normally describe his symptoms, offer a diagnosis, and suggest a treatment, co-operating only with treatments that concurred with his diagnoses. He fancied himself an informed armchair doctor. He had reference volumes on drugs and diagnostics on his bookshelf and tried to keep up with medical and pharmacological developments in the news, occasionally asking his doctors for some new drug he had read about. (He was known to actually take other people's medication just to study its effects.) His notepads are full of bits of medical data, often tips that he wanted to follow up. More alarmingly, he enjoyed playing the doctor with his friends, as early as the 1950s. In one letter from 1957, from "GOULD'S CLINIC FOR PSYCHO-PSEUMATIC [*sic*] THERAPY," he casually dispensed advice to a friend about barbiturates that he confidently described as "perfectly harmless." Gladys Riskind remembers feeling unwell and seeing Gould open up a black bag lined with shelves full of pills and ask, "What would you like?"

Gould's was a "technological" approach to the body and to medicine. He could not see his problems as symptomatic of an unhealthy lifestyle, and doctors who took this line with him he dismissed as "nature-boy" types. He saw only problems that needed to be fixed, preferably through machines and other tools of modern Western medicine – especially pills. There are medical records and prescription receipts for Gould dating back to the early fifties, and, though what survives is presumably only the tip of the iceberg, especially in the early years, they point to a pattern of dependence on pills to cure every ill. It is likely, though not certain, that at some points Gould became addicted to medications – barbiturate sleeping pills and Valium, for instance, are known to be habit-forming. He *worried* about addiction (he dropped Nembutal for that reason) and as an opponent of the drug culture of the sixties he dreaded acquiring a reputation as a "drug addict" – which, alas, he did. His luggage and pockets bulged with pills in his concert days, and his bathroom was always littered with them. He was often prescribed antibiotics, for it was in his nature to prefer this route to his mother's hot lemonade when he had a cold. His notepads show a reliance on over-the-counter products: painkillers (with or without codeine), laxatives, lozenges, vitamins, as well as dietary supplements like magnesium and potassium, presumably necessitated by his poor diet and side effects of other medications. He tried the ancient folk remedy belladonna, too, a narcotic pain reliever and antispasmodic extracted from the leaves of deadly nightshade. Keith MacMillan saw him take Aspirins to warm up in a poorly heated CBC studio before performing the Goldberg Variations for the first time, in 1954. During the broadcast the studio began to warm up and he became overheated; by about Variation 15 his palms were sweaty, and by the end his hands were slithering on wet keys. ("I messed up a whole run completely.") He later said he would have been in real trouble had Bach written more than thirty variations.

With age, Gould was taking more and more prescription and over-the-counter medications, often in dosages of his own choosing, and in combinations at best unpredictable and sometimes known to cause adverse reactions. He was also taking pills to counteract the side effects of other pills, creating a cycle of dependency. From 1963 his regular drug store was Bowles Pharmacy on Kingston Road – close to Southwood Drive, in the Beach – and his many surviving receipts reveal the vast quantity of his intake. His pharmacy bills were among his largest expenses. Here, for instance, is one typical list of a month's expenses he jotted down in a notepad on September 10, 1979:

Apartment rent: $503.50
Studio rent: $375.00
Studio room service: $441.71
Telephones (apartment, studio, car): $504.44
Bowles Pharmacy: $503.56

Some of Gould's recurring minor medical complaints, such as dizziness and blurred vision, gastrointestinal discomfort, and weight gain, were possibly side effects of medication. And at a certain level of intake it becomes impossible to tell what is a primary symptom and what is a side effect, and the act of juggling medications becomes exponentially more dangerous with each new pill added to the mix. Gould occasionally realized that some particular symptom might be associated with his drug intake, but his solution, unfortunately, was to treat that symptom as yet one more illness requiring yet one more pill. Considering that Gould would, for instance, regularly take Valium or other sedatives before a concert or recording session, it is surprising that only one writer, Richard Kostelanetz, has raised the perfectly reasonable issue of what impact Gould's drug intake might have had on his art. I do not believe that a pharmacological rationale is needed to justify, say, his rapid tempos or baroque prose style, and anyway it would be impossible to determine exactly what medication Gould was taking when, but the notion of a connection is hardly absurd and merits some consideration: what *might* all that medication have done to his thinking and his playing?

Given his genuine medical problems, hypochondriacal assumptions, and pharmaceutical intake, it is hardly surprising that Gould's notepads from the mid-seventies forward include seemingly endless medical documentation: lists of symptoms and self-diagnoses, lists of questions prepared in advance of appointments with doctors, lists of medications, records of blood pressure, pulse rate, and sleeping patterns, and more, most of it couched in detached, pseudo-scientific language. We may as well work through this data from the head down – and what follows does not include problems already discussed or indicate the many times specific symptoms were reiterated over a period of years in changing combinations.

Gould reported two unexplained problems in the fall of 1976: what he called "back of head" phenomenon and "*pressure-point awareness*" – the latter (whatever it was) being "sensit[ive] to *hand-washing, walking, driving*," and having "reached point of relatively sharp pain when sitting down or walking; in any case, is precursor and accomp[animent] to light vertigo." He told a friend in the mid-seventies that an inner-ear infection had left him with balance problems that affected him after prolonged work sessions or even after laughing or talking animatedly, and he took to reporting this as

A page typical of the medical documents among Gould's private papers. Dated just before Christmas, 1977, it is a list of symptoms he jotted down in preparation for a visit to Alexander G. Logan, a Toronto kidney specialist and one of his regular doctors in his later years. He reports (1) escalating blood pressure, (1A) chills and shivering, (2) plugged nostrils and some difficulty in breathing, (3) gastro-intestinal troubles that he associates with a hiatal hernia, and (4) several months in which he was sleeping only three to four hours at a stretch. The list also refers to a "Barium meal test" and, in the margin, mysteriously, to "Sea Salts." (*Estate of Glenn Gould.*)

"labyrinthitis," an inflammation or dysfunction within the cavities and canals of the inner ear that is defined by the acute onset of vertigo commonly associated with head or body movement, sometimes leading to nausea, vomiting, or malaise. He later reported "pressure at left temple" and "decided unsteadiness" when rising from a seated position, bad enough at time to make "even brief city *trips hazardous. Piano-playing impossible*"; he cancelled at least one CBC recording session because of "inner-ear troubles." He was seen to stumble in his later years, and noted in his diary in 1980 that he "fell en route to the bathroom in mid-sleep this a.m." and hurt his left knee. (Or was his intake of pills to blame?)

His eyes worried him. In the spring of 1976 he noted concern about a possible infection ("l. eye being 'glued' shut upon waking"), and that fall noted, "*Left eye* is *constantly bloodshot.*" In later years he reported a "sty-like sensation" and "puffiness in eyes," and this from around 1980: "Eye dry sore (after rubbing etc.) and/or teary, filmy, vision less sharp, 'speck of sand' syn[drome] = bloodshot, gen[era]l darkening in eye-tone esp. left side." In the fall of 1976 he also reported that "*Ringing in ears continues,*" along with this more cryptic note: "Pulse-sync in ears (crickets in summer, sleet in fall)." In the later seventies he reported on several occasions "General stuffiness and at times, inhalation insufficiency," as well as nasal blockage, sore throats, difficulty breathing after animated conversation, and "snorting while inhaling." There are hints of dental problems around the fall of 1978, references to sensitivity of the teeth and pain that sometimes radiates into the face and head, as well as "locked muscles" in the mouth, and unexplained references to esophageal problems. In late December 1977 he noted, "*Throat-Neck*: myalgia, etc., as background[.] greatly increased jerks, spasms, stiffness in past w[ee]k. Does it rep[resent] gland problem?" And around 1980 he noted, "Tongue evidences black markings for w[ee]ks."

That was just from the neck up. In the mid-seventies he noted "burning in upper chest [and] throat," "curious *sore* and/or *weak* spot . . . on r. side [of chest]," and, in late December 1977, "*Chest* – periodic lightness and pain – quasi muscular, on occ[asion] – ribs sore from time to time – no known on-setting incident." He also reported incidents of breathlessness and fatigue. In the early eighties he made notes about "palpitations" and "arm-heat," and about waking up with a rapid and irregular heartbeat. Strange abdominal pains persisted through his last years, yielding notations like this: "tight, gas-pocket sensation"; "frequently bloated at base of rib-cage – temporarily relieved by release of gas which happens freq[uently] esp[ecially] on rising, etc"; "spasm in left upper abdomen"; "lower abdomen ache after eating (sometimes) or even drinking, gas-like, penetrates to back when esp[ecially] severe"; "indigestion-like pains reaching into throat"; "Recent month's lower abdomen problem – liquid consumption triggers pockets of 'ulcer-like' – pain through to back (– congestive sensation re bending over)." In April 1977 he reported "excruciating" pain in his torso when lying down or getting into his car; his sleep was affected, and he noted an intense "spasm effect on waking," especially on his right side. He diagnosed a "hiatal hernia" at least as early as the spring of 1976, and took antacids regularly: "*Phillips* [Milk of Magnesia] a *staple* of the *diet*."

Around the time his uric acid level was being treated, Gould complained of frequent and sometimes painful urination, of bladder pressure that interfered with sleep, and, in fall 1978, of awakening sometimes to find his clothing damp from urine, "unprecedented since childhood." In the late seventies he reported "pulsating or throbbing" aches and sometimes intense pain in the genital area, "typically in penis and/or left side of testes," when sitting down or crossing his legs, and this was sometimes referred down one leg to create a "throbbing toe sensation." By about 1980, he was noticing "nodules" on the left side of the scrotum. He asked, "Could there be some *purely local* inflammation – poss[ibly] set off orig[inally] by the excess diathermy applied to the lower back – which has triggered chain reaction" – this from a pianist who sat on a chair with no seat and a support bar that ran front to back along his crotch. He reported hemorrhoids, abdominal cramps and gas, "rectal pressure" and allied discomfort when sitting, and "*irregular* bowel mov[emen]ts generally . . . primarily *loose* as opposed to *formed* bowel mov[emen]ts." Dr.

Philip Klotz, a urologist Gould consulted twice in 1978, told Ostwald that "Glenn was very, very worried about his prostate." He confided these worries to his notepads, even when medical tests revealed nothing; around 1980 he reported with grim triumph that his doctors "observed 'puffy' prostate" that "seemed larger than recollected."

Finally, there were problems with his skin and extremities in his last years, including a "psoriasis episode" and concerns about "discoloration re fingers," "circulation re fingers," and *"some finger pains."** He worried about *"'sleep'-sensation* in left foot and (either) hand," about "ankle-foot phenomenon" and "flat-footed-like sensations," about "hot-flash sensation, prim[arily] in right foot but, as of yesterday also left wrist," and "neural sensation, hyper-activity-like, radiates down leg (usually left) to *toe*" while lying down.

The volume of these complaints is astonishing, especially as they are in addition to the very real problems, like hypertension, for which Gould was being treated at the same time. And no complaint ever appeared in isolation. In a "symptomology" that he jotted down sometime around February 1980, he reported all of the following problems in a single day: "Slight Rib Cage syndrome," especially while laughing; "immense fullness in upper abdomen," along with the release of gas; "some neuralgic reference in *right* toes"; "feet flatness and back of leg syndrome"; "chest-throat indigestion discomfort"; "air-pocket, right abdomen"; "some minor discomfort in right side"; and finally, "burning sensation during urination (restricted flow) upon wake-up [at one p.m.] . . . also, some pressure in rectum upon returning to bed." Small wonder that Gould was convinced he was constantly ravaged by disease.

In a notepad a few years earlier he had wondered if he could find *"anyone* who might *evaluate* all the disparate *evidence* and *formulate a theory accordingly.*" But everyone had the same theory: he was a hypochondriac who pathologized every trivial, passing creak, ache, and twinge that the middle-aged male body is prone to, especially a

---

* Gould claimed that his fingers were so sensitive that they were stiffened by air conditioning and swimming, which, he said, "ruins my hands for days afterwards."

body that has for years been poorly fed, inadequately exercised, denied fresh air and sun, over-medicated, and subjected to considerable physical and emotional stress at home and on the job.

Gould knew, at least theoretically, that the mind could make a hell of heaven where the body was concerned. Andrew Kazdin heard him talk openly about his fears that emotional stress would yield physical symptoms – he knew all about this from his illness-plagued concert days – and he was aware and afraid of the potentially destructive power of repressed emotions like anger. Yet he often could not see the mind-body connection in his own case. The filmmaker John McGreevy remembered him calling, before a filming session, to announce that he had five of six symptoms of sub-clinical polio, and would call back if the sixth and deciding symptom appeared. In the end, however, he simply showed up as planned. "It was pre-concert nerves," McGreevy concluded, "exaggerated in the most baroque way." In any event, Gould's claims that he "scarcely had so much as a sniffle" after 1964 and that "my hypochondria pretty well ended with the last of my live concerts" were plainly absurd. He continued to get sick, and to think he was sick even when he wasn't. We can only imagine the torment he might have endured had he lived to old age; we might almost be glad that he was spared it.

"You see what kind of neurotic you're dealing with."

On the basis of his hypochondria some people have questioned Gould's mental health. He had at least one passing episode of real mental illness according to Peter Ostwald, who saw it at first hand. In late December 1959, Gould called Ostwald to report that "people were spying on him from the roof of an adjacent building, shining lights into his windows, making strange noises, and sending him coded messages. He said he could hear them talking about him and wondered if this was part of a plot involving an illegal business deal." Around the same time, John Roberts recalled, Gould reported hearing voices talking to him, and had a particular cabinet moved out of a room because, he said, "I didn't like it, it was looking at me, it was staring at me." Ostwald concluded that he "was probably suffering from a brief paranoid delusional episode," and if so it was likely caused by excess intake or improper combination of drugs. (This was just after the initial Steinway injury, when he was perhaps over-medicating himself.) In any case, the episode stands out, because nothing resembling mental illness of this order was ever regularly a part of Gould's life.

He acknowledged that he was neurotic, and he certainly had a healthy share of demons and the elevated sensitivities one would expect in an artist. Some of his doctors and friends suggested that he might benefit from psychiatric counselling, and while he did not take offence at the idea he never really accepted it. Ostwald found that Gould did consult a psychiatrist, Dr. Albert E. Moll, at McGill University in Montreal, apparently around August 1955, shortly after his recording of the Goldberg Variations – a period in his life when he was under an unusual amount of pressure. Moll recommended four psychiatrists in Toronto, and Gould, according to some lighthearted comments he made to Jock Carroll in 1956, visited one of them. The psychiatrist, he recalled, found nothing physically, sexually, or environmentally wrong, "so it was just a question of tranquilizers – bigger and better pills." This sounds like a tall tale. Gould never did enter therapy; the closest he came to it was seeking out psychological insights through conversations with friends like Dr. Joseph Stephens, a psychiatrist and harpsichordist who spoke to Gould regularly for seventeen years. Some of his doctors believed that he would have benefited from psychiatric treatment for hypochondria, but it is difficult to imagine him being a successful patient, talking frankly about personal problems and accepting advice; presumably he would have treated a psychiatrist like all the other professionals to whom he felt confident dictating terms. In later life he poked fun at psychiatry and its jargon through fictitious characters like Dr. S. F. Lemming and Dr. Wolfgang von Krankmeister.

Gould lived permanently with a great deal of generalized anxiety, and he admitted to suffering bouts of depression during his concert years. Aspects of the classical definitions of the saturnine or melancholic temperament can certainly be seen in his personality: a need for solitude alongside a resentment of loneliness; a passionate insistence on a life of the mind, even if "inwardness" sometimes acts as a drag on one's life; total immersion in work and a compulsion to chronicle that work, as well as a capacity for juggling minutiae; a self-consciousness that is vigilant and unforgiving, always worried about real or perceived weaknesses of the will; complex relations with other people marked by secretiveness, caution, and manipulativeness, and the masking of negative feelings (like hostility or superiority) with outward geniality; difficulty forming intimate personal bonds and a tendency to connect better with things rather than people, including a tendency to revere certain privileged objects; an obsession with death; stubbornness; a certain physical "slowness" and blundering; avoidance of eye contact. Hypochondria, too – "melancholics make the best addicts," as Susan Sontag wrote. Gould's fear of losing control of his emotions, and his repression of powerful emotions like anger, could be linked to a depressive temperament – one definition of depression is indeed "anger turned inward" – as could his insomnia, chronic tension, and poor eating habits.

Gould manifested a variety of obsessional, schizoid, and narcissistic traits, too, hardly surprising given his fragility, sensitivity, and advanced intellect – and these are in addition to his hypochondria. The obsessional traits are plain to see. He sought to control every aspect of his mind, body, and environment, and was a perfectionist in every aspect of his work. He was inhibited emotionally and exalted intellect at the expense of instinct, tending to rationalize and overintellectualize and to be rigid and uncompromising in his thinking. Fearing the unexpected, he was cautious and punctual, valued precision in all things, always planned and prepared. He found it difficult to "let go," a personality trait that became an aesthetic position – witness his distrust of improvisation and "chance music," for instance. He needed the security of ritual and routine in order to function productively. A case in point: his famous chair, the familiarity of which obviously gave him comfort and confidence.

We can include "numeromania" among his obsessional traits, the tendency to count things and record the results, in an effort to deal with the stress of multiplicity and disorder, to give oneself the illusion of controlling the world by keeping accounts of it. His papers reveal a lifelong cataloguing instinct, of which his hypochondriacal note-taking was but one example. In 1959 the journalist Pierre Berton wrote that Gould would literally count the seconds until lunch hour when he was in public school; he also liked to track his class's highest and average marks on tests and assignments. In high school he began to keep track of the word count as he wrote an essay (still a habit at the end of his life), and he numbered and dated the bars as he composed his score of his String Quartet. In his last years, he would not only track his blood pressure and pulse rate and sleeping patterns in detail, but calculate three- and five- and seven- and ten-day averages and sometimes plot his findings on graphs. Sometimes he would track and graph weather statistics in different Canadian cities throughout a day – keeping records of his environment seemed to bring him some comfort.

Gould loved making lists. Often he would write out lists of daily, weekly, and seasonal tasks, crossing them off when completed, and in some of these lists he included even the trivialities of his day, allotting five minutes for shaving, five minutes for brushing his teeth, fifteen minutes for taking laundry to the cleaners, and so on. He might even break down a half-hour practising session into segments of twelve, ten, or eight minutes. He made lists of people to be called, in numbered order, sometimes noting how long each call should take. He made lists of letters to be written and checked them off as they were done, then made lists of the finished letters and checked them off as they were mailed; he did likewise with his bills. When he travelled he drew up detailed packing lists (admittedly he required a lot of gear) and duly checked off each item. He made long lists of his accounts and of the performance of various stocks in his portfolio. When he stopped keeping his diary in 1980, he made an index of it and placed it at the front.

Gould also manifested traits of a schizoid nature. He was solitary and shy, and found intimacy difficult. To many people he seemed detached and withdrawn emotionally, sometimes cold and inaccessible. He feared confrontation because to confront someone is to bring out emotions on both sides, the prospect of which often embarrassed and frightened him; he preferred to keep some distance between himself and the outside world, including other people. "For me the presence of people is a distraction," he said, explaining his preference for contact by telephone. He was reluctant to look people in the eye more than glancingly, even when regaling someone with an anecdote: to do so is, of course, to confront that person's personality and feelings directly. Even on television, when speaking unscripted about something personal, he sometimes had trouble looking right at the camera. In the CBC documentary *Variations on Glenn Gould*, while talking about the origins of radio, he notes "that incredible, spine-tingling sense of awareness of some other human voice and persona," and while uttering these emotional words he keeps averting his eyes.

Like the typical schizoid person, Gould tended to find satisfaction and meaning more in his inner reality than in the outside world (though hardly to the extent that would define schizophrenia). But his preference for solitude was coupled with an urgent, barely containable desire to communicate unilaterally. In his tendency to launch into long, torrential, self-centred monologues, some friends and acquaintances detected at once a desire to express and a desire to throw up a protective layer – of words in this case – to keep the other person at a distance. Peter Ostwald saw a combination of two impulses in Gould: "stay with me" and "keep your distance," a nice summary of an essential schizoid dilemma. As we have already seen, Gould was in the classic predicament of people of this temperament in that he feared love and closeness not because he did not desire them but because they contained the risk of being swallowed up. Gould also had the schizoid's paradoxical combination of vulnerability with superiority in his relations with others – a certain helplessness but also the feeling of being the centre of the universe. Gould was out of touch with his body – another schizoid trait – even though he was constantly examining it; he agreed with Proust that the possession of a body is a great danger to the mind. He was reflective and drawn to abstract thinking, which requires a certain detachment from ordinary feeling and permits emotional expression and communication in a removed, impersonal way – and it is no coincidence that he was attracted to the electronic media. Schizoids also have a propensity to create their own idiosyncratic and rigid images of what the world should be like, and Gould's world view, formed in adolescence and little changed thereafter, certainly fit this profile.

That Gould had narcissistic traits, too, is hardly in doubt. He was self-absorbed and stubbornly independent. Though not as immune to the feelings of others as legend would have it, he did put his own needs first most of the time, and could be dictatorial: he thought that his needs should be *your* needs, too. His intellect and aesthetic were powerfully self-referential and he found it almost impossibly difficult to accept or even to understand contrasting opinions. "I took it for granted that everyone shared my passion for overcast skies," he said. "It came as quite a shock when I discovered that there were actually people who preferred sunshine." When offered advice, he would simply shrug and say, "You can't fight City Hall!" When he sought feedback it was for validation, not correction; he had an enormous need for approval and praise – for those pats on the head from his mother. When treating a friend to a recording or videotape, or at a playback in the recording studio, he would conduct and grimace and sing along and provide a running commentary sometimes filled with praise for his own achievement. "As you listened his eyes seldom left your face," Geoffrey Payzant recalled. "He would have positioned you and himself so as not to miss any detail of your spontaneous reaction." And he wanted only one kind of spontaneous reaction: unalloyed praise, to which he might respond with vociferous agreement. He believed the flattery, because his faith in his own productions was absolute.

Gould often demonstrated a failure of empathy, a difficulty appreciating what others were feeling, particularly when it was not a feeling he shared. As a lecturer, for instance, he was a poor judge of his audiences, seemingly unable to detect when he was boring or confusing them with dense, technical prose or trying their patience with heavy-handed attempts at humour. In private, his jokes and anecdotes were sometimes so long and tortuous that he lost his listeners, and the more he became caught up in his own invention the funnier he seemed to find them. Certainly his phone calls at all hours suggest that he was oblivious to his listener's schedule. He apparently felt certain that the person on the other end of the line wanted to do nothing more at midnight than listen for an hour or two while he read a new essay or played alternative takes from a new recording session or rattled on about some new enthusiasm. The CBC producer Mario Prizek remembered Gould singing him a complete one-act opera over the phone. He had high expectations of others, a sense of entitlement, and he was not above taking advantage of a friendship or working relationship in order to get help with, say, one of those quotidian errands at which he was so hopeless – asking one of his secretaries to pick up laundry, for instance – and some of his friends felt manipulated.

There was a (mild) paranoid component in Gould's psychology, an oversensitivity to the potentially destructive influence of other people and ideas; hence his desire for solitude and self-sufficiency. He could seem paranoid in situations where he did not feel in control. When he came upon a group of people who were laughing, for instance, he might wonder if they were laughing at him, and he fired a cleaning woman whom he suspected of gossiping about him. He was concerned about his personal security, especially where over-ardent fans were concerned. Andrew Kazdin wrote of one young female fan who, in the late sixties, wrote letters to Gould and sought to meet him. She showed up at the offices of Columbia Records, in New York, when Gould happened to be there, and Kazdin recalled seeing him "cowering in a crouched position behind the door" when the woman's presence was announced. An unexpected knock on his door might provoke a worried phone call to the building manager, and one Halloween, when some trick-or-treaters threw milk at the CBC building, Gould was so upset that he cancelled a taping session.

Like many schizoid people, he was empathetic and benevolent in the abstract, as his political and social views reveal. He had difficulty reading the feelings of individuals, yet he had a real social conscience, loved animals, was deeply disturbed by troubles around the world that he saw on the evening news. But this same abstract thinking led to some disturbing claims. He wrote, for instance, in a 1974 self-interview, that a war "engaged in by computer-aimed missiles is a slightly better, slightly less objectionable war than one fought by clubs or spears," because "the adrenal response of the participants" is less involved, and he told Andrew Kazdin that, while he could not imagine himself picking up a weapon and engaging in hand-to-hand combat, he could imagine himself in a deep bunker masterminding a war from behind a console of machines. He even said that "the Orwellian world holds no particular terrors for me," and his ethical approach to art led him to take seriously the potential menace that certain kinds of art could pose – hence the puritanical censoriousness of his aesthetic. "The Soviets are a bit roughhewn as to method, I'll admit," he wrote, "but their concerns are absolutely justified." Only a sheltered aesthete with a detached and abstracted view of the world could fail to realize the frightening implications of such remarks.

Gould sometimes compartmentalized his relationships in order to control them. Some have suggested that he made lists of what information he shared with different people in order to keep account of his relationships and track down any leaks or betrayals. He seems, in his own mind, to have slotted people into the categories that best suited *him*. Though he worked for a decade on films with Bruno Monsaingeon, who is a professional violinist, he never heard him play the violin, except once by accident, and he took no interest in Joseph Stephens's harpsichord playing, though Stephens was accomplished enough to give a cycle of concerts featuring all of Bach's keyboard works. When his relationship with the record producer

Paul Myers became close in the mid-sixties, he decided to work with another producer in order to keep the friendship out of the workplace. He worked well with his subsequent producer, Andrew Kazdin, for fifteen years, probably because, as friends recall, he had him pigeon-holed as a producer. Kazdin's own memoirs do not suggest that they ever had a warm friendship: he never once visited Gould's apartment, for instance, and (wrongly) assumed that no one else did either.

It is a commonplace of the Gould literature that he used people and then dropped them when they were no longer useful to him, but the truth was hardly as brutal as that. Some relationships *did* end abruptly. Sometimes close friends of long standing found themselves suddenly shut out of Gould's life, for reasons he would not share. Gladys Riskind says that after more than six years of close friendship Gould simply stopped contacting her, without explanation, and hid behind an answering service. He and Morry Kernerman "parted in a strange and bitter way," Kernerman recalls, after a decade of friendship and musical collaboration, and even after confronting a visibly uncomfortable Gould at a rehearsal Kernerman could get no answer as to why he severed the relationship. His relationship with Greta Kraus ended in a similarly unclear way, and Verna Post, Walter Homburger's former secretary, thinks her own friendship with Gould ended perhaps because she "said something, moved into his personal territory, or embarrassed him somehow." In some such cases Gould left considerable bitterness in his wake, though often the pain of the severed relationship was mutual, suggesting he had been (or *thought* he had been) somehow betrayed or hurt.

Sometimes, where an argument or misunderstanding or humiliation, or some real or perceived slight (usually magnified in his own mind), had introduced a note of awkwardness or embarrassment into a relationship, Gould preferred to withdraw than to confront the situation directly. Incidents of this sort apparently contributed to the cooling of his relationship with his childhood friend Robert Fulford, in his twenties, and the upsetting telephone gag seems to have been a primary motive for his finally ending a decades-long friendship with Joan Maxwell. Most who knew him felt that they had to tread carefully, because he could easily take something innocent the wrong way, and because he was acutely sensitive to criticism about some aspects of his work. Harvey Olnick, for instance, saw little of Gould after criticizing his interpretations of late Beethoven in the mid-fifties, and John Beckwith offended him with some of his published criticism, particularly on the subject of Richard Strauss. Anton Kuerti visited him backstage after the Brahms concerto with Bernstein in 1962, and joked, "After what we heard tonight, maybe it *is* time to retire." Gould shot him a look that said "*Et tu, Brute?*" and never spoke to him again. He stopped corresponding with the critic B. H. Haggin, one of his biggest supporters, after Haggin began to critique his Mozart recordings in the mid-sixties. He stopped seeing Vincent Tovell, whom he had known since 1959, after the 1964 CBC television recital *An Anthology of Variation*, which Tovell directed. Tovell had had to confront Gould about the length and verbosity of his spoken commentary, and though Gould agreed to cuts and revisions, he was so sensitive to criticism of his writing he terminated the relationship. A few years later, when he mentioned his latest writings to Keith MacMillan, MacMillan teased him by expressing the hope that they would be "in English." Offended, Gould quickly ended the conversation and a few days later sent MacMillan a curt note stating that in future he should be contacted through his manager. He ended years of contact with Peter Ostwald and Joseph Stephens in 1977, apparently after detecting their lack of enthusiasm for his recent projects when they visited him in Toronto.

Gould's supposed ruthlessness about relationships has been exaggerated, however, for like everyone else he had relationships that ran a logical course and ended naturally and amicably, and like everyone else he had colleagues and acquaintances and friends of varying degrees of closeness and did not welcome every person he knew into his circle of intimates. There were many perfectly innocuous cases in which he stopped seeing someone after a project they had been involved in ended and there was no basis for continued contact – hardly cases of people being "dropped" after being "used."

In the early sixties, as his concert career was winding down, and especially after 1964, when he was definitively shedding one life for another, Gould narrowed his circle of acquaintances considerably, and many people who had known him up to that time, in either a personal or professional capacity, found that they stopped seeing or hearing from him. Some resented his withdrawal, especially as there were no formal farewells, but in many cases the relationships ended naturally once he stopped travelling widely and appearing in public, and anyway his truly close friends and professional colleagues were not a part of this process.

In some cases the end of a relationship with Gould was a relief, for he could be engulfing and controlling as a boss or friend. As Ray Roberts put it, "he would sort of burn people up." His single-minded commitment to his work, and his intense, seemingly boundless concentration on whatever task was at hand, could exhaust his colleagues. Tom Shipton, one of his editors in the later seventies, says that Gould expected others to keep up with his own furious pace. But Shipton, like some others, did not resent Gould's demands; rather, he felt bad at the thought of letting Gould down. Shipton sometimes reluctantly feigned illness in order to take a day off, knowing that Gould would not want a sick person anywhere near his studio, and he was not the only overworked technician to resort to that ruse so as not to disappoint the boss, for Gould did feel let down at the thought that someone might not live for his art to the degree he did.

Given that Gould was hypochondriacal, and had obsessional, schizoid, narcissistic, and perhaps melancholic traits, is a diagnosis of personality disorder or mental illness, of real psychological damage, warranted? Some, like Peter Ostwald, have concluded that he was tormented by terrible psychological problems: "While onlookers were satisfied to conclude tolerantly that Glenn's style of life was just another way of being human, Glenn – we now understand – often experienced it as a nightmare." But Gould's neuroses, though potent, do not tell the whole story.

Yes, he had melancholic traits – he was introverted, a brooder. But he cannot be considered chronically, clinically depressed. When he became depressed it was in response to some circumstance that was *depressing*, like his long immobilization in a body cast in 1960, and the depression would lift when circumstances improved. His private papers and the testimony of those who knew him most intimately do not suggest that he fought depression as a daily fact of life; he functioned at a very high level and was immensely productive, even while dealing with anxieties and physical problems. He was not gloomy or embittered or malicious, or prone to feelings of misery or hopelessness, he did not lack self-esteem or live with self-reproach, he did not indulge in black humour or caustic irony; in fact, he was usually upbeat, often excited and joyous, even during periods of tribulation and stress. For all his problems he remained a focused and optimistic person who worked confidently and with considerable success toward his stated artistic and personal and moral goals.

Yes, he had obsessional traits, but not to the extent that one should question his sanity. Some consider his arm-soaking to have been a neurotic, obsessional ritual, but it was merely functional: he soaked his arms because he had a great deal of work-related musculoskeletal tension, and he was not the only musician to use this therapy; he can hardly be compared with the obsessive-compulsive who washes his hands fifty times a day for no good reason. He was not necessarily *ruled* by his obsessional tendencies. It gave him a sense of comfort and control to plan out in detail the activities of his day, for instance, but he was not fixated on keeping to his schedule. Moreover, his obsessiveness was channelled in productive, artistic ways, and was responsible for much of what was most impressive and characteristic in his work – the fantastic, almost superhuman precision of his piano technique, for instance, or his fussiness about the action of his piano, or his analytical grasp of the music he played, or his meticulousness as an editor of recordings and radio documentaries. In this sense, his obsessional traits were adaptive as much as neurotic. Gould was a Vermeer, a Stravinsky, a Beckett, a Kubrick – an artist for whom obsessiveness was a crucial tool.

Yes, he had schizoid traits, but we have already seen that while he found intimacy difficult he did not find it impossible and managed to have genuinely close relationships, though often with precisely those people most reluctant to talk openly to biographers. He was isolated, but only to the degree he considered necessary to his creative work, and under the right circumstances, with the right people, he enjoyed nothing more than hanging around and shooting the breeze. He abhorred large groups of people – "I'm rather alarmed when I don't know what will happen," he told an interviewer in 1964, "as in a crowd, for example" – yet he dealt successfully, if reluctantly, with public situations when he had to; this was a man, after all, who played the piano, lectured, and hammed it up in front of thousands of people for more than fifteen years. That he quitted the concert circuit in order to cultivate a life that kept him away from crowds does not necessarily indicate that he was agoraphobic or a victim of "social phobia," merely that, unlike most of us, he had the will and the resources to live without compromising his preferences.

Yes, he had narcissistic traits, but he was also widely perceived as warm and considerate, could be an extraordinarily loyal and supportive friend, and was thoughtful and kind on countless occasions. Sometimes shyness made him *seem* narcissistic. Bruno Monsaingeon recalled that Gould could not face the farewell party his crew had organized after their filming sessions in 1974, but not because he did not appreciate their work: he was simply too shy, and wrote them warm personal letters instead. The technicians and others who worked for him recall that Gould almost never expressed praise or thanks, yet his 1980 diary reveals that he greatly appreciated his colleagues, even if he was embarrassed to say so to their faces. On May 27, 1980, he wrote that Lorne Tulk's editing "is as fluent as ever," that "he's an immensely gifted editor," that he wished he could work with him more often. On June 7 he wrote that "[Tom] Shipton's [editing] work is absolutely marvelous," and on August 21 that Jean Sarrazin was "unquest[ionably] one of the finest editors I've ever encountered." Moreover, far from taking their work for granted, he wrote admiringly, albeit to himself, of their willingness to work long hours with real dedication despite other commitments. The 1980 diary also reveals that when he did feel the need to replace someone whose work was not satisfactory, he did so with regret, not merely ruthlessly.

How selfish Gould was depends on whom you talk to. Andrew Kazdin and Joseph Stephens, for instance, have both recalled that Gould's late-night phone calls never began with him wondering if it was a convenient time to talk, yet others have recalled that his every call began with precisely this question (was it merely rhetorical?). Much writing about Gould has leaned heavily on recollections from people who were not among his closest friends even though they may have spent a great deal of time with him, in person or on the phone, over many years. Some such sources remember only a narcissist whose conversation consisted of interminable monologues about himself, his ideas, and his activities, and who seemed to take no real interest in the person on the other end of the line except as a sounding-board. That was certainly the reality for one class of Gould's friends. But he had other, closer relationships, with people in whom he took a genuine interest, that endured for many years with give and take on both sides – ordinary friendships, in other words, which did not necessarily come to an abrupt end whenever some conflict or tension arose. To the extent compatible with his shyness and the necessary degree of solitude, he was a good and real friend who valued close emotional bonds. Lorne Tulk decided, after ten years of working on radio documentaries and recordings, that he needed to take a sabbatical from Gould's intensity and perfectionism, and so he worked for him only sporadically in Gould's last five years. Gould regretted the loss, but did not, as legend demands, cut Tulk out of his life. Their close friendship continued as before – indeed, Gould came to speak of him as the brother he never had. They spoke almost daily, and Gould confided in him about the most sensitive aspects of his private life in his last years. John Roberts admits that it was "a whole career" being Gould's friend, but adds, "when I needed him he was there."

Gould could not escape his neuroses, to be sure, but he was at least aware of them and able to laugh at them, which gave him some measure of control over them, and they were balanced by many compensatory features of his personality. Many gifted artists and intellectuals are rendered creatively impotent, severely damaged if not ultimately destroyed, by their eccentricities and demons, but Gould does not belong in this company or qualify as self-destructive. Even when it comes to the hypochondria that undoubtedly contributed to his premature death, his motivations must be taken into account: significantly, he medicated himself only in response to perceived medical problems, however misguided his diagnoses may have been; he never, as far as can be determined, took drugs to get high, to dull his senses, to lose himself. His psyche was not simply a matrix of torments that he sought to escape; he fought his psychological issues to a draw. For all his anxieties and neuroses, his personal limitations and failures, Gould coped, he got things done, he led a professional life of astonishing productivity and success and a private life that afforded him more satisfaction than is usually recognized.

**"All good Canadians would rise with irate
displeasure at the slighting inference that I was
anything other than the archetype of the well scrubbed,
gentlemanly boy next door."**

His eccentricities have stood out in much writing about him because they are colourful, newsworthy, yet the Gould that most people remember was also very much his parents' son: the quintessential Nice Canadian Boy, at heart a man of decency and integrity. For every person who suffered at the hand of his neuroses there was one who found him warm, sweet, and lovable, much as people remember him as a child. Paul Myers wrote that in person Gould was "quietly spoken and with almost old-fashioned good manners," and his Toronto piano tuner, Verne Edquist, whom he would give several months' notice where possible about an upcoming job, called him "a real gentleman – polite, considerate." He was unfailingly polite, and like his parents observed simple courtesies – for instance, sending a donation to All Saints' Church (Kingsway) after making a recording on the church's organ. Considering his workload and his professional status, he was remarkably generous with his time when it came to answering fan mail and doing favours for friends and even strangers, and he often returned small acts of kindness: he treated Dr. Stanley E. Greben, a Toronto psychiatrist, and his wife to what Greben recalls as a very pleasant dinner at a good local restaurant, simply because he had spent five minutes on the phone with Gould recommending an ear, nose, and throat specialist. He once granted a dreaded face-to-face interview simply because he could not refuse the interviewer, who had travelled all the way from London to see him. He was gracious and solicitous with women; if taking a young woman out for dinner, he would arrive punctually at her house, come to the door, chat with her mother. For a loner he was surprisingly friendly. "He was really jolly," Tim Page recalled, "and a really damned good companion."

Gould did not play the prima donna, a fact that is reiterated again and again by those who knew him; rather, he usually came across as modest, unpretentious. He was "Glenn" to just about everyone who exchanged more than a few sentences with him, "Dr. Gould" to no one. (Many of his posthumous fans call him "Glenn," apparently reflexively.) Though he could be "difficult" where his idiosyncratic needs proved hard to accommodate – with Steinway and Sons, for instance – one searches in vain for, say, the loftiness of Stokowski, the cruelty of Bernstein, the arrogance of Rubinstein, the waspishness of Stravinsky. He was disgusted by uppity behaviour in others, by the "opera capes and temper tantrums" of Toscanini, for instance, and seems to have been determined not to behave like a typical world-class artist. He demanded respect, to be sure, and was disappointed or petulant or angry when things went wrong, but he did not indulge in tantrums in order to reinforce his celebrity stature. In private, he enjoyed the company of people who were not artists or intellectuals, whom he sought out for genuine companionship, not as an audience to sit at his feet; he enjoyed talking to them about everything except his own work. One of his neighbours in his apartment building remembered him as funny, talkative, and surprisingly gregarious. In his later years he would visit Jessie at her home in Oshawa, where, she recalled, "he would curl up on the chesterfield in his stocking feet and while I served five or so pots of tea he would relate numerous anecdotes, play guessing games, catch up on family news and through his word pictures draw me into a world of minds far beyond my comprehension. During these times he accepted me as an equal, never demeaning or holier than thou." Lorne Tulk wrote that his first meeting with Gould included a lot of friendly getting-to-know-you conversation: "Here was this person with a huge international reputation and a staff technician who had just met, and we were talking as if we'd always known each other." Gould, he realized, "had an incredible ability to make people immediately feel at ease."

Gould knew he was a superior person in many ways, but tried not to behave as such. He did not make racial or economic or class distinctions between people, had no snobbery about wealth or status, and did not condescend to "ordinary" people. Those who served him in restaurants and hotels, for instance, remember a pleasant man who did not want to be fussed over and gave no hint of being a famous artist. Geoffrey Payzant recounted an occasion in the late seventies when a CBC technician innocently asked Gould – asked *Glenn Gould* – if he could recommend a good model of apartment-size upright piano. "And I thought, Oh my God, what can Glenn Gould say in reply to that? Well, what he said was as respectful and as kind and considerate as anything you could imagine. He took this as a serious request and gave serious, useful information in reply. Now, I was just impressed out of my boots – I thought this was marvellous."

Andrew Kazdin recalled that when the baritone Cornelis Opthof became exhausted while recording some Schoenberg songs, and asked if they could "rest for a minute," Gould immediately and courteously replied, "Why, of course," waited precisely sixty seconds, then announced that work would resume. But for the most part, those who worked with Gould, even those who found the work itself exhausting, found him a personable and accommodating boss. "He was the soul of patience in the studio and in the editing room," says the CBC producer James Kent. "There was no display of 'tempera-ment.'" Even Kazdin noted that when he conveyed to Gould in writing that he was feeling overworked, in their first years record-ing in Toronto, Gould at once hired an assistant and "was somewhat hurt and saddened that this matter had to take the form of a letter." Many of his technicians and secretaries recall their time with him as enjoyable and remember his idiosyncrasies as more lovable than oppressive. There was often an atmosphere of high spirits when he was recording or filming, and where the work was gruelling he was usually alert to the need periodically to relax the crew with rest breaks, games, jokes, or his own improvisations or renderings of show tunes on the piano. A camera assistant was moved to write to him in 1978, after a film project, simply to tell him how much the crew had enjoyed the project, and CBC staffers sometimes wrote to him just to say that it had been a pleasure to work with him.

As a young man Gould occasionally performed for charitable pur-poses, and over the years he quietly donated money to many musical and charitable organizations. Privately he helped many people. The pianist Antonin Kubalek emigrated from Czechoslovakia in the summer of 1968, and for several years found his new life in Canada a struggle. Gould heard him play on CBC radio in 1969, heard of his plight, and the following year sent him a substantial cheque; later he wrote on Kubalek's behalf to the Royal Conservatory of Music and advised him on concert management – all of this before meeting him in person.

He could be open and solicitous with his friends. Jessie Greig found him "tender and kind and gentle," and he was actively involved in her life and interested in her teaching. She remembered him once running his hand down her arm and saying, after a beloved aunt had died, "Jessie, I'll always be good to you." Despite his feelings about public situations, he was an eager witness at John Roberts's wedding, in 1962, for which he insisted on donning a morning suit, and he was godfather to several of his friends' children. He was loyal about fol-lowing and supporting his friends' careers, even those friends who played Liszt and Rachmaninov. Whenever Ray Dudley appeared live on the radio, for instance, Gould, as Dudley wrote, "would telephone the minute the performance was finished." (Surprisingly, he was often full of praise for others' performances of music he hated.) Gould wrote warm letters of reference for musician friends, former secretaries, and others, and was not standoffish toward the former schoolmates and old family friends and Uptergrove neighbours who wrote to him from time to time.

He was supportive of friends who were in mourning, experiencing marital strains, or otherwise in difficult straits. "I will never forget his solicitude," Vincent Tovell said, recalling the time of his mother's sudden death. When a close friend was attacked on the street and badly injured in the late fifties, Gould wrote reassuringly to his parents, who lived overseas, and sent them some autographed albums. (He was always generous in making gifts of his albums.) Though he feared sick people and hospitals he did not neglect friends who were ill. In 1963, when Lois Marshall had a throat infection and was ordered not to sing or even speak for a month, Gould called her up often to keep her company, gently telling her not to say anything and then proceeding to entertain her with news and stories; he cheered Joan Maxwell, too, with daily phone calls when she was hospitalized after back surgery. When Barbara Little was diagnosed with a brain tumour in 1978, Gould had several high-profile friends who had lived through a similar diagnosis – including Marshall McLuhan – call her and offer their reassurance, and after she had an operation he was among the first friends to call. Some personal gestures were perhaps difficult for him, given his emotional reticence, but for every story of the detached and self-absorbed Gould there is one that has him tenderly wiping tears from the eyes of a distraught friend, or at least doing what he could. Gladys Riskind remembers "one particular time appearing on his doorstep in despair, and the only way he knew to comfort me was to play for me." (As a child he was observed improvising for his mother as a way of apologizing for misbehaving.) Compassion – a crucial theme of *The Three-Cornered World*, incidentally – was a feeling he greatly prized.

There are stories of personality clashes when Gould played concertos and chamber music – with the Juilliard String Quartet, for instance. He seems actually to have been a less flexible collaborator as a young man; he could be "a little dictator" at times, said Otto Joachim. (Recall the frequent criticism about his "overwhelming" his partners in chamber music at Stratford.) In 1954, Alexander Schneider and Zara Nelsova were annoyed at their young colleague's precocious confidence when it came to Beethoven's "Ghost" Trio, which he was playing for the first time but about which he already had many strange but firm ideas. When Schneider said that he had played the trio at least four or five hundred times, Gould replied loftily, "My position has always been that quality is more important than quantity."* Eventually, Nelsova recalled, she and Schneider managed to talk him out of most of his ideas.

Mostly, however, his fellow-musicians marvelled at his open-mindedness, sensitivity, and spirit of co-operation in collaborations, especially in his later years, and in spite of his strong and idiosyncratic musical personality. Most of the singers he worked with, as well as instrumentalists of the status of Yehudi Menuhin, Leonard Rose, and Jaime Laredo, reported smooth, rewarding collaborations, with Gould willing to try new things whether they were his ideas or not. Some have recalled capitulating to his interpretation of a piece, though not because he pulled rank, using his talent and status to bully, but because they found his ideas too musically compelling to resist. Kerstin Meyer told an interviewer that "it felt completely natural," was "a pure joy," to sing with Gould. She was surprised, in fact, that he was such a good accompanist and was so willing to subordinate his ego; many first-rank pianists are not. "He knew what he wanted,

---

* Schneider, who said that he had never before encountered a pianist who knew the violin repertoire by heart, also objected because Gould did not play with a score in front of him, and so Gould, as Nelsova recalled, "brought it with him into the concert hall and sat on it." When he performed Brahms's F-minor piano quintet with the Montreal String Quartet in 1957, the quartet also asked him to use a score, for appearance's sake, so he put a score on the piano and turned a page from time to time, without regard for where he actually was in the music.

but I never felt pressured – the operative word was collaboration," said the Canadian soprano Roxolana Roslak, who worked with Gould in the later 1970s. "His musical influence was, of course, enormous, but curiously it did not stifle my own expression. Quite the contrary, he had the ability to create such an atmosphere of enthusiasm and discovery, that one felt that anything was possible, and more important – attainable." In 1973 he asked the Canadian clarinetist James Campbell to participate in a CBC television program in which Gould was to perform, for the first time in his career, a piece by Debussy, the *Première rapsodie*. Campbell remembers that, to his surprise, Gould treated him as an equal throughout the collaboration, asking for and deferring to his opinions on interpretation on many occasions, though at the time Campbell was in his early twenties and still a student.

An anecdote related by Morry Kernerman says a great deal about Gould's basic decency, even at the height of his international fame. The Toronto Bach Society found it was having financial trouble in its first season, so Kernerman asked Gould, on short notice, to help out by appearing in their season-end concert in May 1958. Gould agreed, ensuring that Eaton Auditorium was full, and he played his best in Bach's Partitas Nos. 1 and 6. He refused to accept a fee, and at the end of the concert his father presented the society with a donation. The society's debt was wiped out, and when its chairman sent Gould a small honorarium as a token of appreciation he returned the cheque. "I said no fee and I meant it!" he wrote. "Please use this to buy epaulettes for the choristers or some suitable and significant embroidery." If the musicians' union protested, he was willing, grudgingly, to accept a payment of union scale – "but not one cent more." The society gave him an inscribed book, *Early Russian Icons*, as gift, and it was still in his possession when he died.

Stories like this can easily be multiplied. Many people, by their own reports, felt not just entertained but nourished by contact with Gould, for all his evident faults. "Being with him I rose above myself," says Gladys Riskind, who is not a musician but found that she could talk to Gould for hours at a time, even for the better part of a day, and never run out of things to say. "When I left him I always felt like a better person. I could pull out the best that was in myself."

"Well, I'm a ham, as you know . . ."

The Scottish, Stephen Leacock wrote, "always seem to me to prefer adversity to sunshine," and Gould liked to claim a "dour hieland heart." Yet he had an uproarious sense of humour – and not a subtle, sophisticated humour, but an innocent, childlike playfulness, a healthy sense of the absurd, and a fondness for sheer silliness, make-believe, and dress-up. A thread of humour ran throughout his personality and relationships and work, even his performing. Few in the grimly serious, conservative world of classical music have ever acted the little boy and had as much fun in public as did Glenn Gould. He had a sharp intellect and a quick wit, but his humour, unlike that of many intelligent and witty people, was without cruelty or spite; he used it to relax, occasionally to provoke, never to wound. And he liked to have it run both ways. He enjoyed being the butt as well as the source of a joke, as long the intent was not malicious. Kazdin wrote that Gould could "freeze the air" in a jocular situation by suddenly not getting the joke, or perceiving some troubling subtext. Playing practical jokes on him was not a good idea, either: the loss of control in such situations upset him. Nevertheless, humour was one more default position of Gould's personality, and for his friends and colleagues as well as his fans it was one of his most endearing and refreshing traits.

In conversation, in meetings, in interviews, in the studio – in most interpersonal situations he liked to keep the atmosphere light, filled with his trademark cackling laugh. He seemed to be always "on"; to take his phone call was to be entertained for an hour or two. Everyone in his circle – record producers and musical collaborators, accountants and lawyers, assistants and secretaries – got drawn into his whimsies and usually learned to respond in kind. It was difficult to be in his circle if you had no sense of humour. In 1958 he and some friends formed the Lower Rosedale Shakespeare Reading Society, which would meet in John Roberts's apartment and elsewhere to read plays, play games, chat. Gould joined in enthusiastically, and was able to lose himself in comic shenanigans for surprisingly long periods of time; they offered him needed respite from his work and his anxieties. He had outrageous pet names for some of his friends, and loved to puncture pretension and pomposity. Robert Fulford recalled the teenage Gould's pleasure at a local funeral home's daily "death notices" on the radio – the lugubrious organ music, the earnest announcer. He was particularly delighted when it was solemnly intoned, "There are no death notices today."

His surviving papers include many, sometimes remarkably involved, specimens of private humour that he worked up for himself and friends – joke memos, stories set in verse, monologues and scripts, little songs. There was, for instance, a two-page draft of an interview with "the eminent musicologist and opera buff, Boris Gouldowsky," and, in April 1977, some strange made-up dialogue between Roxolana Roslak and the CBC producer James Kent, who, Kent says, barely knew each other. (The dialogue ends with this stage direction: "The sound of heavy breathing is heard.") Even his notes to his assistant might take the form of elaborate lists of "Robertsiana" in which the most trivial errands were described in highfalutin language. He loved to write long, verbose, mock-pompous letters. A friend's engagement in 1957 yielded a long formal letter from the "HERBERT GOULD AGENCY: Escort Services, marriage counseling, Divorce attorney. Our motto: 'low fidelity and high frequency.'" Another of his letterheads was "GOULD PORTFO-LIO MANAGEMENT AND INVESTMENT COUNSELLING SERVICES, INC." To Paul Myers he wrote a three-page introduction to a ficti-tious record company, "Notmuch Records Inc. (A Voice of the Turtle Execusound Company)" – a dig at the esoteric Nonesuch label. When the daughter of his secretary Jill R. Cobb drew him a little picture, in 1975, he responded with a formal lawyer's letter of thanks signed "G. Lenherb." He wrote poems for Cobb's children, too, and for (or about) the children and pets of other friends. Joan

Maxwell, whose married name was Rempel, merited a longer poem, beginning:

> There once was a singer named Rempel,
> Who regarded all art as a Tempel,
> i.e. Rock she abhorred
> but Aida adored
> And preached opera as would Aimee Semple.

He drafted a long twelve-tone song in 1980 involving Menuhin (who was a practitioner of yoga), Menuhin's wife Diana, and the composers Bruch and Mahler, which began: "While standing on his head, one morning in Gstaad/Yehudi said: 'For me, the works of Mahler count for naught.'" Perhaps the two had debated about Mahler and the poem was Gould's reply. Amid the most serious work on *A Letter from Stalingrad* he made a vocal sketch on a text, presumably culled from a newspaper, that begins, "Sex Cited in Chicken Seizures," not a phrase one expects to read in a biography of Glenn Gould.

All of this spilled into the workplace, where Gould could be riotous fun. There was a persistent, often infectious – occasionally tiresome – streak of joshing and good humour in his interactions with his colleagues, which can be seen in outtakes and other bits of audio and video never intended to be seen in public and in fly-on-the-wall documents like the NFB films. His producers and technicians and collaborators speak of recording sessions filled with laughter even where the work was serious and demanding – "We were down on the floor doing animal noises," Margaret Pacsu told a CBC interviewer. Otto Joachim recalled rehearsing at Stratford with Oscar Shumsky and Leonard Rose "when Glenn Gould walked in, with 'Guten Morgen, Herr Doktor!' – that was about all he could say in German," and from that moment the rehearsal degenerated into horseplay. "We never played another note. End of rehearsal." When he was recording Brahms's F-minor piano quintet with the Montreal String Quartet in 1957, the twelve-hour session was, in Joachim's words, "a free-for-all circus" that included impromptu parody-performances of

Wagner, complete with vocals and staging. In a letter to one of his former secretaries, Avril Rustage-Johnston, in 1979, Gould recalled that their work together "consisted of two-thirds anecdotal material and one-third work" – all of which he, of course, paid for.

A note of humour, or at least lightness, was always part of Gould's public persona, in his onstage lectures, in his liner notes and other writings, in his broadcasts, in such compositional confections as *So You Want to Write a Fugue?* and the Lieberson Madrigal. After retiring from concert life, however, he increasingly liberated his humorous side. In 1965, he wrote three witty articles for *High Fidelity/Musical America* under the pseudonym of the conductor Dr. Herbert von Hochmeister (loosely based on Karajan), and in later years he published seriously intended though lighthearted articles and reviews with titles like "'Oh, for Heaven's Sake, Cynthia, There Must Be Something Else On!'"; "Liszt's Lament? Beethoven's Bagatelle? Or Rosemary's Babies?"; "Data Bank on the Upward-Scuttling Mahler"; "The Future and 'Flat-Foot Floogie'"; "A Festschrift for 'Ernst Who???'"; "The Grass Is Always Greener in the Outtakes"; "Back to Bach (and Belly to Belly)"; and "A Hawk, a Dove, and a Rabbit Called Franz Joseph." His first sustained piece of written humour was "The Aftermath of Breton," which was begun in 1966 and went through several versions. The centrepiece of the article is a report on controversies surrounding the publication of a (fictitious) book on music, *The Consonant Choirloft*, by a certain "Lapierre Breton." It was a parody of Pierre Berton's *The Comfortable Pew*, which was a frank and controversial critique of religion in Canada published in 1965, and which gave Gould a pretext for a tongue-in-cheek look at Canadian music and criticism. The whole exercise was very convoluted and "inside," which is probably why he never saw it published. A spoof for radio followed in 1967 and *was* later published: "Conference at Port Chillkoot" was a parody of a music critics' conference, set in Alaska and featured thinly disguised portraits of real Canadian and American critics. It included a choral number the text of which ("From Chillkoot's icy glacier,/O'er Chillkoot's lowering fjord . . .") parodied a famous nineteenth-century missionary hymn ("From Greenland's icy mountains,/From India's coral strand . . .").

More humour writing soon followed. His liner notes for his 1967 album of the Beethoven-Liszt Fifth Symphony consisted of four imaginary reviews by fictitious critics of various nationalities (British, German, American, Hungarian) and persuasions (historical, analytical, psychiatric, socio-political). His liner notes for his 1973 Grieg-Bizet album closed with "A CONFIDENTIAL CAUTION TO CRITICS" in which he noted his genealogical connection to Grieg so as to guide those critics who might otherwise miss the "unquestionable authority" and "incontrovertible authenticity" of his interpretation of Grieg's piano sonata. He published two amusingly self-deprecating interviews with himself, one on his ambivalent views of Beethoven, in 1970, the other on the moral underpinnings of his aesthetic, in 1974. And he wrote book reviews in the 1970s that, while insightful, have a charming lightness of touch. His humour writing, like his writing generally, greatly improved with time.

As a child Gould enjoyed playing make-believe and putting on funny voices, sometimes mimicking (never maliciously) his friends and neighbours and teachers. (He was a fan of Rich Little.) Around 1950 he, John Beckwith, and Ray Dudley made a private recording of a three-hand, *prestissimo* reading of Chopin's Étude in A Minor, Op. 10/No. 2, preceded by a little skit in which Gould, for once, played straight man, interviewing Beckwith who, in dialect, played Vladimir Horowitz. (The recording survives.) As an adult he made all sorts of private recordings, some alone, some with friends, in which he documented the sort of play-acting he liked to indulge in privately, and by the early sixties it was clear that he would be incapable of keeping his fondness for hamming at bay forever in public – recall the "Piano Lesson with Glenn Gould" in Vancouver, and the "Panorama of Music of the 20's" at Stratford. In the later sixties he sometimes played fictitious characters in promotional recordings requested by Columbia Records, and in the early seventies he got up the nerve to appear on CBC radio and television in character, occasionally in what were intended to be serious statements of his ideas (presumably he subscribed to the spoonful-of-sugar theory).

He developed several recurring characters based on broad ethnic stereotypes, and from the mid-sixties they increasingly infiltrated his CBC broadcasts. There was a silly-ass, imperviously Edwardian British conductor, originally named Sir Humphrey Price-Davies and later incarnated as Sir Nigel Twitt-Thornwaite, based on models like Sir Thomas Beecham and Sir Adrian Boult, undoubtedly also on some of the transplanted British musicians Gould encountered growing up in Toronto, and on a pompous musicologist once played by Peter Ustinov. He trotted out a few other variations on the same theme over the years – for instance, Jonathan Wynan, a BBC producer and athlete. There was a series of intellectual Germans and Austrians: the conductor Hochmeister, the arrogant psychiatrist Dr. Wolfgang von Krankmeister, and the avant-garde composer and musicologist Dr. Karlheinz Klopweisser, whose interests included "the resonance of silence," specifically "*German* silence, which is of course organic, as opposed to French silence, which is ornamental." (Klopweisser was partly based on Stockhausen.) There was a New York cabby, an early-Brando-type mumbler with a "dese-dem-dose" accent, whom Gould encountered in 1966 and immediately added to his dramatic arsenal in various forms, usually dressed in a leather jacket and sometimes of a beatnik disposition – the boxer Dominico Pastrano, the actor Myron Chianti, and Theodore Slutz, a downtown New York critic with a taste for the avant-garde. And there was a gruff, inscrutable Scot with an impenetrable brogue, who turned up as the athlete Duncan Haig-Guinness and later as a radio technician of the same name.

Gould's humour, like so much about him, was identifiably Canadian, particularly in his writings. As a schoolboy he became familiar with the works of Stephen Leacock and with Paul Hiebert's fictional poetess Sarah Binks, "The Sweet Songstress of Saskatchewan,"*

---

* Some time in the late fifties, Gould made a sixteen-bar sketch for (apparently) a vocal duet based on one of Binks's hilariously awful poems, "The Farmer and the Farmer's Wife."

and he was likely familiar with Robertson Davies and other Canadian humorists. Certain recurring features of his humour fall entirely within this tradition: his fondness for tackling sophisticated themes in rural (often Arctic) settings; his tendency to convey innocuous circumstances in the tones of high drama, blowing up the mundane and banal to mock-heroic stature; his witty use of euphemism and understatement, and fondness for undercutting what he purported soberly to be elevating; his use of thinly disguised parody; and a knowing corniness of a sort that can still be seen in comedy on Canadian radio and television. Even the details are distinctively Canadian, including his fondness for colourful, self-parodying names and titles. Hiebert had "*The Claim Jumper*, the official organ of the Quagmire Bureau of Mines," and Davies had "the Skunk's Misery *Trombone*, a lively little paper with a rather limited circulation." Gould had "*Insight*, Digest of the North Dakota Psychiatrists Association," "*Rhapsodya*, Journal of the All-Union Musical Workers of Budapest," "*Field and Theme – The Country Gentleman's Guide to Music and the Garden*," "*The Village Grass Is Greener*," and "*The Great Slave Smelt*," as well as the "*Port Chillkoot Packet*," an obvious nod to Orillia's real-life newspaper, the *Packet and Times*. Here is Leacock, in *Sunshine Sketches of a Little Town*:

> Of course, Pupkin would never have thought of considering himself on an intellectual par with Mallory Tompkins. That would have been ridiculous. Mallory Tompkins had read all sorts of things and had half a mind to write a novel himself – either that or a play. All he needed, he said, was to have a chance to get away somewhere by himself and think. Every time he went away to the city Pupkin expected that he might return with the novel all finished; but though he often came back with his eyes red from thinking, the novel as yet remained incomplete.

Here is Hiebert, analyzing Sarah Binks's early poem "The Parson's Patch":

Here we have already the Sarah we have learned to love, sweetly lyrical, deeply moralizing. But her touch is unsure. "A onion, a lettuce" is weak, some of the lines do not quite scan, and her rhyming of "visible" with "contemplation" is not in the best traditions of Saskatchewan literature.

And here is Gould:

I had scarcely begun the first supper show of my gala season at the Maude Harbour Festival when, as was my habit, I glanced toward the boxes. And there, seated on one marked "Live Bait – Do Not Refrigerate," was a vision of such loveliness that it instantly erased from my mind the memory of all four amorous adventures which had befallen me between lunch and five o'clock tea. Delightful as the company of those ladies may have been, I realized at once that my future, my fate, my destiny, belonged to the dazzling enchantress who now, with such demure grace, hid her bubble gum beneath the crate of worms on which she sat and attempted to come to terms with the ardor of my gaze. I resolved to address every note of my performance to her and her alone and to inquire into the county's statutory-rape provisions at intermission.

That is the opening paragraph of "Memories of Maude Harbour, or, Variations on a Theme of Arthur Rubinstein," published in 1980, a spot-on parody of Rubinstein's self-congratulatory autobiography, *My Young Years*, and perhaps Gould's masterpiece in the comic vein.

Gould, naturally, thought *all* his humour was brilliantly funny, though much of it is as awful as it sounds, particularly the ethnic humour. His English accents, for instance, call to mind one of Robertson Davies' quips about amateur theatricals: "Their English accents were not very well assumed, their English slang was derived from hearing people who had read Wodehouse talk about him." (Ironically, Gould's Scottish accent was his least convincing.) His

comedy could be heavy-handed, and was often laboured and atten-
uated; he got so caught up in laughing at himself that he did not
know when to stop. "Glenn was not an actor," Robert Silverman
said. "He was a college-variety ham." And that is precisely right. Yet
even when his writing or play-acting was at its most awful – and
sometimes *especially* then – there is something charming and refreshing and satisfying about the spectacle of one of the world's premier
classical musicians lost in comic reverie in public. It is difficult to
imagine, say, Pollini or Karajan or Schwarzkopf onstage with kooky
hat and funny accent, and this is surely one reason why Gould has
proved attractive to the general public. He takes some of the stuff-
ing out of a pretentious and poker-faced field, without undercutting
his eminent qualifications in that field.

Gould's humour might be interpreted as a mask behind which
he hid in order to protect his true feelings and avoid real interaction
and intimacy, and on many occasions he turned to humour when
compelled to confront someone. When Columbia Records owed
him money in 1965, he wrote to them, in his best fractured English,
in the guise of Herbert von Hochmeister: "HAVING NOT PLEASURE
KNOWING YOU WHILE HOPING SUCH FOR COMING SOON –
FINDING COURAGE BREAK IN YOUR PEACE ASKING MONEY PLEASE.
ON BEHALF CLIENT MR. GLENN GOULD DO SO – SINCE CLIENT NOT
TOO QUICK WHERE MONEY MATTERS AND ALSO SHY." Mostly,
though, Gould was simply in love with play. Light badinage and
playacting relaxed and reassured him, made private situations more
enjoyable and public situations more tolerable, but never precluded
intimacy with close friends.

That humour, moreover, is strikingly apparent throughout the
Gould discography – no performer has ever explored the possibilities for wit and parody in the classical repertoire to the degree Gould
did. In his high-comic cycle of Mozart's sonatas, and some of
Beethoven's early piano pieces, he indulged in all sorts of quirky
ornaments and cheeky turns of phrase, in up-and-down arpeggios
that come off like vaudeville crosstalk. He brought out the parodis-
tic qualities of works like Mozart's famous "Turkish Rondo" and

Schoenberg's neo-Baroque Suite, Op. 25, and liked to poke fun at commonplaces of interpretation. His fast, clipped reading of the popular first prelude from Bach's *Well-Tempered Clavier* is a studied refusal to offer the expected "poetic" reading, and his reading of Beethoven's "Appassionata" Sonata parodies just those rhetorical aspects of the "heroic" middle-period Beethoven that he most despised. There is even a hint of self-parody in such projects as his recording of the Beethoven-Liszt Fifth Symphony, his busy, over-dubbed recording of Wagner's *Meistersinger* Prelude, and his solo-piano version of Ravel's *La Valse* – projects in which he seems knowingly, with a wink, to step outside the repertoire characteristic of him, as though to confront his detractors head-on. Gould was a nose-thumber as well as a serious artist, and his contrarian stance relative to hallowed classical-music canons and conventions was in many ways profoundly subversive, not just fun.

"I was good at fughettas – it was like solving a puzzle."

Gould loved games. As a child he competed passionately, and John Roberts recalls that even as an adult "he would shriek with glee" if he was winning at Monopoly – and he usually was. He enjoyed mixing his conversations and work sessions with parlour games of all sorts: association games (If you were a dog, what kind of dog would you be? If you were a key, what key would you be?),* role-playing games (I'll be Mozart, you be Beethoven, let's have a con-versation), mental-telepathy games, musical games, novelties like the Lüscher Color Test, which purports to assess your personality according to your colour preferences, even little quizzes in popular magazines. Guessing games were his favourites, especially Twenty Questions, which everyone who knew him recalls as an unavoidable, occasionally exhausting part of the Gould Experience. There were

---

* Gould, by his own admission, would be a collie, and would be either F minor or B minor (he was not quite sure).

also guessing games of his own devising. The notepads from his last decade include notes relating to musical guessing games that he was either posing or answering, and one of them includes this revealing answer: "Unfortunately, I can't remember a note of Musorgsky." (He could often be tripped up with the most popular Romantic warhorses of the repertoire.) He loved guessing even outside the formality of a game. Many of his phone calls, even long-distance, began with, "Guess what happened to me today?" – and he really meant it. One friend recalls sitting in Gould's cubicle at the CBC when they heard approaching footsteps; Gould would not even allow her to see who was coming until they first had guessed. As a child, on the streetcar, he used to guess what other passengers did for a living. Games have long been viewed as harmless ways of getting rid of aggressive and competitive impulses, which Gould undoubtedly had, and some, like Andrew Kazdin, believe that Gould's fondness for guessing games reflected a delight in exercising power – I know something you don't. But his enjoyment of games seems to have been mostly innocent, and besides, he enjoyed being the one who guessed, at which task he was never known to give up or lose patience.

The pervasiveness of guessing and game playing in Gould's life suggests that these were not merely relaxing pastimes for him but processes hard-wired into his brain. Games have also long been viewed as manifestations of the impulse to order, and are consistent with an obsessional temperament; Gould's own obsessive tendency was often channelled in ways that suggest game playing. The stock market could well have been a game to him as much as it was a source of income and security – it was *fun*. (One of his first acts on a typical day was to call his broker.) He enjoyed trying to outwit the experts, often succeeding, and tracked the progress of his stock portfolio in loving detail. He seemed to relish real-life opportunities to exercise his obsessiveness. He would pore over his contracts and royalty statements with fanatical precision. Among his papers is a truly virtuosic seventeen-page letter that he wrote to Kazdin, in 1977, which includes thirty-four separate reports of questionable royalty calculations for various albums in countries all over the world. Of course he took his business affairs seriously, but when he began to compare unit-royalty rates and reporting dates in Chile with those in New Zealand, or to fuss over his participation in "greatest hits" packages in Norway and South Africa, his tongue was surely edging toward his cheek. In such documents – and there are many of them – he was obviously ferreting out trivial discrepancies as much *pour le sport* as for the income involved, which was often trivial, and he loved to boast of his findings in his replies to Columbia Records, whose accountants must have dreaded sending out his semi-annual statements.

Obsessional traits like game playing were symptomatic of a fantastically busy brain that never shut off. Gould was McLuhan's "oral-aural man," unable to be silent, totally involved mentally with whatever he was doing. No wonder he had trouble sleeping. (What is more, many of his dreams had to do with work, as though his brain kept working while he slept.) He always had to be *doing something* with his brain, the way a person with too much physical energy, forced to sit still, will tap a foot or twirl a pencil. When there was no work being done, he had to find other outlets – hence the persistent doodling (a habit from childhood),* the obsessive list-making, the games and puzzles. When he tried his hand at verse it was always in rhyming couplets, limericks, haikus, and other set forms: fitting new ideas into a given pattern was just the sort of puzzle-solving challenge he craved. The music he loved most was contrapuntal – music, as he told Tim Page in 1982, "with an explosion of simultaneous ideas." Music, in other words, that was most like a puzzle. His brain was attuned to counterpoint even in day-to-day life. He was fond of eavesdropping on several conversations at once in restaurants and other public places, and he was able to talk

---

* In one doodle from his school years, he stacked the words *Gould, Guerrero*, and *Greig* vertically, with all three words growing out of the same large capital *G*. I leave the psychoanalyzing of this morsel to others.

on the phone while drafting an article and listening to music, and to keep track of all three streams of input. In ordinary conversation, the unusual organizing power of his mind was apparent. "His was the most brilliant mind I have ever encountered," Avril Rustage-Johnston wrote. "No matter how intricate a path he wove in his discussions, with parentheses inside parentheses, I never heard him lose his way, or stop for a moment to say, 'Where was I?' Having rerouted a story in the interests of clarification or enlargement, he was able to return to the precise word at which he had left off, perhaps after five minutes of non-stop talking, without a moment's hesitation."

Fugues and twelve-tone works gave pleasure to Gould's puzzle-solving brain because they need to be analyzed, *figured out*, to be fully appreciated, while more intuitive types of music – fantasias, aleatory pieces, jazz improvisations – disturbed him the way an unmade bed disturbs a neat freak. You can't wing it when you're making a puzzle; you have to put every piece in its rightful place in order to succeed. Gould's seemingly paradoxical love for the most Romantic music of all – Wagner, Strauss, Mahler, and their contemporaries – derived from the density of texture in this music, and he said as much when he praised late-Romantic counterpoint. This was music that, like the largest works of Bach, was so contrapuntally rich that one got lost in it: to hear everything that was in it stretched the analytical capacities of the ear and brain to their limits. And what is Gould's fondness, at the piano, for revealing (or inventing) strands of counterpoint if not a delight in figuring out a puzzle and making the solution clearly perceptible to his listeners? The transparency of Gould's piano style was all about opening up the music, setting out the constituent parts of its structure for the listener's delectation; one critic compared his playing to a chess master who could see many moves ahead. And he looked always for new unifying elements to add to the puzzle. For instance, he grew increasingly fond of exploring proportional tempos in the music he played – that is, creating mathematically precise rhythmic relationships between different movements or parts of a piece. His 1981 recording of the

Goldberg Variations is the best-known case, though the practice pervades his later recordings. And when he played continuo, he was not content simply to strum chords; he might add new counterpoints, or play a kind of piano reduction of the full score.

It was this same puzzle-solving brain that drew Gould to recording and editing. His producers have testified that he had an uncanny knack for keeping track of the characteristics of different takes in his mind and for knowing in advance which splices would work where. He was a true, ideal recording artist who did not need the continuity of the concert setting in order to craft a unified performance of a work. "At a certain point in his life, montage became to him second nature, in order to separate the moment of the physical act (playing) from the artistic decision," wrote Bruno Monsaingeon. "Very few people are able to work in segments and still give a unity to all these segments. Gould could keep a complete view of the total work and an abstract one, very coherent from the first to the last note, and still do one segment at a time." For Gould it was a pity that the fad for quadraphonic technology in the early seventies passed quickly, for he was naturally drawn to its possibilities and complexities; it would have allowed him, in effect, to juggle both horizontal and vertical dimensions of the editing process at the same time, a complexity he finally did encounter, in a different way, in the recordings he made using "acoustic orchestration" – a three- rather than two-dimensional puzzle. He admired the synthesizer artist's ability to build up a performance section by section, line by line, or literally note by note, and he likely would have loved this ultimate puzzle-solving challenge himself, had he been able to craft a piano performance this way without musically inferior results.

No wonder he loved movies so much and spoke of recording by analogy with filmmaking: a film is a great puzzle, built up out of bits and pieces of material created out of sequence. He dreamed of directing a film, and though he admitted having not much visual sense – in public school he got Cs and Ds in art – he was in some ways a natural for the film medium. He might have made a great *documentary* filmmaker, and it is a pity he never had an opportunity to try his hand at the visual counterpart of "contrapuntal radio." He jumped at whatever chance to direct came his way. In 1975 he was asked to contribute to World Music Week, and in lieu of giving a paper he created a half-hour videotape on the subject of "contrapuntal radio," for which he reused the title *Radio as Music*. It purports to be a behind-the-scenes look at Gould in a studio at work on *The Quiet in the Land*, but in fact he scripted the whole thing, even the mundane chit-chat. Outtakes from the program show him enjoying the whole process immensely, though his "co-stars," who were not actors or even hams, were obviously rattled. His technician, Donald Logan, was unable even to ask if anyone wanted coffee without being compelled to do multiple takes of precisely scripted lines. Much of *Radio as Music* looks posed and stilted as a result, but Gould was having too much fun making his movie to notice.

His composing, too, tended to resemble puzzle-solving, and that is why as a serious composer he did not succeed. What he possessed as a composer was a capacity for the ingenious development of germinal musical ideas, precisely the facility he exercised so obsessively in the String Quartet. In that work Gould concocted a great puzzle for himself to solve, but he was less successful in writing great melodies, contriving colourful and idiomatic string textures, crafting a compelling large-scale drama. What he *lacked* as a composer, in short, was inspiration, that special spark that animates a piece of music into something other than a technical exercise, and what ended his composing career may have been his realization of this. The only later works he completed were humorous pastiches: exercises, once again. In his subsequent development of "contrapuntal radio," though, Gould created a new genre of "musical composition" of precisely the sort that best suited him. In his radio style the crucial gift required was not inspiration – say, plucking a great tune out of thin air – but the ability to forge resonant new syntheses out of "found footage." "Contrapuntal radio" requires not a composer so much as a great and imaginative editor, someone with a native gift for solving puzzles, and in this congenial medium Gould did his greatest, most original composing. For the creative work demanded by broadcasting and recording, he had not just skill but positive genius.

Opposite: Gould in the 30th Street studio in New York, during his last photo session for CBS Masterworks, June 18, 1980. *(Photograph by Don Hunstein. Sony Classical.)*

PART SIX

THE LAST PURITAN

In Transition, 1975–82

"One of the finest of all halls acoustically."

With his artistic and technical standards ever rising, Gould found himself chafing more and more against the limitations of the organizations he worked for, and sought greater control over his career. That, for him, meant working close to home as much as possible. He came to resent the twenty-or-so trips he had to make each year in order to record in New York, a city he described as "one of the most depressing places on earth," and where, if he were compelled to live in the city, he "would have a crack-up for sure." In 1970, when the direct Toronto–New York rail service he relied on was discontinued, he chose to move his whole recording operation to Toronto. After a test in December 1970, he decided he would thenceforth record in Eaton Auditorium, on the seventh floor of the Eaton's department store (now College Park), an Art Moderne building downtown at College and Yonge streets. (The store opened in 1930; the auditorium above it, with a seating capacity of 1,275, had its first concert in the spring of 1931.) Its acoustic, drier than that of Columbia's 30th Street studio, suited his repertoire and style. The familiarity of the hall probably offered a psychological boost, too: site of his first professional recitals as an organist and pianist, it was home turf. He had his first session there on January 10, 1971, when he recorded some of the final preludes and fugues from Bach's *Well-Tempered Clavier*.

In order to record in Toronto he had to become, in effect, his own business manager. He had to buy his own recording equipment: at that time there was none of suitable quality in Toronto. In a letter to his insurance company on February 1, 1971, he listed seventeen major pieces of new equipment: tape recorders, amplifiers, microphones, speakers, a mixer, and custom-made pieces including a talk-and-playback system – all of it valued at about $14,000. In later years, he acquired still more equipment, including a Dolby sound system and four Dolby noise-reduction units, and he leased an eight-track tape recorder as well as a mixing board. By 1977, he was insuring about $60,000 worth of recording equipment, and he never stopped adding to the list. Andrew Kazdin, who rightly doubted that Gould ever earned back the money he put out, said, "I wish CBS had equipment as good as he has." Gould was also responsible for booking Eaton Auditorium, transporting his equipment from his studio to the hall and back for each session, engaging his local piano tuner, Verne Edquist (whom he had known since 1961), and keeping track of expenses. Columbia Masterworks paid for the hall, the tuner, and Kazdin's engineering fees, and paid Gould a nominal fee for renting his equipment and his piano, CD 318, which was stored in the hall between sessions; Gould himself bore the cost of transporting his equipment and donated his post-production services for supervising his own editing. Under the new arrangement everyone was happy: union restrictions that obtained in New York were circumvented, Masterworks saved money on expenses, and Gould, though a little out of pocket, could make recordings without leaving home.

He continued to arrange about twenty sessions per year. It was necessary to record after the department store closed for the day, which suited him fine. In his concert days he had often been compelled to record in the morning and early afternoon; now a typical session started in the late afternoon or early evening and wrapped up by eleven or midnight, sometimes at one or two in the morning (contrary to legend, he did not record in the middle of the night).

At first the equipment was handled by Lorne Tulk – Gould never lugged anything, ever – but when it became clear almost at once that more help was needed, Gould hired Ray Roberts, an old friend of Tulk's, as a studio attendant. A resourceful, reliable, even-tempered man who was then employed as a salesman for Coca-Cola, Roberts took responsibility for the recording equipment, sometimes with his son's help, became Gould's liaison with electronics manufacturers and suppliers, and was soon helping out at the sessions in other ways. He knew his way around an automobile, too, and began to look after Gould's revolving stable of cars. Eventually he became Gould's personal assistant, in his own words a "glorified gofer" – running errands, travelling with Gould on business trips, and acting as his spokesman where Gould preferred not to deal with people or institutions in person.*

Once the recording equipment was set up, only Gould, Kazdin, and Edquist were present. Visitors were forbidden, though a night watchman employed by Eaton's patrolled the premises, since occasionally a shoplifter was discovered hiding out in the hall. The sessions were broken up by stories and jokes and rounds of Twenty Questions and other games, and by hand-soaking sessions in the bathroom, for which Gould had an electric kettle put by. The work was fuelled by "double-doubles" (coffee with two sugars and two creams) procured from a Fran's across the street, to which Gould might repair for his daily meal after a session. The piano was set on the floor between the apron of the stage and the first row of seats; the microphones were placed closer to the piano than they had been in New York; and the piano's lid was removed, so that the microphones "looked down" on the soundboard. The result, in Gould's view, was "a very lovely and very clear sound," though also an

---

* Roberts has said that he felt the end of this relationship was imminent in Gould's last years, and some notes in Gould's papers from mid-1977, including a draft of a letter of reference for Roberts, suggest that he might have been looking for a new assistant at that time; however, at the time of Gould's death Roberts was still working for him.

enhancement of his vocalizing, only slightly improved by the placement of a sound-absorbent screen to his right that partially shielded
his face from the microphones. Four tape recorders ran during the
sessions: two provided the high-quality tapes that were edited back
in New York to create the masters; one provided a tape of lower
quality that Gould kept in Toronto in order to devise the editing
plan; and one provided a temporary tape that allowed him to hear
playbacks immediately during the recording session and so to match
the tempo and volume of a take perfectly when recording an insert.

By this time, he had become so fussy a recording artist that at a
typical session he might spend fifty minutes or more out of an hour
studying playbacks, and by his last years, he said, he rarely averaged
more than two minutes' worth of finished product for every hour he
spent recording. Listening to his copies of the session tapes at home,
he prepared a detailed splicing plan, which he wrote into a score and
then conveyed by phone to Kazdin, who spliced the final master tape
at his own home in New York; Gould then approved or corrected the
master tape, sometimes after listening to it over the phone line.

Even as his standards rose throughout the seventies his output
of recordings remained impressive:

- Hindemith, Sonatas for Horn, Bass Tuba, Trumpet, Alto Horn,
  and Trombone, with the Philadelphia Brass Ensemble (respec-
  tively, Mason Jones, Abe Torchinsky, Gilbert Johnson, Mason
  Jones, and Henry Charles Smith) (recorded in 1975–76/released
  in 1976).
- Bach, Six Sonatas for Violin and Harpsichord, with Jaime
  Laredo (1975–76/1976).
- Bach, Six English Suites (1971, 1973–76/1977).
- Sibelius, Three Sonatines, Op. 67; *Kyllikki*: Three Lyric Pieces
  (1976–77/1977).
- Hindemith, *Das Marienleben*, original 1923 version, with
  Roxolana Roslak, soprano (1976–77/1978).
- Bach, Seven Toccatas, in two volumes (1963, 1976, 1979/1979,
  1980).

- Bach, Preludes, Fughettas, and Fugues (1979–80/1980).
- Beethoven, Piano Sonatas, Opp. 2/Nos. 1–3 and 28 ("Pastoral") (1974, 1976, 1979/1980).
- *The Glenn Gould Silver Jubilee Album* (released in 1980), comprising: Scarlatti, Sonatas, L. 463 in D Major, L. 413 in D Minor, and L. 486 in G Major (recorded in 1968); C. P. E. Bach, Würtemberg Sonata No. 1 in A Minor (1968); Gould, *So You Want to Write a Fugue?* (1963); Scriabin, Two Pieces, Op. 57 (1972); Strauss, *Ophelia-Lieder*, with Elisabeth Schwarzkopf, soprano (1966);* Beethoven-Liszt, *Pastoral Symphony*, first movement (1968); and *A Glenn Gould Fantasy* (1980).

Beginning with the three sonatas released in 1973, Gould had something of a Hindemith fit in the 1970s. His recordings of *Das Marienleben*, an eighty-minute cycle of fifteen songs, and of the five brass sonatas – hardly staples of the piano repertoire – as well as his liner notes and contemporaneous television performances of Hindemith, reveal a deep new commitment to that composer. (He considered moving on from the brass sonatas to those for woodwind and string instruments with piano.) He had performed *Das Marienleben* as a "theatrical occasion" at Stratford, in 1962: Lois Marshall sang, and the actor John Horton (Gould had tried to get Christopher Plummer) read the original Rilke poems, in English translation, before each song. In 1971 he sought to recreate that event for CBC radio, and though he could not accommodate Marshall's schedule he did not lose interest in what he called "the greatest song cycle ever written." In 1975, driving around in the middle of the night, he heard a Ukrainian-born Canadian soprano, Roxolana Roslak, on CBC radio, and was so impressed that he hired her at once to perform Strauss's *Ophelia-Lieder* and parts of *Das Marienleben*

---

* Schwarzkopf approved the release of the *Ophelia-Lieder*, but she has never permitted the release of the four other Strauss songs she recorded with Gould in January 1966. Judging from the producer's notes, the Ophelia songs were the only ones for which many takes and inserts were recorded.

with him that year on television, and he insisted that she record *Das Marienleben* with him even though CBS wanted him to use a better-known singer from its own stable. He considered her, as he wrote in one of his notepads, "among the most gifted vocal artists of this generation," and they developed a close friendship, which shows in the often haunting intensity of their recording.

Gould's last analogue album celebrated his twenty-fifth year as a Columbia recording artist. It gave him an excuse to release some odds and ends still in Columbia's vaults from his various abandoned recording projects, and it included *A Glenn Gould Fantasy*, a humorous documentary, completed in August 1980, that he recorded and edited in his own studio. In it he revived three of his alter egos – Sir Nigel Twitt-Thornwaite, Dr. Karlheinz Klopweisser, and Theodore Slutz – to create a wide-ranging four-way conversation; a fourth character – Duncan Haig-Guinness – appears as a studio technician, and the conversation is moderated by Margaret Pacsu, who brought along a character of her own, the Hungarian Marxist musicologist Márta Hortaványi. The *Fantasy* allowed Gould to tackle some pet topics and create yet another "position paper" in a lighthearted setting. The humour is sometimes groan-inducing, though Gould's self-deprecation, as usual, is attractive: in one busy sequence of overlapping dialogue, Sir Nigel can be heard, perfectly clearly, to insist, "Mr. Gould, of course, has this *absurd* notion that one can concentrate on the multiplicity of vocal impressions, and it's absolute nonsense, of course, as well as *complete affectation*, in my view."

The *Fantasy* closes with a self-contained, ten-minute showpiece that had been on his mind for fifteen years. In 1965, a year after Gould gave his last concert, Vladimir Horowitz ended twelve years of self-imposed retirement from concerts with a highly publicized "Historic Return" at Carnegie Hall. It was an event that ran contrary to everything Gould believed in, and a year later he was already talking of parodying the "Historic Return," and the whole institution of the public concert, in some kind of album, which would allow him to use some unreleased recordings in a "delightfully zany" way. He wrote detailed letters on the subject to Columbia Records over the years, but some executives were firmly against the idea, which they considered undignified – and besides, Horowitz was a Columbia artist. Some, according to Kazdin, expressed the view that Gould was not as funny as he thought he was. Gould finally got his way in the *Fantasy*, which concludes with "Glenn Gould's Hysteric Return." (In the end nothing beyond that title alluded to Horowitz, who had returned to RCA in 1975.) The "Hysteric Return" features Gould in performance with the Aklavik Philharmonic on an oil rig in the Arctic Ocean, in a "characteristic" program of Romantic and Impressionist showpieces – he pulled out the CBC's tape of Weber's *Konzertstück*, from 1951, for this purpose. During his encore, Ravel's *La Valse*, reports of a new oil find cause a mass exodus in his audience, which consists mostly of executives of Geyser Petroleum; Gould himself plays the deep-voiced chairman of the board, interviewed by Pacsu's American reporter Cassie Mackerel. At the end of his encore, Gould is alone on the rig in the howling wind, taking his bows to the barking of a lone seal.

"Confront a TV type with threats of diminution, augmentation, and canon at inversion and he'll freeze at the thought of showing the unshowable."

Gould remained under the management of Walter Homburger for twenty years, to the benefit of both. But Homburger's business was primarily concerts – in 1962 he became managing director of the Toronto Symphony – and Gould, after leaving concert life behind, came to feel that he needed a manager more attuned to the electronic media. On April 1, 1968, he severed his ties with Homburger and signed with the biggest classical-music agency in the world, Columbia Artists Management Inc. (CAMI), in New York, and became a personal client of Ronald Wilford. Notoriously secretive and camera-shy, Wilford had a reputation as a ruthless, even Machiavellian, businessman; he was nicknamed the "Silver Fox," and

Horowitz and his wife privately referred to him "the barracuda." He became CAMI's president in 1970, and eventually he was arguably the most powerful man in the classical-music business, with, among much else, a virtual monopoly on the world's top conductors. He and CAMI have been key figures in the growing corporatization of classical music over the past forty years. Lacking artistic credentials or musical experience, Wilford was not – as, for instance, Goddard Lieberson was – an executive with an enlightened attitude toward the relationship between art and commerce, but Gould was presumably attracted by his international connections. His papers, in any event, are silent on the circumstances in which he joined CAMI and on his break with Homburger, with whom he remained cordial.

As soon as he signed with CAMI, Gould began excitedly to plan making classical-music films for television in Europe. Inevitably he set his sights on another of Wilford's star clients: Herbert von Karajan. He and Karajan had remained in touch since their last concert together in 1959, and were eager to collaborate. Like Stokowski, Karajan was a passionate technophile who, even in old age, advocated new technologies like the videocassette, digital recording, the compact disc, and the laser disc. Gould admired his media work, particularly the five innovative, visually striking films he made in the mid-sixties with the French director Henri-Georges Clouzot, which, influenced by the spontaneity of the French "New Wave," captured rehearsals and performances in a cinematic style that had nothing to do with the concert hall. Gould made tentative plans to fly (yes, fly) to Europe in spring 1969 to make films of Bach and Beethoven concertos with Karajan and the Berlin Philharmonic, and perhaps also a film in which the two would alternate roles as conductor and soloist in works by Bach or Mozart, or take turns conducting from the keyboard. In the end, he refused to travel so far from home, balked at a schedule too short for his liking (it required filming the "Emperor" Concerto in one day), and came down with the flu; Karajan, moreover, insisted on owning the films himself, while Gould, too, wanted to control his film work rather than simply work for a flat fee. Plans for Karajan to come to Toronto for filming also failed to materialize.

Gould was besieged with film offers after signing with CAMI, from networks in the United States, Britain, France, Germany, Australia, and Japan. In 1971 he proposed working again with Humphrey Burton at the BBC, on a program devoted to Haydn, including piano sonatas as well as "something symphonic, directed from the harpsichord." The same year, he made detailed plans for an NBC program on "the birth, development, decline and death of the piano concerto," in which he would lecture, perform, and conduct from the harpsichord, in works from the eighteenth through twentieth centuries. But neither project came to fruition. In 1972, Felix Schmidt, music editor of *Der Spiegel*, proposed a "relaxed and conversational" documentary for Südwestfunk, in Baden-Baden. It was to offer a portrait of Gould's personality and musical imagination, including performances, interviews, and behind-the-scenes footage, with (as Gould insisted) no hint of the sort of "proscenium-arch psychology" that "turns television-films into concerts with pictures." Plans were made for filming in Toronto, Wawa, and New York, in spring 1973, but Gould backed out, citing "labyrinthitis" and other medical problems, though the real issue was money: Schmidt wanted to sign him for a flat fee, while Gould sought remuneration for reruns and international distribution.

Wilford, as hoped, was opening many doors in the world of mass media, but Gould, reluctant to leave the house and making strict artistic and financial demands, was letting lucrative, high-profile projects slip away. Meanwhile, he still had a home at the CBC – though he hardly needed the most powerful manager in the business for that. In fall 1974, he created a ten-week radio series to celebrate the centenary of the birth of Arnold Schoenberg, his most comprehensive exploration ever of the composer's life and music (his scripts amount to a small book on the subject). The series culminated, on November 19, with the premiere of his latest documentary, *Schoenberg: The First Hundred Years – A Documentary*

Fantasy. Long dissatisfied with his more conventional, more "linear" 1962 documentary on Schoenberg, he now crafted a subtler, more fluid *mélange* of music and interviews according to the principles of "contrapuntal radio." The Casals and Schoenberg documentaries were the first projects completed under the terms of a new contract he made with the CBC to reflect the growing sophistication of his work as a broadcaster, and his by now excessive demands on the Corporation's time and facilities. He was now making recordings in Toronto with his own equipment, and felt he would be better off making radio programs, too, under his own auspices. In 1973, with *The Quiet in the Land* still in production, he signed an agreement that called for him to produce one major documentary per year from 1974 through 1978,* for which he could use the CBC's facilities to collect raw material but would do post-production work in his own studio with his own technicians, then deliver a finished program to the CBC. Once again his fee hardly covered his labour, but he now had unprecedented creative freedom.

Gould's CBC television projects, too, were becoming more ambitious. In 1973, he conceived a set of programs for the series *Musicamera*, each one dealing with musical developments in a particular decade of the twentieth century. There were to be seven programs in all, under the collective title *Music in Our Time*, though only four were made: "The Age of Ecstasy, 1900–1910" (1974); "The Flight from Order, 1910–1920" (1975); "New Faces, Old Forms, 1920–1930" (1975); and "The Artist as Artisan, 1930–1940" (1977). The series allowed Gould to proselytize on behalf of some favourite composers, to offer new interpretations of works he had already recorded, like Berg's Sonata, and to play all sorts of solo,

---

* In December 1975 he also completed a short documentary on Ernst Krenek for the BBC radio series *Music Weekly*, in which he read a text based on his recently published review of Krenek's book *Horizons Circled*. He considered this documentary relatively accessible but it was still not what the BBC had expected: they found his counterpoint of text and music difficult to follow. Gould refused to allow it to be remixed, so it never aired.

vocal, and chamber music for the first time in public.* The mandate of the series required that he participate in performances of uncharacteristic repertoire, including, despite his "general francophobia," Debussy's *Première rapsodie*, with the clarinetist James Campbell, Poulenc's "choreographic concerto" *Aubade*, and what he called "my transcription of Ravel's transcription" of *La Valse*, a tour de force in which he restored many of the orchestral details Ravel had purposely left out of his solo-piano arrangement. And in staged excerpts from Walton's satirical *Façade*, Gould hammed it up in costume as a dotty Englishman and an incomprehensible Scot. Each program featured his own commentary, which, though mostly concise and accessible, was sometimes flippant and tart. (He described Stravinsky's *Soldier's Tale* as a "jazz-age *Dr. Faustus*" with "a sort of 'I'll Take You Home Again, Kathleen' sub-plot," and compared the composer's complex rhythms to "Josquin Des Prez rescored for *Sesame Street*.") Technically the series was adventurous – swirling "light sculptures" formed a backdrop to music by Scriabin, for instance – and Gould was closely involved with the production at every stage.

He was now outgrowing the editing facilities he had rented since the mid-sixties, and anyway was required to vacate them in 1976 when Film House reorganized its rental space. He found new digs at the Inn on the Park, a posh hotel then in the Four Seasons chain ("obviously for capitalists," as one of Margaret Atwood's characters quipped), located at 1100 Eglinton Avenue East, in nearby Don

---

* In preparing to join in Webern's Concerto, Op. 24, Gould studied and memorized the whole score – all nine parts, not just the piano part – and even wrote out his own piano reduction of it. But as the taping drew near he discovered that he had to do some extra practising in order to isolate the piano part – he had studied the score too well. Bruno Monsaingeon recalled hearing Gould play through the concerto twice, the first time in his reduction of the whole score, the second time playing only the piano part while singing the other parts as best he could. Both times he played from memory – testimony to the extraordinary, computer-like facility of his brain. Monsaingeon also heard Gould play a movement from a Mendelssohn string quartet by memory after hearing it once on the radio.

Mills. (He loved the anonymity of the suburbs.) In September 1976, he leased a four-hundred-square-foot suite there, No. 215, and would maintain it as his studio for the rest of his life. Situated on the ground floor away from the busy parts of the hotel, and close to a side entrance adjoining the parking lot, the suite was private; moreover, the hotel offered round-the-clock room service. (A typical month's room-service tab, which he noted down in January 1980: $1,173.40.) The hotel was close to several parks and creeks and the West Don River, providing Gould with welcome proximity to natural settings. "I made a point of not interfering with his stays at the hotel," recalls Isadore Sharp, the founder, chairman, and CEO of Four Seasons Hotels and Resorts. "He enjoyed being at the Inn because the staff respected his privacy." Indeed, the front desk would not even admit that he was a guest. He, in turn, was considerate and friendly with the staff, and is still remembered fondly there by veteran employees. The hotel became his second home – he sometimes slept there, in another room – though from the mid-seventies on he was also staying from time to time at the Hampton Court Hotel at 415 Jarvis Street, near the CBC studios. There he had found a precious, elusive commodity: a mattress that pampered his aching back.

"The French nation has known worse crises than my absence."

In 1965, in a record shop in Moscow, a young Parisian violinist named Bruno Monsaingeon discovered, for the first time, an album by Glenn Gould, whose name he only vaguely recognized. Listening to that record – the Melodiya release of Gould's 1957 Vienna performance of Bach's Three-Part Sinfonias – he had what he likened to a religious experience: he heard a voice that said to him, "Come and follow me." Six years later – by which time he had some experience making music programs for the Office de radiodiffusion-télévision française (ORTF) and had his own ideas about music on television – he wrote to Gould to solicit his co-operation in a projected series of programs featuring "great personalities" of music. Gould agreed to meet him in Toronto, in July 1972, and afterwards told him, "I would feel very comfortable making films with you." Monsaingeon would be one of his closest colleagues and most devoted champions through the last decade of Gould's life.

By the end of 1972 they were hammering out details for a series of four films to be broadcast as part of the ORTF series *Chemins de la musique*. Monsaingeon offered what Gould wanted: control over content, which meant an uncritical portrait; discussion of serious musical issues in addition to filmed performances; high technical and artistic standards; filming in Toronto, on a generous schedule; and a satisfactory financial deal, a fee of $12,000 plus rights covering broadcast and distribution in other countries. Originally scheduled for fall 1973 but postponed after Gould reported shoulder problems, the films were shot in six weeks in January and February 1974, with a French crew, in the studio of Robert Lawrence Productions as well as at Eaton Auditorium and the CBC, and edited in Paris. The series aired in France in November and December 1974, and garnered a great deal of attention. (It helped that there was a television strike in France and nothing else to watch.) Gould had never given a concert in France, and was not especially well known there, but Monsaingeon's films won him a new and lasting reputation; even CBS was surprised at how sales of his records, including a special album featuring music used in the films, took off in France after the broadcasts.

Running about two and a half hours in total, the films offer a thoughtful synthesis of Gould's ideas and present him in a winning light. For one thing, he is refreshingly unscripted: the wide-ranging subject matter of the interview segments was plotted out in advance, but the actual conversations were conducted impromptu and edited together from multiple takes. (Gould had actually considered reading lines in French from a teleprompter.) The film is visually stark, though appropriately Gouldian – conversations and performances take place against a plain white background – and among the performances, which range from Byrd and Gibbons to Wagner and

Webern, are new, highly subjective readings of Bach's E-minor partita and Berg's Sonata. The second episode, "L'Alchimiste," offers a staged portrait of Gould at work in the studio. In one sequence, the CBC producer James Kent, who had some acting experience, plays Gould's record producer during a mock-recording of Bach's A-major English Suite, which Gould had recorded and edited for real some months before; at one point Gould makes a finger slip intentionally in order to force a retake. (Andrew Kazdin was offended at not having been asked to portray himself, but Gould liked to keep his real working life out of the public eye.) In another sequence, he makes a multi-track recording of Scriabin's Two Pieces, Op. 57, then "conducts" Lorne Tulk during a playback in order to convey instructions for a provisional "acoustic orchestration."

The Germans did not lose interest in Gould. Felix Schmidt found backing for his proposed television portrait from a company amenable to Gould's financial demands: Beta Film, a subsidiary of the Munich-based conglomerate Unitel. Filming was scheduled for fall 1975, then postponed at least twice before being abandoned in 1976. Gould's papers reveal his mounting displeasure with Schmidt's "apparently incurable bent towards sensationalising his subject matter." Schmidt wanted to include segments on Gould's youth, family, and lifestyle, including scenes filmed in his apartment, but Gould scorned the autobiographical approach. At the same time, Karajan wanted to make films with Gould during the Berlin Philharmonic's American tour in the fall of 1976, but despite good intentions the negotiations failed, and failed again when the orchestra returned to North America two years later. Gould was simply unwilling to accept the economics of recording with a major orchestra: he refused to tape more than ten or at most fifteen minutes of music per day.*

---

* As his papers reveal, his German film projects might have included, in addition to his usual repertoire, several of Bach's Brandenburg Concertos, Haydn's D-major concerto, Beethoven's "Les Adieux" Sonata, Fauré's *Ballade*, Berg's Chamber Concerto, and Hindemith's *Kammermusik* No. 2.

But there was still Bruno Monsaingeon. The weeks spent filming for the ORTF, Gould told him, had been "among the happiest of my professional life," and even while those films were in production they were already planning to work together again, with the music of Bach as their subject. They discussed a project related to *The Well-Tempered Clavier*, but by 1976 they had settled on a series of five programs featuring performances linked by historical and analytical commentary, this time to be shot on videotape rather than film. Toward the end of that year, Gould began to plot out the programs, and by mid-1977 he had settled on his topics: fugue, chamber music, suite, concerto, and variations. (He considered but rejected a program on the early and improvisational Bach, the sides of Bach that interested him least.) Monsaingeon now had support from Metronom, a film and television production company in Munich, and Gould secured a good financial deal. Originally thinking of making one film per year, he eventually came up with a very ambitious schedule calling for completion of all five between 1978 and 1980. As it turned out, the Bach series was delayed by what he called an "inflammatory neck condition" but what was, in fact, a far more serious problem.

"Fingers don't have much to do with playing the piano."

Arthur Rubinstein was once asked on television what he would wish for if he were given a second chance at life; he replied, "to be born with Glenn Gould's hands." Gould was born with good hands for the piano, to be sure: his fingers, even the weaker ones, were unusually long, flexible, and strong. (They were graceful and beautiful, too.) But as we have already seen, his hands were a source of pain and anxiety. Even as a toddler he shielded them from potential injury; as an adult he claimed they were unusually sensitive to cold air and damp, that the circulation in them was poor, that he was prone to all sorts of pain, stiffness, and swelling. He frequently swaddled and rubbed and soaked his hands, and tried a succession of pills and therapies, including dipping them in melted paraffin wax ("makes me feel that I have new hands"). Some of this was neurotic: the hand-soaking, for instance, was so ingrained a habit that, as Margaret Pacsu recalled, he immersed them until they were red before recording interview segments for the *Silver Jubilee Album*, even though he did not have to touch a piano. But there is no question that he had real, persistent problems with his hands – increasingly so, even though he practised and performed less and less with age. Among his notepads from the mid-seventies are references to recurring pain and stiffness in both hands and wrists; "sleepiness" in some fingers of the right hand while lying down or propped up; sharp pains when pushing himself out of a chair; pain in some finger joints, especially on waking or when making certain movements (he thought his anti-hypertensive medications might be to blame); and unexplained problems like "knuckle 'bumps'" and "snapping-straining syndrome." By spring 1977 he was experiencing what he considered serious and potentially crippling problems at the keyboard.

"History: Lack of coordination was first noticed in second w[ee]k of June" – so begins a long, two-part diary devoted to these problems that Gould started in late September 1977 and kept for almost ten months.* In the first entry, he discusses a taping session for the fourth instalment of *Music in Our Time*:

> During 2nd TV taping (first w[ee]k of June) lack of co-ordination was imm[ediately] apparent. Opening theme of Casella was unbalanced – notes appeared to stick and scale-like passages were uneven and uncontrolled. Prok[ofiev] suffered similarly, though

---

* The first part of the diary is ninety pages long, and begins with a twelve-page undated entry (from after mid-September 1977, according to internal evidence) followed by entries dated September 23, 1977, through January 30, 1978. This part is headed only with the initials "p. p." – perhaps meaning "pressure point," a term (unexplained) that Gould used in some later notepads to refer to some particular musculoskeletal problem. The second part of the diary is seventy-two pages long, includes entries dated January 30 through July 12, 1978, and is headed "B[OO]K II."

at this period, problem appeared prim[arily] in dyn[amically] restrained passages. An unpleasant experience, and seemingly immune to solution by ad hoc pressures (thumb indents) etc.

During next 2 w[ee]ks, which separated 2nd taping and commentary, problems increased. It was no longer poss[ible] to play even [a] Bach chorale securely. Parts were unbalanced, progression from note to note insecure. All attempts to apply thumb indents as stabilizers failed; among other symptoms was inability to articulate chords without arpegg[iation] and to control even those chords at any but the most minimal dynamic levels.

Imm[ediately] following commentary taping, a summer-long series of practice experiments began. These freq[uently] involved sessions of 2, 3, or even more, hours.

The "practice experiments" continued for at least a full year, as Gould tried vainly to restore what he felt he had lost: the "extraordinary naturalness, ease, and spontaneity" of his piano technique, which he had always taken for granted. The diary, alas, is rife with idiosyncratic terminology that is often impossible to understand; even the doctors who have studied it, some of them specialists in the medical problems of performing artists, have been stymied by Gould's vocabulary. ("Thumb indents," for instance – does he mean flexed thumbs?) What is clear, however, is Gould's belief that the perfect alignment and co-ordination of his performing mechanism was now compromised.

The diary documents, in exhaustive detail, practice sessions in which he analyzed every part of his performing mechanism – seat, lower and upper back, shoulders, upper arms, elbows, forearms, wrists, hands, fingers – as well as adjoining parts like the neck, head, and chest, and then attempted, by manipulating those parts singly and in combinations, to recover the "gleaming, lustrous sound" that he defined as "the sound of control" – all the time recording the resulting sensations in his diary. He tried everything he could think of: changing the body's centre of gravity this way and that; experimenting with the curvature of the spine; "collapsing" into the keyboard; trying new positions and movements of the neck and shoulders; steadying the elbows; elevating the wrists; facial grimacing; wrinkling and unwrinkling the brow; staring at sheet music. Some experiments were remarkably focused: the diary includes references to "'drooping neck' syndrome," "shoulder-blade protrusion," "arm-pit extension," "thumb-web control." Throughout, there are announcements of new insight and imminent success – on April 8, 1978, for instance, he determined "that *the* common denominator in *all* these problems (famous last words?) was the lack of *constancy* in shoulder elevation" – but no solution proved satisfactory for long.

What he had lost, it emerges from the diary, was psychological as much as physical. Playing the piano had always come to Gould as naturally as breathing; the process of translating musical ideas into physical acts had never been a problem for him. But he could not explain how he did what he did at the piano: his brilliant technique was largely a mystery to him. Though he prized reason in most things, he was compelled to retain an almost mystical faith in his gifts, and did not want to risk jinxing them. He did not like to reflect consciously on technical matters, which is why pianistic shop talk made him anxious, why he did not practise scales or exercises or write fingerings into his scores, why he so obsessively sought a piano action of the utmost responsiveness. "I don't want to think too much about my playing," he told Jock Carroll, in 1956, "or I'll get like that centipede who was asked which foot he moved first and became paralysed, just thinking about it."

Once, when he *did* talk about his playing, Andrew Kazdin recalled, he said that "when he played, he kept a mental image of every key on the piano – not only where each note was, but how it would feel to reach for it and touch it. Once that process (strictly mental) had been accomplished, it was a rather simple matter actually to strike the key with the desired force. In this way, he held the concept of technique to include both parts of the process – the mental preparation and the physical execution." Another of his specific mental images, he said, was of producing tones not by pushing the keys down but by *pulling them up* – physically impossible, but psychologically significant considering his reluctance to treat the piano as a percussion instrument. Another image, obviously a legacy from Alberto Guerrero, was of the forearms extending back beyond the spine, thus bypassing the upper arms and shoulders. In his diary he revealed yet another image: "The motto 'still point of the turning world' defines it, and was used sotto voce many times. It related to the revelation (?) that fingers, ideally, should not be required to move – only, so to speak, to 'be there' – and that all other adjustments should be accommodated by body-adjustments." It was the sustaining mental imagery that was apparently lost in 1977: as he told John Roberts, his hands had become "out of sync" with his mind. His year-long experimentation at the keyboard was a search for the mental imagery of a fully co-ordinated playing mechanism, and his diary reveals that he often undertook a practice session only after spending several days away from the piano thinking about that imagery. (Here is an explanation for his claim, repeated to various interviewers over the years, that he played better after being away from the piano for a time.)

The neurologist Frank R. Wilson, medical director of the Peter F. Ostwald Health Program for Performing Artists at the University of California at San Francisco, published an article in 2000 in which he defended the startling thesis "that in biomechanical terms Gould may have been almost completely unsuited for a career at the piano" – meaning that the innate structure of his hands put him biomechanically at risk for a repetitive-strain disorder like "focal dystonia" (occupational cramp). Wilson found some compelling evidence in Gould's diary and in his photos and filmed performances. He observed, for instance, that when his middle and ring fingers rested side by side, the fingertips would converge and sometimes even overlap, and he noted that those two fingers rarely separated laterally at the keyboard – both of which are traits common to performers with focal dystonia.

Wilson's research implies that Gould's musical predilections might have been allied to the physiology of his hands – that, for instance, he might have avoided Romantic music demanding much lateral stretching of the hands for instinctive physical reasons as well as musical ones. One should not be too reductive about this: Gould's aesthetic and moral disdain for, say, the music of Liszt did not merely rationalize an inability to play it. There is enough evidence to show that he could have played any piece of piano music to which he applied himself – he did, after all, leave a note-perfect (if tepid) recording of Scriabin's Fifth Sonata, which Sviatoslav Richter nominated as the most difficult piece in the whole piano repertoire.* And there is the testimony of colleagues like Jaime Laredo, who recalled that he was open-mouthed as he listened to Gould play transcriptions between takes in their recording sessions; he thought Gould's technique superior to that of *any* other pianist. "He really did have a magnificent technique," Charles Rosen said. "He could have developed terrific octaves quite easily if he'd wanted to. He just didn't want to." In an interoffice memo from 1981, a Steinway and Sons employee referred to Gould as the one pianist of his generation with "complete tonal command" – comparable to Horowitz – and more than one critic and fellow-musician considered his technique to have been perfect, perhaps the greatest of the age.

Still, to acknowledge that Gould could have played Chopin's études or Liszt's B-minor sonata or the Rachmaninov Third does not mean that he was physically (never mind temperamentally) suited to making a career of such music. His recordings show that he was not at home here. Significantly, whenever he had to perform a piece that demanded great bravura, like Beethoven's "Appassionata" or "Hammerklavier" sonata, Brahms's D-minor concerto, or Scriabin's Fifth, he always managed to find a musical or moral rationale for undercutting its virtuosity. He might, for instance, claim to seek a "symphonic" or "architectural" approach, to put "continuity" before

---

* Pianists can still take heart, though: Andrew Kazdin's log for the Scriabin recording shows more than a dozen takes and inserts devoted to the sonata's knuckle-busting closing pages. Among Gould's private audio tapes in the National Library of Canada is an amusing one, from the early fifties, in which he breaks off practising in the middle of one of the most difficult bravura passages of Strauss's *Burleske*, wearily sighs "Oh, my!" and shuffles away from the piano.

"contrast," but whatever the rationale, the result was always a slower-than-usual tempo and a general broadening and smoothing out of the music: uncharacteristic over-pedalling, for instance, in the angular first movement of the "Hammerklavier," and even in the fugal finale; and moderately paced, measured realizations of the punishing octave trills in the Brahms concerto. In such cases, Gould's musical choices may well have been partly, subconsciously, motivated by an instinct to protect hands that were not ideally suited to the demands of such music. It does not belittle his musical ideas and interpretations to suggest that his aesthetic system fitted his physiology; in fact, only a perfect symbiosis of physical and mental proclivities can really explain his extraordinarily high level of achievement as a pianist.

If Wilson's biomechanical analysis of Gould's hands is correct, then Gould, had he played works like the Brahms D-minor and the Scriabin Fifth in concert a hundred times a year, might indeed have ended up debilitated by focal dystonia, the condition that derailed the careers of the American pianists Leon Fleisher and Gary Graffman. But it is difficult to believe that was Gould's problem in 1977–78, when he was recording at most a couple of times per month and practising very little – hardly overusing his hands. Focal dystonia, moreover, once established, normally worsens as one continues playing, but there is no evidence that Gould's problem worsened through the year documented in his diary. Wilson offers only the somewhat contrived conclusion that if Gould did have focal dystonia "his subsequent return to the recording studio would represent an unprecedented example of a musician's recovery (or partial recovery) from that disorder through retraining."

So why *did* he suddenly begin obsessing about his hands in 1977? First, we need to ask whether Gould, the anxiety revealed by his diary notwithstanding, even *had* a major new physical problem at all. What exactly did he mean when he reported "instability" and "unevenness" and "lack of control" in his playing? Was he really, as he seems to imply, suddenly playing poorly, or was he detecting problems so minuscule that no one but he would ever have noticed them? Was his "insecure" rendering of that Bach chorale in fact a performance that any of his colleagues would kill to give? There appear to be no recordings of his practice sessions in 1977–78, so we will probably never know for sure. But considering his reluctance to accept anything less than perfection in his playing, it is entirely possible he was set on his year-long quest by perceived problems that would have been undetectable to any other ears. It is worth emphasizing that in the few years before the period of the diary Gould was doing some of the most controlled and subtle and inspired playing of his career – in, for instance, Bach's English Suites and Hindemith's sonatas, in the Wagner and Sibelius albums, in Bach sonatas with Leonard Rose and Jaime Laredo, in the first set of films with Bruno Monsaingeon. ("He never played a wrong note," Laredo recalled of their sessions together.) And after he resumed recording in spring 1979, he continued to give great performances – in Monsaingeon's Bach films, in sonatas by Haydn and Beethoven and Strauss. There are Bach recordings from his last years in which his control of touch and tone is so immaculate as to be almost superhuman.

It is possible the problems were side effects of medication, which in the mid-seventies he was taking in increasing amounts and varying combinations. One can detect a slight tremor in his hands at times in the Bach films, particularly in his 1981 film of the Goldberg Variations – presumably evidence of over-medication. Perhaps more likely is that the experiments of 1977–78 were but another, though extreme, manifestation of Gould's tendency to exaggerate and pathologize every passing bodily sensation he could not benignly explain. If this is so, then the motivation for the experiments might have been nothing more medically profound than middle age. Gould was just about to turn forty-five when he began keeping the diary, typically an age at which a professional pianist is at or just past his technical prime. Certainly his body was middle-aged in other respects in the mid-seventies: he had hypertension; he had more discomfort and less stamina in recording sessions when it came to his back shoulders, and arms, as Verne Edquist noticed; he had been prescribed reading glasses. But if Gould did notice one day in 1977 that his playing was only 99 per cent of what it had been, he wasn't likely to conclude (let alone *accept*) that something as natural and routine as middle-age decline was the culprit.

Gould thought he was exploring the problem rationally, objectively. In the diary he records his experiments using the passive voice ("During mid-summer, much effort was directed to the hand knuckles"; "experiments with elevated wrist were tried") and referring to himself in the third person, as "the writer" – only gradually does he begin to use the first-person singular. But his insight into the human body was negligible, as the doctors who have studied the diary have confirmed. For all his pseudo-scientific jargon and attempted objectivity, his experiments, doomed to fail, succeeded only in making him increasingly anxious about his continuing problems. Indeed the experiments themselves may have been the problem. Whatever the source of the physical insecurity Gould initially perceived – focal dystonia, medication, middle age – he was forced to do precisely what he always tried to avoid doing: think about technique. (Within the diary itself are some notes suggesting that he had more success when he was concentrating on the music than when he was concentrating on his body.) "Part of the secret in playing the piano is to separate yourself from the instrument in every possible way," he said in 1981. "I have to find a way of standing outside myself while at the same time being totally committed to what I'm doing." He meant that he could not afford to get caught up in the physical minutiae of playing, but had to focus his attention at a higher level, on the imagery underlying his approach to the keyboard. Getting caught up in the physical minutiae of playing is precisely what he did in his diary, however, and once begun, the process snowballed. As he had always feared, he became the centipede.

The diary includes vague references to other "times of crises" in Gould's career: 1957 (in Russia), 1959 (on tour), 1965, 1966, May 1967, and 1969. These, presumably, were other periods in which his hands and mind were "out of sync," yet they were some of his busiest years as a concert and recording artist, and nothing in his body of work in those years hints at anything that could be called a crisis in his playing. Whatever problems he perceived at those times, they did not lay him up, perhaps because his schedule did not allow him to give in to obsessive worry and experimentation. An anecdote from the conductor Boris Brott is revealing. One day during taping of the third *Music in Our Time* program, in 1975, Gould watched the proceedings while sitting on the floor propped up on his hands. Unaware of where Gould was, Brott stepped backwards at one point and felt his heel land, lightly but unmistakably, on "something squishy." Gould let out a cry and blanched, and the room went dead quiet, but then the pianist who had fretted over his precious hands since infancy merely shook the afflicted hand, smiled, and said, "It's all right. Don't worry." Had someone stepped on Gould's hand, say, at home, at a time when he had no recordings or broadcasts pending, the incident might have launched him into days or weeks of hypochondriacal panic. But in the midst of a complicated taping session for a major program involving expensive facilities and many artists and technicians, he simply did not have the luxury – and was not prima donna enough – to indulge his hypochondria.

In 1977, however, he could. At the end of March, Eaton Auditorium was closed for extensive renovations. Gould recorded prolifically in January, February, and March that year, knowing that he would be shut out of the hall for at least twelve months. It was precisely in spring 1977 that he became aware of problems with his playing, which raises the question: did the loss of Eaton Auditorium and the hiatus in his recording give him "permission" to let his anxieties about his hands run riot? Frankly, that sounds like Gould. And just as the onset of the problems was convenient, so was their mysterious disappearance (the diary simply peters out without solution). When the hall became available to him again, in May 1979, he was ready to resume recording, with Bach's G-major and C-minor toccatas.* Perhaps, in the end, he simply cut the Gordian knot – became aware that he was creating rather than solving a problem, stopped

---

* He actually resumed recording on April 23, on which date he recorded two of Strauss's Op. 3 pieces (Nos. 1 and 3) at St. Lawrence Hall, in downtown Toronto.

experimenting and diarizing, and found his technique right where he had left it.

According to Wilson, Gould's later films do show some changes in his hands. In the film of the Goldberg Variations, in particular, Wilson observed frequent curling of the fourth and fifth fingers, typical of pianists with focal dystonia, and noted occasional strain in execution. And a CBC production assistant noticed that Gould seemed to have problems with dexterity while making *The Question of Instrument*. Nevertheless, Gould did not live long enough to come close to losing his fabled technique. But even 99 per cent of potential was not good enough for him, and if he did perceive some small decline in his powers in middle age it would certainly explain his decision to bring his performing career to a halt by his early fifties. He was not the kind of performer able to allow himself to age gracefully in public; he was only willing to be heard at his best, and would have found any decline in his technique traumatic. Gould had always insisted that "one does not play the piano with one's fingers, one plays the piano with one's mind," that "fingers don't have much to do with playing the piano." Yet the spectre of even a slight decline in the piano technique he took for granted threw him into a year-long panic. Fingers may not have much to do with playing the piano but, as even Gould realized, they help.

"Father and Vera have been up to some new tricks."

On July 26, 1975, Florence Gould died of a stroke. She was eighty-three years old and had suffered from failing health, including hypertension, for some time. She was stricken just as Bert was arriving home one evening, and succumbed after several days in a coma, during which time Gould desperately sought advice from friends like Joseph Stephens. Publicly, his response to his mother's death was restrained, dignified; he kept a tight rein on his emotions. There was a brief hiatus in his work, but by early September he had resumed his correspondence and was back in the recording studio.

("The reaction to pain, to suffering, is such a personal thing," he once wrote; "it does not necessarily entail the dissipation of order. It can be depicted by an attempt to invoke an artistic order to compensate distress.") He spoke about his mother's death only to close friends, who saw the pain that he would not expose in public. "He was really devastated by her death," Jessie Greig recalled. "It was a very traumatic experience for him." She added that Gould came to appreciate only after his mother's death how much his parents had done for him. Lorne Tulk saw him in tears: "That was the only time ever I saw him in a state where he wasn't really thinking." His grief was exacerbated by guilt, for despite his fear and concern after his mother suffered her stroke he could not, as he told Tulk, overcome his anxiety and visit her in the hospital, a failure that haunted him.

Peter Ostwald and others have suggested that Gould's problems at the piano in 1977–78 might have been a delayed reaction to the loss of his mother, his first piano teacher, though the timing and circumstances of those problems do not make this connection convincing, and the theory exaggerates the degree to which the adult Gould was psychologically tied to his mother. Still, Florence was his first and greatest champion, and he never stopped sharing his triumphs and travails with her or seeking her approval. He continued to see his parents from time to time as an adult, and spoke to his mother on the phone (he shared his reviews with her). That relationship was intensely private and is little documented, but was certainly among the closest and most important of Gould's life. He dreamed often about his mother after she died, and in some of those dreams she looked down on him from the hereafter. Her death was a watershed in his life; it made him more introspective in his last years, more aware of his own mortality.

It also drew him closer to the Greig side of his family, especially to Jessie, who became, in his last years, almost a surrogate for his mother. Now it was Jessie whom he would call in order to read his latest reviews, always asking, "Now who would have enjoyed this?" – meaning his mother. "Over the years Glenn and I became closer and the phone calls became almost daily," Jessie wrote. "They even followed me to my summer retreats." Gould began to visit her more often at home in Oshawa, too. After his mother's death, he told Jessie, he came to know for the first time what the loving support of a family could mean. He developed a renewed interest in his mother's genealogy and in the whole Greig-Grieg connection, and with Jessie's help compiled a large file on the subject, which included the 1952 booklet *Grieg and his Scottish Ancestry*, by J. Russell Greig. Through Jessie he now kept up on news of various branches of the Greigs.

Gould had no such interest in the Gold side of his family. In the wake of his mother's death he had been deeply concerned about and solicitous toward Bert, who took his wife's death hard, but Gould's relationship with his father became irrevocably strained in his last years. In the late seventies, Bert became involved with Vera Dobson (1909–99), the widow of one of his cousins and long a friend of the family. Vera was clearly good for Bert, but Gould and Jessie were both deeply disturbed by the relationship, even though Gould himself had earlier said that Bert needed someone to look after him (Gould knew that *he* could not do it). When the couple announced in 1979 that they planned to marry, a schism developed within the family. One of Gould's notepads, from early summer 1979, includes three pages in which he sought to organize his thoughts in preparation for a confrontation with his father:

(1)
– hope I'm not speaking out of turn
– If I am, say so, and I'll break off imm[ediately]
– have kept silent till now
– re socializing activities
– [added later in margin] don't mean it as advice; really; just as a comment.
– which does not mean that I have not observed things
(2)
– must tell you, I find it *out of char*[acter]

– which may repres[ent] nothing other than my ability to assess char[acter] [read "inability"?]
(re Vera) – obv[iously] an energetic lady, trem[endously] so for her age; (theatres, and parties and what not etc)
– and I notice a trem[endous] diff[erence] in you in that respect; Greece trip as opposed to other times

(3)

– my point is that I'm not sure it's *approp[riate]* for a person of your age to change their spots so radically, if indeed, that's what you're doing
– (but) you do seem to take on a similar kind of *manic activity*, and I think, at your age, one should be *reducing* not *accel[erating]* the *pace of one's life*.

(4)

– all love relationships are *addictive* – just as much so as *alcohol* or *tobacco*.
– one dev[elops] what one thinks of as an *intense* need to be *with* a *partic[ular] person*, to *translate* all your *activity*, *everything* that you *do* in the course of a *day*, for ex[ample], and, while that may be a *fasc[inating] exercise in com[munication?]*, it's also *exhausting* and it has one other, g[rea]t *disadv[antage] to wit* – that it distracts you from contemp[lation], from looking inward. [added later:] , to really meditate upon the shape of your life – one doesn't do that, because one thinks one is starting one's life.

(5)

– at *your age*, at *any age*, that's *what one should be doing, in my opinion* [i.e., "looking inward"].
– And that's why *late marriages*, such as *Uncle Willard's*, for ex[ample], *very seldom work*: when *you've* been *married* to *somebody* for a *long time*, the *communication* aspect *changes*, and a more normal pattern emerges, but when a *relationship* is *new* there's a much g[rea]ter *intensity*, and the best [?] engines are overtaxed comparatively. (Reprise re Greece if necc[essary])

(6)
– (?) Now, I just hope you know what you're doing.

Clearly Gould assumed that everyone must find intense new relationships as potentially disturbing and overwhelming as he did. With Jessie feeding him the family gossip, he formed an image of Bert being dominated and changed by a more extroverted woman. In his 1980 diary he reported one story in which Bert arrived at someone's house *wearing a red sweater*, and another in which Bert has cuffs removed from a pair of trousers – "Vera's orders, app[arently]." This was Gould's idea of immodest behaviour in need of correction. His concern about Bert's health and lifestyle and propriety obviously disguised bitterness and even a kind of panic at the perceived betrayal of his late mother. As the wedding loomed, Gould made many anxious attempts to formulate a letter to his father, including this politely disapproving one, on December 2, 1979:

> Dear Father:
> I've had an opportunity to give some thought to the matter of your wedding and specifically to the invitation to serve as your 'best man'. I'm sure that, under the circumstances, you would prefer to arrange a private service – one in which any such conventional ceremonial gesture would be inappropriate; in any case, while I appreciate your kindness in extending the invitation, I regret that I must decline.
> Needless to say, I wish you every happiness, and I would ask you to pass on my good wishes to Mrs. Dobson.
> Love,
> Glenn

In another draft, in January 1980, Gould crossed out "Love" and replaced it with "Sincerely." Finally, convinced that any such letter would be hurtful, Gould telephoned his regrets instead, and was greatly relieved when the matter was behind him.

Gould and his father never had a particularly warm relationship.

"I am very proud of you and the work you are doing," Bert wrote during his son's trip to Russia in 1957. "Every thinking Canadian has reason to thank you. Your music may have a very real part in establishing a better feeling between east and west. We do hope and pray that it will, and that it will bring new hope and faith to a people to whom music has been a very real part of their lives for generations." That reads more like best wishes from the Kiwanis Club than a thumbs-up from Dad, but then Gould's relations with his father were always somewhat distant and formal. His classically Oedipal closeness to his mother during childhood may have been a sore spot, a source of accumulated tension or hostility; Bert's "betrayal" of Florence after her death certainly seems to have brought long-simmering resentment to the surface. It did not help that Gould, like Jessie, believed that when Bert sold the beloved cottage on Lake Simcoe in early 1975, he hastened Florence's death.

Gould's notepads from 1979 and 1980 include many references to family troubles. The marriage was the subject of much discussion within the family, and Gould and Jessie would commiserate (and swap blood-pressure readings) after one of them had had a family encounter. Jessie's relations with Bert also became strained. She and Gould were worried and hurt by what they perceived as changes in Bert's personality, and it shows in the petty complaints Gould confided to his friends and to his papers. One day the couple is "on their best behaviour," the next they are engaged in their "latest mischief." In Uxbridge they are "enlisting" the family's support for their cause, while back in the Beach they are taking "vengeance" against Jessie and have "dropped" and "banished" the loyal housekeeper Elsie, who had somehow given offence. Gould begins referring to Bert as "his nibs," records evidence of his "changed spots," remarks that he "is really quite unhinged," refuses to answer the door when he hears Bert's knock (his "unmistakable calling-card"), even laments – on the basis of one sherry – that Bert is now drinking.

Bert and Vera were married in Don Mills on January 19, 1980. Gould did not attend. After the wedding Bert sold the house on Southwood Drive and moved into Vera's house at 61 Norden

Crescent, in Don Mills, just north of the Inn on the Park. As he packed up the old house, he put aside Gould's mementoes, which Ray Roberts picked up in batches – at one point he told his son gruffly to "get your man down to the house tomorrow." Vera attempted to keep peace within the family after the wedding, and welcomed Gould to visit them at home, but the polite letters about the couple's new life and the cheery postcards from their winter holidays in Florida, especially when signed "Vera B. Gould," must have further rankled. (Bert invited him to visit them in Florida, to enjoy the beautiful, sunny weather. Did he really know that little about his own son?) Gould clearly did not like Vera. He resented her lack of reserve, her efforts to become a second mother to him, her attempts to capitalize on his celebrity, her opinion that he was "weird." At least that was the image of Vera he was getting through Jessie, and according to the testimony of people who knew Vera that image was absurd.

Gould's relationship with his father deteriorated so badly that he could report a polite two-minute conversation between them as a real achievement. He jotted down two pages of notes based on a phone call with Jessie, who had just spoken with Bert about Gould's feelings – including this exchange:

> Jessie Greig: He's a really fine, serious, gentle person. You've got to treat him like a man, not a child. If you listen, he's got a great deal to say.
>
> Bert Gould: He's got far too much to say.

Alternately amused and angered by Bert and Vera, Gould eventually had little to do with them, though he never completely severed contact, and never stopped caring about his father's well-being.

"The dawning of a new age."

Had Gould lived longer, the period around his late forties would probably still be viewed as transitional – in some ways traumatic, in others liberating. His last decade was stimulated by relationships old and new, many of which provided both companionship and artistic opportunity. But in his last decade he also experienced major losses that were particularly devastating to someone uncomfortable with change. In addition to his mother, his childhood home and cottage, and to a degree his father, he lost friends and colleagues as well as institutions, places, and objects that had long been important to him.

For one thing, the mutually satisfying relationship with Columbia Records was showing signs of strain. The company was changing. By the mid-sixties it was having serious financial problems: sales of formerly reliable types of popular music – jazz, country, "middle-of-the-road," Broadway cast albums – were fading as folk, protest, and especially rock music accounted for more and more of the record market. In 1966, Clive Davis, who had joined Columbia as a corporate lawyer in 1960 and had, he admitted, "no musical credentials," became president of the company and established a regime focused on the bottom line, where classical music was a duty rather than a passion. The market share of classical music, which had actually grown through Gould's early years with Columbia, was now dropping precipitously, and Davis considered Goddard Lieberson's enlightened philosophy of happily taking a loss on the classics to be an outdated, burdensome luxury. He pushed Columbia to take the same leadership role in rock that it had once taken in classical, jazz, and popular music. By the late sixties, when rock was accounting for more album sales than all other types of music put together, Columbia's profits and market share were exploding thanks to its stellar rock catalogue, and that suited the parent company, CBS, just fine. Through Gould's later years the atmosphere at Columbia, and CBS generally, grew increasingly corporate – a trend neatly symbolized by "Black Rock," the forbidding office tower in midtown Manhattan that became CBS's headquarters in 1965.

Clive Davis was fired from Columbia in 1973 and was briefly replaced by Lieberson, who was brought out of retirement. "His return was like a Greek tragedy," Schuyler Chapin recalled. "He was the last musician to run a record label. The industry had been taken over by bean-counters and lawyers." Not even Lieberson, by this time, could combat what Norman Lebrecht has called "the Coca-Colisation of classical music." Publicly, Gould continued to express gratitude toward the company, but privately he felt increasingly alienated from it. Old friends like Paul Myers were leaving, while the new corporate executives did not give him the support or camaraderie he was used to. ("He was talking to strangers on the telephone," Myers says.) In a draft letter in one of his notepads, from spring 1978, he complained that he was being treated poorly in matters like royalties and marketing compared with other classical musicians, and in his 1980 diary he complained about CBS Masterworks's "insular N[orth] A[merican] philosophy" and about quality-control problems with some of his recent albums. As he celebrated his twenty-fifth anniversary with Columbia in 1980, he noted that only two contract artists had been with the label longer, the pianist Rudolf Serkin and the violinist Isaac Stern, but he felt that his loyalty was not much appreciated. Shortly after signing with Ronald Wilford, in fact, he had contemplated moving to Karajan's label, Deutsche Grammophon, and a decade later he considered following Paul Myers to Decca. But he doubted he could continue to record at home, with the freedom and control he wanted, at a European label, and according to friends he did feel loyalty toward the company that had signed him as an unknown and supported his idiosyncratic demands for years. When the time came, in 1980, to renew his recording contract, he hemmed and hawed but signed, though he confided to his diary that he was determined to let his contract lapse in 1983.

Given these circumstances, Gould considered taking the logical step of producing his own recordings. Since 1964 he had made dozens of albums with Andrew Kazdin, for whose gifts as a producer he had boundless admiration – a view widely shared in the business. (Kazdin holds degrees in both music and engineering.) But as his papers, the recollections of his friends, and Kazdin's memoirs suggest, their personal relationship was not warm, and could be tense when their egos clashed. Kazdin was hurt when a *New York Times* writer, researching a profile of him in 1976, told him she had come away with poor "vibrations" after speaking to Gould, the musician with whom Kazdin had worked the longest, but Gould, by this time, was unhappy with the relationship and seeking some way to bring it to an end. The opportunity came in December 1979, when Kazdin, at the climax of what he called "my own personal crisis" at CBS Masterworks, was fired. (Gould's response, when Kazdin told him, was "Well, congratulations!") They had last worked together in October 1979 on Gould's album of preludes, fughettas, and fugues by Bach, and were scheduled to record again in the last week of December. But just before Christmas, Gould phoned to say that CBS had refused to allow him to work with Kazdin on a free-lance basis; he had either to take a new CBS producer or become his own producer, and had chosen the latter. (This was a fib.) Gould gave him the don't-be-a-stranger line, and quickly terminated the call. "I never heard from him again," Kazdin wrote. "Thus ended our fifteen-year relationship. No regrets, no emotion, no thank-yous."

Gould had long wanted to strike out on his own, and at this point he still had Paul Myers to support this move within the company, but from Kazdin's perspective the break was abrupt and inexplicable, and there was mutual animosity afterward. In Gould's later correspondence there are some sarcastic references to Kazdin, and in his 1980 diary he reported some tense encounters between Kazdin and CBS staff, in part because, he wrote, Kazdin was slow to return a Gould tape. (Concern about various tapes in Kazdin's possession was, according to Myers, the main reason Gould gave for not severing ties with Kazdin earlier than he did.) In anticipation of his return to Eaton Auditorium as his own producer, Gould made several drafts of a speech he presumably intended to read out to his colleagues at the first session, on January 11, 1980. In the speech he sought "to celeb[rate] the coming of a new era – the dawning of a new age – an age which has already been designated by some historians with the initials A.K. – and, by others with the initials A.A.K."

("After Kazdin," obviously – he also referred to this "new era" as the "Fourth Reich.") Kazdin is treated throughout the speech to some not-very-kind ribbing, suggesting that, from Gould's perspective, his departure was a relief.

Gould's first task as producer was to complete his album of preludes, fughettas, and fugues. On this and later recordings at Eaton Auditorium, he worked with various local technicians, particularly Jean Sarrazin, and his sessions now often lasted longer, regularly running as late a four in the morning. Now responsible for all of his post-production work, including the finished master tape, he worked with editors borrowed from the CBC and occasionally from a local studio, billing CBS for the costs. His private papers suggest that he paid a price in anxiety for Kazdin's departure: the technical "gremlins" that plagued his recording sessions were now his responsibility alone to fix; moreover, his various editors in Toronto, though excellent, were not always available when he needed them, nor were they always able to make sense (as Kazdin had) of his idiosyncratic organizational system.

This new independence was spoiled by the threatened loss of another old friend, Eaton Auditorium. In 1977, concerned that the closure of the hall might turn out to be permanent, Gould had made a sound test in the just-completed Leah Posluns Theatre in North York (just north of Toronto), and in the years that followed he made occasional tests in other places: Convocation Hall at the University of Toronto, St. Lawrence Hall, the Orillia Opera House, the studio of the Vanguard Recording Society, in New York, and elsewhere. When he and Kazdin were permitted to return to Eaton Auditorium in spring 1979, they found a dusty, partially gutted, unlit, unheated hall with missing walls, boarded-up doors, no green room or bathroom – and this was *after* some cleanup had been done. They had to rig up a bare light bulb, surround the piano with space heaters, take their bathroom breaks who-knows-where, and Gould often had to play in an overcoat and scarf, but they continued to record there nonetheless, and one can quite easily imagine

Gould working happily in a setting so conspicuously devoid of concert-hall glamour.

In January 1980, however, the company that owned the historic Eaton's building received the city's consent to convert the seventh floor to office space after a market study had shown that the auditorium was unlikely ever to be financially viable again. (The process, however, was stalled, thanks to the lobbying of The Friends of the Eaton Auditorium and other parties, including Gould himself.) Then, in January 1981, he was told that for insurance reasons he could no longer use open-flame propane heaters in the hall. (In his concert days he had once scorched a hotel carpet with his heater.) His last sessions in Eaton Auditorium were in August 1981, when he recorded Beethoven's E-flat-major sonata, Op. 27/No. 1, and Bach's Italian Concerto, and while the hall was still not literally closed to him when he died, he worked throughout his last years under the assumption that its loss might be imminent.*

"My magnum opus is still several drawing boards away."

The 1974 *Music of Today* series on Schoenberg was Gould's last ambitious project created for CBC radio;† thereafter he made only a handful of relatively modest appearances – twice to promote new

---

* After years of lobbying and court battles, Eaton Auditorium and its adjoining Round Room restaurant and other facilities were saved from demolition. The whole seventh floor of College Park (the former Eaton's College Street store) was refurbished at great expense, renamed The Carlu, after the architect who originally designed it, and reopened to the public in May 2003.

† In a 1980 interview, Gould said, "Now I am drafting an idea that I don't really expect to get to work on for a year or so, but at that point I intend to do a radio equivalent of Tallis's sixty-four-voice motet [*laughs*] – but I don't want to say anything more about that, as it will probably jinx the whole project if I do!" Nothing related to such a project seems to survive among his papers.

CBS recordings, once to host the series *Arts National* for a week, tackling subjects ranging from Gibbons to Barbra Streisand.* In December 1981 he made his last appearance on CBC radio, in the series *Booktime*, reading excerpts from *The Three-Cornered World*. As for television, he still hoped to finish the series *Music in Our Time* by 1980 – at which point he could have added an eighth program, on music of the seventies. His papers from the mid-seventies reveal that the fifth, sixth, and seventh programs would have included songs, chamber and orchestral music, ballets, and electronic works by many post-war composers with whom he had never before been associated, and would have include his only performances of non-Canadian music from the post-war period, perhaps including Boulez's Second Sonata (which he considered intellectually intriguing but cold), Cage's Sonatas and Interludes for Prepared Piano, Copland's Piano Sonata, solo and concerted works by Henze, Ruggles' *Evocations*, and Shostakovich's Preludes and Fugues.

Of all pianists, Gould was the one who least needed his hands in order to keep busy, so he was not idle while he dealt with the problems of 1977–78. His main occupation at that time was the last and longest of his "contrapuntal radio documentaries": *The Bourgeois Hero*, a profile of Richard Strauss. He began working on it in 1976, and taped interviews over the next two years with an international cast of eight representing a wide spectrum of opinion about Strauss, an "embarrassment of riches" that comprised two composers, two

---

* In "Streisand as Schwarzkopf," a perceptive review of the 1976 album *Classical Barbra*, Gould described Streisand's voice as "one of the natural wonders of the age," and later he called her "probably the greatest singing-actress since Maria Callas." He ended his review by offering to work with her (she was a Columbia artist) on a second classical album, for which he suggested songs by Dowland and Musorgsky and Bach's Cantata 54. "I will certainly talk to Barbra about your almost incredible offer," wrote Claus Ogerman, the arranger, conductor, and producer for *Classical Barbra*, "so don't be surprised if a telegram will someday order you to the coast whenever a second album is in the making." But there is nothing more on the subject in Gould's papers, and Streisand never has made a second classical album. According to several of Gould's friends, he contacted Streisand's representatives directly, without result.

conductors, and four writers. By the summer of 1978 he was drafting the script, and in March 1979, after six and a half "maniacal" months of post-production work with five editors (mostly Tom Shipton), the program – two years overdue – was finished. It was broadcast, in two parts (approximately forty-four and fifty minutes), on April 2 and 9, 1979.

Gould, with a nod to the subtitle of Strauss's last opera, *Capriccio*, called his show "a conversation piece in two acts," tracing Strauss's life and career, the development of his musical language, his relationships with famous colleagues and with the Nazi regime, his place in nineteenth- and twentieth-century music, and his prospects for posterity. Throughout, Gould stresses the dichotomies in Strauss's personality and work (encapsulated in the title *The Bourgeois Hero*) and explores "Strauss' relationship to the zeitgeist" – long one of his favourite subjects. The result is a superb mix of biography and criticism, the form of which parallels Strauss's own life: the first act flamboyant, the second restrained. (In all of Gould's radio portraits there is close connection of subject, form, and style.) Once again, Gould crafted quasi-conversational montages out of his interviews and set them against a seamless backdrop of music. "It's as though they are still sitting around the summer cottage at twilight," he said in a press release. "They are each with their own thoughts, and slowly become more involved in the conversation. Then, when they've said almost all they want to say, they slowly back off."

The program is less ostentatiously contrapuntal than Gould's earlier documentaries, though it is still technically complicated and demanded an obsessive attention to detail, even by his standards: he bragged to the critic William Littler of one speech, lasting just two minutes forty-three seconds, in which he made 131 edits – about one per second. His intention, however, was not to show off his virtuosity as a radio artist, but to attain a new level of fluency and subtlety and finesse. (In one evocative passage, for instance, he uses a Mahlerian moment in Strauss's *Alpine Symphony* to contradict a speaker who claims that Strauss was divorced from the modernistic tendencies represented by Mahler.) As elegant and beautiful in its own way as Strauss's autumnal late music, *The Bourgeois Hero* is one of Gould's masterpieces.

He never produced the fifth documentary demanded by his 1973 contract. In 1978, John Fraser, then the Peking correspondent for the *Globe and Mail*, wrote to him suggesting that he add to his Solitude Trilogy a fourth program, about China. Gould was interested enough to formulate a considered reply, proposing that he use China as a means to explore "the political dimension of isolation." He even thought up a title: "The Last Puritans." But he never developed the idea, in part because his travelling to China was out of the question. As he wrote to Fraser, "even if a slow boat to China did exist, I would not be on it."

"The piano, though miraculously improved, is still not fully returned to health."

Gould was threatened with the loss of yet another old friend in the 1970s: his beloved Steinway, CD 318. The instrument underwent thorough repairs in early 1971, and was, Gould said, "restored to its glories as of yore." In September of that year, his plan to record concertos in Cleveland confirmed, he shipped the piano there, only to have it shipped back when he cancelled. It arrived at Eaton's on October 20, though was only taken up to the auditorium on October 26 (a delay Gould later deemed suspect). At some point, probably while first being unloaded at Eaton's – no one ever found out for sure – the crate containing the piano was dropped. Verne Edquist, the first to hear the news, alerted Gould, who appeared in the auditorium as CD 318 was uncrated. His despair was visible as it became obvious it had been seriously damaged. As he reported on December 12 to David Rubin, the manager of Steinway's Concert and Artist department, "The piano was apparently dropped with great force and the point of impact would appear to be the front right (treble) corner." The instrument's lid was split and otherwise damaged, its plate was "fractured in four critical places," its sound-board was "split at the treble end," some pins and screws were bent, and the key frame and action were put "completely out of alignment."

For more than a year CD 318 was in Steinway's factory in New York being repaired. When it came time, in March 1972, to begin recording four suites by Handel, for which he had done his practising on the piano, Gould decided to record them on a harpsichord, because he thought it would be fun. (It was, so much so that he considered completing *The Art of Fugue* on the harpsichord.) CD 318 did not return to Toronto until November 1972; Gould's first recordings on it were French Suites by Bach and works by Mozart. At the time he extolled the "miraculous rebirth of the instrument," though in reality it would never again be the reliable friend it had been. For one thing, the action was now heavier, and he found it more difficult to achieve the effects he desired; he noted that, as a result, his tempos in his first recordings on the restored CD 318 were slower than usual.

Like its owner, CD 318 became something of a hypochondriac. Throughout the 1970s, it was in and out of repairs, sometimes in Toronto, sometimes in New York, sometimes for months at a time. Both Verne Edquist, in Toronto, and Franz Mohr, at Steinway, worked on it at different times. Gould's private papers from this period include many notes about the piano's health. The basic sound quality he had always prized was not lost, though he complained of new tonal anomalies like a persistent "horrendous buzz," which Edquist blamed on Mohr's "penchant for acidizing the hammers." But the action never felt quite right again after 1971, and Gould's technicians struggled vainly to give him what he wanted but could not have: CD 318, circa 1960. After each repair he would declare the piano reborn, only to begin grumbling again soon after. In June 1980, when he removed the action from the piano and drove it down to the Steinway factory, he lamented to his diary, "I'm inclined to feel that 318 is a lost cause." Still, he continued to use it when he could; his last Toronto recording, of Bach's Italian Concerto, was made on the instrument. CD 318 was never a wreck, but it eventually became so difficult for Gould to get exactly what he wanted from it that the effort was counterproductive.

After 1971, he borrowed other congenial Steinways wherever he could find them – in New York, at the CBC – and made test tapes of this or that instrument. Some of his later recordings, like Beethoven's C-major sonata, Op. 2/No. 3, and his second Bach film with Bruno Monsaingeon, were made on more than one piano; he recorded Strauss's Op. 3 pieces on two different pianos in two different halls. (In such cases, the recordings were equalized in order to minimize tonal differences between the pianos.) He was testing Steinways as late as May 1981, but never found one to replace his old friend permanently, not even instruments that had served artists like Rachmaninov and Horowitz. As always he found the new Steinways, especially the American ones, ranged from "terrible to pathetic" in tone or action or both, and he was not the only Steinway artist to complain at this time: the seventies is generally considered to have been the low point in the company's history. In 1972, after more than a century of family ownership, Steinway was sold to CBS Musical Instruments, and in the years that followed the company, like Columbia Records, was increasingly run as a corporation, and was rife with dissension. More and more Steinway artists and technicians complained of poor service and quality-control problems in the new pianos, including too-heavy actions. Gould's old friends in the company were mostly gone, and David Rubin, according to Steinway historian Susan Goldenberg, had an "edgy" relationship with many pianists and a haughty attitude toward his product. It was Rubin who ended Steinway's long-standing practice of loaning pianos to select artists for extended periods, which is why Gould purchased CD 318 outright in February 1973 (he paid $5,900). CBS sold Steinway in 1985 – too late for Gould, who in his last decade found it a less accommodating company with a less acceptable product.

He tested other pianos – German Steinways, Bechsteins – and finally defected to Yamaha. Steinway's hegemony in the concert-grand business was being seriously challenged in quality and price by the Japanese, Yamaha in particular, and Bill Evans had recommended Yamaha pianos to Gould in the early seventies. He first tried a Yamaha around the turn of 1981 at the Ostrovsky Piano and Organ Company in midtown Manhattan, and was deeply impressed by the piano's action, which had the responsiveness and the minimal aftertouch he craved. According to Daniel Mansolino, then a piano technician and rebuilder at Ostrovsky's, Gould said, on his first day in the store, "The action is the best in the world; don't change anything." He also liked "the intimacy, clarity, and brightness" of the Yamaha's tone, and though he did not consider the sound completely satisfactory – he found the bass unfocused, for one thing – he knew he could work with it. The important thing was that he had at last found a piano whose action reminded him of CD 318 in its prime. As he wrote in his 1980 diary, "if I can get a Yamaha that doesn't buzz and does what I ask of it, I'll take it."

In February 1981 he began playing a Yamaha while working on his first digital recording, in New York, of the last six sonatas of Haydn.* The following month he purchased a Yamaha CF Concert Grand from Ostrovsky's – built in Japan in 1975 – and used this piano in all of the digital recordings he made in New York in the last two years of his life. Mansolino, himself a professional (non-classical) pianist and organist as well as a composer and producer, served as Gould's piano technician in New York and spent hundreds of congenial hours in his company. ("Dan," he said, "you are the only one who can shake my hand, smoke, and eat meat in my presence.") As usual, though, Gould solicited input wherever he could. He sometimes called Verne Edquist to discuss the Yamaha's adjustments, but also had Mansolino fly up to Toronto for a week in June 1981 to work on the ailing CD 318.

No piano in its native state suited Gould perfectly, but he considered the Yamaha particularly amenable to the customized adjustments he demanded. During the Haydn sessions and the subsequent

---

* He had already recorded the first two sonatas for this album, Nos. 60 and 61, on a Steinway, at the 30th Street studio in New York, in October 1980.

recording and filming of the Goldberg Variations, Gould and Mansolino experimented with the new piano, whose action attained Gould's ideal by February 1982, when he recorded Brahms's Ballades, Op. 10. That ideal departed in important respects from factory specifications, and all of the special adjustments he demanded had the same effect of maximizing responsiveness while minimizing effort. In outtakes from the Goldberg film, he can be seen telling Mansolino, "Think harpsichord – I want a harpsichord," and he complains when he feels that the action is not fast enough to accommodate his rapid cross-hand passages and "machine-gun" trills. Mansolino has said that, in fact, "Gould's pianistic technique exceeded the limits of what a 'modern' piano action can do at its best."

Gould's fussiness with the action of his new piano was not frivolous, for, as Mansolino observed with astonishment, his ears and fingers were "miraculous," so uncannily sensitive that he could hear and feel minuscule flaws in the piano's action and tone that no other professional pianist could detect and that caused other piano technicians to shake their heads in disbelief when told about them.* Mansolino marvelled at Gould's absolute control in both striking and releasing keys, and at his ability to "memorize" instantly the voicing of a piano and so compensate by playing brighter notes softer, duller notes louder – something he saw him do on his first visit to Ostrovsky's after running his hands up and down the keyboard a couple of times. Gould noticed the smallest problems caused by misadjustment, temperature, or humidity, and as Mansolino recalled, "I had learned to look for the improbable the second day we worked together."

Glenn Gould was now a de facto Yamaha artist and purchased a second piano from the Yamaha dealer in Toronto. For the company,

---

* Likewise, Verne Edquist recalled that Gould could detect tuning problems before he could, and the CBS engineers who worked on his digital recordings in New York were amazed to discover that he could discriminate, by ear, between recordings made on Sony and Mitsubishi digital recording systems, even though the technical specifications of the two systems were identical.

proud to add a pianist of his stature to its comparatively small roster of A-list artists, this was a marketing windfall. He politely told Steinway that he was using a Yamaha merely as a stop-gap measure – likely a fib – and Steinway kept trying to win him back, offering new pianos for him to try and volunteering to built him a new piano from scratch. They even asked to see for themselves what he liked so much about his Yamaha, but he would not let them examine it. He said he wanted to remain a Steinway artist, but when he was sent an updated Steinway Artist release form in August 1981, he did not return it. It is still among his papers, unsigned.

"It occurred to me on one of my rare re-listenings to that early recording that it was very nice, but that perhaps a little bit like thirty very interesting but somewhat independent-minded pieces going their own way."

Bruno Monsaingeon began shooting *Glenn Gould Plays Bach* in November 1979. For the first film, *The Question of Instrument*, Gould opted for a recital of works in several forms (fugue, fantasy, suite), linked by commentary on Bach's idealism and "instrumental indifference"; it closes with the complete Partita No. 4 in D Major – one of Gould's greatest performances. In the second film, *An Art of the Fugue*, shot a year later, he deals insightfully with Bach's development as a fugal craftsman. In the sequence that forms the centrepiece of the film, he simultaneously plays and analyzes the E-major fugue from Book Two of *The Well-Tempered Clavier* – a feat of extraordinary mental agility and pianistic command, given the piece's structural density and ingenuity. The film closes with the unfinished final Contrapunctus from *The Art of Fugue*, which Gould called "the most extraordinary piece that a human mind ever conceived." He had never played it before, and was intimidated: "It's the most difficult thing I've ever approached," he said. After considering four radically different interpretations, he opted for an elegiac, deeply introspective reading, and was, Monsaingeon recalled, "transported" as he played it, particularly near the end, where Bach introduces a four-note motif based on the letters of his surname. But despite great performances and (usually) penetrating commentary, these two films are less engaging than the ORTF series, and the fault is Gould's. This time he scripted the conversation segments down to the last comma, and instead of memorizing his lines he relied, very obviously, on cue cards, as did Monsaingeon; as a result, the conversations are stilted, the efforts at humour laboured. As in *Radio as Music* and some other later productions, Gould's obsessiveness was proving counter-productive in some ways, at least in those situations (such as conversation) in which spontaneity pays dividends.

The first two Bach films were co-productions of Clasart (as Metronom was now renamed) and the CBC, but while Clasart willingly acceded to Gould's demand for a schedule permitting no more than ten minutes of finished music per day, the CBC grew annoyed at his lavish use of studio time – his insistence, for example, on stopping to watch playbacks between takes. The situation was exacerbated by technical problems in the CBC's Studio 7 – camera and tape-recorder failures, distortion on audio tracks, a lumpy, pitted studio floor. In November 1979, the CBC producer Mario Prizek was moved to type a four-page memo noting "the deplorable state" of Studio 7 and "the inadequate maintenance of the production hardware," which caused delays "shameful and shaming" in the presence of the European co-producers. Gould's 1980 diary notes "disasters" and "gen[era]l chaos" at the CBC, and in the middle of filming *An Art of the Fugue* he and Monsaingeon decamped for another Toronto studio. Later, Studio 7 was closed due to high asbestos levels, delaying the mixing of that film. The whole program, Gould wrote, "has been a comedy of errors from the beginning."

The CBC was another old friend that had begun to slip away. John Roberts departed as head of radio music in 1975, and Gould was never as comfortable with succeeding regimes at either radio or television. As the papers from his last years reveal, he sensed that the network was increasingly less enthusiastic about making and promoting the kinds of musical programs that interested him, on the assumption that they were too highbrow for most viewers. The technical problems on the Bach films – surely a major factor in his decision not to complete *Music in Our Time* – were the last straw; it is unlikely he would have worked again for CBC television. When it came time to shoot the next instalment of *Glenn Gould Plays Bach*, the CBC bowed out and Clasart alone produced.

The third and fourth Bach films were to have dealt with chamber music and concertos, and the series was to have ended with a program on variation form, but the threatened lost of yet another old friend led Gould and Monsaingeon to move up that projected fifth film. Columbia Records' 30th Street studio in New York, where Gould had made his early Columbia albums, was slated to be demolished. His New York trip in June 1980 reminded him of what a "terrific hall" it was, with its "rare mix of clarity and fidelity with qualities of warmth and spaciousness," and he decided to make a recording and film there before it was too late. And so, in six sessions in April and May 1981, he took up anew the work through which he had first found international fame: the Goldberg Variations. The production was technically complicated – CBS engineers recorded the sessions for an album as Monsaingeon's crew shot – but Gould was in high spirits throughout. He horsed around with the crew between takes, once agreeing to play Duke Ellington's "Caravan" for a technician who had asked if he took requests; he began to make a canon out of the melody before breaking off in laughter. The outtakes reveal his enjoyment of the filmmaking process. He had fun faking in sequences where he had to pantomime at the keyboard in order to synchronize visuals with an existing soundtrack. In the passage of overlapping thirds and sixths at the end of Variation 23, for instance, he followed Bach's tricky disposition of the hands for the visual track, but used easier fingering – cheated, in other words – to get a cleaner take for the soundtrack. The outtakes also reveal occasional finger slips and at least one prominent "Oh, shit!"

He was thrilled with the finished film, with the way the "the camera was absolutely wedded to the piano, and the visual architecture grows with each succeeding variation." The film makes no concessions to concert-hall aesthetics. It opens with Gould, in the control booth, introducing his interpretation with several minutes of faux-casual conversation. The performance itself begins with a self-conscious allusion to its "film-ness": Gould is glimpsed in the distance, through the glass of the booth, and the camera slowly zooms in on him as he begins the opening Aria; only midway through the Aria is Gould shot from within the studio proper. He is casually, a little raggedly, dressed, in stocking feet and dark-blue Viyella shirt with another shirt beneath – the flapping of his open cuffs gave him some trouble in cross-hand passages – and wearing glasses, as he had done, for the first time in public, in *An Art of the Fugue*. The fallboard of the piano (where YAMAHA is written) is removed, giving his fingers more room to manoeuvre and putting him in closer contact with the piano's action.

Gould was fussier about a recording than he was about the soundtrack of a film, and for the purposes of the Goldberg album he held retake sessions in April and May* – after which, despite public lobbying to which he lent his support, the 30th Street studio was closed. He was still spending many hours polishing the recording, with at least three local editors, well into his last summer, long after the film was first shown on television, in France, on January 2, 1982. (Monsaingeon described the public response as "very positive, even delirious on occasion.") His musical and technical standards were now fantastically high, and he was surely also driven by a desire to top the bestselling album that had first made his name and had been in print for more than a quarter of a century. His papers show

---

* There was some sharing of expenses between Clasart and CBS, but the film and album are two legally separate entities. Though they document the same basic interpretation, the latter is not literally the soundtrack of the former. There are some differences between the two performances not only in editing standards but in musical detail – a phrase here, an ornament there.

him correcting even the tiniest unwanted accents, the slightest flaws of contrapuntal balance, the most fleetingly uneven figuration. According to one of his editors, Kevin Doyle, he was achieving splices on his analogue copies of the tapes that the New York technicians, even with their digital equipment, deemed impossible.

The album was released in September 1982 and attracted a great deal of attention. The reviews, many of which accompanied fiftieth-birthday profiles and retrospectives, were glowing, and Gould promoted the album enthusiastically. In August he recorded a scripted interview about his new interpretation for CBS to use for promotional purposes. The interviewer was Tim Page, whom he had met in fall 1980 when Page was a young classical-and-new-music coordinator for the *Soho News*, a New York arts journal. At that time Page had conducted a delightful telephone interview with Gould – unscripted, though later edited and expanded – for the *Soho News*, and the two had become fast friends.

Comparing his two recordings of the Goldberg Variations in the CBS interview, Gould admitted to finding the 1955 version too pianistic, which was to him a dirty word; he singled out the dark twenty-fifth variation, "which sounds remarkably like a Chopin nocturne." And he found much of that recording "just too fast for comfort." The 1981 version comes across as more meditative, more expansive, more introspective, particularly in the three G-minor variations and in the framing Arias. Tonally the later recording is more austere (this may have had as much to do with Gould's new piano as with his fingers), and is considerably more calculated in terms of phrasing, balance, expressive nuance, and ornamentation. There are countless differences of detail between the two interpretations, and wholly new tempos in some variations. In 1955 Gould took no repeats but in 1981 he repeated the first strain in the nine canons and in four other variations that feature formal counterpoint. More fundamentally, the 1981 version represents an effort to communicate the work as a single unified structure, not as a miscellany of thirty related but independent pieces. Most crucially, each variation is linked by some proportional rhythmic relationship to the

Gould's chart of the rhythmic scheme that unifies his 1981 interpretation of the Goldberg Variations, showing relationships between the pulses of consecutive variations, as well as the rhythmic relationship each variation has to the opening Aria. (*Estate of Glenn Gould.*)

variations that precede and follow it; as a result, a continuity of "pulse-rate," at some rhythmic level, binds the work together.

The 1981 recording is intellectually more commanding but not free of the showing off that characterized the earlier one. Most of the virtuosic variations (starting with the astonishing No. 5) still fly by at freakishly fast tempos, as though he sought to dispel any doubts (including his own?) that at fifty he could still compete with himself at twenty-two. (The rhythmic continuity makes the performance seem more expansive than it really is.) In fact, though the Goldberg Variations became Gould's signature piece it was not his favourite piece or even his favourite piece by Bach. Some of it he ranked among the "silliest" of Bach: Variation 14 was "one of the giddiest bits of neo-Scarlatti-ism imaginable"; Variation 17 was "slightly empty-headed"; Variations 28 and 29 were "capricious" and "balcony-pleasing." The encyclopaedic range of the work, which musicians have marvelled at for centuries, apparently disturbed Gould. "As a piece, as a concept, I don't really think it quite works," he told Joseph Roddy in 1981, and his unified interpretation that year represented his effort somehow to incorporate the "silly" side logically into the whole.

But within a week of the album's release Gould was dead, and it was easy then to hear it as "autumnal," as his "testament"; in the decades since, sentimentality about his untimely death has given the 1981 recording, and the Goldberg Variations generally, an exaggerated prominence within the Gould *oeuvre*. A better candidate for the summit of his Bach discography might be his two-record set of the English Suites, released in 1977: his Bach was never more thoughtfully creative, more intimate or more strongly characterized, and never attained a superior balance between high-modernist orderliness and Romantic flexibility. In any event, Gould had no plans to die at fifty, and his second recording of the Goldberg Variations became his testament only through a sad fluke of fate.

"The world has had enough of Glenn Gould."

"I do not think I will be making piano records in a few years," Gould said to Tim Page in summer 1982. "When I have recorded all I want to play, I will move on to other things." For years he had been telling people he would stop making piano recordings at age fifty – a threat that seems to have alarmed his fans more than it did him. He never wanted to be tied to the piano and had no problem imagining a career away from it, though he could not live without playing altogether, he admitted. He said he had run out of music, having largely recorded the piano music that interested him. Normally this would sound astonishing in a fiftyish pianist who had yet to take up Schubert or Schumann, Chopin or Liszt, Debussy or Ravel, Rachmaninov or Bartók, but then (to crib from Kenneth Tynan) Gould always had the courage of his restrictions.

Bruno Monsaingeon has reported seeing Gould literally don blinkers – "You know, what horses wear" – while driving Longfellow through midtown Manhattan, so intent was he on shutting out Times Square and the X-rated movie houses and the rest of New York's street life. (No peripheral vision – just what Gould's driving needed.) The anecdote is irresistible metaphorically, for Gould ranks among the most blinkered, least inclusive of thinkers. There is a famous line, the subject of much interpretation, among the fragments of the Greek poet Archilochus: "The fox knows many things, but the hedgehog knows one big thing." For Isaiah Berlin, the hedgehogs were those "who relate everything to a single central vision, one system, less or more coherent or articulate, in terms of which they understand, think and feel," who accept or reject things on the basis of "one unchanging, all-embracing, sometimes self-contradictory and incomplete, at times fanatical, unitary inner vision." Gould, clearly, was a hedgehog, and might have liked the analogy: his taste in animals ran more to the dowdy than the noble beasts. He never abandoned the strictly exclusive intellectual and aesthetic and ethical premises he formulated in his teens, and was disdainful of artists and thinkers like Stravinsky – the foxes – who celebrated life's variety and multitude and so, in his view, lacked consistency of vision. Gould did not develop as a thinker and musician in the sense of challenging his own premises; his career, rather, involved the constant refining of a fixed set of values and practices.

That mindset, of course, was the source of Gould's strength as an artist, but it had drawbacks that became increasingly apparent as he grew older. He had begun to repeat himself more and more in his writings, broadcasts, films, and interviews. As he approached fifty he was still taking potshots at Monteverdi and Beethoven and Stravinsky, at the supposed emptiness and hedonism and superficiality of early-Romantic piano music, without bringing any new insight to these subjects. "I happen not to like the Mozart concertos," he told an interviewer in 1980. "I don't believe any of them really work as structures." He thought the solo parts especially were "very badly written." He was still the precocious teenager in the conservatory cafeteria telling his chums that Mozart couldn't write a concerto, and presumably still smirking and thinking himself devilishly clever and *outré*, but with time these positions sounded less and less like reasoned arguments, more and more like hardened prejudices supported by wilful ignorance. Monsaingeon recalled begging Gould at least to acquaint himself with Mozart's string quartets and quintets, but he declined. Even on pet topics close to his heart – the idealism of Bach, early music on the modern piano, recording versus concert life, "contrapuntal radio" – he was not finding much new to say, only new media in which to say it. The Monsaingeon films, the later CBC radio appearances, the *Glenn Gould Fantasy*, and the like include a good deal of old news, and some of his unrealized projects, like the German television portrait, would have included still more.

Some of Gould's comments from his last years – "I've *done* all that," "I don't want to do that act again" – suggest that, though he never lost his enthusiasm for his work or his confidence in what he did, he knew he was at a turning point in his career and needed to find new things to say and do. The need to repeat old news was somewhat obviated by the appearance of the only book about him to be published while he was alive: *Glenn Gould, Music and Mind*. The author, Geoffrey Payzant, was a professor of philosophy at the University of Toronto, and an organist, who had known his subject slightly since 1956, when, as editor of the *Canadian Music Journal*, he had published Gould's first article. In 1974, long interested in musical aesthetics, Payzant began to look closely at Gould's ideas about music and the media, at first in a series of public lectures. His book was published by Van Nostrand Reinhold, in Toronto, in spring 1978. Gould provided bibliographical assistance, and checked the text at various stages to correct factual errors, but by mutual consent the book was Payzant's alone; the two met face to face on the subject only shortly before publication, to go over photographs. However, in one of his cheekiest moves as a writer, Gould reviewed it – positively – himself, in the third person, in the *Globe and Mail*. *Glenn Gould, Music and Mind* is a serious but concise and accessible introduction to the Gould aesthetic, "not by any definition a biography," as Payzant has always maintained, "but a study of the ideas of a profound and innovative musical thinker." Largely uncritical, it is a book Gould himself might have written. Indeed, just before he died Gould told Payzant gratefully that he had done less writing in recent years precisely because of the book, presumably meaning that it had made a definitive statement about his aesthetic.

The five digital albums Gould recorded in his last years* hint that he was indeed planning to enter a new phase of his life:

---

* The Haydn and Bach albums were released while Gould was still alive, and the post-production work on the two Beethoven sonatas was completed though that album was released only posthumously, but the posthumously released Brahms and Strauss albums were apparently not completed to his satisfaction when he died: his notepads show that he had plans to do further editing for these two albums in late September, October, and early November 1982. Moreover, his 1981 recording of Bach's Italian Concerto, though edited and mixed in September 1981, apparently did not satisfy him, according to friends. His last surviving notepad indicates a plan to "check Italian" on what turned out to be the Saturday after his death.

- Haydn, Sonatas Nos. 56 and 58–62 (recorded in 1980–81/ released in 1982).
- Bach, Goldberg Variations (1981/1982).
- Brahms, Ballades, Op. 10; Rhapsodies, Op. 79 (1982/1983).
- Beethoven, Sonatas, Opp. 26 and 27/No. 1 (1979, 1981/1983).
- Strauss, Sonata in B Minor, Op. 5; Five Piano Pieces, Op. 3 (1979, 1982/1984).

This mix of repertoire suggests a tying-up of loose ends in preparation for retirement. Gould was partially fulfilling his long-standing desire to record Haydn's sonatas, taking up some of the congenial music by Brahms that he had not yet performed, finally setting down what little piano music his beloved Strauss had composed, getting back to his commitment to record a complete cycle of Beethoven's sonatas. That cycle was on his mind throughout his last decade. In the mid-seventies he considered recording Beethoven's minor, early Op. 49 sonatas, and as late as 1980 he returned to his old idea of an album featuring the sonatas he loved best, Opp. 78, 79, 81a ("Les Adieux"), 90, and 101. He made plans to release, in 1981, an album of Beethoven's Opp. 7 and 22 sonatas, neither of which had interested him before – he called Op. 22 the one "dud" among the early sonatas – but he recorded only the second and third movements of Op. 22, in July 1979 (they have never been released). It is doubtful that his Beethoven cycle would ever have been literally complete: he declined to record the "Hammerklavier" after his unsatisfying experience with it on the radio in 1970, and he confessed that he could not see himself recording the heroic, popular "Waldstein" Sonata. And yet, there is the "Waldstein," along with the Op. 54 sonata and the "Hammerklavier," in a list of projected recordings from summer 1979.*

---

* According to John Roberts, Gould also considered, from time to time, recording Beethoven's monumental Diabelli Variations, which he had never performed in concert.

Even with his beloved Bach there was a sense of tying up loose ends in, for instance, his 1980 album of short preludes, fughettas, and fugues. He had always planned to record all of Bach's keyboard music for Columbia, and by the end of his life he was running out of important works. In 1979 and 1980, in Toronto, he recorded minor Bach pieces for two albums, neither completed. One was to have comprised various fantasies and fugues; the other, tentatively entitled *Bach in the Italian Style* or *The Italian Bach*, was to have included mostly early works based on Italian subjects or models. These pieces did not much interest or challenge Gould. He saved the Bach he loved for Monsaingeon's camera, and his last Bach recordings, for all their polish and beauty, are mostly pro forma.

On the digital recordings he made in New York from 1980 to 1982, Gould shared the producing credit with a CBS Masterworks producer, Samuel H. Carter, though Carter admits that Gould alone was in charge of the sessions and made all the post-production decisions. After a search for another New York studio the Brahms and Strauss albums were recorded at RCA's Studio A – including his last session as a pianist, on September 3, 1982, when he recorded the piano sonata that Strauss wrote at the age of sixteen. Though in its early years digital technology was often criticized for producing dry, flat, tinny recordings, Gould loved the "clarity and immediacy" of the digital sound. In all of the late recordings made under his own supervision, he preferred an even drier acoustic and even closer microphone perspectives than before, particularly in Bach; the lovely sheen of his early Bach is gone, replaced by a more transparent, analytical sound. Some listeners find his later Bach recordings clinical and over-calculated, yet they remain expressive and deeply probing. He was seeking a recorded sound that offered the listener a closer, more intimate engagement with the music, though it also cruelly exposed Gould's playing, making almost superhuman demands on his pianistic control. That he met these demands spectacularly must make us wonder, once again, about those hand problems back in 1977–78.

Even as he talked of having run out of music and of retiring from performing at age fifty, Gould did not stop thinking about making new piano recordings – clearly, he had not made a definitive decision about retirement when he died. To friends and colleagues, and in his private notes, he considered all sorts of future recording projects in his last years.* If he *was* planning to make more piano recordings while allowing his CBS contract to lapse in 1983, he obviously intended to exert more control over them. He had been micromanaging his own recordings in Toronto since 1970, and in his last years considered taking the next logical step: making them at his own expense, then licensing the master tapes to the highest bidder. To Andrew Kazdin, in 1979, he gave the scheme a twist: announcing his retirement at fifty but continuing to make recordings *in secret*, stockpiling them until their value had risen significantly, then auctioning them off. He considered one day making films, too, under his own auspices, like Karajan, hiring technical crews as necessary, directing productions himself, and keeping all rights to the finished products. According to Bruno Monsaingeon, his testament as a pianist was to have been a recital of works by Haydn, Beethoven, Mendelssohn, Brahms, Sibelius, Strauss, and Schoenberg, filmed in an empty Carnegie Hall – the perfect Gouldian "historic return."

He even considered moonlighting as a producer for other musicians. In August 1973, as a favour, he had produced his friend Antonin Kubalek's recording of piano music by Erich Wolfgang

---

* These included rerecording the Two- and Three-Part Inventions, the G-major partita, and other Bach works, perhaps even the whole *Well-Tempered Clavier*; recording the complete *Art of Fugue* on the piano; completing his Bach-concerto cycle with No. 6 in F major; and rerecording concertos (Bach's D-minor, Beethoven's Second) that existed only in monaural sound. He considered recording Brahms's C-major and F-minor sonatas; short pieces by Scriabin; the Six Impromptus, Op. 5, by Sibelius; the *Suite "Den Luciferiske,"* Op. 45, by Nielsen; and perhaps more music by Hindemith. And he considered chamber-music projects including Beethoven's cello-and-piano works, with Leonard Rose; violin sonatas by Busoni, Grieg, and Strauss, with Jaime Laredo or Gidon Kremer; and songs by Strauss and Mahler.

Korngold – it was released on the small Genesis Records label – and had enjoyed the process: he took childlike delight in pushing buttons and calling out "Take 1!" Late in life his thoughts turned to Sviatoslav Richter, whom he considered a genius but whose recordings, many of them made in concert, he thought technically poor. While filming the Goldberg Variations, he broached the subject of producing Richter recordings with Monsaingeon, who knew Richter and passed on the message that summer. Richter, who considered *Gould* a genius, was intrigued, but was unwilling to travel to North America, and Gould was unwilling to travel to Europe. Presumably with a twinkle in his eye, Richter finally agreed to record in Toronto under Gould's supervision if Gould would agree to give a recital at his festival in Tours, France – and that was the end of that.

Through recordings and films, Gould could continue to enjoy wide international exposure while becoming, in essence, a private, self-contained, boutique operation – Glenn Gould's Olde-Tyme Musicke Shoppe. One of the top classical artists of his day, under high-powered management, he could have commanded whatever resources he wanted within the business, but he wanted only to work at home, with his own equipment, with his local piano tuner and an editor borrowed from the CBC. He wanted to work and to disseminate his work on his own terms, even if the circumstances lacked glamour or prestige. This desire to make homemade recordings reflected his temperament, of course, but also showed a sound understanding of the aesthetic and logistical implications of musical life in the electronic age. It did not matter where he lived or how he worked; as long as he could produce master tapes and finished films, he could communicate with the rest of the world. He would have worked happily in the digital world of today, commanding a world-class musical franchise from his desktop, with total control over his work. As the rock singer Prince once said, in light of his feuds with his record label, "If you don't own the masters, the master owns you."

"It's been fascinating to get to know Toronto after all these years."

For Gould, finding new things to say and do in his last years meant jumping at chances to do interesting work away from the piano and the recording studio. In 1978, the Toronto filmmaker John McGreevy, whom Gould had known since the late sixties through the CBC, asked him to serve as writer and on-camera tour guide in the second instalment of *Cities*, a series of thirteen hour-long programs that introduced major cities of the world through a local celebrity's eyes – *Studs Terkel's Chicago, Jonathan Miller's London*, and so on. Gould cheerfully referred to himself as "possibly the worst tourist guide you could find," and confessed that he "didn't know a damn thing about the city." He had never lived anywhere else, it is true, but even in 1978 the Toronto he knew and admired was the Toronto he remembered from the thirties and forties. Since the 1950s it had been one of the fastest-growing cities in the world, and perhaps no other city of its size had been transformed so rapidly into a modern, ethnically diverse metropolis. To those who were born in Toronto in the early thirties, the broadcaster Peter Gzowski wrote in 1969, "It is our town, and we are the first people who are enjoying it as it grows near to its real potential as a city." Gould was an exception: he largely ignored the New Toronto when he was not actually disparaging its "horrors." He liked the city to the extent that it still reminded him of his sober, peaceful, complacent life in the Beach before the war.

Still, he eagerly accepted McGreevy's proposal – it would be a challenge, and sounded like fun. (He received a fee of $20,000, plus royalties.) Shot in August and September 1978, the program "was a great joy to make," Gould wrote to a friend; "indeed, it occupied some of the most hilarious weeks of my life." McGreevy managed to get Gould outside even during the day, and tried to shoot quickly and unobtrusively in deference to Gould's anxiety in public situations. He was truly frightened while shooting a sequence at Old Fort

York, where he stood before some grenadier guards in period dress as they fired off cannons and guns – he had been promised that they would *not* fire, and predictably worried that he would lose his hearing. "Glenn prizes personal anonymity more passionately than anyone I know," a friend told a reporter at the time. "I think he got a big kick out of making that film. But I imagine he saw enough new faces during those two weeks to last a lifetime."

Gould insisted from the start that the film would not be auto-biographical. The Beach is conspicuously absent from his tour, as are his apartment and studio and regular haunts, and the personal anecdotes are all innocuous and well sanitized. Yet the program is still revealing, and entertaining, precisely because of the tension between Gould's temperament and the New Toronto: his admira-tion for the "City of Churches"; his profession of love for the anony-mous suburbs of North York; his bemusement at the Mariposa Folk Festival and the hippies of Yorkville; his embarrassment at the sleaze and glitz of the Yonge Street strip downtown; his disbelief as he strolls, presumably for the first time, through the vast mall of the Eaton Centre, muttering "It's absurd! It's absolutely absurd!" The New Toronto was a clean, comfortable, safe, functional city by comparison with, say, New York in the seventies, though still not quite dull enough for Gould's taste.

Much of the film comes across as conventional travelogue, revealing not an old hand but a tourist in his own hometown (a researcher had to feed him information while he prepared his script). He leads the viewer past the two city halls and Nathan Phillips Square, the CN Tower, the Bay Street financial district, the Canadian National Exhibition, the Ontario Science Centre, Kensington Market, the Toronto Islands, and so on, yet admits in the first speech of the film that he is unfamiliar with most of these places. The series called for spontaneous narrative, but Gould insisted on writing a script, producing an essay of some forty-five thousand words, about *ten times* as much text as an hour-long film could accommodate. "You can't cut a word," he at first announced, though he proved gracious about the need for editing. The massive original essay has not survived – presumably it was cut up and discarded in the process of being pared down – but Gould noted some planned but unrealized sequences in other of his papers: visits to Casa Loma, Grenadier Pond, Massey Hall, and McKenzie House; trips to the tony neighbourhood of Rosedale and to the suburb of Don Mills; an exploration of the underground city (had he ever been on the subway?); a conversation with Marshall McLuhan; and a presumably staged segment showing him recording in Eaton Auditorium. He was fascinated by the production process, and while preparing the script made notes about camera shots, dissolves, and so on, but McGreevy remained firmly in charge of both filming and post-production. He charitably invented a technical excuse to edit out an apparently awful sequence in which Gould got into an argument, on Yonge Street, with his New York–cabbie alter ego, but he allowed Gould to ham it up in period costume at the piano, early in the film, as a sort of mad professor playing *Enoch Arden*. And he wisely retained a charming image that has since become iconic: the great pianist, at dawn, in the Toronto Zoo, singing Mahler's "St. Anthony's Sermon to the Fishes" to some indifferent elephants.

The completed film received a lot of press at home, some of it mildly hostile ("Dracula lives as tour guide to Toronto"). Some people felt that Gould was hardly an ideal host, some found his tone sarcastic, some carped when, true to form, he declined to appear at a private screening of the film a week before it first aired on the CBC on September 27, 1979. ("Gould doesn't show at his party" ran one of the newspaper headlines.) But *Glenn Gould's Toronto*, like the whole *Cities* series, proved immensely popular even long after its initial run. Gould and McGreevy talked about one future project, a film on the Arctic that would have required that Gould travel to the far North, but it was not to be.

"One of these times I'll write my autobiography, which will certainly be fiction."

Gould wanted not just to write but to be a real Writer. As the end of his pianistic career loomed his literary efforts became more ambitious, and he produced an impressive volume of writing in various forms – essays, memoirs, reviews, humour. Through the 1970s he still contributed liner notes to some albums, though now only when he had some special point of view to put before the public: championing unfamiliar repertoire (Byrd and Gibbons, Grieg and Bizet, Sibelius); explaining the premises behind his Mozart cycle and his Wagner transcriptions; making a case for the much-maligned music of Hindemith. He had a productive relationship with the *Piano Quarterly*, whose editor, Robert Silverman, gave him *carte blanche* to contribute any article, on any subject, at any length. His first contribution, a self-interview about Beethoven, ran in the Fall 1972 issue, and a dozen more articles and interviews followed over the next decade. At the same time, he was contributing occasionally to the *Globe and Mail*, the *New York Times*, the *Canada Music Book*, *High Fidelity/Musical America*, *Look*, the *New Republic*, and other publications. He continued to write on pet topics. His last completed piece of writing was a short script, dated July 26, 1982, for a CBS Masterworks in-house video project in which various people were asked to answer the question, What does the process of recording mean to you? In a notepad from that same month he began drafting what sounds like a promotional essay for the Brahms album he was then editing; it includes yet more tiresome slander about the "distasteful" and "mechanistic" and "cloyingly sentimental" piano music of the early nineteenth century.

But he was finding new subjects, too – often reviewing assignments provided an excuse – and in his forties he blossomed as a literary craftsman, managing mostly to avoid, even when writing on complicated musical subjects, the verbose, tangled prose that had plagued his earlier writing. He was now a more disciplined writer, and when he indulged in pompous rhetoric or wince-inducing wordplay it was for self-deprecating laughs. (The only Grammy Award he won in his lifetime was for his essay "Hindemith: Will His Time Come? Again?" which was printed on the back of his 1973 album of that composer's sonatas. He kept it in his storage room as a paperweight.) He developed a reviewing style that was both pointed and engaging, his humour improved greatly, and he discovered a gift for memoir. The longest and perhaps best article he ever wrote was "Stokowski in Six Scenes," begun shortly after the conductor's death in September 1977.* Though its autobiographical elements are carefully laundered, the essay is colourful, witty, insightful, and in form, pace, and tone masterly – the best of Gould the raconteur, in polished form.

This new interest in writing memoirs was a symptom of Gould's introspection in his last years. He seems to have felt an urge to document his career as a concert and recording pianist as he was preparing to put that part of his life behind him. He would never have written an intimate, tell-all autobiography, but his autobiographical writing was sometimes more revealing than he may have realized. In one of his *Arts National* programs for CBC radio, he paid tribute to another favourite conductor, Josef Krips. This script and the Stokowski article led him to consider writing a more substantial essay devoted to his encounters with conductors over the years, under the title "The Wands of Youth."† He made several sketches for an essay that might have included musical memories from childhood, some involving his mother and the organ; portraits of various conductors of his acquaintance; his musical and temperamental

---

* The essay was commissioned by the *New York Times Magazine*, which published it in May 1978, and paid Gould $10,000, but he angered them by – naively? – allowing the *Piano Quarterly* to publish parts of the essay first. The magazine refused to publish anything by him after that.

† One draft of the Stokowski article, in fact, bears the title "The Wands of Youth I: Remembering Stokowski." Never one to resist a pun, whether good or lousy, Gould obviously stole this title from *The Wand of Youth*, the title Edward Elgar gave to two orchestral suites he composed in 1907 and 1908 based on themes he had jotted down in childhood.

clashes with certain conductors, including Szell and Bernstein; his "Bach problems" with Dimitri Mitropoulos and Malcolm Sargent; his own conducting of Bach from the keyboard; an "essay against the concerto"; and comments on the end of his concert career. He made several lists of his various concert performances and cancellations and of the sixty-three conductors he had worked with, and actually began to draft "The Wands of Youth" in May 1978, but he did not get far before abandoning it.

When Robert Silverman suggested that Gould contribute autobiographical writing to the *Piano Quarterly*, he had the idea of writing his memoirs in sections, starting with one season of his concert career and then working backward and forward to compile a diary of his life. Around spring 1982 he began to work on a three-part essay entitled "A Season on the Road," which was to deal with his 1958–59 season, including his illness-plagued tour of Europe. He got no further than drafting a ruminative preamble and noting down highlights of that season in point form, but the project remained open. In fact, the last page of his last surviving notepad – perhaps the last words he ever committed to paper – is a list of American orchestras with which he had performed.

John Roberts, Tim Page, and other friends suggested over the years that he collect his writings into an anthology, but even in his late forties he did not think the time right, partly because he was superstitious: he thought it unlucky when his life was far from over. Yet among his notes from this period are several lists of his own writings, organized by genre and with word counts attached – perhaps, after all, he *was* considering an anthology, or at least taking stock of his literary output. Among these lists are plans for essays that he contemplated but never wrote, some of them intended to be as long as ten or twelve thousand words, some incorporating earlier writings. They include an essay on pianists he admired, including Schnabel, Tureck, Weissenberg, Gulda, and Richter, with perhaps a separate essay on Schnabel; major new essays on Mozart, Beethoven, Strauss, Schoenberg, and his own Solitude Trilogy; "the longest possible essay" on *Metamorphosen*; an expanded essay on Barbra

Streisand; an essay on the nature of editing in music, radio, and film ("The Louds on the Cutting-Room Floor"); an essay on interpretation; and, as he told Silverman, a "sequel" to Carol Montparker's 1981 book *The Anatomy of a New York Debut Recital*.

Gould still had ambitions to compose, too. His admirers never stopped talking about him as a composer, and he was not eager to correct them, but only a few sporadic efforts survive from his later years. There are a few sketches for dour, highly chromatic tonal music, always with that tangled counterpoint he seemed unable to resist, a few stabs at twelve-tone music, and some little comic pieces and parodies written for his friends. There are unexplained oddities, too, like a sketch for some strange music for flute, contrabassoon, and double bass, as well as a manuscript of the opening bars of one of Strauss's Op. 3 piano pieces scored for a chamber orchestra. Some of Gould's friends recall that he again talked about composing in earnest after retiring as a performer. Jessie Greig said he "was fascinated by the book of Revelation in the Bible, and he was going to write something akin to Handel's *Messiah*," and John Roberts recalls his desire to set some of the Psalms. But that was wishful thinking at best – it had been almost twenty years since he had completed a substantial piece of music, assuming that *So You Want to Write a Fugue?* even qualifies.

"I've always been a cinema-buff."

In September 1971, Gould received in the mail, unsolicited, a copy of Kurt Vonnegut's novel *Slaughterhouse-Five*, and shortly after an explanatory letter from George Roy Hill, the director of *Butch Cassidy and the Sundance Kid*, who was completing a film version of the Vonnegut novel for Universal. He wanted Gould to supervise the music, and in fact was already using Gould's Bach recordings in his rough cut. *Slaughterhouse-Five* is the story of Billy Pilgrim, a young American soldier who, as a prisoner near the end of Second World War, witnesses the fire-bombing of Dresden. Through that catastrophe Billy becomes "unstuck in time," and though he goes on to a superficially normal middle-class life in the suburban Midwest of the 1950s, he develops, in his mind, a time-travelling and dimension-shattering fantasy life, "time-tripping" between the war and a planet he calls Tralfamadore. "The dominant and recurring theme of the book is Dresden itself and I would like the musical theme to be in the same baroque style as the city," Hill wrote, on September 20. "I have been thinking of using Bach and possibly improvisations on Bach themes throughout the film. Since my knowledge of Bach is closely associated with all your Bach recordings, I thought of you and hope to ask your advice and possibly determine with you whether you would be interested in participating in some capacity in this project." Though he appreciated its anti-war theme Gould disliked the novel. He loved the movies, however, and loved a challenge. He met with Hill one evening in a motel room near the Toronto airport, and though he would formulate a characteristic eighteen-page critique of Universal's standard composers contract, he signed on to the project, for a fee of $17,500, and for ten weeks beginning in December was at the studio's disposal.

At first he envisioned a soundtrack that was as complicated and virtuosic as the film itself – "I conceived of vast montages," he told William Littler – but Hill's mantra was "Keep it simple." In the end, the film included less than fifteen minutes' worth of Bach's music, much of it simply taken from Gould's Columbia recordings, edited as required. The slow movement from Bach's F-minor clavier concerto became "Billy's Theme": at the beginning of the film it accompanies images of the shell-shocked Billy wandering through the Ardennes forest in winter; later it is associated with some of his reveries. Two of the Goldberg variations were used, most strikingly Variation 25 in G minor, which hauntingly underscores the burning of Dresden. In several scenes, Gould created audio "zooms" to mimic movement within the film frame – "acoustic orchestration," once again. The only really substantial music he had to concoct was a five-minute sequence for the arrival of the American prisoners at the Dresden train station and their subsequent march through the city. The finale of the D-major clavier concerto, with Gould on piano, forms the soundtrack for the train station, the Brandenburg Concerto No. 4 in G Major for the march; to bridge the musical disparity between those pieces, Gould wrote a brilliant harpsichord cadenza. The cadenza begins just as the soldiers step out of the train station, beneath the sign reading "Dresden," and throughout the film Gould uses the harpsichord as a musical metaphor for the historic city. He recorded this sequence under Andrew Kazdin's supervision, in New York, conducting from keyboard, with musicians from the New York Philharmonic.

Hill said he was thrilled with the soundtrack ("it exceeds everything I had hoped for"), and though Gould received praise in some high-profile reviews, *Slaughterhouse-Five* was not a very happy experience for him. Hill had final control over all matters including music, and Gould felt constrained: the film made "some very particular demands," he discreetly told a reporter when it was released, in March 1972. He was not fond of the film itself. (He reviewed it on CBC radio in August 1972, and discussed it in a self-interview in 1974.) He admired Hill's craftsmanship, but not the film's morals – "pessimism, combined with a hedonistic cop-out," was its hallmark, he wrote – or its sex and violence. "It's not a work of art that one can love," he wrote, and in the end he tried to dissociate himself from the project: "even an idealist can misread the intentions of a shooting script."

Still, having seen movie-making from the inside, he was anxious to do more.* He even dreamed of directing a film himself some day. The young Orson Welles quipped that a movie set was "the greatest electric train set a boy ever had," and it is easy to imagine Gould being happy as a filmmaker. (His colleagues report that he had fun on the set while making music programs – he enjoyed the hustle and bustle behind the scenes, the cameras, the lights, the makeup.) In

---

* His Bach recordings were used in the English director Mike Hodges's science-fiction film *The Terminal Man*, released by Warner Brothers in 1974. He received a fee of $15,000 but was not involved with the production.

1974, he trotted out Sir Nigel Twitt-Thornwaite, Myron Chianti, and Dr. Karlheinz Klopweisser to make three minute-long television commercials promoting the radio series CBC *Tuesday Night*, and among his papers are two typed pages of notes on costumes and makeup, sound and music, set design and props, blocking and camera movements – he could not resist the opportunity to direct, as he would a year later in *Radio as Music*, during which he had a high old time playing director with friends at the CBC. Near the end of his life he talked of writing a screenplay based on Thomas Mann's *The Confessions of Felix Krull*, and another based on *The Three-Cornered World*, though he admitted having difficulty turning its "wispy, dreamlike atmosphere" into action.

John McGreevy points out that Gould was very sensitive to the relation of image and sound and might have made a fine film composer. McGreevy came to Gould with a musical problem in 1975. He was completing *Mandelstam's Witness*, a one-woman television drama based on the memoirs of Nadezhda Mandelstam, the widow of a Soviet poet who was a victim of Stalin's purges. McGreevy could not decide what music to use in this film. Gould joined him at the CBC late one evening (it was Christmas Eve, and Gould had nothing else to do), and after viewing the film twice he made a suggestion: imagine there was an unseen cello student in the next apartment, practising bits of the slow movement from Shostakovich's cello concerto as the film unfolded, then, finally, performing the movement as the closing credits rolled. It was, McGreevy recalls, an inspired idea, and he duly gave Gould credit as "music consultant."

Early in 1982, Gould was asked to write a score for *The Wars*, a film based on the novel by Canadian writer Timothy Findley, and directed by the English theatre director Robin Phillips, who had run the Stratford Festival from 1975 to 1980. The film was a co-production of Nielsen-Ferns, the National Film Board of Canada, and Polyphon, in West Germany, and Gould was already a friend of the producer, Richard Nielsen (Nielsen-Ferns had co-produced *Glenn Gould's Toronto*). *The Wars* is the story of a traumatized Canadian soldier in the First World War, Robert Ross, who defies orders and rescues a group of horses in a kind of symbolic act of goodness. Gould loved the book – its anti-war message, its themes of compassion and redemption, its sensitivity to the suffering of animals – and was deeply impressed by Phillips's rough cut. He needed reassurance on only one point: that the dead horse in one battlefield sequence was not killed especially for the film. It wasn't, Nielsen assured him – it came from an abattoir – so Gould signed on, and was deeply committed to the project.

Phillips had wanted an intimate, classical score appropriate to the period, perhaps for piano alone, which is why Nielsen had suggested Gould. Given the opportunity to write whatever he wanted, Gould chose to arrange existing music – to rely on craft, in other words, rather than inspiration, a revealing choice for someone who still harboured ambitions to compose. In the end, he forged an evocative, subtly unified network of recurring motifs, variations on themes mostly by Brahms and Strauss, with other period music including popular songs of the day ("Tipperary," "The Grand Old Duke of York") and Protestant hymns ("Eternal Father, Strong to Save," "All People That on Earth Do Dwell").

The score includes piano performances, some taken from Gould's CBS recordings, other instrumental numbers, including Gould's "first professional exposure to the harmonica," and vocal numbers for which he supervised the recording in the spring of 1982, working with adult and children's choirs and some individual choirboys at St. Martin-in-the-Fields, a local Anglican church. This time he was intimately involved with every detail of the editing and mixing of the soundtrack, and Nielsen and Phillips marvelled at his skill and fanatical precision as an editor, at his ability to create a rhythmically perfect union of action and music almost frame by frame. Nielsen watched him tweak recorded tapes ever so slightly in order to underscore precisely what was on the screen. "I still have no idea how he'd do it," he said, "even though he did it right in front of me."

The sombre *Largo* theme from Strauss's piano piece Op. 3/No. 3 frames the film, but the most important classical theme is that of Brahms's tender Intermezzo in E-flat Major, Op. 117/No. 1, which

Gould called "Rowena's Theme." When it first appears in the film, it is associated with Robert's beloved, disabled sister Rowena, who dies before he goes off to war – and according to Nielsen and Phillips, Gould developed one of his obsessive adolescent crushes on Rowena, and was for a time watching one of her scenes every day at breakfast. (Brahms, incidentally, noted that the piece was based on a Scottish folk song, "Sleep Softly, My Child.") The theme is woven throughout the score. In its original key, it is associated with images of farewell, longing, remembrance; Gould, in one of his working papers, wrote, "If you want the musical-mystical-metaphorical significance, E Flat Major is a key which composers have frequently associated with the idea of resurrection." (He was probably thinking of Mahler's Second Symphony.) The theme also appears in E-flat *minor*, usually in a haunting version for one or two choirboys when someone dies – Rowena, Robert's friend Harris, soldiers in combat, even a horse. The theme hovers over the score like the Angel of Death. The score is in fact unified harmonically, with E-flat (major and minor) as principal key. The most important hymn, "Abide With Me," appears in E-flat, and when Gould needed a new theme for the sequence involving Harris's ashes he chose Brahms's dark Intermezzo in E-flat Minor, Op. 118/No. 6. And the Strauss theme is in C minor, the relative minor of E-flat major. Music that stands outside this key scheme tends to come in sequences parenthetical to the main action, like that of Robert's recovery at a country home in England.

Gould was in his element creating this score: he was solving a puzzle once more, taking found material and manipulating it to new creative ends. He had fun showing off his cleverness, indulging in variations of Schoenbergian subtlety that were surely lost on most viewers. At one point, for instance, "Abide With Me" is woven into a canon on a minor-key variant of "Rowena's Theme," in a duet for cello and double bass. He actually signed one of his sketches "A. Schönberg, opus posth."

According to Otto Friedrich, Jessie Greig heard angry tirades from Gould on the subject of *The Wars*, but both Nielsen and

Phillips remember a smooth and creatively exciting collaboration, and both loved Gould's music, which was just what they had envisioned when they hired him. Phillips maintains that the only point of contention came when he insisted on the need for hard-driving "tension music" during the war sequences, which Gould stubbornly refused to believe was necessary. Gould enjoyed and was proud of his work, and admired the dour, poetic, elegantly constructed film. "I think it's a remarkably fine picture," he wrote to a friend when it was nearly finished; "very understated, rather slow-moving, interesting particularly for what it leaves unsaid and unshown. It's a sort of Canadian 'Winter-Light' – the only Bergman film I can relate to – though not quite as well sustained structurally." In summer 1982 he showed *The Wars* to many people in Toronto and New York, anyone he could steer into a screening room. Among his papers are notes in which he organizes about forty minutes' worth of the music to fit the two sides of a record, and he screened the film for executives at CBS Masterworks, who showed some interest in a soundtrack album. But the film received mixed reviews, and was not picked up for American distribution, so plans for an album were dropped. *The Wars* rather quickly fell from view even in Canada, and has only rarely been seen since. Gould was spared this disappointment: it was released only after his death.

"Conductors live a long time, you know. It'll give me several more years to look forward to."

Gould had a direct physical response to music: he could not play or hear or imagine music without bobbing and weaving, waving his arms, singing. He had a profound knowledge of the orchestral repertoire; his thinking about music was never bound up solely with the piano. He numbered many conductors among his musical heroes, and modelled his tightly controlled approach to rhythm on orchestral performance – pianists, he said, were too indulgent in this respect. In his day he was a rare exponent of transcriptions, and from Guerrero, Schnabel, and others he inherited the venerable Romantic premise that one should play the piano as though it were an imaginary orchestra. He was a *conductorly* pianist, and it would have been strange had he not tried his hand at conducting.

He did so, in fact, as early as 1939, in a concert for the Business Men's Bible Class in Uxbridge. "By special request," according to the local newspaper, "a short song service was conducted in a most capable manner by little six year old Glenn Gould: without a trace of self-consciousness or shyness, in a perfectly natural manner but with striking ability he took the great audience in hand like a seasoned veteran, not only conducting but accompanying the songs on the piano, the audience responding the great enthusiasm." Gould directed small ensembles from the keyboard in some concerts and broadcasts, but really conducted for the first time in 1957 on the CBC television program *Chrysler Festival*, leading a pickup orchestra in the fourth movement ("Urlicht") of Mahler's Second Symphony, with Maureen Forrester singing. Later that year, he conducted Mozart's Symphony No. 1 and Schubert's "Tragic" Symphony (No. 4) with the CBC Vancouver Orchestra (in a radio studio, not in public). He was already envisioning a second career as a conductor, but his efforts in 1957 revealed an unexpected problem: after conducting "I was practically crippled for playing the piano," he said a year later. "I found that one uses an entirely different set of muscular coordination in conducting, and it's something I learned as a rather hard experience, because I had to cancel a couple of concerts as a pianist when I found this out too late." He made occasional plans to conduct after that – in Toronto, in Vancouver, in St. Louis – but always cancelled.

"You have undoubtedly heard by now of my temporary retirement as a conductor," he wrote to Vladimir Golschmann, conductor of the St. Louis Symphony, in 1958. "My retirement after a successful career of one concert which was at once my debut and my farewell appearance will, I am sure, be an irreparable loss in the music world. The one logical alternative is to retire from the piano and devote myself to conducting, which I am seriously considering."

He was considering no such thing – not in 1958, anyway. But his thoughts did turn seriously to conducting in the last years of his life, once it became clear that his demands in terms of studio time were making concerto films economically unfeasible. In his last years he envisioned solving the problem technologically, through over-dubbing on multi-track tape: he and Karajan could record concertos by taping the piano and orchestral parts separately after first conferring on matters of interpretation. He went as far as drawing up a provisional plan for recording Beethoven's Second Piano Concerto in this way, and summarized the possibilities in these terms: "Thesis and Resolution: That HvK and G.G. could have a meeting of the minds without a meeting. Antithesis and Retribution: The result could sound goddam awful." Whether he presented this proposal to Karajan, however, is unknown.*

Inevitably, Gould hit upon the idea of doing it all himself – playing the piano and conducting the orchestra on separate tracks. He chatted for hours on the subject (on New Year's Eve – again, he had nothing else to do) with his old friend Victor Di Bello, a conductor who had worked at the Stratford Festival during Gould's last years there. Finally, he hired Di Bello to serve as orchestral manager for an experimental session in which he would test his abilities as a conductor. Di Bello hired the Hamilton Philharmonic; Gould, through American friends, hired a young Juilliard student, Jon Klibonoff, to stand in for himself at the piano; and one afternoon in April 1982, in great secrecy, they all met to run through Beethoven's Second Piano Concerto.

Gould's interpretation of the concerto had changed since he recorded it in 1957. He took a slower tempo in the first movement, using the extra time to animate the music's latent counterpoint and

---

* The two remained in touch, on good terms, and earnestly intent on working together. Samuel Carter says that Gould, at the time of his death, was still planning to record with Karajan (including the "Emperor" Concerto) in the future, and Elliette von Karajan, the conductor's widow, told the Italian magazine *L'Espresso*, late in 2002, that her husband had been planning to travel to Toronto to record Bach concertos around the time Gould died.

to dissect the component parts of themes and phrases. At the start of the session, for instance, he spent time with the concertmaster fussing over the articulation of the small but important violin phrase in bars 2–4, trying out various *détaché* bowings even though the phrase is marked legato in the score. The second movement, with its powerfully expressive theme and Romantic piano textures, was always a favourite of Gould's – "the magnificent, glowing Adagio." His tempo was already slow in the 1957 recording, but now, as he told the orchestra, he wanted "to treat it almost like a Wesleyan hymn," and to conduct it not with three slow beats to the bar, but with *twelve* moderate beats, beating each of the four sixteenth notes into which each quarter note subdivides.

There was only one problem: Gould didn't know how to conduct, not really, and the sort of impromptu flailing he indulged in at the piano was no preparation for the task of leading an ensemble. In take after take of the *Adagio* the orchestra breaks down. Gould lacked the technique to convey his idiosyncratic intentions clearly and to maintain ensemble and continuity. It did not help that he never used a baton and insisted on conducting primarily with his left hand, which confused and annoyed musicians, whether he was conducting on a podium or from the keyboard. The *Chrysler Festival* appearance offers the only videotape of Gould conducting away from the piano, and it shows his technique to have been stiff and vague. In Hamilton, one of the musicians told him they were sometimes seeing *three* (rather than four) beats per quarter note, and Gould's response was to encourage them to, in effect, pay no attention to him. Still, he was a great musician, with great enthusiasm for the music at hand, of which he knew every note, and by flailing and singing and cajoling and explaining he did manage to convey his interpretations, and to lead decent takes of the first movement and eventually the second.

He was not happy with the session in Hamilton. To Victor Di Bello he complained about the "sideman mentality" that prevailed among professional orchestras – the cynicism and complacency of the players, the strict union rules, and so on. If he was going to continue to conduct, it would have to be with pickup ensembles of committed and sympathetic players. And so, in summer 1982, when he decided to conduct the original thirteen-part, chamber-orchestra version of Wagner's *Siegfried Idyll*, Di Bello hand-picked some of the best local performers, including members of the Toronto Symphony and musicians who had worked with Gould before. They recorded July 27–29, in St. Lawrence Hall. Gould paid the musicians and covered all the expenses himself, and this time the sessions were properly recorded by Kevin Doyle, a local engineer who worked on various of Gould's late recording projects. Gould went into the sessions unsure of what the result might be, but in the editing stage he came to feel that the recording was fit for release, and so scheduled an additional session, on September 8, to fix a few problem spots. It would be his last recording session.

He arrived at the sessions, with Ray Roberts, in his big Lincoln. He would emerge, wrote Timothy Maloney, one of the clarinetists, "wearing layers of shapeless dark jackets, flannel shirts and pants (plural) despite the summer's heat, and carrying a large, green, plastic garbage bag containing his musical score, note pads and paraphernalia." Wholly dedicated to the music at hand, Gould was not interested, like so many conductors, in matters of power and personality, and so came across as unpretentious. "What struck me the most about my encounter with Glenn was his unfailing politeness and encouragement to the musicians," Maloney wrote. "He was animated, resourceful, inspiring and *sympathique* throughout. He did his best to make us all feel like partners in the endeavour rather than sidemen to his maestro. We were all on a first-name basis. In fact, he had taken the time to commit everyone's name to memory before meeting us, and he made sure to shake everyone's hand at the end of the final session, something none of us expected." Gould was chummy with the musicians (that was the case in Hamilton, too), and found ways to keep them amused and energized during long sessions that went on late into the night. During one break, they all sat around, at his suggestion, thinking up names for their group – "Gould's Ghouls," "The Siegfried Idyllers," "The Academy of St. Lawrence-in-the-Market."

Gould's languorous approach to the *Siegfried Idyll* had not changed over the years, and for orchestral musicians it was a cruel interpretation – Wagner's long-breathed lyricism coupled with Gould's slow tempo made impossible demands on hands and lungs and lips. There is tenderness and poignancy in this performance, and Gould sometimes achieves extraordinary precision, but it is not quite the wondrous, dreamy meditation of his piano recording; at times it plods, and the players' struggles are palpable. Problems with tuning and balance and entries were to be expected at such a slow tempo, and were exacerbated by Gould's insecurity as a conductor. "His gestures were generally sweeping and extravagant," Maloney wrote, "sometimes more in response to the music than actually leading it." Other players report that he tended to get swept up in the music, his gestures consequently becoming less precise as a take unfolded. According to Maloney, the players often compensated by slipping into "chamber-music mode," communicating among themselves with their faces and bodies in order to keep together. But, again, Gould managed to inspire his musicians despite his lack of technique. He was ebullient during the sessions, and the players came away from the experience mostly enthusiastic. The bassist Charles Elliott says it was the most inspiring experience he ever had with a conductor, and Maloney wrote that Gould was "an instinctive communicator who always made music come alive."

The miking, like the interpretation, was cruel – so tight that one can almost taste the oboe reeds. Gould sought transparency rather than blend; he wanted to clarify the counterpoint, to make each instrument heard. (According to Kevin Doyle five microphones were used.) Gould was initially uncertain about the close pickup but eventually adored it; it gave him an intimacy of sound that matched his interpretation. To Doyle he described the effect as "wearing your heart on your sleeve." When the recording was finally released in 1990, the clinical sound disturbed many critics, to say nothing of the interpretation.* But the recording was just what Gould had wanted. At the end of one take, he cried out, "Gorgeous! Magnificent! Heartbreaking!"

"This is the most exhilarating experience of my life," he said of the Wagner sessions. He was now certain that, whether or not his pianistic career was winding down for good, he would make more recordings as a conductor. The prospect opened up a whole new repertoire to him as a creative interpreter. To judge from his two conducting experiments in 1982, and his piano performances of orchestral music by Beethoven, Wagner, and others, he would have offered orchestral performances no less personal and refreshing – and maddening – than his piano recordings. In the last months of his life, in his notepads, he made lists of some of the orchestral works he was considering conducting for future recordings, and they reveal his extraordinary enthusiasm at the prospect of this new career, and his astonishing ambition.† He began to compile some of

---

* In his 1997 book *The Compleat Conductor*, the American composer and conductor Gunther Schuller, deploring the phenomenon of the pianist turned conductor, singled out this recording as "probably the most inept, amateurish, wrong-headed rendition of a major classic ever put to vinyl."

† Those works included Bach's Orchestral Suites, Brandenburg Concertos, D-minor clavier concerto, and Cantata 54; concerti grossi by Handel; three overtures by Gluck (including *Alceste*); six middle- and late-period symphonies by Haydn; Beethoven's Second and Eighth symphonies, first three piano concertos, and *Große Fuge*, plus four overtures (*Egmont, Fidelio, Coriolan*, and either the third *Leonore* or *King Stephen*); Schubert's Fifth Symphony; Mendelssohn's "Scotch" and "Italian" and "Reformation" symphonies, plus four overtures (*The Hebrides, Calm Sea and Prosperous Voyage, Die schöne Melusine*, and *Ruy Blas*); Wagner's *Wesendonk-Lieder*, plus three overtures (*Faust, The Flying Dutchman*, and *Die Meistersinger*); Brahms's Third Symphony, Violin Concerto, *Variations on a Theme of Haydn, Tragic Overture, Alto Rhapsody*, and perhaps *Song of Destiny*; Strauss's *Till Eulenspiegels lustige Streiche, Don Juan, Metamorphosen*, Oboe Concerto, and Four Last Songs, plus the Suite from *Le bourgeois gentilhomme* and perhaps one of the suites based on keyboard music by Couperin; Sibelius's First, Fifth, and Seventh symphonies, plus *Luonnotar*, a tone poem with solo soprano; Schoenberg's two chamber symphonies, his chamber-orchestra arrangement of the "Lied der Waldtaube" from *Gurrelieder*, *Verklärte Nacht*, and *Pelleas und Melisande*; Webern's Passacaglia and Symphony; and Krenek's *Symphonic Elegy* for strings on the death of Webern.

these pieces into "sample programs" and "dream programs," presumably with an eye to future albums. Moreover, some of his conducting projects, including Wagner's *Siegfried Idyll*, were to be tied in with films by Bruno Monsaingeon, who said that Gould planned to bring his career as a performer to an end in 1985 with a film and recording of Bach's monumental B-minor Mass.

Those lists make for mouth-watering, heartbreaking reading – there is no more poignant might-have-been than Gould's planned conducting career. When he died he was not just idly speculating about conducting but making firm plans to begin this new phase of his career. In spring and summer 1982 he began to calculate projected expenses for conducting ventures he wanted to undertake in 1982 and 1983 – including Beethoven's Second Piano Concerto, again in Hamilton – and in the fall Victor Di Bello rounded up thirty-eight musicians for recordings in which Gould would conduct two overtures, Mendelssohn's *Hebrides* and Beethoven's *Coriolan*. Di Bello booked St. Lawrence Hall again, for October 25 and November 8, 1982.

"These are the happiest days of my life."

When he talked about giving up performance altogether, Gould envisioned an idyllic retirement in which he would live alone, away from the city, writing and composing, realizing some of his bucolic ambitions, like Glenn Gould's Puppy Farm, and performing only "for the fleas on the rocks in Muskoka." He was never happier than he was in his early twenties, living at the family cottage, playing for an audience of one and composing his String Quartet, and he longed to return to that life. He professed a fondness for the "neo-Thoreauvian way of life," and shared the Romantic view that it was the countryside not the city that inspired and nourished creativity. As long as he was a performer he was compelled to live in the city, but he told Monsaingeon that after 1985 they would no longer communicate in person, only by phone.

Some of his papers from the mid-seventies suggest that he might have been looking to give up his penthouse in favour of another apartment, or a house, in a less built-up part of Toronto – he said he could think better in the suburbs than he could downtown – and from time to time in the last twenty years of his life he expressed an interest in buying property in rural settings he found attractive: Bonavista Bay and Middle Cove, in Newfoundland; the town of Baddeck, on Bras d'Or Lake in Cape Breton Island; Grand Manan Island, in the Bay of Fundy. He was particularly fond of Manitoulin Island, which he considered an almost mystical place, as have the Indians who have long inhabited it. But he was never quite ready to leave the city behind permanently until the late seventies, when he began to think more seriously about retirement. After his mother's death he actually scouted property on Manitoulin, and considered buying land on one of the islands he loved off the Carolinas.

With his mother's death, his hand problems, his family troubles, the various losses of his later forties, his apparently worsening health, and probably the realization he would never enjoy a long-term romantic relationship, it is no surprise that Gould became more introspective in his later years. Yet his geniality and exuberance and sense of humour never diminished. He was still maintaining a furious workload, still boundlessly enthusiastic about his ideas and projects, still full of plans for the future, still enjoying the companionship of friends. He was still plagued by anxieties, too, but he was looking confidently ahead. "These are the happiest days of my life," he said to Tim Page a few weeks before his death, when he was in high spirits and working busily on writings and orchestral recordings and films and all the other projects that were to figure in the next phase of his career. Said Ray Roberts, "He had the next ten years planned."

By his own admission he was preoccupied with death throughout his life, and increasingly so with age. Stephen Posen, his lawyer from 1972, recalled that Gould was superstitious about drawing up a will. "He considered it bad luck, but at one point, about two years before he died, he felt he ought to do it. He was resistant to spending too much time on it, and when I pointed out that I was under obligation to explain certain things to him, he would go only as far as was necessary. When I asked him questions about the proper use of his assets, about memorialization or the advancement of causes which were important to him, he said, 'Look, just do it this way. When we are in our eighties we will make a perfect will. Those are your instructions, sir.' And that was the end of it." Much has been made of Gould's decision to divide his entire estate between the Salvation Army and the Toronto Humane Society, which have quietly reaped millions of dollars since his death, but that was a spur-of-the-moment decision never intended to be permanent. Compelled to name beneficiaries, he said, "out of the blue," as Posen recalled, "'Okay, there are unfortunate people and unfortunate animals,'" and that was that; he provided a life interest in a fifty-thousand-dollar trust fund for his father, but made no other provisions for the people in his life. But he did not plan to die at fifty, and did not think he was putting his affairs permanently in order. "Today I made a will," he said to John Roberts, after leaving Posen's office, "but it's not a *real* will. One day I'm going to make a real will."

Gould did remark, to more than one acquaintance, that he did not think he would live much past fifty, but this was hardly a "premonition" – if anything, it was a rare flash of insight into his destructive hypochondria. Roberts says that Gould was always "a man in a hurry," who seemed driven by the assumption that he did not have many years before him, but that did not stop him from confidently telling people that he planned to live to a hundred and ten. Neither he nor anyone else thought he was near death in the summer of 1982, though he had begun to look permanently ill. He had always seemed frail and pasty and underfed, but he looked worse and worse through his last decade. Acquaintances who saw him in his late forties for the first time in years were shocked at his deterioration. His complexion was sickly, his hair was thinning and greying, he was paunchy and wrinkled, he was more stooped than usual. He looked tired – his eyes were perpetually bloodshot – he moved more slowly and clumsily than before and he was having problems with his eyesight. His last photographs were taken in Toronto, by Don Hunstein, in September 1981, to accompany a profile in the December issue of *Esquire*, and while he appears tired and blood-shot in them he does not seem deathly ill.* But according to friends his appearance deteriorated further in the year after those pictures were taken. Jessie Greig was alarmed by his appearance in summer 1982 – "I'm *so* tired, Jessie," he said to her, adding that he had begun to have trouble remembering things, and was experiencing worsening circulation.

He was confiding medical problems to his notepads: musculoskeletal aches, hypertension, gastro-intestinal complaints, high levels of uric acid, difficulty sleeping, and all sorts of other physical problems from head to toe. Yet he was never able to see any connection between his health and his lifestyle, which was becoming ever more ascetic, ever harder on his body. He was still doctor-shopping and still taking increasingly alarming amounts of medication. His surviving pharmacy receipts for January through September 1982 indicate that he was prescribed more than *two thousand* pills in that period, which is to say about seven or eight per day, and not innocuous medications: he was regularly taking Valium, Aldomet, allopurinol, and Librax. In the *Esquire* photos, in fact, he looks not just tired but a little drugged. From at least 1976 he was gaining weight significantly, probably due to his medication: he was looking not so much heavy as puffy.

Gould feared that hypertension would kill him, for on both sides of his family there was a history of high blood pressure and of deaths by stroke. Yet his lineage was, if anything, cause for optimism. His mother had lived to eighty-three; his father would survive several strokes and outlive him by almost fifteen years, dying in 1996 at age

---

* His last photos for CBS Masterworks were taken at the 30th Street studio, by Don Hunstein on June 18, 1980; some of them appeared on his last album covers. They already show a deterioration in Gould's health, though according to his 1980 diary the photos were taken after he had been sleeping "miserably" for days. The last video images of Gould are in the April-May 1981 film of the Goldberg Variations.

ninety-four; and Jessie lived to seventy. His grandfather, Thomas Gould, despite his hypochondria, lived to eighty-six, and his Grandmother Gould lived almost to ninety. Many other ancestors in both the Gold and Greig families lived into their sixties, seventies, and eighties. (The Scots especially, as John Kenneth Galbraith's memoirs remind us, were "made to last.") Gould's great-great-great-great-grandfather, Isaac Gold, who was born almost *two hundred years* before he was, lived into his eighties. Nothing in Gould's family tree, in short, should have led him expect, even while nursing high blood pressure, to die anytime soon.

He turned fifty on Saturday, September 25, 1982, an event that was marked by published tributes, many tied to reviews of the new album of the Goldberg Variations, though there were no parties or public celebrations. Both Bert Gould and CBS Masterworks had wanted to celebrate the landmark in some way, but Gould had scotched all such plans. He was in good spirits the weekend of September 25–26, when he spoke by phone to many friends who had called up with birthday greetings, though he was curt during a brief meeting with Bert and Vera in the parking lot of his building (she had knitted him a sweater and baked some cookies). Gould was thrilled by Edward Rothstein's sympathetic article about him in the *New York Times*, and read it over the phone to many people. Everyone who spoke to him that weekend (and there were many) recalls that he was bubbling over with enthusiasm, for his conducting plans especially. His only complaint was a persistent cold that had plagued him all summer, and for which his papers document a steady stream of drugstore products – Vicks cough syrup, Neo Citran, Phenogram CV expectorant, 222s (an over-the-counter painkiller with some codeine), antibiotics, and at least one a small prescription of Percodan.

The afternoon of Monday, September 27, he was sleeping in a room at the Inn on the Park, and awoke feeling "not right." He had a bad headache and felt numb down his left leg. He thought at once it was a stroke and summoned Ray Roberts, who called Dr. John Percival. But the doctor, to whom Gould must have seemed like the

Gould in the Steinway display at the Eaton's department store, in Eaton Centre, downtown Toronto, during his last documented photo session, in September 1981. Two other images from this session were published in the December 1981 issue of *Esquire*. *(Photograph by Don Hunstein.)*

Boy Who Cried Wolf, was not unduly concerned. Gould continued to feel worse and his speech became less clear as the afternoon wore on. Roberts called the doctor several more times, and Percival, unable to come to the Inn, insisted that they call an ambulance. Finally, Roberts got Gould down to his car in a wheelchair and drove him to Toronto General Hospital, on College Street downtown. Peter Ostwald studied the hospital's records for his biography:

> Examined at 8:44 P.M. in the emergency room, Glenn was found to have muscular weakness over the left side of his body, including his face, and some inequality of the deep tendon reflexes. There was no diminution in his responsiveness to sensory stimulation, touch, pain, or change in position. He was drowsy, but had no difficulty speaking. His blood pressure was 124/90 and the pulse rate 104 per minute. A preliminary diagnosis of cerebro-vascular-accident (stroke) with left-sided paralysis was made. It was suspected that the cause might be a blood clot in one of the arteries supplying the right side of the brain, and he was admitted to the neurology department for further observation. . . . The neurology staff concurred with the diagnosis of a right frontal brain infarction due to a blood clot causing paralysis of the left side of the body. There was no evidence of a hemorrhage but a CAT scan of the brain was recommended. It showed enlarged ventricles but no signs of acute bleeding.

Gould's headache was worse the next day, as was his vision, and he was still paralyzed on the left side. Though he was sleeping a lot, he was able to talk and watch television and even to discuss financial matters with Ray Roberts and play a game of Twenty Questions over the phone. By this time, friends and family members were gathering at the hospital, and Gould was able to spend some time with his father and with Jessie Greig among others. (He was worried about the effect his stroke might have on his father's well-being.) By that evening, however, he was beginning to show signs of confusion and disorientation. The next morning, Wednesday, September 29, his headache was still worse, he was barely able to move or speak, and he was having trouble swallowing. He was in and out of consciousness and becoming increasingly incoherent. "He started to ramble – lose control," Ray Roberts recalled. "I can remember having to leave him. He was getting more and more upset, and he was asking me to do things that I couldn't possibly do. And I had to leave. I just knew instinctively that I couldn't be there. And I can still hear him calling me." "Another CAT scan was ordered," wrote Ostwald. "It showed that the midline structures of the brain had shifted markedly from right to left, confirming the clinical impression of massive right-sided swelling. A blood-flow study revealed that there was no blood passing through the right internal carotid artery, one of the major blood vessels supplying the brain. . . . Chest X-rays showed that fluid was collecting in the chest cavity." Medication did little to reduce the intracranial pressure, and by that evening Gould was comatose in the intensive-care unit.

On Thursday, September 30, Gould was completely unconscious and relying on a breathing tube; he was beset by more physical complications, and administered more medication. An electroencephalogram revealed a significant reduction of brain activity. He had often expressed horror at the prospect of ever having to live with some dire physical or mental disability, and now it was becoming clear that even if he did survive he would indeed be gravely impaired. His family and friends were stunned by the prognosis, and Bert was devastated, at one point lamenting, "Why him and not me?" In the first days of October, it became clear that Gould had suffered massive and irreversible brain damage and could no longer breathe unassisted. Only then did the hospital release news of his illness to the public. "On Sunday, October 3," Ostwald wrote, "Glenn's blood pressure had risen to 220/125 and he developed a nosebleed, both probably in reaction to the enormous amount of pressure building up inside his head. There was no longer any hope of recovery, and it was suggested that life-support systems be withdrawn because the patient was in essence 'brain-dead.'" Bert agreed, but as October 3 was Vera's birthday they delayed until the following morning. On

Monday, October 4, he was taken off life support, and at 11:00 a.m. he was pronounced dead.

An autopsy was performed two hours later, revealing a blood clot filling the right cavernous sinus, a large vein that drains blood from the brain and within which lies the internal carotid artery; the clot, probably caused by an infection, was about ten days old – this was the "cold" and sinus pressure Gould had complained of around the time of his birthday. A smaller, younger clot was found within the internal carotid artery, too – that was the immediate cause of Gould's stroke. The autopsy, Ostwald noted, also revealed "a minor degree of arteriosclerosis," "some enlargement of the left side of the heart consistent with chronic hypertension," and "a mildly fatty liver" probably due to "dietary insufficiency." However, "no physical abnormalities were found in the kidneys, prostate, bones, joints, muscles, or other parts of the body that Glenn so often had complained about."

Gould's friends and colleagues paid respects at a funeral home, though his funeral service, on a miserable, rainy, appropriately Gouldian day, was a private affair attended only by his immediate family and a handful of friends. He was buried not far from his St. Clair Avenue apartment building, in Mount Pleasant Cemetery, next to his mother and, eventually, Bert. His grave is marked by a modest headstone, flat on the ground, bearing only his name and dates and the first three bars of the Goldberg Variations (the carver left off the ornaments). By the time the memorial service was held in St. Paul's Cathedral on October 15, the press and the public airwaves were rife with stories about Gould, and the widespread shock and sorrow at his untimely death was already being transformed into a new interest in his life and work. By the first anniversary of his death, his recordings were already being rereleased, his writings were being collected, and plans were afoot for commemorative volumes and other tributes. The extraordinary posthumous life of Glenn Gould had begun.

Opposite: The storage room of Gould's midtown Toronto apartment, shortly after his death. (*Photograph by Lorne Tulk.*)

NOTES ON SOURCES
& ACKNOWLEDGEMENTS

Archival and private sources

My most important source was the Glenn Gould Archive, archival fond
MUS 109 in the Music Division of the National Library of Canada (NLC),*
in Ottawa, which includes most of the personal effects that were in Gould's
possession at the time of his death. Over a period of more than ten years,
I have examined this material on site and through photocopies and micro-
films, and have used the databases and other resources on the NLC's Gould
Web site <http://www.gould.nlc-bnc.ca/egould.htm>. For this book, I
studied all of Gould's handwritten papers (notepads, diaries, etc.), unpublished writings, compositional sketches, incoming and outgoing correspondence, genealogical papers, school and conservatory and Kiwanis
Music Festival records, concert programs, press clippings, recording-
session logs, promotional material, awards and honours, and medical
records. I also studied many of his business and financial records, travel
records, drafts for published writings, and annotated scores, as well as
indexes of the books, recordings, videotapes, photographs, and artifacts he
owned when he died.

I further drew on the Manuscript Collection of the Music Division
(MUS 229) as well as the archival fonds for Walter Homburger (MUS 259),
Otto Joachim (MUS 270), Sir Ernest MacMillan (MUS 7), Keith MacMillan

---

* A bill merging the NLC and the National Archives of Canada into a new institution, the Library and Archives of Canada, was tabled in the House of Commons in
May 2003, just as this book was being completed.

(MUS 239), Eric McLean (MUS 173), Oskar Morawetz (MUS 76), Geoffrey Payzant (MUS 174), and Steinway and Sons (MUS 258).

I am grateful for the extraordinary generosity of the NLC's staff. In addition to examining papers myself, I used research undertaken by Cheryl Gillard, who reviewed many of Gould's medical, financial, and travel records on my behalf and responded to countless queries over the years. I am indebted to her, to her colleagues in the Music Division – Jeannine Barriault, Richard Green, Timothy Maloney, Maureen Nevins – and to Lise Vézeau of the NLC's interlibrary-loan division.

The Canadian federal government's file on Gould's tour of Russia is housed in the National Archives of Canada, Government of Canada Files, RG 25 (External Affairs), Series G-2, Volume 7271, File 10417-S-40. Copies of these documents were made available to me by Robert Desjardins and Hector Mackenzie, both of the Department of Foreign Affairs and International Trade.

I gratefully acknowledge information received under Canada's Access to Information Act from the Canadian Security Intelligence Service (CSIS), the National Archives of Canada, and the Royal Canadian Mounted Police (RCMP), and under the United States's Freedom of Information-Privacy Acts from the Federal Bureau of Investigation (FBI) of the Department of Justice and from Department of State files in the National Archives in Washington.

My thanks to Keith Harrington, in Southampton, England, for his research into the history of the Gold family. I also acknowledge assistance in genealogical research from the Archives of Ontario, the Family History Centre of the Church of Jesus Christ of Latter-Day Saints (Victoria), Allan McGillivray (Uxbridge-Scott Township Museum and Archives), Ellen Millar (Simcoe County Archives), Mrs. G. M. Turner (Hampshire Record Office), and the Victoria Genealogical Society. Records on the Gold/ Gould name-change were supplied by the Office of the Registrar General, Ministry of Consumer and Business Services, Ontario.

I gratefully acknowledge the input of persons representing other archives and institutions: Robert J. Barg (Yamaha Canada Music, Toronto); Tom Belton (Archives of Ontario, Toronto); Johanna Blask (Paul Sacher Foundation, Basel); Lisa Brant, Jane Edmonds, and Kathleen Walsh (Stratford Festival Archives); Suzanne Eggleston Lovejoy (Irving S. Gilmore Music Library, Yale University); Myra Emsley (Hart House, University of Toronto); Peter B. Goodrich (Steinway and Sons, New York); Barbara Haws and Richard Wandel (New York Philharmonic); Carol Jacobs (Cleveland Orchestra); Jane Klain (Museum of Television and Radio, New York); Steve Lacoste (Los Angeles Philharmonic); Hilde A. Limondjian

(Metropolitan Museum of Art, New York); Richard Lingner (Isabella Stewart Gardner Museum, Boston); Kathleen McMorrow (Faculty of Music Library, University of Toronto); Denise Restout (The Landowska Center, Lakeville, Connecticut); Jonathan Summers (National Sound Archive, British Library, London); Karen White (Written Archives Centre, BBC, London); and Jan Wilson (American Symphony Orchestra League, New York).

I am also grateful to many individuals who contribtuted to this book in various ways over the years. Besides those acknowledged elsewhere, they include Jonathan Bellman, Ray Chrunyk, Robert Craft, Jim Curtis, Renate Fleck, Corey Hamm, Marcia Hennessy, Dale Innes, Helmut Kallmann, Sean Malone, Matthew McFarlane, Bruno Monsaingeon, Hele Montagna, Sadako Nguyen, Natalia Novik, John Oswald, Jeffrey Smyth, Michaela Steber, Bob Trenholm, Christopher Weait, Natalie Webster, and Reg Whitaker.

Interviews

I conducted close to a hundred interviews for this book, most between February 2001 and May 2002, one as late as May 2003. In many cases, there was follow-up conversation and correspondence, and some interviewees shared Gould materials in their possession.

I conducted in-person interviews with Angela Addison, Hugh Davidson, Peter Heron, Barbara and Carl Little, Harvey Rempel, and Robert and Sara Turner.

I conducted telephone interviews with Gordon Bacque, Robert J. Barg, Fran Barrault, Coenraad Bloemendal, Jean Brown (née Trott), James Campbell, Norman Campbell, Samuel H. Carter, Schuyler Chapin, Mark Childs, Jill R. Cobb, Ann Coulter, Richard Coulter, James Deak, Richard Dorsey, Kevin Doyle, Fran and Ray Dudley, Verne Edquist, Charles Elliott, Susan Englebert, Dr. A.A. Epstein, Ellen Faull, Victor Feldbrill, Patrick Fleck, Lea Foli, Sam Gesser, Norman Glick, Dr. William E. Goodman, Dr. Stanley E. Greben, Stuart Hamilton, Ken Haslam, Sylvia Hunter, Becky Hutchings, Mélisande Irvine (née Guerrero), David Jaeger, Otto Joachim, Gilbert Johnson, Mason Jones, Morry Kernerman, the late Karen Kieser, William Knorp, Susan Kocsis, Ilona Kombrink, Antonin Kubalek, Louis Lane, Ronald Laurie, Naomi Lightbourn, Kurt Loebel, Donald Logan, Ian Macdonald, John McGreevy, Edna Meyers, Franz Mohr, Oskar Morawetz, Ruth Morawetz, Marguerite Mousseau, Paul Myers, William Needles, Richard Nielsen, Tim Page, Robin Phillips,

Laura Pogson, the late Margaret Privitello, Gladys Riskind (née Shenner), John P. L. Roberts, Charles Rosen, David W. Rubin, Jean Sarrazin, Ezra Schabas, Marianne Schroeder, Suzanne Shulman, Howard Scott, Dr. William Shipman, Tom Shipton, Robert Skelton, Janet Somerville, Steven Staryk, Henry Z. Steinway, Dr. Joseph Stephens, Robert Sunter, Lamont Tilden, Eric Till, Vincent Tovell, Lorne Tulk, Helen Vanni, and Peter Yazbeck.

I communicated in writing with Edward J. Bond, James Kent, Nicholas Kilburn, Richard Kostelanetz, Daniel Mansolino, Verna Post (née Sandercock), Isadore Sharp, and Dr. Herbert J. Vear. Several people supplied me with copies of unpublished interviews they conducted: Angela Addison (interviews with various people in the Uptergrove and Orillia areas), Rhona Bergman (with Stephen Posen), Jörgen Lundmark (with Kerstin Meyer), Junichi Miyazawa (with Daniel Mansolino and Eric McLuhan), and Elke Regehr (with Russell Oberlin). Patricia MacMillan shared her late husband Keith MacMillan's then unpublished memoir "Me and Glenn Gould," and Harvey Rempel shared notes on Gould made by his late wife Joan Maxwell.

I also drew on interviews with Gould's family members, friends, and colleagues that appeared in the previous Gould biographies and in the books *Glenn Gould: Variations* and *The Idea of Gould* (all cited below); in *Glenn Gould*, a booklet published by the Centre Culturel Canadien, in Paris, at the time of their Gould exhibition in 1986; in the panel discussion "Gould the Communicator," held at the NLC on May 25, 1988, and published in the *Bulletin of the Glenn Gould Society* (October 1989); in the special Gould issue of the Swiss magazine *Du* (April 1990); in the film *Thirty Two Short Films about Glenn Gould* (Rhombus Media, 1993); and in the television documentaries *Glenn Gould: A Portrait* (CBC, 1985), *Glenn Gould: Extasis* (Radio-Canada, 1998), *Glenn Gould: The Shadow Genuis* (CBC, in their series *Life & Times*, 1998), and *Glenn Gould: The Russian Journey* (DocuTainment Plus Productions, et. al., 2002). The NLC supplied me with dubs of interviews with Victor Di Bello, Nicholas Goldschmidt, Bert Gould, Jessie Greig, Walter Homburger, and Roxolana Roslak, conducted for *Glenn Gould: A Portrait*.

Writings by Gould

I list only published books and interviews here, though I also studied broadcasts and films for which Gould wrote scripts, and uncollected writings published since 1995 in the Glenn Gould Foundation's magazine, *GlennGould*, which I edit. (Contents of past issues of the magazine are listed at www.glenngould.ca/index.nn.html. For a comprehensive Gould bibliography, see the NLC's Gould Web site.) Among the interviews I include conversations both impromptu and scripted, as well as articles that feature a significant interview or photographic component. I include only major pieces, however, not all of the articles written by reporters who chatted with Gould – I read scores of these among the press clippings in his papers – nor interviews collected in *Glenn Gould: Variations*, *The Glenn Gould Reader*, and *The Art of Glenn Gould*.

Books

Glenn Gould, et. al., *Glenn Gould: Variations*, edited by John McGreevy (1983).

The Glenn Gould Reader, edited by Tim Page (1984).

Non, je ne suis pas du tout un excentrique, edited by Bruno Monsaingeon (1986).

Glenn Gould: Selected Letters, edited by John P. L. Roberts and Ghyslaine Guertin (1992).

La Série Schönberg [1974 CBC radio scripts], edited by Ghyslaine Guertin (1998).

The Art of Glenn Gould: Reflections of a Musical Genius, edited by John P. L. Roberts (1999).

Journal d'une crise, suivi de Correpondance de concert [hand-related diaries, 1977-78, and letters from the concert years], edited by Bruno Monsaingeon (2002).

Interviews

Gladys Shenner, "The Genius Who Doesn't Want to Play," *Maclean's* (April 28, 1956).

Gordon Parks, "Music World's Young Wonder," *Life* (March 12, 1956).

Jock Carroll, "'I don't think I'm at all eccentric,' says Glenn Gould," *Weekend Magazine* (July 7, 1956).

"Glenn Gould Interviewed by Hugh Thomson," [CBC radio, 1958] *GlennGould* (Fall 2001).

At Home with Glenn Gould [with Vincent Tovell, CBC radio, 1959], released on CD by the Glenn Gould Foundation (1996).

Joseph Roddy, "Apollonian," *New Yorker* (May 14, 1960); reprinted in *Glenn Gould: Variations*.

Betty Lee, "The Odd, Restless Way of Glenn Gould," *Globe Magazine* (December 1, 1962).

"Ten Minutes with Glenn Gould: A Conversation with Vincent Tovell" [CBC television, 1962], *GlennGould* (Spring 2003).

New York Philharmonic intermission radio interview with James Fassett (February 2, 1963), excerpt released on CD by Sony Classical, in *The Glenn Gould Silver Jubilee Album* (1998).

"Bach's Keyboard Partitas: A Conversation with Glenn Gould" [with David Johnson, liner notes, 1963], *GlennGould* (Fall 1998).

Alfred Bester, "The Zany Genius of Glenn Gould," *Holiday* (April 1964).

Pat Moore, "Interview with Glenn Gould, the Pianist" [CBC radio, 1964], *GlennGould* (Fall 1998).

Richard Kostelanetz, "The Glenn Gould Variations," *Esquire* (November 1967); reprinted in *Glenn Gould: Variations* and in Kostelanetz's *Three Canadian Geniuses: Glenn Gould, Marshall McLuhan, Northrop Frye* (2001).

Glenn Gould: Concert Dropout [with John McClure, 1968], *GlennGould* (Fall 2001); released on LP by Columbia/CBS Masterworks (1968, 1984).

James Kent, "Glenn Gould & Wolfgang Amadeus Mozart," *Canadian Composer* (March 1969).

"Where Music and Film Meet: Glenn Gould in Conversation with Norman McLaren" [CBC radio, 1969], *GlennGould* (Spring 2002).

Gladys Houck, "Glenn Gould: Talking about Television – and Beethoven," *Canadian Composer* (January 1971).

Peter Goddard, "Glenn Gould is a Conjurer," *Canadian Composer* (March 1972).

"The Scene: Glenn Gould on Competitive Sport" [CBC radio, 1972] *GlennGould* (Spring 2003).

Tony Thomas, "Glenn Gould," *Canadian Stereo Guide* (Summer 1973).

William Littler, " 'Retired' pianist Glenn Gould is busier than ever . . . ," *Toronto Star* (December 8, 1973).

Jonathan Cott, *Conversations with Glenn Gould* [*Rolling Stone* interview, 1974] (1984).

Norman Snider, "Glenn Gould at 45," *Toronto Life* (May 1978).

"CBC Radio Script from 1978," *GlennGould* (Spring 1996).

Interview [1978] in Yehudi Menuhin and Curtis W. Davis, *The Music of Man* (1979), based on their television series.

Elyse Mach, *Great Pianists Speak for Themselves* (1980).

Andrew Stephen, "A Rare Meeting with the Bobby Fischer of Music," *Sunday Times* (March 16, 1980).

"*Mostly Music*: Glenn Gould in Conversation with Barclay McMillan" [CBC radio, 1980], *GlennGould* (Spring 2002).

Martin Meyer, "Interview: Glenn Gould, '. . . the inner movement of music . . . ,'" in German, *FonoForum* (June 1981); in English, *GlennGould* (Fall 1995).

Joseph Roddy, "Glenn Gould," *People Weekly* (November 30, 1981).

Laurence Shames, "Glenn Gould: Music for Piano and a Different Drummer," *Esquire* (December 1981).

"On Bach's Goldberg Variations: Glenn Gould in Conversation with Tim Page (1982)," *GlennGould* (Spring 2001); released on CD by Sony Classical, in *Glenn Gould: A State of Wonder* (2002).

"Glenn Gould: A Last Interview" [1982], in David Dubal, *Reflections from the Keyboard: The World of the Concert Pianist* (1984).

I also studied unpublished interviews, some for radio and television, made available to me by the NLC and CBC and by individuals including John A. Miller, Tim Page, and Jörg Scheuvens.

Gould's recordings, radio and television broadcasts, and films

All of Gould's Columbia/CBS studio recordings, and a generous selection of his concert, radio, television, and film performances, were released, beginning in 1992, by Sony Classical in a Glenn Gould Edition. The same year, Sony Classical began releasing a Glenn Gould Collection on videotape and laser disc, comprising most of his television and film performances. These comprehensive series, completed in the mid-1990s, were my principal sources for Gould performances. I used several other Sony Classical CDs outside the Edition: *Glenn Gould: The Composer* (1992); *The Glenn Gould Silver Jubilee Album* (1994); the April 6, 1962, New York performance of Brahms's D-minor concerto (1998); and *Glenn Gould: A State of Wonder* (2002), which includes both recordings of the Goldberg Variations and outtakes from the 1955 recording sessions.

Between 1993 and 1999, CBC Records released six individual Gould CDs, compilations of broadcasts (both concert and studio performances) from 1951 to 1955. CBC Records has also released boxed sets of CDs of the radio documentaries of the Solitude Trilogy (1992) and of the radio portraits of Stokowski and Casals (2001). Gould's first recordings, the 1953

Hallmark sessions, have been rereleased most recently by VAI Audio, in *Glenn Gould: His First Recordings (1947-1953)* (2001), along with some private recordings that are misattributed to Gould and Alberto Guerrero. I studied all of these recordings.

Among unauthorized releases, I benefitted particularly from the following: the nineteen CDs of live and broadcast performances released by Music and Arts Programs of America between 1987 and 1991; *Glenn Gould: Concert de Moscou*, May 12, 1957 (Le Chant du Monde/Harmonic Mundi, 1983); *Glenn Gould in Stockholm, 1958* (BIS, 1986); a 1988 Melodram CD that includes chamber music by Beethoven (with Oscar Shumsky and Leonard Rose) from a Stratford Festival concert on August 7, 1960; and a 1995 Artistotipia/M-Classic Records CD of concerts in Berlin and Vienna, May–June, 1957.

I also studied private recordings, unreleased concert recordings, CBC radio and television programs, promotional recordings for Columbia/CBS, outtakes, and other audio-visual sources. For access to such material, I am indebted to Ray Roberts and the Estate of Glenn Gould; the CBC, particularly Ken Puley (radio archives) and Roy Harris (television archives); Richard Green, of the NLC's Music Division; and individuals including John Beckwith, Eitan Cornfield, Jed Distler, Yosif Feyginberg, Louis Lane, R. D. (Doug) Lloyd, Jörgen Lundmark, Fred Maroth, John A. Miller, Junichi Miyazawa, Jack Saul, Jörg Scheuvens, Ates Tanin, and Vladimir Tropp.

Compositions by Gould

The cadenzas to Beethoven's C-major concerto were published by Barger and Barclay in 1958 but are no longer in print. *So You Want to Write a Fugue?* was published by Schirmer in 1964 and remains in print. To date the following works have been published by B. Schott's Söhne, in Mainz: *5 Short Piano Pieces* and *2 Pieces* (1995); *Sonata for Bassoon and Piano* (1996); Lieberson Madrigal (1997); String Quartet (1999); *Sonata for Piano* (2003); and the transcription of Wagner's *Siegfried Idyll* (2003). Other compositions and arrangements, including uncompleted works and juvenilia, have been published in facsimile in *GlennGould*. As to Gould's film scores: *Slaughterhouse-Five* and *The Terminal Man* are both available commercially, and a videotape copy of *The Wars* was kindly made available to me by the film's producer, Richard Nielsen, through his television-production company Norflicks.

Writings about Gould

I list only those books that made a direct impact on mine, and only major articles and book chapters that include reminscences of people who knew Gould personally. "*BGGS*" refers to the *Bulletin of the Glenn Gould Society* (Groningen, The Netherlands, 1982-92).

Books

Geoffrey Payzant, *Glenn Gould, Music and Mind* (1978, 1984).
Glenn Gould: Variations, edited by John McGreevy (1983).
Michel Schneider, *Glenn Gould piano solo: Aria et trente variations* (1988).
Glenn Gould, pluriel, edited by Ghyslaine Guertin (1988).
Otto Friedrich, *Glenn Gould: A Life and Variations* (1989).
Andrew Kazdin, *Glenn Gould at Work: Creative Lying* (1989).
Jens Hagestedt, *Wie spielt Glenn Gould? Zu einer Theorie der Interpretation* (1991).
Elizabeth Angilette, *Philosopher at the Keyboard: Glenn Gould* (1992).
Nancy Canning, *A Glenn Gould Catalog* [discography] (1992).
NLC, *Glenn Gould: Descriptive Catalogue of the Glenn Gould Papers*, edited by Ruth Pincoe and Stephen C. Willis, 2 vols. (1992).
Michael Stegemann, *Glenn Gould: Leben und Werk* (1992).
Jock Carroll, *Glenn Gould: Some Portraits of the Artist as a Young Man* (1995).
Peter F. Ostwald, *Glenn Gould: The Ecstasy and Tragedy of Genius* (1997).
Carmelo di Gennaro, *Glenn Gould: L'immaginazione al pianoforte* (1999).
Rhona Bergman, *The Idea of Gould* (1999).
Glenn Gould: A Life in Pictures, introduction by Tim Page (2002).

My own previous book, *Glenn Gould: The Performer in the Work* (Oxford: Clarendon Press, 1997), based on a Ph.D. dissertation I completed in 1996 at the University of California at Berkeley, is a scholarly study of Gould's piano style, interpretations, and aesthetic ideas.

I learned much from biographies and autobiographies of contemporary classical musicians and others who either knew Gould or helped me to understand his times and milieu, including Louis Applebaum, Leonard Bernstein, Schuyler Chapin, Van Cliburn, Leonard Cohen, Bill Evans, Maureen Forrester, Northrop Frye, Robert Fulford, Gary Graffman, William Kapell, Herbert von Karajan, Josef Krips, Stephen Leacock, Sir Ernest MacMillan, Marshall McLuhan, Yehudi Menuhin, Boyd Neel, Elisabeth Schwarzkopf, Leo Smith, Ben Sonnenberg, Steven Staryk, Isaac Stern, Jon Vickers, and Healey Willan.

Articles and book chapters

Angela Addison, "The Ultimate Soloist: A Portrait of Glenn Gould," *BGGS* (October 1988).

Pierre Berton, "The Boy Who Broke the Rules," *1967: The Last Good Year* (1997)

Humphrey Burton, "The Glenn Gould I Knew," *GlennGould* (Fall 2000).

Robin Elliott, "Glenn Gould and the Canadian Composer," *Notations* (September 1992).

Robert Fulford: "Growing up Gould," *Saturday Night* (December 1982); reprinted in *Glenn Gould: Variations*.

Robert Fulford, "The Genius Who Lived Next Door," in *Best Seat in the House: Memoirs of a Lucky Man* (1988).

Allan M. Gould, "Glenn Gould: The Way He Was," *CBC Radio Guide* (January 1983).

Jacques Hétu, "Variations et variantes," in *Glenn Gould, pluriel*; in English in *GlennGould* (Fall 1995).

Silvia Kind, "Glenn Gould, the Man," *BGGS* (October 1988).

Junichi Miyazawa, "An Interview with Jaime Laredo," *BGGS* (October 1989).

Daniel Kunzi, "An Interview with Leonard Rose," *BGGS* (October 1990).

Gene Lees, "Glenn Gould: A Memory," *Gene Lees Jazzletter* (July 1998).

Kurt Loebel, "Glenn Gould off the Record," *Clavier* (April 1984).

Keith MacMillan, "Me and Glenn Gould" [1990], *GlennGould* (Fall 2002).

Bruno Monsaingeon, "Encounters with Glenn Gould," *GlennGould* (Spring 2000).

Tim Page, "Glenn Gould: The Last Months," *GlennGould* [1984], (Spring 2001).

"Albert Pratz Remembers the Young Glenn Gould" [1982], *GlennGould* (Fall 2002).

Avril Rustage-Johnson, untitled reminiscence in Peter Gzowski, *The Morningside Papers* (1985).

Robert Silverman, "Money and the Pianist," *BGGS* (March 1988).

James Strecker, "Glenn Gould: Man, Musician, and Legacy – Nine Canadians talk about the legendary pianist," *BGGS* (1991).

Lorne Tulk, "Remembering Glenn Gould," *GlennGould* (Fall 2000).

Selective list of other sources consulted

Postlude (in the form of a Prelude)

Peter Foster, "If Glenn Gould Were Alive Today ...," *Toronto Life* (October 1999); Robert Fulford "Ladies and Gentlemen ... Glenn Gould Has Left the Building," *Saturday Night* (September 1992); and Carl Sagan, et. al., *Murmurs of Earth: The Voyager Interstellar Record* (1978).

Part 1, Beach Boy

On the milieu in which Gould was raised, I read standard histories of Toronto by G. P. de T. Glazebrook, William Kilbourn, James Lemon, Bruce West, and others, as well as books on the Beach neighbourhood, Uxbridge, Orillia, and the Lake Simcoe area, including H. Higgins, *The Life and Times of Joseph Gould, Ex-Member of the Canadian Parliament* (1887). Especially useful were two articles by Robert Fulford: "Whose Beach?" in *Accidental City: The Transformation of Toronto* (1995); and "Beach Boy," in *The Toronto Book: An Anthology of Writings Pase and Present*, edited by William Kilbourn (1976). My background reading further included books on the Scots in Canada; on religious life in Canada, Ontario, and Toronto; on Canadian Methodism and Presbyterianism, the United Church, and the social gospel; and on the Canadian experience of the Depression and the Second World War. I learned much about Gould's milieu by reading mid- and late-twentieth-century Canadian fiction, too. Allan McGillivray, of the Uxbridge-Scott Township Museum and Archives, supplied much useful information, including newspaper clippings, about the Gold and Greig families in Uxbridge. On the Gold/Gould name change, I read John Beckwith's "Master Glen Gold," *GlennGould* (Spring 1997), and a handful of books on Jewish life in Canada and Toronto in the early twentieth century.

On music in Canada and Toronto particularly in the first half of Gould's life, I made copious use of the second edition of the *Encyclopedia of Music in Canada* (1992); read standard histories by Clifford Ford, Timothy J. McGee, and George A. Proctor; and drew on such periodicals as the *Canadian Review of Music and Art* (1942-48), *The Canadian Music Journal* (1956-62), and the *Canada Music Book* (1970-76). Other useful sources included John Beckwith, *Music Papers: Articles and Talks by a Canadian Composer, 1961-1994* (1997); Beckwith's chapters on music in *The Culture of Contemporary Canada*, edited by Julian Park (1957), and *The Arts in Canada: A Stock-Taking at Mid-Century*, edited by Malcolm Ross (1958); *Canadian Music in the 1930s and 1940s*, edited by Beverley Cavanagh (1986); Arnold Edinborough, *A Personal History of the Toronto Symphony Orchestra* (ca.

1973); Robin Elliott, *Counterpoint to a City: The First One Hundred Years of the Women's Musical Club of Toronto* (1997); Murray Ginsberg, *They Loved to Play: Memories of the Golden Age in Canadian Music* (1998); William Kilbourn, *Intimate Grandeur: One Hundred Years at Massey Hall* (1993); Eric Koch, *The Brothers Hambourg* (1997); Gordana Lazarevich, *The Musical World of Frances James and Murray Adaskin* (1988); Sir Ernest MacMillan, *MacMillan on Music: Essays on Music*, edited by Carl Morey (1997); *Music in Canada*, edited by Ernest Macmillan (1955); Carl Morey, "The Beginnings of Modernism in Toronto," in *Célébration*, edited by Godfrey Ridout and Talivaldis Kenins (1984); R. Murray Schafer, *On Canadian Music* (1984); and *Aspects of Music in Canada*, edited by Arnold Walter (1969).

On Alberto Guerrero: John Beckwith undertook a great deal of original archival research, in Toronto, New York, and Chile, while I was writing this book, and generously shared the results with me. Two documentaries about Guerrero proved useful: one in Ken Winters' CBC radio series *Five Great Music Teachers*, from the late 1990s; and *The Music Teacher*, directed by Patricia Fogliato (White Pine Pictures, 2001, for its television series *A Scattering of Seeds: The Creation of Canada*). Chilean sources included Samuel Claro and Jorge Urrutia Blondel, *Historia de la Musica en Chile* (1973), and Daniel Quiroga, "Los Hermanos García Guerrero," *Revista Musical Chilena* (May 1946). I read two brief articles by Guerrero published in the Toronto/Royal Conservatory's magazine: "Promenade" (Winter Term, 1932) and "The Discrepancy Between Performance and Technique" (October 1950).

On Guerrero and Gould: William Aide, *Starting from Porcupine* (1996); John Beckwith, "Shattering a Few Myths," in *Glenn Gould: Variations*; John Beckwith, "Glenn Gould, the Early Years: Addenda and Corrigenda," *GlennGould* (Fall 1996); and Ray Dudley, "Alberto Guerrero and Glenn Gould: My View," *New Journal for Music* (Summer 1990).

Part 2, National Treasure
On Gould and the Stratford Festival: Brandon Flowers, "Glenn Gould at the Stratford Festival, 1953-1964," *GlennGould* (Fall 1999); and John Pettigrew and Jamie Portman, *Stratford: The First Thirty Years*, 2 vols. (1985).

On the cultural context of Gould's early professional life, I studied the Massey Commission's *Report* (1951) and some of the literature it engendered, and read books on Canada and Canadian arts and culture in the early postwar period. Three collections of essays by Northrop Frye were influential: *The Bush Garden* (1971), *Divisions on a Ground* (1982), and *Mythologizing Canada* (1997).

On the CBC: Karen Kieser, "Glenn Gould and the CBC," *Classical Music Magazine* (March 1995); Knowlton Nash, *The Microphone Wars: A History of Triumph and Betrayal at the CBC* (1994); Michael Nolan, *Foundations: Alan Plaunt and the Early Days of CBC Radio* (1986); and Mary Vipond, *The Mass Media in Canada* (1989, 1992).

On Gould's String Quartet: Robert William Andrew [Robin] Elliott, *The String Quartet in Canada* (Ph.D. dissertation, University of Toronto, 1990); Robin Elliott, "'So You Want to Write a String Quartet?': Glenn Gould's Opus 1," *GlennGould* (Spring 1997); and Robert A. Skelton, *Weinzweig, Gould, Schafer: Three Canadian String Quartets* (D.M. dissertation, Indiana University, 1976).

Part 3, Vaudevillian
On Gould's early years at Columbia Records: Schuyler Chapin, "Remembering Goddard Lieberson: The Legendary Recording Executive as Artist and Businessman," *Symphony* (January/February 1991); John Culshaw, *Ring Resounding* (1967); John Culshaw, "The Mellow Knob, or The Rise of Records and the Decline of the Concert Hall as Foreseen by Glenn Gould," *Records and Recording* (November 1966); Evan Eisenberg, *The Recording Angel: The Experience of Music from Aristotle to Zappa* (1987), especially "Glenn Gould"; Roland Gelatt, *The Fabulous Phonograph* (1955, 1965, 1977); the privately published book *Essays by Goddard Lieberson* (1957); and Robert Offergeld's tribute to Columbia and Lieberson in *Hi-Fi/Stereo Review* (January 1965).

On Gould's tour of Russia: Truman Capote, *The Muses Are Heard* (1956); Sofia Moshevich, "Glenn Gould and the Russians," *GlennGould* (Fall 1997); and Boris Schwarz, *Music and Musical Life in Soviet Russia* (1972, 1983).

On the National Film Board of Canada: D. B. Jones, *Movies and Memoranda: An Interpretative History of the National Film Board of Canada* (1981).

On Steinway and Sons: D. W. Fostle, *The Steinway Saga: An American Dynasty* (1995); Susan Goldenberg, *Steinway from Glory to Controversy: The Family, the Business, the Piano* (1996); Franz Mohr, with Edith Schaeffer, *My Life with the Great Pianists* (1992, 1995); and Ronald V. Ratcliffe, *Steinway* (1989).

Documents from the files of the ABC relating to Gould's planned 1960 tour of Australia were brought to light by Brett Allen-Bayes.

I also benefitted from books on the international classical-music culture of the mid- and late twentieth century, particularly two books by Joseph Horowitz, *Understanding Toscanini* (1987) and *The Ivory Trade: Music and the Business of Music at the Van Cliburn International Piano Competition* (1990), and two books by Norman Lebrecht, *The Maestro Myth: Great Conductors in Pursuit of Power* (1991) and *When the Music Stops ...: Managers, Maestros and the Corporate Murder of Classical Music* (1996).

Part 4, Renaissance Man

On the media and communications theory in Canada, in addition to writings by and about Marshall McLuhan, my sources included Robert E. Babe, *Canadian Communication Thought: Ten Foundational Writers* (2000); Peter Hall, "Innis, McLuhan and the Toronto Tradition," *Cities in Civilization* (1998); *Mass Media in Canada*, edited by John A. Irving (1962); Arthur Kroker, *Technology and the Canadian Mind: Innis/McLuhan/Grant* (1984); S. Timothy Maloney, "Three Canadian Legacies to the World of Ideas: Marshall McLuhan, Northrop Frye, and Glenn Gould," *Australian Canadian Studies* (Spring 2002); Jean Le Moyne, *Convergence: Essays from Quebec* (1961, in English 1966); and Paul Théberge, "Counterpoint: Glenn Gould and Marshall McLuhan," *BGGS* (October 1987).

On Gould as a radio artist and the influences on his radio style: *Andrew Allan: A Self-Portrait*, edited by Harry J. Boyle (1974); *All the Bright Company: Radio Drama Produced by Andrew Allan*, edited by Howard Fink and John Jackson (1987); István Anhalt, *Alternative Voices: Essays on Contemporary Vocal and Choral Composition* (1984); István Anhalt, "The Making of 'Cento,'" *Canada Music Book* (Spring-Summer 1970); Robert Fulford, "Glenn Gould in the Age of Radio," *GlennGould* (Spring 2000); Richard Kostelanetz, "Glenn Gould as a Radio Composer" [1982], *Three Canadian Geniuses: Glenn Gould, Marshall McLuhan, Northrop Frye* (2001); Gerald Nachman, *Raised on Radio* (1998); and *The Road to Victory: Radio Plays of Gerald Noxon*, edited by Howard Fink and John Jackson (1989).

On the Canadian North and *The Idea of North*: Howard Fink, "Glenn Gould's *Idea of North*: The Arctic Archetype and the Creation of a Syncretic Genre," *GlennGould* (Fall 1997); Jim Lotz, *Northern Realities: Canada-U.S. Exploitation of the Canadian North* (1971); R. A. J. Phillips, *Canada's North* (1967); and the three articles on *The Idea of North* published in *Essays on Canadian Writing* (Fall 1996).

On *The Quiet in the Land*: Matthew McFarlane, "Glenn Gould, Jean Le Moyne, and Pierre Teilhard de Chardin: Common Visionaries," *GlennGould* (Fall 2002).

Part 5, A Portrait of the Artist

Ann Davis, *The Logic of Ecstasy: Canadian Mystical Painting 1920-1940* (1992); Susan Sontag, *Under the Sign of Saturn* (1980); Anthony Storr, *The*

Dynamics of Creation (1972); and contributions to a panel on "Glenn Gould and the Doctors" by Helen Mesaros and Lynne Walter, *GlennGould* (Fall 2000).

Part 6, The Last Puritan
On Gould's hand problems: John P. L. Roberts, "A Pianist's Hands: The Implications of the Secret Diaries of Glenn Gould," *GlennGould* (Spring 2003); and Frank R. Wilson, "Glenn Gould's Hand," in *Medical Problems of the Instrumentalist Musician*, edited by Raoul Tubiana and Peter C. Amadio (2000).

On Gould's relationship with Columbia/CBS in his post-concert years: Clive Davis, with James Willwerth, *Clive: Inside the Record Business* (1975); and Robert Metz, CBS: *Reflections in a Bloodshot Eye* (1975).

Other sources: Isaiah Berlin, *The Hedgehog and the Fox: An Essay on Tolstoy's View of History* (1953); William Black, "A Matter of Ifs," *Piano Quarterly* (Fall 1988); Ken Forfia, "Glenn Gould's Workshop," *Piano & Keyboard* (September/October 1995); and S. Timothy Maloney's lecture "Glenn Gould as Conductor" (1998).

Photographs and Facsimiles

For supplying copies of photographs and facsimiles, granting me permission to use them, or otherwise assisting with the illustrations in this book, I gratefully acknowledge the Archives of Ontario; Lynda Barnett (Design Library, CBC, Toronto); the *Beacon Herald* (Stratford); Lucy Brock, Ute Krebs, and Susannah Reid (akg-images, London); Ellen Charendoff and Jane Edmonds (Stratford Festival Archives); Walter Curtin; Doubleday Canada (Toronto); Erica-Sommer Dudley (European American Music Distributors, Miami); Cheryl Gillard and the Glenn Gould Archive (Music Division, NLC, Ottawa); the Estate of Glenn Gould (Toronto), in particular Stephen Posen and Malcolm Lester; the Glenn Gould Foundation (Toronto), in particular John A. Miller; V. Tony Hauser; Don Hunstein; Andrea Knight; Allan McGillivray (Uxbridge-Scott Township Museum and Archives); Ruth Morawetz; Carl Morey; Kong Njo (art director, McClelland & Stewart); Natalie Pancer (Sony Classical, Toronto); the late Margaret Privitello; Karin Rees-Hofem and Elisabeth Schneider (Schott Musik International, Mainz); Marianne Scharwenka; Sean Smith (York University Archives and Special Collections, Toronto); Lorne Tulk; Wendy Watts (*Toronto Star*); and Jay Wilson.

Acknowledgements

"Any notable figure has only to empty his Xeroxed memos into the publisher's office to have a biography available in a few hours," McLuhan once
wrote. If only it were so. In reality, I discovered, writing a biography of a
major figure recently deceased is inconceivable without input from scores of
people willing to give generously of their time and energy. Despite the best
efforts of my memory and my files, I doubt that I have succeeded in thank-
ing every person who contributed to this book, though such was my intent.
I can only apologize abjectly to anyone whose help, somehow, I neglected to
note. But everyone who contributed to my research should know that I am
grateful – without them, this book would have been a lean and spindly thing.

Thanks are still due to a few people besides all those mentioned above,
starting with the broadcaster Shelagh Rogers, who, on the morning of
September 26, 1999, at Glenn Gould Studio in Toronto, innocently
planted the seed from which this book grew.

I am enormously grateful to the Estate of Glenn Gould and its executor, Stephen Posen, for supporting this project from the beginning, without
requesting any authority over my text in return – specifically, for giving me
unrestricted access to Gould materials in the National Library of Canada
and elsewhere, for allowing me to quote from Gould's unpublished writings, and for permitting me to reproduce photographs and facsimiles.
Thanks also, at the Estate, to Malcolm Lester and David T. Ullmann.

I owe an enormous debt to John A. Miller, executive director of the
Glenn Gould Foundation, who has supported my research on Gould in

countless ways over the years, and has fed me more useful information than I can possibly keep track of; he alone, moreover, was responsible for my finding a publisher for this book.

McClelland & Stewart offered me a contract for this book before a word of it had been written, despite my want of credentials as a writer for the trade-book market, and for this show of confidence I thank the president and publisher, Douglas M. Gibson, and the associate publisher, non-fiction, and managing editor, Jonathan Webb. Seeing the book through its various stages of production, from editing and proofreading to promotion and licensing, was far less onerous than I had imagined it would be, for which I am indebted to the professionalism, openness, and good humour of Alex Schultz, the senior editor; Adam Levin, the copy editor; and Marilyn Biderman, director of rights and contracts.

I am grateful to those persons who read parts – in several cases *all* – of the book in manuscript, and whose comments averted many errors and misunderstandings: William Aide, John Beckwith, Ray Dudley, Dr. David Goldbloom, Stuart Hamilton, Otto Joachim, Nicholas Kilburn, Timothy Maloney, John A. Miller, Carl Morey, Tim Page, Gladys Riskind, John P. L. Roberts, Ezra Schabas, Vincent Tovell, and Lorne Tulk.

Thanks also to my friends Janet Munsil and Neil Reimer, for their comments on the manuscript; to Dr. Arthur J. MacGregor and Karen Wreggitt, for their expert ministrations; to the Saturday Breakfast Club (Linda Hunt, Lois Kelly, Don Miller, Mary Mouat, and Gwen Taylor); and to Billy, Sandy, and everyone at Re-Bar and the Seahorses Café, where some of my pleasantest working hours were spent.

Finally, I am deeply indebted to my partner, Sharon Bristow, for supporting my work on this book unwaveringly and in countless ways over the past four years, through desolate and manic patches as well as more even-keeled times. She was there when I needed help clarifying my foggy first thoughts about Gould's life, and she was still there when I needed an intelligent non-musician's feedback on the finished text. To her and to the loyal companions named with her on the dedication page, my love and thanks for helping to make this project – and everything else – worthwhile.

Brentwood Bay, B.C.
August 6, 2003

Index

A page number in italic (e.g., *51*) indicates a facsimile page. The italic letter *n* following a page number (e.g., *72n*) indicates that the information is in a footnote. Where the index includes both discussions of composers and Gould recordings of their works, the composers are listed by full name first, and the Gould recordings next (e.g., "Anhalt, István" appears immediately before "Anhalt recording by Gould").